to Mum & Dad

Dedicated to the eradication of extreme poverty

Introduction

When I came back to Hungerford 1991, it's fair to say I had a lot more time than I had money. I had just left my previous job and was doing odd jobs for my Dad. One such job was the weekly trip to Cash & Carry where I found that, in addition to various cheap produce, I could buy myself a big sack of spuds for about 3 quid. After about a month of mashed potatoes I started to experiment and I jotted down the few recipes that didn't either turn into mush or set off the smoke alarm. A few pages became 50 then 100 and after a while I was on a mission.

As much as I've always enjoyed my food, I've always been acutely aware of the amount of starving people there are in our world of plenty – particularly kids. There are 170 million underfed children in the world today. Hunger and dirty water lead to malnourishment and disease. A child dies every 3 seconds from malnourishment or disease. 50 children will have died before you have finished reading this introduction. It's not acceptable. It deserves to be front page news every day and the reason it isn't, is because it has become acceptable.

For those of you old enough to remember Live Aid in 1985 there was a harrowing video played to the tune of 'Drive' (…who's gonna take you home tonight?') by The Cars. There were children too weak to walk and emotional scenes of grieving parents burying tiny coffins. At the end was a lingering shot of a baby girl, flies around her eyes, staring at the camera – apparently hours from death. 20 years later at Live 8 Bob Geldof introduced a beautiful young lady to the crowd. Same person. I felt the tears rolling down my face. What it meant was that someone's contribution had saved her life. I decided to turn my (now very large) collection of recipes into a book and give all the proceeds to Save the Children or any other charity that could help save lives.

The main killers are malaria, pneumonia, diarrhoea and measles. These are all preventable diseases. Yet to provide free healthcare for all children in Africa would cost less than £1.50 per child for a year – the price of a cup of coffee.

Sir Bob, Sir Bono, 'the' Richard Curtis and many others are trying to get governments to change their policy to Aid and to cancel debts of money that we can live without – their efforts deserve support. But don't think that your 2 or 3 pounds a month won't make a difference, it will. That's why they ask you for it. Apart from creating a life what can you do that's better than saving a life? You've already helped by buying this book, if you like it, tell your friends. Better still, get involved.

It's not about charity - it's about justice.

By the way, don't confuse me with a professional cook. I'm just a bloke who spent a lot of time pratting about in the kitchen. There were times when I didn't write a recipe down for a few days after I cooked it – so if you follow a recipe to the letter and it doesn't quite work out …… don't tell anyone.

www.savethechildren.org.uk

Acknowledgements

My mother **Anne Curtis**.
Richard Bennett of Kerridge Properties.
Your generosity will help a lot of people

Marjorie & Teresa –
I couldn't have done it without you

Susie Bond –
for your illustrations

Chris Caswell –
for the back cover photo

You –
*thanks for buying this book,
I hope you enjoy it*

Chapters

About this Book

- Every recipe starts with **one pound of potatoes,** that's 4 medium sized potatoes – hence the snappy title

- There are many varieties of potato which basically fall into 3 categories, **waxy, floury** and **new.** Where a specific category is required I have specified it in the first line

- You **don't need to peel** new potatoes – just scrub them to remove dirt

- 'cubed' means ¾" – 1" shapes, **diced** means ¼ " to ½"

- make your **own stock** – you'll notice the difference

- the **choice** of oil, fat, salt and pepper is **crucial** to the taste

- don't use mishapen, wrinkled or green potatoes

- try not to remove too much potato when peeling – **the tastiest parts,** which also contain the most nutrients, are **near the skin**

- With so many recipes I've tried to use as few words as possible. It's **brief** but **to the point**

- Why Potatoes? They're readily available, they're nutritious, they're versatile and best of all, **they're cheap**

CONVERSION CHART (TO THE NEAREST ROUND FIGURE)		
1 oz	=	25 grams
4 oz (¼ lb)	=	115 grams
8 oz (½ lb)	=	225 grams
12 oz (¾ lb)	=	350 grams
16 oz (1 lb)	=	450 grams
¼ pint = 5 fluid oz	=	150 ml
½ pint = 10 fluid oz	=	300 ml
1 pint = 20 fluid oz	=	600 ml
1 tablespoon	=	3 teaspoons
1 level tablespoon	=	15 ml
2 level tablespoons	=	1 fl oz

Appetizers

PARTY BAKED POTATOES

1 lb small (floury) potatoes –
washed and pricked
¼ lb gravadlax – flaked
1 tbsp fresh dill – chopped
4 spring onions – trimmed and finely sliced
1 tbsp creamed horseradish
3 tbsp sour cream
1 tsp lemon juice
1 tbsp extra virgin olive oil

1. Pre-heat oven to GM6/200°c/400°f
2. Bake the potatoes for 40 mins.
Remove and allow to cool slightly
3. Halve the potatoes and scoop out the flesh and
place in a bowl. Add the remaining ingredients
(except the oil). Season and mix well
4. Brush the potato skins with oil and put on a
baking tray. Spoon the filling into the skins
– cover and bake for 10 mins

PAPRIKA POTATOES

1 lb new potatoes – scrubbed, boiled &
cut into small wedges
3 tsp paprika
1 tsp cumin
Olive oil for frying

1. Put the paprika and cumin in a small dish,
season and mix
2. Heat a good quantity of the oil in a large
pan and fry potatoes until browned.
Remove and drain on kitchen paper
3. Transfer the wedges to a mixing bowl and
sprinkle on the paprika mixture ensuring
the potatoes are coated

POTATO & CHIVE SAUCE

1 lb potatoes – peeled & diced
2 onions – peeled & chopped
10 fl oz whipping cream
1 bunch chives – finely chopped

1. Boil the potatoes & onions until potatoes
are soft
2. Drain thoroughly, put back into the pan &
add the cream. Warm gradually until hot.
3. Remove from heat & purée in a food
processor, Season well and add the chives
(serve warm as a sauce or refrigerate and
use as a dip)

POTATO PRAWN COCKTAIL

1 lb new potatoes – scrubbed, boiled
and diced
10 oz frozen prawns – defrosted, cooked
and drained
6 tbsp mayonnaise
2 tbsp double cream
2½ tbsp tomato purée
1 tbsp lemon juice
1 tsp Worcester sauce
4 large cos lettuce leaves – shredded

1. Place the mayonnaise, cream, purée, lemon
juice and Worcester sauce in a bowl.
Season lightly and mix well
2. Add the potatoes and prawns while they are
still warm. Mix thoroughly. Cover with cling
film and refrigerate for at least 3 hours
3. Serve in dishes layered with the lettuce

MACAROON BARS

1 lb potatoes – boiled & mashed
4 oz desiccated coconut
Icing sugar
8 oz cooking chocolate - melted

1. Allow potatoes to cool
2. Spread coconut on a baking tray and place
under a pre-heated grill. Keep turning the
coconut until it is golden brown. Allow to cool
3. Place the potatoes in a bowl and start to
mix in the sifted icing sugar. Keep adding
the sugar until you have a very stiff paste
(similar consistency to marzipan)
4. Shape into small oblongs and cover
(while still moist) with the melted chocolate
and then the coconut

BAKED POTATO SKINS

1 lb (floury) potatoes – washed & pricked
Butter - for brushing

1. *Pre-heat oven to GM6/200°c/400°f*
2. *Bake the potatoes for 1 hour*
3. *Remove the potatoes and cut in half lengthwise. Remove the flesh and set aside*
4. *Turn oven up to GM8/230°c/450°f*
5. *Slice the skins into strips about 1" wide and put on a baking tray. Brush with plenty of butter and season*
6. *Bake for about 10 mins until crisp*

POTATO FRUIT & NUT

1 lb (waxy) potatoes – washed and cut into wedges
6 oz dried apricots – chopped
6 oz walnuts – shelled and broken up
4 tbsp walnut oil
1 tbsp white wine vinegar
1 tsp sugar

1. *Boil the potatoes for 15-18 mins. Drain*
2. *Put the oil, vinegar and sugar in a screw top jar. Season and shake vigorously to mix*
3. *Put the potatoes in a bowl, add the apricots and walnuts. Mix well and pour on the dressing*

FILLED NEW POTATOES

1 lb small new potatoes – scrubbed and boiled
¼ lb cream cheese
2 tbsp fresh dill – chopped
2 oz smoked salmon – cut into small pieces

1. *Allow the potatoes to cool until warm then cut a cross in the top of each one to a depth of half of the potato. Squeeze the base of each potato to open the top*
2. *Mix the dill with the cream cheese and spoon some of the cheese mixture into each potato and top with a piece of salmon*

ROASTED NEW POTATOES WITH SAGE AND HAM

1 lb new potatoes – scrubbed
Fresh sage leaves - 2 for each potato
Parma ham – cut into strips - 1 for each potato
2 tbsp olive oil

1. *Pre-heat oven to GM6/200°c/400°f*
2. *Wrap 2 sage leaves round each potato and a strip of ham around the sage*
3. *Put half the oil in a small roasting pan, add the potatoes, drizzle with the remaining oil and season. Roast for 45 mins*

CLASSIC NEW POTATOES

1 lb new potatoes – scrubbed
1 handful fresh mint – chopped
3 oz full fat butter – cut into small cubes

1. *Boil the potatoes with half the mint for 16-18 mins*
2. *Drain and allow to cool for 5 mins*
3. *Serve, sprinkled with the rest of the mint and butter*

POTATO & CHESTNUT PUREE

1 lb potatoes – peeled & cubed
1 lb chestnuts
9 fl oz milk

1. *Slash each chestnut with a knife and boil for 5 mins*
2. *Drain and allow to cool slightly. Remove all skin*
3. *Warm the milk in a pan, add the chestnuts and cook on a low heat for 20 mins. Drain and keep the milk*
4. *At the same time boil the potatoes for 20 mins. Drain*
5. *Alternate cubes of potatoes with chestnuts in a large food processor. Season and pour in the milk and blitz to a purée*

9

POTATO PUREE

1 lb (waxy) potatoes – peeled & cubed
4 oz unsalted butter
2 fl oz double cream

1. Boil the potatoes until they start to soften. Drain
2. Put the potatoes in a food blender and add a little of the butter and cream
3. While the motor is running add the remaining butter and cream and process until the desired consistency is reached. (Serve warm as a sauce or refrigerate and use as a dip)

SUGARED POTATOES

1 lb new potatoes – scrubbed, boiled, drained & halved
1 oz butter
1 oz sugar

1. Melt the butter in a small pan and stir in the sugar
2. Add the potatoes to the pan and stir over a low heat until the potatoes are golden brown

FRIED POTATO SKINS

1 lb (floury) potatoes – halved
Sunflower or corn oil for frying

1. Scoop out most of the potato flesh and cut the skins into strips
2. Heat the oil to 180°c add the skins in a chip basket and fry until crisp and golden
3. Remove, drain and season. Serve with a dip

POTATO & ARTICHOKE PUREE

1 lb potatoes – peeled & cut into chunks
1 lb Jerusalem artichoke – peeled and cut into pieces
4 tbsp double cream
1 oz butter

1. Boil the potatoes and artichoke together for 20 mins then drain thoroughly
2. Put in a blender, season and add the butter and cream. Blitz until it becomes a smooth puree (Serve warm as a sauce or refrigerate and use as a dip)

MINT & POTATO PARCELS

1 lb new potatoes – scrubbed & halved
2 tbsp fresh mint – chopped
1 oz butter

1. Pre-heat oven to GM6/200°c/400°f
2. Mix the potatoes with the butter and mint. Season and place in a large piece of tin foil. Wrap the foil around the potatoes to form a parcel and bake for 45 mins

VEGETABLE DIP

1 lb potatoes – peeled & chopped
2 carrots – peeled & chopped
1 aubergine – pre-cooked, peeled & chopped
1 onion – peeled & chopped
2 cloves garlic – crushed
6 fl oz chicken stock
1 tbsp fresh thyme – chopped
1 tbsp fresh parsley – chopped

1. Heat the oil and fry the onion until it starts to soften
2. Add the garlic and fry for 1 more minute
3. Add the herbs, season, stir and cook for 1 more minute
4. Add the remaining ingredients and enough stock to just cover. Bring to the boil and simmer covered for about 20 mins or until soft. Stir occasionally and ensure the liquid covers the vegetables
5. Drain off the liquid and reserve. Transfer the potato mixture to a food processor, season and blitz to a purée (adding some of the reserved liquid if you wish)
6. Place in a bowl, cover with cling firm and refrigerate for 2 hours before serving

POTATO & CELERIAC PUREE

1 lb potatoes – peeled, cut into chunks
  & boiled
1 lb celeriac – peeled, cut into chunks & boiled
2 fl oz double cream
2 fl oz milk
2 oz butter

1. *Put all the ingredients into a blender (in*
   2 batches if necessary) season and mix
   until smooth
   (This puree can be served hot with meat or
   refrigerated and used as a dip)

POTATO & PARSNIP DIP

1 lb potatoes – peeled, boiled, drained
  & chopped
1 lb parsnips – peeled, boiled, drained & chopped
2 tbsp single cream
1 tbsp fresh thyme – chopped
1 oz butter

1. *Put the parsnips in a blender and blitz to a purée*
2. *Mash the potatoes with the butter,*
   season and add the thyme
3. *Mix the potatoes with the parsnips and the*
   cream and blitz again until a smooth purée
   is formed
4. *Put in a bowl, cover with cling film and*
   refrigerate for 2 hours before use

SOUR CREAM POTATOES
WITH BACON

1 lb new potatoes – boiled & drained
3 rashers bacon – cooked until crisp & chopped
into small pieces
1 small tub sour cream
2 tbsp fresh chives – chopped

1. *Scoop out a little hole from each potato*
   and fill with sour cream till overflowing
2. *Arrrange the potatoes on a plate and*
   sprinkle with the bacon and chives. Season

POTATO SAMOSAS

Filling
4 medium potatoes, peeled & diced
3 carrots peeled and cut into small dices
1 tsp salt
¾ tsp ground cumin
¾ tsp ground coriander
1 tsp ground turmeric
¼ tsp chilli powder
4 fl oz boiling water
5 spinach leaves finely chopped
Pastry
12 oz self-raising wholemeal flour
½ tsp fine sea salt
3 oz margarine
⅓ pint cold water
a dash of milk

1. *Pre-heat oven to GM6/200°c/400°f*
2. *Put all the fillings ingredients except the*
   spinach into the boiling water. Cover and
   simmer for 10 mins
3. *Add the spinach and simmer without the*
   cover for about 5 mins, adding more
   water if needed
4. *Meanwhile make the pastry. Sift the flour*
   and salt into a large mixing bowl. Put in
   the margarine until the mixture resembles
   fine crumbs. Stir in enough water to make
   a soft dough then shape it into a ball and
   divide it into 3 portions
5. *Place one of the portions on a floured*
   board and roll into a rectangle about 7 x 9
   inches. Spread ⅓ of the vegetable mix
   along the length of the rectangle. Bring
   the long edges together moistening each
   edge with a little milk to make them stick.
   Dust with a little flour and cut the rectangle
   to make 3 squares
6. *Repeat with the rest of the dough and*
   vegetable mixture
7. *Grease and flour a baking sheet. Place*
   the 9 samosas onto it and cook for about
   25 mins

POTATO SAMOSAS (2)

Filling
1 lb potatoes – boiled & mashed
3 tomatoes – peeled, deseeded & chopped
4 oz peas – cooked
2 tsp coriander seeds – ground
1 tsp cumin seeds – ground
½ tsp fenugreek seeds – ground
1 tsp ground black pepper

Pastry
1 lb plain flour
3½ oz margarine
7 fl oz milk
½ tsp turmeric
½ tsp salt
1 tsp lemon juice

Filling
Roast the spices for 1-2 mins on a high
heat then mix well with the potatoes, peas
and tomatoes. Season

Pastry
Sift the flour, salt and turmeric into a large
mixing bowl. Rub in the margarine until
the mixture resembles fine crumbs. Stir in
sufficient milk to make a soft dough.
Place it in the fridge for 15 mins

1. *Pre-heat oven to GM5/190°c/375°f*

2. *Roll out the pastry and cut into 5 " circles
(you should end up with about 15) Cut each
circle in half and put 1 tbsp of the potato
mixture on each. Brush the edges with milk
and lemon juice (mixed) and fold each half
over to make a triangle. Seal well and crimp
the edges. Bake until crispy*

PEPPER & POTATO DIP

1 lb potatoes – peeled, boiled and diced
3 red peppers – de-seeded and chopped
1 onion – peeled & chopped
3 cloves garlic – crushed
2 tbsp lemon juice
4 tbsp mayonnaise
2 tbsp olive oil

1. *Heat the oil and fry the peppers and onion
gently for 2-3 mins until softened*

2. *Put all the ingredients into a liquidiser,
season and process until smooth*

3. *Put the mixture into a bowl, cover with
cling film and refrigerate for at least 2 hours*

SPICY POTATO PARCELS

Filling
1 lb potatoes – boiled & mashed
2 cloves garlic – crushed
½ tsp cumin
½ fenugreek seeds
¼ tsp chilli powder
1½ tbsp lemon juice
1 tbsp milk
1 tbsp fresh coriander – chopped
1 egg

Pastry
6 oz wholemeal flour
3 oz plain flour
2½ oz butter
1 tbsp cumin seeds
4 fl oz warm water

1. *Pre-heat oven to GM4/180°c/350°f*

2. *To make the filling – combine all the ingredients
(except milk and egg) into the mash*

3. *To make the pastry – sift the flours into a mixing
bowl and add the seeds then rub in the butter
until you have a mixture like breadcrumbs*

4. *Add sufficient water to make a dough.
Press the dough into a ball and knead until
smooth, Put in cling film and put in the
fridge for 15 mins*

5. *Whisk the egg and milk together*

6. *Roll the pastry until fairly thin and cut
out circles about 4" and put 1 tbsp of
the mixture into the middle of each then
seal over. Put each parcel onto a greased
oven tray, sealed side down. Brush the
parcels with the egg and milk mixture
and make several slits in each. Bake for
20-25 mins*

MOROCCAN POTATO TRIANGLES

Filling
1 lb potatoes – boiled & mashed
1 onion – peeled & chopped
2 cloves garlic – crushed
2 tsp ground cumin
½ tsp ground fenugreek seeds
½ tsp chilli powder
2 tsp lemon juice
2 eggs – hard boiled & chopped

Pastry
10 sheets filo pastry
3 oz butter – melted
2 tsp cumin seeds
1 tbsp olive oil

1. *Heat the oil and cook the onion and garlic until soft. Stir in the spices and cook for 2-3 mins, stirring continuously*
2. *Mix together all the filling ingredients in a large bowl and allow to cool*
3. *Pre-heat the oven to GM6/200°c/400°f*
4. *Layer 2 sheets of filo together and brush with butter. Cut layered sheets lengthways into 4. Put 1 tbsp of filling at the end of each strip and fold a corner end of the pastry diagonally across the filling to the other edge to form a triangle. Cut and put aside. Continue folding & cutting in this manner to the end of the strip. Use up all the pastry and filling in this way ensuring all edges are sealed with melted butter.*
5. *Put the triangles on a greased oven tray and bake for 20 mins until lightly browned*

POTATO & ARTICHOKE PUREE (2)

1 lb potatoes – peeled & cut into quarters
2 Jerusalem artichokes – peeled & cut into quarters
5 tsp double cream
2 tbsp chopped parsley
2 oz unsalted butter

1. *Put the potatoes and artichoke in salted boiling water for 15-20 mins. Drain*
2. *Put back into the pan and cook on a low heat for 1-2 mins to remove moisture*

3. *Put mixture into a food processor, add the butter and cream and blitz to a puree. Season and add the parsley*

   (Pour onto meat while hot or refrigerate and use as a dip)

ITALIAN POTATO SLICE

1 lb potatoes – peeled & thinly sliced
2 oz mozzarella cheese – thinly sliced
1 oz parmesan cheese – grated
1 small onion – sliced thinly into rings
3 cloves garlic – crushed
1 fl oz milk
1½ oz butter

1. *Pre-heat oven to GM6/200°c/400°f*
2. *Melt the butter in a small pan and gently fry the garlic for 2 mins. (keep a small amount of butter for later)*
3. *Grease the base of a cake tin and cover it with one third of the potatoes. Add half the onion, half the butter, half of the cheese. Season, add another third of potatoes and repeat*
4. *Pour on the milk and dot with some butter. Bake for 1 hour*
5. *Remove, stand for 5 mins, then cut into slices*

FRENCH POTATO TOASTIES

1 lb potatoes – unpeeled, boiled & drained
8 small thick slices cooked ham
6 oz cheese - cut into 4 slices
1 oz butter
2 tbsp olive oil

1. *Allow the potatoes to cool slightly, peel then cut each one in half and cut a large slice from each (ie 8 slices in total)*
2. *Make 4 sandwiches with the potato on the outside and the cheese on the inside with 2 slices of ham between the potatoes and the cheese. Season*
3. *Melt the butter in a pan and add the oil, when hot add the sandwiches and fry until the potato is browned and the cheese begins to melt*

CHILLI PEPPER & POTATO DIP

1 lb potatoes - peeled, boiled, drained & chopped
2 red peppers - halved lengthways, cored & seeded
2 cloves garlic – crushed
2 small red chillies – trimmed, seeded & chopped
2 tbsp single cream
1 tbsp olive oil

1. *Put the peppers skin side up under a pre-heated grill. Remove from the heat when the skin starts to blacken and put into a plastic food bag. Seal and leave for 5 mins. Remove and peel off the skin. Chop*

2. *While the peppers are cooking heat the oil and gently fry the garlic and chilli for 2-3 mins*

3. *Put all the ingredients in a food processor and blitz to a purée (add more cream if needed)*

4. *Put the purée in a bowl, cover it with cling film and refrigerate for 2 hours before serving*

POTATO SCALLOPS

1 lb small potatoes – peeled & very finely sliced
7 fl oz milk - heated
1 oz butter
1½ tbsp flour

1. *Pre-heat oven to GM4/180°c/350°f*

2. *Add a layer of potatoes to the base of a greased casserole dish. Season, sprinkle with a little flour and dot with a little butter*

3. *Repeat until the potatoes are used up. Dot with butter and pour in the hot milk*

4. *Cover and bake for 45 mins*

5. *Remove the lid and cook for 15 more mins until browned*

PARMESAN POTATO PURÉE

1 lb (waxy) potatoes – peeled & cubed
4 oz parmesan cheese - grated
4 oz unsalted butter
2 fl oz double cream

1. *Boil the potatoes until they start to soften. Drain. Add the cheese*

2. *Put the potatoes in a food blender and add a little of the butter and cream*

3. *While the motor is running add the remaining butter and cream and process until the desired consistency is reached.*

4. *Cover with cling film, refrigerate for at least 3 hours and use as a dip (or it could be served warm as a sauce)*

FRIED NEW POTATOES WITH SPICY CENTRES

1 lb small new potatoes – scrubbed & boiled for 12-13 mins
3 fl oz mayonnaise
1 tsp curry powder
Olive oil for frying

1. *Drain the potatoes and leave to cool*

2. *Cut a slice off each potato and remove about a tablespoon of potato from the centre*

3. *Deep fry the potatoes until brown and drain on kitchen paper*

4. *Mix the chilli powder with the mayonnaise and fill each centre*

It's all French to me:

Pomme de terre is French for potato, a pomme is an apple, a pomme de terre is an apple of the ground, and chips are pommes frites or fried apple

Soups

POTATO SOUP

1 lb potatoes – peeled and sliced
2 medium onions – peeled and sliced
1 stick celery – washed and sliced
2 pints chicken stock
½ pint milk
1 oz butter

1. Melt the butter in a saucepan and add the vegetables. Cover and cook for 5 mins, stirring occasionally
2. Season well and add the stock. Bring to the boil and simmer for 30 mins, then liquidise
3. Put into a clean saucepan, add the milk and season, then boil gently for 15 mins until desired consistency is reached

LEEK & POTATO SOUP

1 lb potatoes – peeled & diced
3 large leeks – thinly sliced
1 medium onion – peeled & chopped
1½ pints vegetable stock
½ pint milk
1 tbsp dried mixed herbs
1 oz butter

1. Heat the butter in a large pan and gently fry the potatoes, leeks and onions for 5 mins
2. Add the stock and the herbs, season and bring to the boil. Cover and simmer for ½ hour
3. Liquidise the soup and return to a clean pan. Gradually add the milk and season. Heat slowly

CHILLED WATERCRESS VICHYSSOISE

1 lb potatoes – peeled & diced
9 oz leeks – trimmed & sliced
1 onion – peeled & chopped
2 pints chicken stock
¼ pt single cream
2 bunches watercress – washed, stalks removed
 & chopped
1 oz butter

1. Fry the onion & leek in melted butter until soft
2. Add potatoes, stock, season & stir well
3. Bring to boil, cover & simmer for ½ an hour
4. Add the watercress to pan & simmer for 2 mins (keep some for a garnish)
5. Blend mixture in food processor till it's a smooth purée. Stir in cream whilst blending and season. Put the soup into the fridge until chilled

ONION FAMILY SOUP

1 lb potatoes – peeled & cubed
3 leeks – washed, trimmed & sliced
1 onion – peeled & sliced
4 shallots – peeled & sliced
2 cloves garlic – crushed
1½ pints vegetable stock
2 tbsp olive oil

1. Heat the oil and gently fry the potatoes, onion, leeks, shallots for 5 mins
2. Add the garlic and fry for 3 more mins
3. Add the stock, season & bring to the boil then simmer for 20 mins
4. Put the mixture in a food processor and liquidise
5. Return to a clean pan, season and slowly re-heat

GARLIC & POTATO SOUP

1 lb potatoes – peeled & diced
25 cloves garlic – papery skin removed
3 pints vegetable stock

1. Pre-heat oven to GM5/190°c/375°f
2. Put the garlic cloves on a baking tray and cover with foil. Bake for 40 mins
3. Boil the potatoes for 10 mins, drain and add to the stock in a large pan. Season
4. Squeeze the pulp from the garlic cloves add to the soup and simmer for 10 mins
5. Put the soup, in batches if necessary, into a food processor and liquidise. Return to a clean pan, season and gradually re-heat. Simmer until desired consistency is reached

POTATO & CELERY SOUP

1 lb potatoes - peeled & chopped
5 sticks celery - cut into 1" pieces
2 onions - peeled & chopped
1 pint chicken stock
¼ pint milk
2 tbsps cream
2 oz cheddar cheese - grated
1 oz butter

1. Melt the butter in a large pan. Add the celery & onion, cook gently for 4-5 mins
2. Add the potatoes and stock and season. Bring to the boil & simmer gently for 20 mins. Blitz to a purée in a liquidiser
3. Return to the pan, add the milk, re-heat stir in the cream and add a little more seasoning
4. Serve hot topped with grated cheese

MIXED VEGETABLE SOUP

1 lb potatoes – peeled & chopped
3 onions – peeled & chopped
3 carrots – peeled & chopped
5 sticks celery – trimmed & chopped
3 cloves garlic – crushed
3 pints chicken stock

1. Put all the ingredients in a large pan, season well and stir
2. Bring to the boil and simmer for 35 – 40 mins
3. Transfer to a blender and liquidise, Return to a clean pan, adjust the seasoning and gradually re-heat

POTATO & TURNIP SOUP

1 lb potatoes - peeled & chopped
1 large turnip - peeled & chopped
1 medium onion - peeled & chopped
1 pint chicken stock
1½ pints milk
2 bay leaves
1 tbsp mixed herbs (dried)
1 tbsp chopped fresh parsley

1. Put the potatoes, turnip and onion in a large pan and add the mixed herbs, chicken stock & the bay leaves
2. Bring to the boil and simmer for 25 mins
3. Remove the bay leaves, cool slightly then blitz to a purée in a food processor
4. Put the soup in a clean pan, mix in the milk and season
5. Slowly re-heat and add the parsley

POTATO, LEEK & ONION SOUP

1 lb potatoes – peeled & sliced
1 lb onions – peeled & thinly sliced
1 lb leeks – trimmed, peeled & thinly sliced
4 fl oz double cream
3 pints chicken stock
4 oz butter

1. Melt the butter in a large saucepan and cook the onions and leeks for 5 mins until soft
2. Add the potatoes and the stock, season, boil then reduce to a simmer for 15 mins
3. Put the soup (in batches) in a food processor and liquidise
4. Return to a clean pan, add the cream, check seasoning and slowly re-heat

POTATO & WATERCRESS SOUP

1 lb potatoes – peeled & diced
4 bunches watercress – washed & finely chopped
1 onion – peeled & chopped
2 pints milk
1 pint chicken stock
2 oz butter

1. Melt the butter and gently fry the potatoes and onion for 5 mins
2. Stir in the milk, stock and watercress. Season, bring to the boil and simmer for 30 mins
3. Put in a food processor and liquidise. Return to a clean pan. Season and slowly re-heat

CHICKPEA & SPICY POTATO SOUP

1 lb potatoes – peeled & diced
1 large tin chickpeas – drained & rinsed
1 large tin chopped tomatoes
2 onions – peeled & finely chopped
3 cloves garlic – crushed
4 oz frozen peas
¼ tsp chilli powder
¼ tsp turmeric
½ tsp curry powder
¼ tsp garam masala
1 tbsp olive oil
2 pints water

1. Heat the oil and gently cook the onion and garlic for 5 mins
2. Add the potatoes and the spices. Cook for 2 mins
3. Add the tomatoes and water. Season, bring to the boil then cover and simmer for 30 mins
4. Add the chickpeas and peas. Cook for 15 mins

LEEK & POTATO SOUP (2)

1 lb potatoes – peeled & diced
1 lb leeks – trimmed & sliced
2 pints chicken stock
5 oz bacon – rind removed & chopped
¼ pint single cream
1 oz butter
1 bay leaf
1 tbsp cornflour

1. Dry fry bacon in large pan until the fat begins to run
2. Add the butter & leeks – cook till soft
3. Add the potatoes, stock & bring to boil
4. Season, add bay leaf, cover & simmer for 25 mins
5. Remove bay leaf – blitz in food processor till smooth
6. Blend cornflour with little water, add it, & the cream to the soup
7. Season and re-heat slowly

CABBAGE & POTATO SOUP

1 lb potatoes – peeled and cubed
1 Savoy cabbage – finely shredded
2 onions – peeled & finely chopped
3 pints chicken stock
2 oz butter

1. Melt the butter in a large saucepan and fry the onion for 5 mins until soft
2. Add the potatoes and cook for 5 more mins
3. Add the stock, season bring to the boil and simmer for 20 mins
4. Add the cabbage and simmer for 5 more mins
5. Put the mixture in a food processor and liquidise (in batches if necessary)
6. Return to a clean pan, season & slowly re-heat

POTATO & PEA SOUP

1 lb potatoes – peeled & diced
½ lb frozen peas
5 shallots – peeled & finely chopped
3 cloves garlic – crushed
2 pints chicken stock
2 tbsp olive oil

1. Heat the oil in a pan and cook the shallots for 5 mins
2. Add the garlic and cook for 3 more mins
3. Add the potatoes and stock, bring to the boil then simmer for 15 mins
4. Add the peas, bring back to the boil then simmer for 5 mins

QUICK BEAN & POTATO CHOWDER

1 lb new potatoes – scrubbed, halved & boiled
2 large tins chopped tomatoes
1 large tin kidney beans
1 tsp chilli powder
2 tbsp tomato purée

Put all the ingredients in a large pan, season and heat gently until simmering but not boiling

CAULIFLOWER, CHEESE & POTATO SOUP

1 lb potatoes – peeled & cubed
2 cauliflowers – florets removed & washed
8 oz stilton cheese - crumbled
1 large onion – peeled & chopped
3 cloves garlic – crushed
2 pints chicken stock
2 bay leaves
2 tbsp olive oil

1. *Heat the oil and fry the onion until it starts to soften*

2. *Add the garlic and cook for 1 more minute*

3. *Add the potatoes, florets, bay leaves and stock. Bring to the boil and simmer for 20 mins*

4. *Remove the bay leaves and transfer the soup to a blender and liquidise (in batches if necessary)*

5. *Return to a clean pan, season and gradually re-heat. As the soup heats add the cheese, stirring often*

POTATO & ROASTED GARLIC SOUP

1 lb potatoes – peeled & diced
1 large bulb of garlic – separated & peeled
3 large leeks – trimmed & thinly sliced
1 large onion – peeled & thinly sliced
2 pints chicken stock
4 fl oz single cream
¼ tsp nutmeg
1 tbsp extra virgin olive oil

1. *Pre-heat oven to GM4/180°c/350°f*

2. *Put the garlic on a baking tray, brush with oil and bake for 20 mins*

3. *Heat the oil in a large pan and cook the potato, leek and onion for 3 mins*

4. *Add the garlic and stock. Season and bring to the boil. Cover and simmer for 30 mins*

5. *Put the soup in a food processor, in batches if necessary, and liquidise*

6. *Return to a clean pan, season and add the cream and nutmeg. Stir and re-heat gradually*

POTATO & BUTTERBEAN SOUP

1 lb potatoes – peeled and diced
¼ lb dried butterbeans – soaked overnight
4 sticks celery – trimmed and chopped
2 carrots – peeled and roughly chopped
2 pints beef stock (made with 3 cubes of stock)
1 tbsp fresh thyme – chopped
2 tbsp vegetable oil

1. *Bring the stock to the boil in a large pan and add the butterbeans. Boil rapidly for 2 mins*

2. *Reduce to a very gently simmer for 15 mins*

3. *Heat the oil and fry the potatoes, celery, carrot and onion for 5 mins or until the onion has softened*

4. *Add the vegetables to the beans and add the thyme, season, and stir and bring nearly to the boil. Simmer gently for 40 mins*

POTATOES MINESTRONE

1 lb (waxy) potatoes – peeled & diced
1 large tin haricot beans – drained
¼ lb green beans – trimmed & washed
¼ lb peas
¼ lb macaroni
½ lb belly pork – skin removed & diced
2 onions – peeled & chopped
4 cloves garlic – crushed
2 carrots – peeled & diced
4 sticks celery – trimmed & chopped
3 tbsp fresh parsley – chopped
4 pints beef stock
¼ lb parmesan cheese – grated

1. *Dry fry the pork in a large pan until lightly browned*

2. *Add the onions and garlic and fry until the onion softens*

3. *Add the haricot beans, carrots & celery. Season, stir and pour on the stock. Bring to the boil then cover and simmer gently for an hour*

4. *Add the green beans, peas and macaroni, remove cover and simmer for 30 mins*

5. *Add the parsley adjust the seasoning and stir, sprinkled with cheese*

POTATO, BACON & PEA SOUP

1 lb potatoes – peeled & diced
12 rashers bacon – rind removed & finely chopped
1 lb frozen peas
2 small onions – peeled & chopped
3 tbsp fresh parsley – chopped
2 pints chicken stock

1. Dry fry the bacon until slightly browned
2. Add the potato and onion. Cook gently until the onions are soft
3. Add the stock, bring to the boil then simmer for 20 mins
4. Add the peas, bring to the boil, then simmer for 3 mins
5. Put in a food processor (in batches if necessary) and liquidise
6. Return the soup to a clean pan, season, add the parsley and gently re-heat

SUMMER SOUP

1 lb new potatoes - washed & diced
8 oz carrots peeled - diced
2 onions - peeled & chopped
8 oz courgettes - washed & sliced
1 oz butter
3 pints chicken stock

1. Heat the butter in a large pan and cook the onions and carrots gently for 5 mins, stirring occasionally
2. Add the potatoes, courgettes and stock, season, bring gradually to the boil. Simmer for 15-20 mins or until desired consistency is reached

POTATO & ONION SOUP WITH THYME

1 lb potatoes – peeled & chopped
5 onions – peeled & chopped
3 pints chicken stock
½ pint milk
4 tbsp chopped fresh thyme
3 oz butter

1. Melt the butter in a pan and stir in the potato and onion
2. Add the thyme and seasoning. Cover and heat gently for 10 mins
3. Add the stock and milk and bring to the boil. Reduce to a simmer and heat uncovered for 7-8 mins
4. Blitz to a purée in a blender. Return to a pan and re-heat gently, season. Simmer until desired consistency is reached

TOMATO & POTATO SOUP

1 lb potatoes - peeled and diced
¾ lb tomatoes – chopped
2 leeks – trimmed & sliced
1 oz butter
1 tsp sugar
1 tbsp chopped basil
1½ pints vegetable stock
3 fl oz single cream

1. Melt the butter and gently sauté the leeks for 2-3 mins
2. Add the chopped tomatoes and cook gently for 6-7 mins
3. Add the diced potato, seasoning and sugar. Mix well, cover and simmer for 20-25 mins or until potatoes are tender
4. Liquidise and re-heat in a clean pan. Season and add the cream and herbs. Serve hot

CELERIAC SOUP WITH BACON & CABBAGE

1 lb potatoes – peeled & cubed
1 lb celeriac – peeled & cubed
6 sticks celery – washed & chopped
2 onions – peeled & chopped
6 rashers bacon – fat removed
4 cabbage leaves – washed
2 pints chicken stock
¼ pint cream
2 oz butter
1 tbsp fresh thyme – chopped

1. *Melt the butter and fry the onion for 3 mins*

2. *Add the celeriac and cook for 3 more mins*

3. *Add the potatoes, thyme and stock, season, stir and bring to the boil and simmer for 20 mins*

4. *Grill the bacon and cut into bite sized pieces*

5. *Add half the bacon to the soup and liquidise*

6. *Blanch the cabbage for 3 mins. Drain and shred*

7. *Return the soup to a clean pan, add the cream, season and gently re-heat. Place the cabbage and the remaining bacon in the centre of the soup just before serving*

PARMENTIER SOUP

1 lb potatoes - peeled & thinly sliced
3 oz onions - thinly sliced
2 oz butter
2 chicken stock cubes - crumbled
1 pint milk
½ pint water
1 bay leaf
1 bunch chives - chopped
2 oz cheddar cheese - grated

1. *Melt the butter in a pan, add the potatoes & onion. Cook slowly for about 5 mins*

2. *Mix the stock cubes, milk & water together and add to the pan with the bay leaf. Cover and cook gently for ½ hour*

3. *Liquidise the soup. Return to a clean pan and slowly re-heat*

   Serve hot sprinkled with the cheese & chives

BACON & POTATO SOUP

1 lb potatoes – peeled & cubed
½ lb bacon – rind removed
1 leek – trimmed & sliced
3 sticks celery – trimmed & sliced
1 large onion – peeled & sliced
2 pints chicken stock
1 tbsp fresh sage – chopped
1 tbsp fresh parsley – chopped

1. *Grill the bacon and chop into pieces. Set aside*

2. *Transfer the bacon fat to a pan and fry the potatoes, leek, onion and celery for 5 mins*

3. *Add the stock, seasoning, sage and parsley and bring to the boil. Simmer for 20 mins*

4. *Put half the mixture into a blender and liquidise*

5. *Return it to the pan, season, add the bacon and slowly re-heat*

POTATO, HAM & LENTIL SOUP

1 lb potatoes – peeled & cubed
½ lb smoked ham – cubed
1 lb puy lentils – rinsed
2 onions – peeled & finely chopped
3 cloves garlic – crushed
20 fl oz water
2 tbsp tomato purée
30 fl oz chicken stock
1 tbsp fresh sage – chopped
1 oz butter

1. *Melt the butter and cook the onions and garlic for 5 mins*

2. *Add the lentils, water and sage. Bring to the boil then simmer for 10 mins*

3. *Add the potatoes, tomato purée, ham and stock, stir well. Season and simmer for 30 mins or until desired consistency is reached*

TATTI SOUP

1 lb potatoes – peeled & sliced
½ lb mutton
2 onions – peeled & finely chopped
1 carrots – peeled & grated
2½ pints water

1. *Rinse the mutton and place in a large saucepan. Add the water and bring to the boil, removing any scum*

2. *Add the potatoes, onions and carrots. Season, cover and simmer for 1¾ hours*

3. *Remove the meat and adjust the seasoning. Serve hot*

SAFFRON & FISH SOUP

1 lb potatoes – peeled & diced
1 lb smoked haddock fillet – skin removed
1 onion – peeled & thinly sliced
3 cloves garlic – crushed
3 strands saffron – crushed
1 tbsp Balti curry paste
1½ pints vegetable stock
4 fl oz cream
2 oz butter

1. Pre-heat oven to GM6/200°c/400°f
2. Wrap the fish in foil and bake for 15 mins. Drain the fish and reserve the liquid
3. Meanwhile melt the butter in a large pan and fry the potatoes, onion and garlic for 5 mins
4. Add the saffron and curry paste. Stir and cook for 1 minute
5. Flake the fish and add to the pan. Season and pour in the stock. Bring to the boil and simmer for 15 mins
6. Transfer the soup to a blender and liquidise. Return to a clean pan, add the cream and gradually re-heat

POTATO & TARRAGON SOUP

1 lb potatoes – peeled & diced
2 leeks – trimmed & thinly sliced
3 celery sticks – trimmed, washed & thinly sliced
2 carrots – peeled & thinly sliced
1 onion – peeled & diced
2 cloves garlic – crushed
1 courgette – washed and thinly sliced
3 tbsp fresh tarragon – chopped
2 oz butter
2 pint vegetable stock

1. Heat the butter and gently fry the vegetables (except the courgette) for 5 mins
2. Add the boiling stock and courgette, season and simmer for 10 mins
3. Add the tarragon and simmer for 5 more mins
4. Put half the soup in a blender and liquidise. Return to the pan, season and stir well. Gently re-heat

POTATO & ARTICHOKE SOUP

1 lb potatoes – peeled & cubed
1 lb artichokes – peeled & cubed
1 onion – peeled & chopped
3 cloves garlic – crushed
4 oz mascarpone cheese
2 pints chicken stock
2 oz butter

1. Melt the butter in a large pan and fry the potatoes, artichoke onion and garlic until the onion has softened
2. Season, add the stock and bring to the boil. Simmer for 20 mins
3. Transfer to a blender and liquidise then return to a clean pan. Season, add the cheese and gradually re-heat

POTATO SOUP WITH BROCCOLI FLORETS

1 lb potatoes – peeled and cubed
1 lb broccoli florets – washed
1 pint chicken stock
1 onion – peeled and chopped
2 cloves garlic – crushed
1 oz butter

1. Melt the butter and fry the onion and garlic for 5 mins
2. Add the potatoes, half the broccoli and the stock. Bring to the boil then simmer for 15 mins
3. Transfer to a blender and liquidise
4. Return to a clean pan, season and add the rest of the florets. Simmer for 15 more mins

CREAMED PUMPKIN SOUP

1 lb potatoes – peeled and cubed
1½ lb pumpkin – diced
½ lb carrots – peeled and diced
2 pints chicken stock
2 pints milk
¾ pint double cream
3 oz butter

1. *Melt the butter and gently fry the pumpkin and carrot for 5 mins*

2. *Add the potatoes, season then pour in the stock and milk. Stir well bring to the boil and simmer for 20 mins*

3. *Transfer to a blender and liquidise. Return to a clean pan, season, add the cream and gradually re-heat until almost, but not, boiling. Simmer gently until desired consistency is reached*

COD & POTATO CHOWDER

1 lb potatoes – peeled & diced
1 lb cod fillet – cut into bite sized pieces
1 onion – peeled & finely sliced
1 clove garlic – crushed
1 carrot – peeled and chopped
2 sticks celery – washed, trimmed
& chopped
1 pint milk
½ pint water
2 tbsp olive oil

1. *Heat the oil in a large pan and gently fry the onion, garlic, carrot and celery for 5 mins*

2. *Add the milk, potatoes and fish. Season then bring to the boil. Simmer for 30 mins adding water if needed until the right consistency is reached*

CREAM OF POTATO SOUP

1 lb potatoes –peeled and cut into chunks
1 onion – peeled and chopped
1½ pints chicken stock
6 fl oz single cream
1 tbsp olive oil

1. *Heat the oil and gently fry the onion for 5 mins*

2. *Add the potatoes and stock, season, bring to the boil, then reduce to a simmer and cook for 20 mins*

3. *Blitz the mixture in a blender and return to a clean pan. Add the cream, season and gradually re-heat*

SMOKED HADDOCK CHOWDER

1 lb potatoes – peeled, diced & boiled
1 lb smoked haddock fillet – skin removed
1 onion – peeled and finely chopped
2 sticks celery – washed and chopped
1 pint milk
2 tbsp fresh parsley – chopped
1 oz butter
1 oz flour

1. *Pre-heat oven to GM6/200°c/400°f*

2. *Wrap the fish in tin foil and bake for 10 mins. Remove, drain and keep the liquid*

3. *Melt the butter and fry the onion and celery for 5 mins*

4. *Sprinkle with the flour and stir well*

5. *Add the milk, potatoes and the reserved liquid, bring to the boil and simmer for 10 mins*

6. *Flake the fish and add it along with the parsley. Season and simmer for 10 more mins – reducing until the desired consistency is reached*

CURRIED POTATO & PARSNIP SOUP

1 lb potatoes – peeled & chopped
½ lb parsnips – peeled & chopped
1 small leek – trimmed & sliced thinly
2 rashers bacon – rind removed & chopped
2 tsp curry powder
2 pints chicken stock
1 tbsp fresh coriander – chopped
2 oz butter

1. *Melt the butter and fry the parsnip, leek and bacon for 10-12 mins*

2. *Add the potatoes, curry powder and chicken stock. Season and stir well. Bring to boil & simmer for 20 mins*

3. *Put the mixture into a food processor and liquidise*

4. *Return to a clean pan; adjust the seasoning and re-heat gradually. Serve sprinkled with coriander*

FENNEL & POTATO SOUP

1 lb potatoes – peeled & cut into chunks
2 fennel bulbs – finely chopped
1 onion - peeled & chopped
1¼ pints vegetable stock
3 fl oz double cream
1 tsp fennel seeds – crushed
2 oz butter

1. Melt the butter and fry the onion for 5 mins
2. Add the fennel seeds and cook for 2 mins
3. Add the potatoes and fennel, season and cook gently for 5 more mins.
4. Pour on the stock and simmer for 40 mins
5. Put the soup in a blender and liquidise
6. Return to a clean pan, season, stir in the cream and gently re-heat until almost, but not, boiling

POTATO, BROCCOLI & BLUE CHEESE SOUP

1 lb potatoes – peeled & cubed
4 oz blue cheese – cubed
1 lb broccoli – stalks removed
1½ pints vegetable stock

1. Put the potatoes into a saucepan containing boiling stock. Simmer for 10 mins
2. Add the broccoli and cook for 15 mins
3. Put the mixture into a blender and liquidise
4. Return to a clean pan, add the cheese, season and gently re-heat

CREAM OF WATERCRESS & POTATO SOUP

1 lb potatoes - peeled & chopped
2 bunches watercress - washed & chopped
1 onion - peeled & chopped
1 oz butter
2 pints chicken stock
¼ pint cream
Pinch of nutmeg
1 tbsp flour

1. Melt the butter in a large pan and cook the onion gently until soft. Add the flour and mix well
2. Add the stock, stirring continuously over a medium heat until the soup comes to the boil. Add the potatoes, watercress, nutmeg and seasoning. Simmer gently for ½ hour
3. Blitz the soup to a purée in a food processor. Return to a clean pan and slowly re-heat. Blend in the cream and adjust the seasoning

BACON, PEA & POTATO SOUP

1 lb potatoes – peeled & diced
½ lb smoked bacon – fat removed & chopped
1 leek – washed, trimmed & chopped
1 onion – peeled & finely chopped
1 lb frozen peas
2 pints vegetable stock
2 bay leaves
¼ pint double cream

1. Dry fry the bacon until nearly cooked
2. Add the onion and leek and gently cook for 5 mins (add some butter if needed)
3. Add the stock, bay leaves, seasoning and the potatoes and bring to the boil and simmer for 15 mins
4. Add the peas and half the bacon, return to the boil and simmer for 10 mins
5. Remove the bay leaves, transfer to a blender and liquidise
6. Return to a clean pan, add the cream, season and gradually re-heat. Serve sprinkled with the rest of the bacon

POTATO AND CARROT SOUP

1 lb potatoes – peeled & chopped
½ lb carrots – peeled & chopped
1 onion – peeled & chopped
½ lb mushrooms – sliced
1 stick celery – washed & chopped
2 cloves garlic – crushed
2½ pints chicken stock
1 tbsp fresh thyme – chopped
1 oz butter

1. *Melt the butter and sauté the onion until soft*

2. *Add the potatoes, carrots and garlic – fry for 3 mins*

3. *Add the rest of the ingredients, season then pour over the stock, bring to the boil then simmer for 20 mins*

4. *Blend the vegetables in batches in a food processor, adding more stock if needed*

5. *Return to a clean pan and gradually re-heat*

APPLE & POTATO SOUP

1 lb potatoes – peeled & diced
1 lb cooking apples – peeled, cored & cubed
3 leeks – trimmed & sliced
10 fl oz apple juice
7 fl oz single cream
1 oz butter
2 pints water
¼ tsp nutmeg

1. *Melt the butter and gently fry the leeks until soft*

2. *Add the potatoes, apple and water. Add the nutmeg and season*

3. *Bring to the boil and simmer for 20 mins*

4. *Put the soup into a food processor, in batches if necessary, and liquidise*

5. *Return the soup to a clean pan and add the cream, apple juice. Season and slowly re-heat*

MINESTRONE SOUP

1 lb potatoes – peeled & diced
½ lb bacon – chopped
2 stalks celery – washed, trimmed & sliced
4 carrots – peeled & thinly sliced
2 onions – peeled & sliced
3 courgettes – washed & sliced
1 bunch fresh spinach – washed, trimmed & chopped
½ head cauliflower – washed and florets
    removed & kept
3 tomatoes – skinned & chopped
4 tbsp extra virgin olive oil
Vegetable stock

1. *Heat the oil in a large saucepan and fry the bacon and onion for about 5 mins*

2. *Add all the vegetables and cook for about 10 mins, stirring frequently*

3. *Add enough stock to cover the mixture, season and bring to the boil. Reduce to a simmer and cook for 20 mins*

4. *Add tomatoes and cook for 3 more mins*

CREAM OF POTATO & HADDOCK SOUP

1 lb potatoes – peeled & diced
2 lbs cooked haddock fillet – skinned & diced
2 onions – peeled & finely sliced
3 pints milk
8 tbsp fresh parsley – chopped
5 ozs butter

1. *Melt butter and gently fry the onions for 5 mins*

2. *Add the potatoes and cook for 10 mins.*

3. *Add the milk and fish and bring to boil, simmer for 12-15 mins*

4. *Put the soup in a blender and liquidise*

5. *Clean the pan and return the soup with half of the parsley. Season and re-heat without boiling*

6. *Serve sprinkled with the rest of the parsley*

POTATO & BEETROOT SOUP

1 lb potatoes – peeled & cubed
1 ½ lb cooked beetroot – cubed
2 onions – peeled and finely chopped
2 carrots – peeled & diced
3 pints vegetable stock
2 tbsp tomato purée
2 tbsp vegetable oil

1. *Heat the oil in a large pan and fry the potatoes, onion and carrot for 5 mins*

2. *Add the beetroot, purée and stock. Bring to the boil then simmer for 20 mins*

3. *Put the soup in a blender and liquidise. Return to a clean pan, season and re-heat without boiling, adding more stock if necessary*

FISH & TOMATO SOUP

1 lb new potatoes – scrubbed & quartered
1 lb haddock fillet – skinned
1 onion – peeled & finely chopped
1 small red chilli – seeded & finely chopped
1 red pepper – seeded, cored, skinned and sliced
1 large tin chopped tomatoes
1 tbsp dried oregano
½ tsp paprika
½ pint fish stock
1 tbsp olive oil

1. Pre-heat oven to GM6/200°c/400°f

2. Wrap the fish in tin foil and bake the fish for 10 mins. Remove and drain, reserving the liquid

3. Heat the oil and fry the onion, chilli and pepper for 5 mins

4. Add the potatoes, tomatoes, oregano, paprika and stock. Season and bring to the boil. Simmer for 15 mins

5. Flake the fish, add along with the reserved liquid – cook for 5 more mins

POTATO, COURGETTE & GARLIC SOUP

1 lb potatoes – peeled & cut into chunks
5 courgettes – washed & chopped
1 whole head of garlic – wrapped in silver foil
2 onions – peeled & chopped
4 pints vegetable stock
5 tbsp vegetable oil

1. Pre-heat oven to GM5/190°c/375°f

2. Roast the garlic in the oven for 15 mins. Remove foil, allow to cool slightly then squeeze out the garlic pulp and put to one side

3. Meanwhile heat the oil and slowly cook the onions for 5 mins

4. Add the courgettes and garlic and cook for 5 more mins

5. Add the potatoes and stock and bring to the boil, reduce to a simmer and cook for 20 mins

6. Put the soup into a blender and liquidize until smooth. Return to a clean pan, season, re-heat, simmer until the desired consistency is reached

HADDOCK, BACON & POTATO CHOWDER

1 lb potatoes – peeled & diced - boiled for 10 mins
1 lb cooked smoked haddock - flaked into 1" pieces
1 small can sweetcorn - drained
1 bunch spring onions - chopped
3 rashers bacon – fat removed and chopped
1 pint white sauce – made from a packet
1 pint milk
¼ pint single cream
2 tbsp fresh parsley – chopped
1 oz butter

1. Melt the butter in a large pan, add the onions & bacon and fry gently for 5 mins

2. Pour on the milk, season, stir & bring to a simmer

3. Add the white sauce, potatoes and sweetcorn. Bring to a simmer and cook for 5 mins

4. Add the fish and simmer for 5 more mins

5. Stir in the cream and parsley and serve

HADDOCK, PRAWN AND POTATO CHOWDER

1 lb potatoes – peeled & diced
1 lb cooked smoked haddock – skinned & diced
5 oz prawns - peeled
5 sticks celery – washed and chopped
½ pints coconut milk
1 pint fish stock
½ pint milk
3 tbsp vegetable oil

1. Heat the oil in a large pan and cook the celery for 5 mins

2. Add the potatoes and cook for a further 3 mins

3. Add the coconut milk and stock. Bring to the boil, cover and simmer for about 15 mins

4. Add the haddock and the milk and simmer uncovered for 6-7 mins until fish starts to flake

5. Stir in the prawns, heat until the prawns are cooked, season and serve

HADDOCK, LEEK AND POTATO CHOWDER

1 lb potatoes – peeled & diced
1 lb cooked smoked Haddock – skinned & diced
5 oz leeks – washed & chopped
1 pint milk
½ pint fish stock
½ oz butter
1 tbsp fresh parsley – chopped

1. Put the potatoes and leek in a large saucepan, add the milk, bring to the boil and simmer for 10 mins
2. Put half the mixture into a blender, add the stock and blitz in into a purée
3. Return to the pan, add the fish, stir and simmer for 10 mins
4. Add the butter, season and stir well. Sprinkle with parsley

CELERIAC AND POTATO SOUP

1 lb potatoes – peeled & cut into 1" chunks
1 lb celeriac – washed, peeled & cut into chunks
10 sticks of celery – washed & chopped
2 pints milk

1. Take a large saucepan and all the ingredients, season and bring nearly to the boil
2. Reduce to a simmer for 25 mins
3. Put the soup into a blender and blitz until smooth. Rinse the pan and push the soup through a sieve into the pan
4. Season and re-heat slowly

POTATO MULLIGATAWNY

1 lb potatoes – peeled & diced
1 large onion – peeled & sliced
1 large tin chopped tomatoes
½ lb courgettes – washed & sliced
2 pints vegetable stock
3 tsp curry powder
1½ tbsp Worcester sauce
1 tbsp vegetable oil

1. Heat the oil and fry the onion until soft
2. Stir in the curry powder and cook for 2-3 mins
3. Add the potatoes, courgettes, tomatoes and stock, season and bring to the boil. Reduce to a simmer for 20 mins
4. Transfer to a blender and liquidise
5. Transfer back to clean pan, adjust seasoning and add Worcester sauce and more stock if necessary consistency is reached

POTATO & CARROT SOUP

1 lb potatoes – peeled & cubed
1 lb carrots – peeled & sliced
2 onions – peeled & sliced
2 pints chicken stock
1 tbsp vegetable oil

1. Heat the oil and fry the onion for 5 mins
2. Add the potatoes and carrots, season and stir well. Pour on the stock and bring to the boil. Simmer for 20 mins
3. Transfer to a food processor and liquidise
4. Return to a clean pan, adjust the seasoning and gently re-heat

POTATO BACON & CELERY SOUP

1 lb potatoes – peeled & cubed
1 large onion – peeled & chopped
6 rashers bacon – fat removed and chopped
3 sticks celery – chopped into 1" pieces
3 cloves garlic – crushed
3 carrots – peeled and cut into 1" pieces
2 pints vegetable stock
3 oz butter
1 bay leaf
1 tbsp fresh thyme – finely chopped

1. Melt the butter in a large pan and gently fry the onion, garlic and bacon until the onion is soft
2. Add the potatoes, carrots, celery, thyme and bay leaf. Cook for 5 mins
3. Add the stock, season & bring to the boil and simmer for about 15 mins

CULLEN SKINK

1 lb potatoes – peeled, boiled & mashed
2 lbs smoked haddock
½ lb leeks – washed & finely sliced
1 onion – peeled & finely sliced
2 egg yolks
¾ pint milk
¾ pint water
½ pint single cream
1 oz butter
2 tbsp fresh parsley – chopped

1. *Place the haddock, skin side up in a pan and cover with the onion, milk and water. Heat till the liquid is simmering and poach for 10 mins. Strain the liquid into another pan and flake the fish*

2. *Mix the potato and leeks into the liquid and simmer for 10 mins. Beat the egg yolk into the cream and stir into the soup. Re-heat gently until slightly thickened. Gently stir in the fish and season*

3. *Stir in the parsley and serve hot, dotted with the butter*

POTATO & PRAWN CHOWDER

1 lb potatoes – peeled & diced
½ lb frozen prawns
1 large tin sweetcorn – drained
1 onion – peeled & finely chopped
1 pint milk
¼ pint chicken stock
1 oz butter
3 oz cheddar cheese – grated

1. *Melt butter in a saucepan and fry the onion for 5 mins.*

2. *Add the potatoes, season, stir and cook for a further 2 mins.*

3. *Pour on the stock and half the milk, bring to the boil and simmer for 15 mins.*

4. *Add the prawns, sweetcorn and remaining milk. Season and gradually re-heat - do not boil. Ensure the prawns are cooked.*

5. *Remove from heat and add the cheese, stirring continuously until it has melted. Serve.*

GOULASH SOUP

1 lb potatoes – peeled & cubed
1 lb stewing beef – cubed
1 onion – peeled and sliced
2 cloves garlic – crushed
1 green pepper – deseeded & sliced
1 large tin chopped tomatoes
2 tbsp tomato purée
2 pints beef stock
1 tbsp red wine vinegar
2 tsp paprika
Pinch of caraway seeds
2 tbsp vegetable oil

1. *Heat the oil in a frying pan and add the beef, pepper, onion, garlic and paprika. Fry for about 5 mins*

2. *Add the vinegar, ½ the stock and the caraway seeds. Bring to the boil then cover and simmer for 1 hour*

3. *Add the remaining stock along with the remaining ingredients. Simmer uncovered for 20 mins*

SMOKED HADDOCK CHOWDER (2)

1 lb potatoes – peeled & diced
1½ lb smoked haddock – skinned, filleted & diced
10 rashers bacon – diced
1 large tin sweetcorn – drained
1 leek – trimmed, washed & sliced
2 pints fish stock
2 pints milk
2 tbsp plain flour
4 tbsp fresh parsley – chopped
2 tbsp vegetable oil

1. *Heat the oil in a pan and fry the bacon until crispy, remove and drain*

2. *Add the potatoes and leek and fry for 5 mins*

3. *Add the sweetcorn and stir in the flour and cook for 1 minute*

4. *Gradually add the stock, bring to the boil then simmer for 15 mins*

5. *Add the haddock and sufficient milk to achieve the desired consistency. Cook for 10 mins then add the parsley and seasoning*

CULLEN SKINK (2)

1 lb potatoes – peeled & chopped
1 lb smoked haddock – washed & cleaned
½ pint milk
½ pint water
1 small onion – peeled & sliced
4 tbsp double cream
1 tbsp fresh parsley – chopped
1 small blade mace
1 oz butter

1. Poach the fish, skin side up in the milk with the onion and mace until just cooked then stand for 10 mins

2. Meanwhile, heat the butter and gently cook the potatoes and onion for about 10 mins

3. Remove the fish, drain, skin, bone and flake. Strain the liquid and reserve

4. Add the liquid to the potatoes

5. Add the mixture to a blender and liquidise

6. Re-heat in a clean pan and add the fish and parsley. Season, serve mixed with double cream

POTATO, HAM & SWEETCORN CHOWDER

1 lb potatoes – peeled & diced
12 oz sweetcorn
1 onion – peeled & chopped
1 red pepper – peeled & chopped
3 sticks celery – washed & chopped
½ lb cooked ham – diced
1 pint vegetable stock
½ pint milk
2 tbsp corn flour (blended with a little of the milk)
1 tbsp vegetable oil

1. Heat the oil in a large pan and gently fry the onion, pepper and celery until soft

2. Add the potato and stock, bring to the boil then simmer for 10 mins

3. Add the sweetcorn and simmer for 5 mins

4. Add the milk, bring to the boil, remove from heat and add the ham and corn flour stirring until thickened

5. Season, re-heat without boiling and serve

BROCCOLI, CHEESE & POTATO SOUP

1 lb potatoes (floury) – peeled & diced
1 large head broccoli – cut into florets
6 oz mature cheddar cheese – grated
2 onions – peeled and thinly sliced
2 cloves garlic – crushed
2 pints milk
2 pints chicken stock
2 oz butter
1 tbsp fresh thyme – chopped

1. Melt the butter and fry the onion and garlic for 5 mins

2. Add the potatoes and thyme, season and stir well

3. Add the stock and bring to the boil and simmer for 10 mins

4. Add the milk and broccoli, return to the boil and simmer for 10 mins

5. Transfer the soup to a blender – in batches if necessary, and liquidise. Return to a clean pan, add the cheese and season. Gradually re-heat but do not boil

POTATO & WATERCRESS SOUP (2)

1 lb potatoes – peeled & diced
2 bunches watercress – stalks removed
2 pints vegetable stock
½ pint double cream
2 shallots – finely chopped
2 tbsp fresh thyme – chopped
1 oz butter

1. Heat the butter and gently fry the shallots until soft

2. Add the watercress stalks and potato. Stir well

3. Add the stock bring to the boil, simmer for 15 mins

4. Add half the watercress leaves, cook for 1 more minute and put the mixture into a blender and liquidise

5. Return to a clean pan and slowly re-heat

6. Season, add the cream and the rest of the leaves, stir and heat for 2 mins

LETTUCE & POTATO SOUP

1 lb potatoes – peeled & diced
2 large lettuces – washed & shredded
2 onions – peeled & chopped
10 fl oz single cream
60 fl oz vegetable stock
2 oz butter

1. Heat the butter in a large pan and gently fry the onions till soft
2. Add the stock and potatoes bring to the boil and simmer for 15 mins
3. Add the lettuce and bring back to the boil. Remove from heat and transfer to a blender. Liquidise
4. Return to a clean pan, season and re-heat
5. Serve with a swirl of cream at the top

POTATO, CHEESE & LEEK SOUP

1 lb potatoes – peeled & cubed
5 leeks – trimmed, washed & chopped
½ lb cheddar cheese – grated
2 pints vegetable stock
2 oz butter
4 tbsp fresh chives – chopped
¼ pint milk

1. Melt the butter and gently fry the potato and leek for 10 mins
2. Season, pour on the stock and bring to the boil and simmer for 20 mins
3. Transfer to a blender and liquidise. Return to a clean pan, season and add the cheese and milk. Re-heat gradually and stir in the chives

POTATO & LEEK SOUP WITH CHEESE

1 lb potatoes – peeled & diced
1 lb leeks – trimmed, washed & sliced
5 oz mature cheese – crumbled
1½ pints vegetable stock
1 pint milk
2 oz butter

1. Melt the butter in a large pan add the potatoes and cook for 6-7 mins
2. Add the leeks and cook for 5 more mins
3. Add the stock and milk, season and bring to the boil. Reduce heat, cover and simmer for about 15 mins or until the desired consistency is reached
4. Stir in the cheese and heat until it has melted

CREAMED POTATO & BROAD BEAN SOUP

1 lb potatoes – peeled & cubed
1 lb broad beans – par boiled, drained & skinned
1 large onion – peeled and chopped
3 pints chicken stock
4 fl oz single cream
1½ tbsp olive oil

1. Heat the oil in a large pan and fry the onion until it begins to soften
2. Add the potatoes and broad beans. Season and pour on the stock. Bring to the boil and simmer for 15-20 mins
3. Transfer to a blender and liquidise. Return the soup to a clean pan and season. Stir in the cream. Gradually re-heat

PORTUGUESE POTATO SOUP

1 lb potatoes – peeled & sliced
1 onion – peeled & sliced
3 cloves garlic – crushed
4 oz Kale (leaves only) – shredded
¾ pint vegetable stock
2 tbsp olive oil

1. Put the stock in a pan and bring to the boil, season and add the potatoes, onion and garlic. Simmer for 15 mins
2. Remove about ⅓ of the potatoes with a slotted spoon and put in a blender. Add some of the stock liquidise and return to the pan. Bring to the boil
3. Season and add the kale and simmer for 5 mins
4. Add the olive oil, stir well and serve

SPICY POTATO SOUP

1 lb potatoes – peeled & chopped
1 onion – peeled & chopped
1 large can cannellini beans – drained
2 pints chicken stock
1 inch fresh ginger – grated
2 tbsp mild curry paste
2 cloves garlic – crushed
1 tbsp vegetable oil

1. Heat the oil and gently fry the onion, garlic and ginger for 5 mins
2. Add the curry paste and cook for 1 more minute
3. Add the potatoes and half the beans, stir well and pour on the stock. Season and bring to the boil then simmer for 20 mins
4. Transfer the soup to a blender and liquidise. Return to a clean pan, season, add the remaining beans and slowly re-heat

POTATO & CABBAGE SOUP

1 lb potatoes – peeled & cubed
1½ lb Savoy cabbage – finely shredded
2 onions – peeled & finely chopped
3 pints vegetable stock
2 oz butter

1. Melt the butter in a large saucepan & fry the onion for 5 mins
2. Add the potatoes & cook for 5 more mins
3. Add the stock, season and bring to the boil and simmer for 15 mins
4. Add the cabbage and simmer for 5 more mins
5. Put the mixture in a food processor and liquidise (in batches if necessary)
6. Return to a clean pan, season and gently re-heat

WATERCRESS & POTATO SOUP

1 lb potatoes – peeled & chopped
1 lb watercress – large stalks removed
2 onions – peeled & finely chopped
4 pints vegetable stock
3 oz butter

1. Take a large pan, heat the butter until melted and gently heat the potatoes and onions for 3-4 mins
2. Add the stock. Simmer for 15 mins.
3. Add the watercress and simmer for 5 more mins
4. Put into a processor (in batches if necessary) and liquidise
5. Return to a clean pan, season & re-heat

POTATO & APPLE SOUP

1 lb potatoes – peeled and cubed
1 lb apples (Cox's or similar) – cored and chopped
½ lb leeks – trimmed and sliced
1½ pints chicken stock
2 oz butter

1. Melt the butter and gently fry the potatoes, apples and leeks until the leeks start to soften.
2. Season and pour in the stock. Bring to the boil and simmer for 20 mins.
3. Transfer to a blender and liquidise. Return to a clean pan, season and gradually re-heat – adding more stock if needed.

CREAMED POTATO & LENTIL SOUP

1 lb potatoes – peeled & cubed
½ lb lentils – washed & drained
1 onion – peeled & finely chopped
2 sticks celery – washed & finely chopped
1 pint chicken stock
½ pint milk
2 oz butter
2 tbsp fresh parsley – chopped

1. Melt the butter and gently fry the potatoes, onion and celery for 10 mins
2. Add the stock and milk, season, bring to the boil then add the lentils and parsley. Return to the boil, cover and simmer on a very low heat for 1 hour
3. Put in a blender and liquidise, return to a clean pan, season and slowly re-heat

POTATO & MUSSEL SOUP

1 lb potatoes – peeled & diced
25 mussels – scrubbed and beards removed
1 clove garlic – crushed
6 fl oz dry white wine
2 oz butter
1 pint chicken stock

1. *Melt the butter and fry the potatoes for 5 mins*
2. *Season, add the stock and bring to the boil. Simmer for 15-18 mins*
3. *Meanwhile put the wine in a frying pan, add the garlic and heat the mussels until they open (throw away any that do not open). Remove the mussels*
4. *Remove ⅓ of the potatoes with a slotted spoon and set aside*
5. *Liquidise the remaining soup then return to a clean pan. Add the wine, season, stir and gradually re-heat*
6. *Add the reserved potatoes and the mussels, continue to heat until the mussels are cooked*

POTATO & SWEETCORN SOUP

1 lb potatoes – peeled & cubed
1 large tin sweetcorn – drained
2 rashers bacon – chopped
4 sticks celery – trimmed & chopped
1 pint chicken stock
½ pint milk
2 oz butter
1½ tbsp corn flour

1. *Melt the butter and fry the onion and bacon for 5 mins*
2. *Add the potatoes and celery - fry for 2 more mins*
3. *Season, stir and pour on the stock & bring back to the boil. Simmer for 15 mins*
4. *Blend the corn flour with a little of the milk. Add to the soup with the remaining milk & sweetcorn. Stir well. Bring back to the boil & simmer for 5 mins*
5. *Transfer half the soup to a blender & liquidise. Return to the pan, season & re-heat*

CHEESE & POTATO SOUP

1 lb potatoes – peeled & chopped
4 oz mature cheddar cheese – grated
1 onion – peeled & chopped
2 sticks celery – trimmed, washed & chopped
1½ pints vegetable stock
2 oz butter

1. *Melt the butter in a pan and gently fry the onion until it starts to soften*
2. *Add the potatoes and celery. Stir, season and cook over a low heat for 10 mins*
3. *Pour in the stock, stir and bring to the boil. Simmer for 15 mins*
4. *Put the soup in a blender and liquidise*
5. *Return to a clean pan, season and add the cheese. Gradually re-heat stirring continually until the cheese has melted*

POTATO & PEA SOUP (2)

1 lb potatoes – peeled & chopped
1 lb frozen peas
1 lb dried split green peas – soaked overnight
2 onions – peeled & chopped
2 pints vegetable stock
2 sticks celery – trimmed & chopped
2 tbsp olive oil

1. *Rinse and drain the split peas and reserve the liquid*
2. *Heat the oil and fry the onion until it starts to soften*
3. *Add the celery and the potatoes, stir and cook for 5 mins*
4. *Add the split peas and the vegetable stock, season, stir and bring to the boil. Simmer for 1 hour, skimming off any scum that rises to the surface*
5. *Add the frozen peas and return to the boil. Simmer for 5 more mins*
6. *Transfer the mixture to a blender (in batches if necessary) and liquidise*
7. *Return the mixture to a clean pan, season and gradually re-heat, adding the reserved liquid if necessary*

CORN & CHICKEN CHOWDER

1 lb potatoes – peeled & diced
½ lb cooked chicken – shredded
1 lb tinned sweetcorn – drained
1 onion – peeled and finely sliced
1 red pepper – cored and finely chopped
¾ pint chicken stock
¾ pint milk
2 tbsp plain flour
1 oz butter

1. *Melt the butter and fry the onion and pepper for 5 mins*

2. *Sprinkle with the flour, stir well and cook for 2 mins*

3. *Add the stock and milk, stir well, season and bring to the boil*

4. *Add all the other ingredients, stir and simmer gently for about 30 mins or until the right consistency is reached*

ROAST POTATO SOUP

1 lb potatoes – peeled & cubed
3 parsnips – peeled & cubed
2 carrots – peeled & cubed
1 onion – peeled & sliced
2 cloves garlic – crushed
1½ pints chicken stock
3 tbsp olive oil
½ tsp cumin
½ tsp turmeric
3 tbsp fresh parsley – chopped

1. *Heat the oven to GM6/200°c/400°f*

2. *In a large mixing bowl mix the vegetables, garlic, spices and oil. Season*

3. *Put the mixture in a roasting tin and place in the oven for about 30 mins*

4. *Put the mixture in a saucepan, season and pour on the stock, bring to the boil then simmer for 5 mins*

5. *Put half the mixture in a food processor and liquidise. Return to the pan and gradually re-heat*

6. *Sprinkle with the parsley and serve*

SEAFOOD CHOWDER

1 lb potatoes – peeled & cubed
1 lb cod fillet – cut into chunks
1 lb prawns – defrosted
1 leek – trimmed & finely chopped
1 onion – peeled & finely chopped
3 cloves garlic – crushed
1 large can sweetcorn – drained
1 tbsp ready made lemongrass
1 tbsp lemon juice
¼ pint milk
16 fl oz fish stock
16 fl oz dry white wine
2 tbsp fresh parsley – chopped
1 tbsp olive oil

1. *Heat the oil and fry the leek and onion until softened*

2. *Add the potatoes, garlic, lemongrass, lemon juice, 1 tbsp of parsley and the wine. Stir well and bring to the boil*

3. *Season, add the milk and stock, return to the boil then simmer for about 10-12 mins*

4. *Add the fish and cook for 3 mins*

5. *Add the sweetcorn, parsley and prawns. Season and cook for a couple more mins – until the prawns and fish are cooked*

CHEESE & POTATO SOUP (2)

1 lb potatoes – peeled & diced
2 carrots – peeled & diced
2 onions – peeled ,& finely chopped
5 oz cheddar cheesed - grated
3 sticks celery washed & finely chopped
1 pint vegetable stock
½ pint milk
1 oz flour
1 oz butter

1. *Put the vegetables in a saucepan add the stock and bring to the boil. Simmer for 20 mins*

2. *Mix the flour with a little milk and add to the soup with the rest of the milk*

3. *Bring to the boil again and simmer for 5 mins*

4. *Remove from heat, season then stir in the butter and cheese and stir until they have melted*

POTATO, LEEK & CELERIAC SOUP

1 lb potatoes – peeled & diced
1 lb celeriac – peeled & diced
2 leeks – trimmed & thinly sliced
1 onion – peeled & thinly sliced
2 pints vegetable stock
2 bay leaves
2 oz butter
1 tbsp fresh parsley – chopped

1. *Melt the butter and fry the onion and leeks until they start to soften*
2. *Add the potatoes, celeriac and bay leaves. Season, stir and then pour on the stock and bring to the boil. Reduce to a simmer and cook for 20 mins*
3. *Remove the bay leaves, add the parsley, stir and transfer to a blender and liquidise*
4. *Return to a clean pan, season and gradually re-heat*

COUNTRY SOUP

1 lb potatoes – peeled & diced
1 carrot – peeled & diced
2 onions – peeled & diced
2 sticks celery – chopped
¼ lb frozen peas
¼ lb tomatoes – chopped
1 clove garlic – crushed
3 rashers bacon – chopped
1 pint ham stock
2 oz pasta twists
2 tbsp fresh parsley – chopped
2 oz butter

1. *Melt the butter and fry the bacon and onion for 2 mins*
2. *Add the potatoes, carrot, celery and pasta. Cook for 2 mins*
3. *Add the tomatoes and garlic, season well, stir then pour on the stock. Bring to the boil then simmer for 15 mins*
4. *Add the peas and parsley, adjust the seasoning and simmer for 5 more mins*

CHUNKY COD & POTATO SOUP

1 lb potatoes – peeled & diced
¾ lb skinless cod fillet – flaked
1 onion – peeled & chopped
2 rashers bacon – rind removed
1½ pints milk
2 tbsp flour
2 tbsp fresh parsley – chopped
1 tbsp vegetable oil

1. *Dry fry the bacon in a large pan. Remove and reserve*
2. *Add the oil, heat and fry the onion until it starts to soften*
3. *Cut the bacon into pieces, add to the pan and stir*
4. *Sprinkle with the flour and stir continually for 1-2 mins*
5. *Drizzle in ¼ pint of milk and stir well to ensure all the flour is mixed*
6. *Add the potatoes and the rest of the milk, season and bring to the boil. Simmer for 10 mins*
7. *Add the fish and the parsley and cook for at least 10 more mins until the fish is cooked*

COTTAGE SOUP

1 lb potatoes – peeled & diced
2 carrots – peeled & diced
2 onions – peeled & diced
½ Savoy cabbage – washed & shredded
4 sticks celery – trimmed, cut into small pieces
2 leeks – trimmed and cut into small pieces
4 rashers bacon – rind removed
1½ pints vegetable stock

1. *Par-boil the cabbage for 5 mins and drain*
2. *Put all the vegetables into a large pan, season and pour on the stock. Bring back to the boil then cover and simmer gently for 30 mins, stirring occasionally and adding more stock if needed*
3. *Dry fry the bacon then cut into small pieces*
4. *When the soup has reached the desired consistency, add the bacon, season and serve*

POTATO & BROAD BEAN SOUP

1 lb potatoes – peeled & sliced
1½ lb broad beans – shelled & washed
1 onion – peeled & finely chopped
2 carrots – peeled & sliced
2 pints vegetable stock
3 tbsp finely chopped parsley
1 oz butter

1. Boil the potatoes, beans and carrots for 20 mins. Drain
2. Melt the butter in a large pan and fry the onion until soft
3. Add the stock, vegetables and parsley. Season and bring to the boil
4. Transfer to a blender and liquidise. Return to a clean pan and re-heat

POTATO & SPLIT PEA SOUP

1 lb waxy potatoes – peeled & grated
½ lb split peas – soaked overnight & drained
1 large onion – peeled & finely chopped
2 sticks celery – washed, trimmed & chopped
¼ lb cooked ham – chopped
3 oz butter
2 pints vegetable stock
2 tbsp fresh parsley – chopped

1. Melt the butter and fry the potatoes, onion, celery and ham for 5 mins
2. Add the split peas, parsley and season. Stir well and pour on the stock. Bring to the boil then reduce to a very gentle simmer
3. Cover and cook for 2 hours

POTATO & BEEF SOUP

1 lb potatoes – peeled and cubed
1 lb stewing beef – cut into cubes
2 large tins chopped tomatoes
4 sticks celery – trimmed and chopped
4 courgettes – trimmed and chopped
1 tbsp fresh thyme – chopped
1 tbsp fresh parsley – chopped
4 pints beef stock

1. Bring the stock to the boil in a large pan, add the beef and return to the boil, skimming off any scum from the surface and simmer for 30 mins
2. Add the celery and herbs. Season and continue to simmer for an hour. Allow the liquid to reduce slightly
3. Add the potatoes, courgettes and tomatoes, season and simmer for 30 mins - again reducing to achieve the desired consistency

POTATO & BROCCOLI SOUP

1 lb potatoes – peeled & cubed
1½ lb broccoli – stalk removed & cut into pieces
1 onion – peeled & sliced
5 fl oz single cream
3 pints light chicken stock
1 tbsp olive oil

1. Heat the oil and fry the onion until soft
2. Bring the stock to the boil in a large pan and add the potatoes and broccoli. Simmer for 20 min
3. Transfer to a blender, in batches if necessary, and liquidise
4. Clean the pan and add the soup. Add the cream, season and gradually re-heat

CHUNKY BROCCOLI & POTATO SOUP

1 lb potatoes – peeled & diced
1½ lb broccoli florets – washed
1½ pints chicken stock
2 onions – peeled and chopped
1½ oz butter

1. Melt the butter in a large pan and fry the onion until it starts to soften
2. Add the stock, season and bring to the boil
3. Add the potatoes and simmer for 10 mins
4. Pour half the soup into a processor, liquidise and pour it back into the pan
5. Add the broccoli and season, stir well. Bring back to the boil and simmer for 10-12 mins

SPRING SOUP

1 lb potatoes – peeled & cubed
3 leeks – washed, trimmed & sliced
1 onion – peeled & sliced
4 shallots – peeled & sliced
2 cloves garlic – crushed
1½ pints vegetable stock
2 tbsp olive oil

1. Heat the oil & gently fry the potatoes, onion, leeks, shallots for 5 mins
2. Add the garlic & fry for 3 more mins
3. Add the stock, bring to the boil & simmer for 20 mins
4. Put the mixture in a food processor & liquidise
5. Return to a clean pan, season & slowly re-heat

POTAGE CRECY

1 lb potatoes – peeled & cubed
1½ lbs carrots – peeled & chopped
2 onions – peeled & finely chopped
2 pints chicken stock
2 oz butter
1 tbsp fresh parsley – chopped
4 tbsp single cream

1. Melt the butter and cook the potatoes, carrots and onion for 5 mins
2. Add the stock and parsley. Season and bring to the boil. Simmer for 20 mins
3. Put the soup in a food processor and liquidise. Return to a clean pan, season and gradually re-heat
4. Serve with a swirl of cream in each bowl

POTATO, BACON & PEA SOUP

1 lb potatoes – peeled & diced
12 rashers bacon – rind removed & finely chopped
1 lb frozen peas
2 small onions – peeled & chopped
3 tbsp fresh parsley – chopped
2 pints chicken stock

1. Dry fry the bacon until slightly browned.
2. Add the potato & onion. Cook gently until the onion softens
3. Add the stock, bring to the boil then simmer for 15 mins
4. Add the peas, bring to the boil then simmer for 5 mins
5. Put in a food processor (in batches if necessary) and liquidise
6. Return the soup to a clean pan, season, add the parsley and gently re-heat

POTATO & GARLIC SOUP

1 lb potatoes – peeled & diced
5 whole garlic bulbs – split into cloves & peeled
½ lb bacon – cut into small pieces
1 tbsp fresh parsley – chopped
5 oz goose fat
4 pints chicken stock

1. Boil the garlic cloves for about 5 mins and drain
2. Melt the fat gently and fry the garlic and bacon for 5 more mins
3. Add the potatoes and cook for 5 more mins – don't let the garlic brown
4. Add the parsley, season and pour on the stock, bring to the boil, skimming the surface if necessary and simmer for 40 mins reducing slightly
5. Transfer to a blender, in batches if necessary, and liquidise
6. Return to a clean pan, season and gradually re-heat. Reduce or add more stock to achieve the desired consistency

POTATO & SPINACH SOUP

1 lb potatoes – peeled & sliced
1 lb spinach - leaves only (washed)
½ lb onions – peeled & thinly sliced
½ lb leeks – trimmed, peeled & thinly sliced
4 fl oz double cream
3 pints chicken stock
4 oz butter

1. *Melt the butter in a large saucepan and cook the onions and leeks for 5 mins*

2. *Add the potatoes and the stock, season, boil then reduce to a simmer for 15 mins*

3. *Add the spinach & simmer for 5 more mins until the spinach wilts*

4. *Put the soup (in batches) in a food processor & liquidise*

5. *Return to a clean pan, add the cream, check seasoning & slowly re-heat*

MARJORIE'S CREAM OF POTATO SOUP

1 lb potatoes – peeled & chopped
2 pints chicken stock
2 oz butter
2 oz flour
1 pint milk
4 fl oz double cream

1. *Melt the butter, add the flour & make a roux with the milk*

2. *Boil the potatoes in the chicken stock for 20 mins. Drain*

3. *Mash the potatoes and add to the sauce, pour on the stock, season & stir*

4. *Place the potato mixture in a blender and blitz until a smooth consistency*

5. *Add cream and re-heat gently*

6. *Check seasoning and serve*

BEETROOT & POTATO SOUP

1 lb (waxy) potatoes – peeled & diced
1 lb raw beetroot – peeled & grated
¾ lb cooked ham – diced
1 large onion – peeled & chopped
4 cloves garlic – crushed
4 sticks celery – trimmed & chopped
3 leeks – trimmed & chopped
4 pints chicken stock
1 tbsp fresh thyme – chopped
1 tbsp olive oil
2 oz butter

1. *Melt the butter in a large pan and fry the onion, garlic and thyme until softened*

2. *Add the beetroot, celery and leeks, stir well, season and pour in the stock. Bring to the boil then reduce to a simmer for 30 mins*

3. *Add the potatoes and ham. Season well and simmer gently for 1 hour*

BACON & POTATO SOUP (2)

1 lb potatoes – peeled & diced
½ lb bacon – rind removed & finely chopped
1 small tin sweetcorn – drained
2 onions – peeled & finely chopped
2 pints chicken stock
1 tbsp dried sage
1 tbsp fresh parsley – chopped
2 bay leaves

1. *Dry fry the bacon until it starts to brown. Remove with a slotted spoon and set aside*

2. *Add the onions and fry gently (adding some oil if needed) until softened*

3. *Add the potatoes and sage, season and stir. Pour on the stock, stir again, add the bay leaves and bring to the boil. Cook over a very low heat for 30 mins*

4. *Remove the bay leaves, add the sweetcorn and parsley and cook for 5 more mins*

POTATO & MUSHROOM SOUP

1 lb potatoes – peeled, chopped, boiled & drained
1½ lb mushrooms – washed & halved
1½ pints chicken stock
½ pint single cream
2 oz butter

1. *Melt the butter and gently fry the mushrooms until they start to soften*

2. *Add the potatoes, season and pour on the stock. Bring to a simmer then remove from the heat*

3. *Transfer the soup to a blender and liquidise*

4. *Return to a clean pan, stir in the cream and slowly re-heat*

POTATO, HAM & BEAN SOUP

1 lb potatoes – peeled & cubed
½ lb smoked ham – cubed
1 small can canellini beans
2 onions – peeled & finely chopped
3 cloves garlic – crushed
2 tbsp tomato purée
2½ pints chicken stock
1 tbsp fresh sage – chopped
1 oz butter

1. Melt the butter and cook the onions and garlic for 5 mins
2. Add the beans, water and sage. Bring to the boil then simmer for 10 mins
3. Add the potatoes, tomato purée, ham and stock. Season and simmer for 30 mins

VICHYSSOISE

1 lb potatoes – peeled & cut into chunks
1 lb leeks – trimmed & sliced
1 onion – peeled & chopped
2 pints chicken stock
6 fl oz cream
1½ oz butter
1 tbsp fresh parsley – finely chopped

1. Boil the potatoes in the stock
2. Meanwhile melt the butter and gently fry the leek and onion until softened
3. Put all the vegetables and stock into a processor and liquidise
4. Allow the soup to cool and refrigerate overnight
5. Just before serving, add the cream, adjust the seasoning and sprinkle with the parsley

CULLEN SKINK (3)

1 lb potatoes – peeled, boiled & mashed
12 oz smoked haddock – skinned & boned
1 onion – peeled & finely chopped
15 fl oz milk
10 fl oz water
1 oz butter

1. Melt the butter and fry the onion until it begins to soften
2. Meanwhile boil the water in a pan
3. Add the fish to the onion, season and pour on the boiling water. Simmer for 10 mins
4. Remove the fish with a slotted spoon and flake it
5. Add the potatoes and milk to the remaining liquid. Season and stir well to mix and bring back to the boil
6. Add the fish and simmer gently for 5 mins

VICHYSSOISE (2)

1 lb potatoes – peeled & chopped
2 onions – peeled & thinly sliced
4 leeks – trimmed & thinly sliced
1 stick celery – trimmed & thinly sliced
2½ pints chicken stock
1½ tbsp fresh parsley
½ pint cream
4 oz butter

1. Melt the butter and gently fry the onions and leeks until they start to soften
2. Add the potatoes, celery and parsley. Season, pour on the stock, stir and bring to the boil. Cover and simmer gently for 30 mins
3. Put the soup in a blender and liquidise. Put it in a large bowl, allow to cool, then cover with cling film and refrigerate for at least 3 hours
4. Stir in the cream and serve

POTATO & BRIE SOUP

1 lb potatoes – peeled & cubed
2 onions – peeled & finely sliced
3 cloves garlic – crushed
1 lb courgettes – washed & sliced
2 pints vegetable stock
1 pint milk
½ lb brie – rind removed & sliced
2 oz butter
3 tbsp double cream

1. Melt the butter and fry the onion and garlic for 5 mins

2. *Add the potatoes, courgettes, season and stir. Add stock. Bring to the boil and simmer for 20 mins*

3. *Add the milk and cheese. Heat gently and stir in the cream once the cheese has melted*

PAT'S POTATO & PARSLEY SOUP

1 lb potatoes – peeled & sliced
4 oz fresh parsley – chopped
1 onion – peeled & chopped
1½ pints vegetable stock
½ pint milk
2 sticks celery – washed, trimmed and chopped
2 oz butter

1. *Melt the butter in a large pan and fry the onion until it starts to soften*

2. *Add the potatoes and celery and fry gently for 5 mins*

3. *Season and pour on the stock and milk. Stir well, bring to the boil and simmer, uncovered for 20 mins*

4. *Add the parsley, stir well then transfer to a blender and liquidise. Return to a clean pan, adjust the seasoning and gradually re-heat*

PEANUT & POTATO SOUP

1 lb potatoes – peeled & cut into cubes
1 onion – peeled & chopped
1 large tin chopped tomatoes
2 pints chicken stock
6 oz peanuts
½ tsp chilli powder
3 tbsp groundnut oil

1. *Heat half the oil and fry the onion till it starts to soften*

2. *Add the potatoes. Season and stir well. Fry for 1 more minute*

3. *Add the tomatoes, peanuts, chilli powder and stock. Bring to the boil then simmer for 20 mins*

4. *Pour the soup into a blender and liquidise*

5. *Return the liquid to a clean pan, season and slowly re-heat*

POTATO & BLUE CHEESE CHOWDER

1 lb potatoes – peeled and diced
¾ lb skinless cod fillet – flaked
6 oz blue cheese – crumbled
1 large tin sweetcorn – drained
½ lb bacon rashers – cut into pieces
1 onion – peeled and diced
1 pint milk
1 tbsp olive oil

1. *Heat the oil and fry the onion until it starts to soften then add the potatoes and sweet corn, stir well*

2. *Season and add the milk. Bring to the boil then simmer for 20 mins*

3. *Meanwhile dry fry the bacon until cooked. Remove with a slotted spoon*

4. *Add the cheese and bacon to the chowder, season and stir. Serve as the cheese begins to melt*

PRAWN & POTATO CHOWDER

1 lb new potatoes – scrubbed & halved
1 lb frozen prawns – defrosted
1 onion – peeled & finely chopped
2 tomatoes – chopped into thin wedges
2 rashers bacon – derinded & chopped
½ pint milk
¼ pint cream
1 pint water

1. *Put the prawns in a small saucepan and pour on the water. Bring to the boil and simmer gently for 15 mins. Drain and reserve the liquid*

2. *Dry fry the bacon until brown and remove with a slotted spoon*

3. *Fry the onion in the bacon fat until it starts to soften*

4. *Add the potatoes and fry for 2 mins*

5. *Season, add the bacon and reserved liquid. Cover and simmer for 30 mins*

6. *Add the prawns, tomatoes and milk. Heat through until the prawns and tomatoes are cooked. Stir in the cream and serve*

POTATO, CHESTNUT & SPROUT SOUP

1 lb potatoes – peeled and diced
¼ lb chestnuts – peeled
1 lb Brussels sprouts – trimmed, peeled and halved
2 onions – peeled and chopped
2 oz butter
2 pints chicken stock

1. Melt the butter and cook the onions until they start to soften
2. Add the potatoes and sprouts, season and cook for 5 mins
3. Pour on the stock and bring to the boil. Simmer for 30 mins
4. Meanwhile boil the chestnuts for about 5 mins, drain and crumble
5. Transfer the potato mixture to a blender and liquidise. Return to a clean pan, season and slowly re-heat – adding more stock if needed
6. Serve sprinkled with the chestnuts

GOULASH SOUP (2)

1 lb potatoes – peeled & cubed
1 lb stewing steak – fat removed & cubed
2 red peppers – de-seeded & cut into squares
1 onion – peeled & sliced
2 cloves garlic – crushed
1 large can chopped tomatoes
1½ pints beef stock
1 tbsp red wine vinegar
2 tbsp tomato purée
2 tsp paprika
¼ tsp caraway seeds
2 tbsp vegetable oil
3 bay leaves

1. Heat the oil and fry the beef, onion, peppers, garlic and paprika for about 5 mins
2. Add the caraway seeds, vinegar, bay leaves and half the stock. Bring to the boil then simmer very gently for about 1 hour
3. Remove the bay leaves and add all the other ingredients, season, bring to the boil then simmer for 20 mins adding more stock if necessary

POTATO & CHICKEN CHOWDER

1 lb potatoes – peeled & diced
1 lb cooked chicken – diced
¼ lb cooked ham – diced
1 large tin sweetcorn – drained
½ lb frozen peas
1 leek – trimmed & thinly sliced
1 tbsp flour
1½ pints milk
1 tbsp vegetable oil

1. Heat the oil and fry the leek until it starts to soften
2. Add the potatoes and the milk, stir, season and bring to the boil then simmer for 10 mins
3. Add the remaining ingredients, return to the boil and simmer for about 10 mins – or until the desired consistency is reached and the potatoes are cooked

CRAB & POTATO CHOWDER

1 lb potatoes – peeled & diced
½ lb crab meat - cooked
¼ lb bacon – cut into pieces
1 onion – peeled & finely chopped
2 pints milk
4 fl oz double cream
2 tbsp plain flour
3 tbsp fresh parsley – chopped
1 oz butter
2 bay leaves

1. Dry fry the bacon until almost cooked.
2. Add the butter and fry the onion until it starts to soften.
3. Add the flour and cook for 1 min – stirring continuously.
4. Add a little of the milk, stir well and gradually stir in the rest of the milk. Add the potatoes and bay leaves. Bring almost to the boil then simmer for 15-18 mins.
5. Remove the bay leaf and add the crab meat and the cream. Season, stir and cook for 2-3 mins (Add a paste of cornflour and milk if you want the chowder to be thicker).

Salads

POTATO SALAD

1 lb new potatoes - scrubbed, boiled & drained
1 medium onion – peeled & finely chopped
5 fl oz mayonnaise
2 fl oz white wine vinegar

1. Slice the potatoes thinly into a basin. Season and add the onion. Mix in the vinegar and leave to cool slightly
2. Mix with the mayonnaise, serve while warm

NEW POTATO SALAD WITH STILTON & TARRAGON

1 lb new potatoes – scrubbed, boiled & drained
2 oz stilton – crumbled
3 fl oz crème fraîche
1 tbsp fresh tarragon – chopped
½ tbsp fresh mint – chopped

1. Allow the potatoes to cool slightly then stir in the cheese and the crème fraîche
2. Allow to cool further then stir in the herbs. Season & serve

POTATO, PEPPER & TOMATO SALAD

1 lb small new potatoes - scrubbed, boiled & drained
4 oz cherry tomatoes – halved
1 small can red peppers (pimento) sliced
8 olives
1 tbsp capers

Dressing
2 tbsp sun dried tomato paste
1 tbsp extra virgin olive oil
1 tbsp lemon juice

1. Mix together all the ingredients for the dressing in a large serving bowl and add the potatoes while still warm. Mix thoroughly and leave to cool
2. Add the tomatoes and peppers stirring gently. Season. Serve cool – scattered with the capers

CORONATION POTATO SALAD

1 lb new potatoes – scrubbed, boiled & drained
3 spring onions – chopped
½ tsp paprika
Cos lettuce leaves

Dressing
2 tsp plain yoghurt
2 tbsp mayonnaise
2 tbsp fresh parsley – chopped
3 tbsp mango chutney
1 tbsp curry paste

1. Allow the potatoes to cool then slice thinly
2. Put all the dressing ingredients into a large serving bowl and mix thoroughly. Season
3. Gently stir in the potatoes so as not to break them up
4. Spoon the mixture over the lettuce leaves and sprinkle with the spring onion and paprika. Serve cold

NEW POTATO & TUNA SALAD

1 lb new potatoes - scrubbed, boiled & drained
3 medium sized tuna steaks
3 large eggs – hard boiled, cooled & quartered
2 baby cos lettuce – leaves torn off
1 red onion – peeled & sliced
¼ lb cherry tomatoes – quartered
¼ lb Kenyan green beans – blanched & cooled
¼ lb asparagus – blanched & cooled
2 tbsp capers

Dressing
6 tbsp extra virgin olive oil
4 tbsp lemon juice

1. Heat 1 tbsp of olive oil in a pan. Season the tuna steaks and fry gently for 5 mins on each side, until cooked
2. Put the olive oil & lemon juice in a screw top jar and shake vigorously to mix
3. Put all the ingredients (except the tuna and eggs) in a large salad bowl and mix together with the dressing. Season
4. Arrange on a plate with the tuna and egg

BEEF & BLUE CHEESE POTATO SALAD

1 lb new potatoes – scrubbed, halved, boiled & drained
1 lb cooked cold roast beef – sliced into strips
½ lb blue cheese – crumbled
¾ lb green beans – trimmed & boiled
½ lb mushrooms – cleaned & sliced
6 tomatoes – skinned & chopped
4 tbsp wholegrain mustard
10 tbsp olive oil
4 tbsp white wine vinegar

1. Use 2 tbsp of oil and fry mushrooms for 2-3 mins
2. Put the mustard, oil and vinegar into a screw top jar, season and shake vigorously to mix
3. Allow the vegetables to cool until just warm
4. Put all the other ingredients (except cheese) in a large bowl, mix well, season and pour over the dressing
5. Serve dotted with the cheese

PESTO POTATO SALAD

1 lb new potatoes – scrubbed, halved, boiled & drained
3 tsp pesto sauce (basil or tomato)
1½ oz fresh parmesan – grated

1. Allow the potatoes to cool until warm. Put in a bowl
2. Season and add the pesto. Mix thoroughly and sprinkle with the cheese

SMOKED MACKEREL & NEW POTATO SALAD

1 lb new potatoes – scrubbed, boiled & sliced
4 smoked mackerel fillets – broken into bite sized pieces
2 tbsp white wine vinegar
1½ tbsp wholegrain mustard
8 spring onions – washed, peeled and sliced
6 tbsp extra virgin olive oil

1. Gently mix the potatoes, fish and spring onion in a large bowl
2. Put the olive oil, vinegar and mustard into a screw top jar and shake vigorously
3. Gently toss the dressing into the potato and fish

MEDITERRANEAN POTATO SALAD

1 lb new potatoes – scrubbed, halved, boiled & drained
1 clove garlic – crushed
2 fl oz olive oil
1 tbsp chives - chopped
1 tbsp basil – chopped
1 tbsp parsley – chopped

1. Put all ingredients except potatoes into a small screw top jar and shake thoroughly
2. Once the potatoes have cooled slightly toss with the dressing. Refridgerate for 1 hour

POTATO & SALMON NICOISE

1 lb new potatoes – scrubbed, boiled for 15 mins, drained and halved
6 oz salmon fillets
¼ cucumber – skinned and diced
1 red onion – peeled & sliced
1 x 8 oz can pimentos – drained and chopped
5 oz black olives - stoned
1 tbsp olive oil

Dressing
6 tbsp extra virgin olive oil
2 cloves garlic – crushed
1 tbsp Dijon mustard
2 tbsp tarragon vinegar

1. Heat the oil and fry the fish for about 5 mins on each side until cooked
2. Put all the dressing ingredients in a jar and shake vigorously to mix
3. Arrange the salmon and warm potatoes on a plate with the other ingredients, season and pour the dressing on top. Serve warm

POTATO & CHICKEN LIVER SALAD

1 lb new potatoes – scrubbed, boiled & drained
8 oz chicken livers – fat removed
3 oz bacon – cut into pieces
3 tbsp white wine
1 tsp balsamic vinegar
1 tsp wholegrain mustard
Olive oil for cooking
6 large lettuce leaves – halved

1. Cut the potatoes into slices and fry in olive oil until slightly browned
2. Meanwhile dry fry the bacon until golden
3. Add the chicken livers, season and fry until cooked. Remove both with a slotted spoon and add to the potatoes
4. Pour the wine and the vinegar into the pan and reduce slightly. Remove from the heat and stir in 3 tbsp of olive oil and the mustard. Season
5. Toss the dressing with the lettuce leaves and serve the potato mixture on a bed of leaves with any remaining dressing drizzled over the top

POTATO & TUNA SALAD

1 lb new potatoes – scrubbed, boiled, drained & diced
1 small tin tuna – drained & flaked
1 small tin kidney beans – drained
1 red onion – peeled and sliced thinly
5 oz cucumber – peeled & diced
6 oz cherry tomatoes – halved

Dressing
4 tbsp mayonnaise
¼ pint coconut cream
Juice and zest of 1 lime

1. Mix all the salad ingredients together in a large salad bowl
2. Whisk together all the dressing ingredients, pour over the salad and gently mix together

POTATO & MACKEREL SALAD

1 lb new potatoes – scrubbed, boiled & drained
10 oz cooked smoked mackerel – flaked
2 cooked beetroots – diced
2 oz rocket
1 tbsp wholegrain mustard
1 tbsp red wine vinegar
2 tbsp extra virgin olive oil

1. Put the oil, vinegar and mustard into a screw top jar and shake well to mix
2. Gently mix the potatoes, mackerel and beetroot in a large bowl, pour over the oil mixture and scatter the rocket over the salad

POTATO SALAD WITH DIJON MAYONNAISE

1 lb new potatoes – scrubbed, boiled, drained & diced
3 tbsp mayonnaise
3 tbsp natural yoghurt
2 rashers bacon – grilled & cut into small pieces
2 tbsp fresh chives –chopped
2 tbsp Dijon mustard

1. Mix the mayonnaise, yoghurt and mustard together. Season and add the potatoes
2. Sprinkle with bacon and chives

ITALIAN POTATO SALAD (1)

1 lb new potatoes – scrubbed, boiled, quartered & cooled
3 oz salami – cut into small pieces
1 red onion – peeled and sliced
1 green pepper – quartered, seeded and skinned
2 tbsp gherkins – cut into pieces
2 tbsp capers – drained
2 oz black olives – halved
3 tbsp extra virgin olive oil

1. Place all the ingredients together in a large bowl and mix thoroughly. Season

CHEESE & POTATO SALAD

1 lb potatoes – boiled & diced
5 oz cheddar cheese – grated
1 lettuce – washed
½ bunch watercress – washed
2 tomatoes – sliced
3 tbsp mayonnaise
1 tbsp white wine vinegar

1. *Blend the mayonnaise and vinegar together then mix with the potatoes*
2. *Arrange the lettuce around a large circular salad dish and layer the tomatoes in the centre*
3. *Sprinkle half the cheese on top of the tomato and add the potatoes. Season. Top with the rest of the cheese and sprinkle with watercress*

GERMAN SAUSAGE SALAD

1 lb new potatoes – scrubbed, boiled, quartered & cooled
1 lb Bratwurst sausage
1 bunch spring onions – trimmed & sliced
6 gherkins – cut into pieces
½ pint mayonnaise
½ pint sour cream
2 tsp Dijon mustardl

1. *Heat the sausages gently in hot water for the recommended time. Drain and slice into bite sized pieces*
2. *Put all the ingredients into a large bowl. Season & mix thoroughly. Serve warm*

POTATO SALAD WITH DILL

1 lb new potatoes – scrubbed & boiled
3 fl oz French dressing
2 tbsp fresh dill leaves - finely chopped
1 tbsp fresh parsley – chopped

1. *Allow the potatoes to cool then cut into dice*
2. *Mix the ingredients thoroughly in a bowl. Season and serve warm*

POTATO, BACON & EGG SALAD

1 lb new potatoes – scrubbed, boiled & drained
8 oz bacon – chopped and fried until crisp
3 eggs – hard boiled and quartered
1 bunch spring onions – trimmed and cut into small pieces
1½ tbsp fresh chives – chopped

Dressing
4 fl oz extra virgin olive oil
3 tbsp red wine vinegar
1 tsp Dijon mustard

1. *Allow the potatoes to cool slightly then cut into pieces*
2. *Put all the dressing ingredients into a jar and shake vigorously until well mixed*
3. *Toss the potatoes, bacon and spring onion gently with the dressing. Season*
4. *Serve onto plates and add the egg and chives*

POTATO & CAMEMBERT SALAD

1 lb new potatoes – scrubbed, halved, boiled & drained
7 oz Camembert – crumbled
3 tbsp dry cider
3 tbsp extra virgin olive oil
2 tbsp fresh chives – chopped

1. *Warm the oil and cider together in a pan. Add the chives and season. Stir in the potatoes and allow to cool then mix in the cheese*

POTATO SALAD (2)

1 lb new potatoes – scrubbed, boiled & diced
3 spring onions – peeled, trimmed & chopped
4 fl oz mayonnaise
1 tbsp chives – snipped

1. *Mix the potatoes, onions and mayonnaise together in a bowl. Season*
2. *Cover with cling film and refrigerate for 1 hour. Remove and sprinkle with the chives*

RUSSIAN SALAD

1 lb potatoes – peeled & diced
1 cauliflower – trimmed & broken into small florets
1 turnip – peeled & diced
2 carrots – peeled, cooked, diced & cooled
1 large beetroot – peeled & diced
4 tomatoes – skinned & chopped
½ pint mayonnaise
8 oz peas – cooked
8 oz tongue – diced
8 oz prawns – peeled & cooked
8 gherkins – chopped
12 anchovies – sliced
12 black olives – halved
3 tbsp capers
3 tbsp lemon juice

1. Boil the potatoes, turnip and carrot for 18 mins. Drain
2. Boil the cauliflower for 10 mins. Drain
3. Mix the lemon juice with the mayonnaise
4. Put the cauliflower florets in the bottom of a large glass and cover with mayonnaise
5. Layer the turnips, carrots, potatoes, peas, beetroot, tomatoes, tongue and prawns on top and with a thin layer of mayonnaise and seasoning between each, finishing with mayonnaise
6. Sprinkle with gherkins, olives, capers and anchovies

CHICKEN & POTATO SALAD

1 lb new potatoes – scrubbed, halved, boiled & drained
12 oz cooked chicken – cut into bit sized pieces
4 oz lettuce – cut into strips
3 eggs – hardboiled and quartered
4 tbsp mayonnaise

1. Allow the potatoes to cool then slice into bite sized pieces
2. Mix the mayonnaise, crème fraîche and dill together in a salad bowl, season and add the potatoes. Sprinkle with parsley just before serving

POTATO, BACON & CHEESE SALAD

1 lb new potatoes – scrubbed & halved
7 oz bacon – rind removed & cut into small pieces
4 oz cheddar cheese – grated
4 eggs – hard boiled, shelled & quartered
6 spring onions – topped, tailed & cut into pieces
6 oz cherry tomatoes – quartered
2 cloves garlic – crushed
6 tbsp extra virgin olive oil
1 tbsp Balsamic vinegar
1 tbsp fresh thyme – chopped

1. Pre-heat oven to GM6/200°c/400°f
2. Put potatoes in a roasting tin and brush with some of the oil. Season and bake for 1 hour. Allow to cool slightly
3. Heat a small amount of oil and fry the bacon till cooked. Remove with a slotted spoon
4. Mix the bacon fat with the rest of the oil, vinegar, garlic and thyme. Season
5. Put the potatoes in a large salad bowl and add the tomatoes, eggs and spring onions. Pour over the dressing and toss gently. Sprinkle with the cheese and bacon pieces. Serve warm

TUNA & POTATO SALAD

1 lb new potatoes – scrubbed & halved
2 small tins tuna – drained
5 oz green beans – washed & trimmed
4 eggs – hard boiled, & quartered
6 cherry tomatoes – quartered
4 oz pitted black olives
4 tsp white wine vinegar
2 tbsp extra virgin olive oil
3 tsp fresh parsley – chopped

1. Boil the potatoes for 12 mins. Add the beans and cook for 5 more mins. Drain.
2. Allow the potatoes to cool slightly then put into a large salad bowl. Add the tuna, beans, eggs, tomatoes and olives. Mix well, season
3. Mix the oil, vinegar and parsley together. Pour over the salad and mix well. Serve warm

SIMPLE ITALIAN POTATO SALAD

1 lb new potatoes – scrubbed, halved, boiled
  & drained
¼ lb cherry tomatoes – washed & halved
¼ lb green beans – trimmed, washed, halved
  & boiled
1 clove garlic – crushed
2 tbsp red wine vinegar
3 tbsp extra virgin olive oil
1 tbsp fresh basil – chopped

1. *Put the vinegar, oil, garlic and basil in a screw top jar, season and shake vigorously to mix*
2. *Mix all the other ingredients (while the potatoes are warm) in a large bowl. Season. Pour on the liquid and mix thoroughly*

POTATO & MACKEREL SALAD (2)

1 lb new potatoes - scrubbed & halved
4 fillets cooked smoked mackerel – flaked
1 lb tomatoes – halved
1 tsp fresh basil – chopped
1 tsp fresh oregano – chopped
3 tbsp extra virgin olive oil
2 tsp course sea salt

1. *Pre-heat oven to GM6/200°c/400°f*
2. *Brush a baking tin with oil then add the potatoes, tomatoes, herbs salt and oil together. Mix well*
3. *Bake for 40 mins. Remove and allow to cool. Mix in the mackerel fillets*

WARM POTATO & ONION SALAD

1 lb new potatoes – scrubbed, halved, boiled
  & drained
2 red onions – peeled and finely sliced
3 tbsp red wine vinegar
4 tbsp extra virgin olive oil
1 tsp dried oregano

1. *Put all the ingredients in a large bowl, season and mix well*

POTATO & SALMON SALAD

1 lb new potatoes – scrubbed, boiled & halved
2 salmon steaks – sliced across each surface
6 lettuce leaves
1½ tbsp extra virgin olive oil
Juice of ½ lemon
Dressing
2 fl oz extra virgin olive oil
1 tbsp white wine vinegar
1 tbsp Dijon mustard
1 tbsp fresh dill – chopped

1. *Coat the salmon steaks in mixed olive oil and lemon, then season. Place on a shallow plate, pour over the rest of the marinade, cover with cling film and refrigerate for 1 hour*
2. *Put the dressing ingredients in a screw top jar and shake vigorously until well mixed*
3. *Heat a small amount of oil and fry the salmon gently for about 5 mins on each side until cooked. Discard the marinade*
4. *Arrange the potatoes on a bed of lettuce leaves, add the cooked salmon, season and drizzle the dressing over*

CONTINENTAL STYLE SALAD

1 lb new potatoes – scrubbed
1 red onion – peeled & sliced
3 eggs – hard boiled & quartered
7 tbsp garlic mayonnaise

1. *Mix all the ingredients together with seasoning in a large bowl*

WINTER SALAD

1 lb potatoes – boiled & sliced
1 medium cauliflower – boiled & broken into
  small pieces
4 oz frozen peas – boiled
3 oz carrots – boiled and sliced
5 fl oz salad cream

1. *Allow the vegetables to cool until just warm*
2. *Mix all the ingredients together with the salad cream. Season and serve*

WARM POTATO & BACON SALAD

1 lb new potatoes – scrubbed, halved, boiled & drained
½ lb bacon – rind removed & cut into pieces
2 red onions – peeled & cut into thin rings
3 cloves garlic – crushed
1 lettuce – stalk cut out & leaves removed
3 tbsp olive oil
Chives

1. Heat the oil and gently fry the bacon for 3 mins
2. Add the garlic and fry for 2 more mins until the bacon is cooked
3. Add the warm potatoes and chives, turn off the heat and mix together
4. Put the potato mixture onto a bed of lettuce, season and scatter with onion

POTATO & AVOCADO SALAD

1 lb new potatoes – scrubbed, boiled & drained
1 large avocado
2 packs cress – washed
Juice of 1 – 2 lemons
2 tbsp extra virgin olive oil

1. Peel the avocado, cut in half and remove the stone. Cut into slices and put into a large salad bowl
2. Cut each potato in half (while still warm) and add to the avocado
3. Mix the oil with the lemon juice & pour on
4. Add the cress and seasoning. Toss gently

SAUSAGE & POTATO SALAD

1 lb (waxy) potatoes – peeled & cut into chunks
½ lb Cumberland sausages
3 spring onions
5 tbsp extra virgin olive oil
2 tbsp red wine vinegar
1 tbsp wholegrain mustard
1 tbsp parsley – chopped
¼ of an Iceberg lettuce – shredded

1. Boil the potatoes, drain and leave to cool slightly
2. Mix together the oil, vinegar and mustard. Season and pour over the potatoes
3. Fry the sausages until cooked and cut into small pieces
4. Toss all the ingredients together in a large bowl. Serve warm on a bed of lettuce, sprinkled with parsley

FISH & POTATO SALAD

1 lb new potatoes – scrubbed, halved, boiled & drained
12 oz smoked haddock, skinned, boned and flaked

Dressing
2 tbsp capers
2 tbsp gherkins – chopped
1 tbsp white wine vinegar
½ tbsp dry English mustard
4 tbsp extra virgin olive oil

1. Put the vinegar, mustard, oil and seasoning in a screw top jar and shake well to mix. Pour the mixture into a bowl and stir in the capers and gherkins
2. Mix the potatoes and fish together in a large salad bowl while the potatoes are still warm and pour the dressing over. Toss gently. Serve warm

POTATO AND TAPENADE SALAD

1 lb new potatoes – scrubbed, halved, boiled & drained
6 rashers bacon – grilled & cut into pieces
4 oz black olives
1 oz jar back olive Tapenade
Juice of 1 lemon
2 tbsp extra virgin olive oil

1. Mix the oil, lemon juice and tapenade in a large bowl. Season
2. Allow the potatoes to cool slightly then add them and the bacon to the mixture
3. Serve scattered with the olives

POTATO, ROQUEFORT & CHICORY SALAD

1 lb new potatoes – scrubbed & boiled
4 oz Roquefort cheese – cut into ½" cubes
1 bulb of chicory
3 walnuts – shelled and broken into small pieces
1 small red onion – peeled and cut into thin slices
1 tsp walnut oil

Dressing
2 tbsp walnut oil
2 tbsp groundnut oil
1 tsp red wine vinegar
1 tsp Dijon mustard

1. *Heat 1 tsp walnut oil and gently fry the walnut pieces for 4-5 mins., tossing continually. Remove and leave to cool*

2. *Trim the base of the chicory bulb then remove and throw away the outer leaves. Halve the bulb, then cut out and throw away the inside. Slice the remaining leaves into long thin strips*

3. *Put all the dressing ingredients in screw top jar, season and shake vigorously to mix*

4. *Manually mix all the salad ingredients in a large bowl, season and pour over the dressing*

POTATO & MINTED YOGHURT SALAD

1 lb new potatoes – scrubbed & boiled
1 lb Greek yoghurt
1 small cucumber – peeled, seeded & cut into small cubes
2 spring onions – trimmed & chopped into small pieces
2 tbsp olive oil
2 tbsp white wine vinegar
3 tsp fresh mint – finely chopped

1. *Beat the olive oil, vinegar and mint into the yoghurt and season with salt only*

2. *Put all the other ingredients into a salad bowl and add the yoghurt. Mix together until the potatoes are coated*

HERBY POTATO SALAD

1 lb new potatoes – scrubbed, quartered, boiled & drained
1 tbsp fresh chives
1 tbsp fresh basil - chopped
1 tbsp fresh tarragon - chopped
1 tbsp fresh parsley - chopped
5 tbsp extra virgin olive oil
1 tbsp white wine vinegar
1 small red onion – peeled and finely sliced

1. *Put the potatoes into a salad bowl while still warm. Mix in all the other ingredients, season and leave to cool*

POTATO & EGG SALAD

1 lb new potatoes – scrubbed, halved, boiled & drained
4 eggs – hard boiled & quartered
1 small can anchovies
4 fl oz mayonnaise

1. *Remove anchovies from can and chop*

2. *Mix the fish oil with the mayonnaise*

3. *Mix all the ingredients together in a large bowl and season*

SAUSAGE AND POTATO SALAD (2)

1 lb new potatoes – scrubbed, boiled & cubed
1 lb sausages – cooked & cut into 1" slices
8 oz broad beans – cooked & drained
6 spring onions – washed & sliced
1 small tin red kidney beans – drained

Dressing
5 tbsp extra virgin olive oil
3 tbsp white wine vinegar
2 tbsp wholegrain mustard

1. *Put all the main ingredients into a large salad bowl and mix together*

2. *Put the dressing ingredients into a screw top jar and shake vigorously to mix*

3. *Season the salad and add the dressing, tossing gently to coat*

POTATO & SMOKED SALMON SALAD

1 lb new potatoes – scrubbed, halved, boiled & drained
5 oz smoked salmon – cut into thin strips
1 avocado
2 spring onions – trimmed and sliced

Dressing
2½ tbsp extra virgin olive oil
2½ tbsp ground nut oil
1 tbsp white wine vinegar
1 tbsp lemon juice

1. Cut the avocado in half lengthways and remove the stone. Remove the peel and cut into long thin strips, then cut the strips in half

2. Put the dressing ingredients in a screw top jar and shake vigorously to mix. Season

3. Gently mix the main ingredients together in a large bowl then pour the dressing over. Season and toss gently to coat

POTATO AND BLACK PUDDING SALAD

1 lb new potatoes- scrubbed, halved and boiled for 15 mins
8 slices black pudding – cut into halves
10 oz chicken livers - washed
10 oz bacon rashers – de-rinded and cut into pieces
5 shallots - peeled & halved
6 lettuce leaves
4 oz butter

1. Melt the butter in a pan and cook the shallots until they soften

2. Add the potatoes and cook for 2 mins

3. Add the bacon and cook until crispy, stirring all the time

4. Add the chicken livers and black pudding, mix well and fry until the livers are cooked

5. Remove from the heat, season and add the lettuce leaves and let the heat from the pan wilt the lettuce

NEW POTATO, RADISH & FENNEL SALAD

1 lb new potatoes – scrubbed and boiled
10 radishes – washed, leaves removed and thinly sliced
2 bulbs of fennel – washed

Dressing
4 tbsp extra virgin olive oil
3 tbsp lemon juice

1. Remove the stalks and outer leaves from the fennel and discard. Thinly slice the bulb and the inner leaves. Boil gently for about 10 mins or until cooked drain & allow to cool slightly

2. Put the olive oil and lemon juice in a screw top jar and shake thoroughly

3. Mix the warm potatoes with the fennel and radish. Season and pour the dressing over. Toss gently to coat

SWEDISH POTATO SALAD

1 lb new potatoes – scrubbed & boiled
2 tbsp mayonnaise
2 tbsp crème fraîche
1 tbsp fresh dill – finely snipped
1 tbsp fresh parsley – chopped

1. Allow the potatoes to cool then slice into bite sized pieces

2. Mix the mayonnaise, crème fraîche and dill together in a salad bowl, season and add the potatoes. Sprinkle with parsley just before serving

ARTICHOKE & POTATO SALAD

1 lb new potatoes – scrubbed and halved
1 6 oz jar artichoke in oil
2 tbsp capers
1 tbsp balsamic vinegar

1. Boil the potatoes for about 20 mins and drain

2. Drain the artichokes and reserve the oil

3. Add the vinegar, capers and 2 tbsp of the reserved oil to the artichokes. Mix in the potatoes and season

WARM CHICKEN & POTATO SALAD

1 lb new potatoes – scrubbed, halved, boiled & drained
3 chicken breasts – skinned
5 oz peas
3 oz broad beans
3 oz French beans
8 spring onions – sliced

Dressing
6 tbsp extra virgin olive oil
3 tbsp wholegrain mustard
2 tbsp runny honey
Juice of 1 lemon

1. Pre-heat oven to GM6/200°c/400°f

2. Put all the dressing ingredients in a screw top jar & shake vigoursly to mix

3. Brush the chicken with some of the dressing and bake for 25 mins

4. Boil the peas and beans in the same pan for 5 mins, drain and cool

5. Cut he chicken into cubes and mix with all the other ingredients

HOT & SPICY POTATO SALAD

1 lb new potatoes – scrubbed, halved, boiled & drained
8 oz green beans – trimmed, tailed & halved
1 small red chilli – de-seeded & sliced thinly
2 cloves garlic – crushed
1 tbsp red wine vinegar
3 tbsp chopped fresh coriander
3 fl oz extra virgin olive oil

1. Blanch the beans and drain

2. Mix all the ingredients thoroughly (except the potatoes & beans)

3. Mix the beans with the potatoes and toss with the dressing. Serve immediately

WARM POTATO SALAD

1 lb new potatoes – scrubbed, boiled, drained & cubed
2 tbsp white wine vinegar
4 fl oz vegetable stock
2 tbsp fresh parsley – chopped
1 small red onion – peeled and finely sliced

1. Mix together the warm vegetable stock with the vinegar and toss gently into the potatoes and onion

2. Season and sprinkle with parsley. Serve warm

POTATO & MUSHROOM SALAD WITH WALNUT OIL

1 lb new potatoes scrubbed & halved
10 medium flat mushrooms - peeled & halved
3 oz bacon – chopped
2 cloves garlic – crushed
6 oz spinach leaves
1 tbsp parsley – chopped
1 tbsp chives – chopped
3 tbsp extra virgin olive oil
1 tbsp walnut oil

Dressing
1 clove garlic - crushed
2 small shallots – chopped finely
1 tbsp white wine vinegar
1 tbsp lemon juice
5 tbsp extra virgin olive oil

1. Put all the dressing ingredients together in a jar and shake well

2. Boil the potatoes for 15-18 mins. Drain and mix with the dressing while still warm. Leave to cool

3. Dry fry the bacon for 2-3 mins

4. Add the oil, fry the mushrooms and garlic for 3-4 mins. Season then add the spinach and the herbs, adding more oil if needed. Stir over a low heat until the spinach wilts

5. Mix in the potatoes and bacon, stir well then spoon onto serving plates. Drizzle the walnut oil on top. Serve warm

SPICY POTATO & CAULIFLOWER SALAD

1 lb potatoes – peeled and cubed
8 slices black pudding – cut into halves
1 cauliflower – broken into florets
2 tsp cumin seeds – ground
2 tbsp whole cumin seeds
2 tsp ground coriander
1 tsp turmeric
½ tsp cayenne pepper
6 tbsp vegetable oil

1. Boil the potatoes for 15 mins and drain
2. Heat the oil and gently fry the whole cumin seeds for 2-3 mins, stirring continually, add the cauliflower florets
3. Lower the heat, cover and let the cauliflower steam for 7-8 mins
4. Add the black pudding, mix well and fry until cooked
5. Add the potatoes and the rest of the spices and season. Stir well and cook under a slow heat for 2-3 mins. Remove from heat and allow to cool slightly. Serve warm

BACON, POTATO & FENNEL SALAD

1 lb new potatoes – scrubbed, boiled & halved
1 lb bacon, rind & fat removed
2 bulbs fennel – cored & finely sliced
½ lb broccoli – stalk removed
10 cherry tomatoes – halved
6 tbsp chopped fresh basil
2 tbsp Balsamic vinegar
8 tbsp extra virgin olive oil

1. Pre-heat the grill
2. Boil the broccoli florets and the fennel separately for 10-12 mins, drain
3. Grill the bacon until browned and cut into strips
4. Put the basil, vinegar and oil into a screw top jar and shake vigorously until mixed
5. Put all the main ingredients in a large bowl and pour over the dressing, season and mix well. Serve while still warm

HARISSA NEW POTATO SALAD

1 lb new potatoes – scrubbed, halved, boiled & drained
1 tsp harissa paste
1½ tbsp extra virgin olive oil

1. Allow the potatoes to cool until warm. Put in a bowl
2. Mix the oil and the paste together and pour onto the potatoes. Mix well

POTATO & CHORIZO SALAD

1 lb new potatoes – scrubbed, halved & boiled
½ lb Chorizo – peeled and chopped
1 bunch spring onions – trimmed & chopped
1 tbsp fresh parsley – chopped
2 tbsp lemon juice
1 tbsp olive oil

1. Heat the oil and fry the chorizo until almost crisp
2. Allow potatoes and chorizo to cool slightly then mix with the other ingredients in a large bowl. Season

SOUTHERN MEDITERRANEAN SALAD

1 lb new potatoes – scrubbed, boiled & drained
1 red pepper – cored, deseeded & cut into strips
1 green pepper – cored, deseeded & cut into strips
2 tbsp sundried tomato purée
Juice of half a lemon
4 oz feta cheese – cut into small cubes
12 green olives – pitted
2 tbsp olive oil

1. Heat the oil in a frying pan and fry the peppers for about 10 min until softened
2. In a large bowl mix the lemon juice with the purée. Add the potatoes and peppers and toss until coated
3. Sprinkle with the cheese and olives

STEAK AND POTATO SALAD

1 lb new potatoes – scrubbed, boiled, drained, cooled & halved
2 steaks (about 10 oz each)
1 red onion – peeled, thinly sliced
½ lb cherry tomatoes – halved
1 red pepper – cored, deseeded & cut into strips
1 yellow pepper – cored, deseeded & cut into strips
¼ lb flat mushrooms – peeled & sliced
3 oz wild rocket
4 tbsp olive oil

Dressing
5 tbsp Balsamic vinegar
2 cloves garlic – chopped
1 tbsp Dijon mustard
6 fl oz plain yoghurt
2 fl oz mayonnaise

1 Brush a frying pan with 1 tbsp of oil and heat. Fry the steaks until just cooked. Remove from heat and allow to cool. Cut into slices

2. Add the remaining oil to the pan and cook the peppers for 5 mins

3. Add the mushrooms and cook for 5 mins. Allow to cool

4. Put all the dressing ingredients in a large bowl and mix thoroughly

3. Put all the main ingredients in the bowl, mix well and pour the dressing over. Season & toss gently to coat

POTATO & CHICKPEA SALAD

1 lb new potatoes – scrubbed, halved, boiled & drained
1 large tin chickpeas – boiled & drained
1 avocado – halved, stoned, sliced (soaked in lemon juice)
3 spring onions – trimmed & finely chopped
1 red chilli – deseeded & finely chopped
Zest of lemon – finely grated
8 large lettuce leaves – washed
6 tbsp olive oil
2 oz Greek yoghurt
Juice of 1 lemon

1. Pre-heat oven to GM6/200°c/400°f

2 Put the potatoes in a large roasting pan and add half the oil. Toss to coat. Roast for 10-15 mins. Remove

2. For the dressing – put the yoghurt, oil and remainder of the lemon juice (not used for avocado) in a bowl and blend together. Season

4. Allow the potatoes and chickpeas to cool until just warm and mix with all the remaining ingredients. Place on a bed of lettuce

5. Pour the dressing on top and serve

SUMMER POTATO SALAD

1 lb new potatoes – scrubbed, boiled, cooled & diced
1 bunch spring onions – trimmed & finely chopped
5 fl oz mayonnaise
1 tsp lemon juice

1. Put the potatoes in a mixing bowl, season with black pepper and add the spring onions

2. Mix the lemon juice with the mayonnaise and add to the potatoes. Mix well until the potatoes are well coated

3. Cover with cling film and refrigerate for an hour before serving

HAM & POTATO SALAD

1 lb new potatoes – scrubbed, halved & boiled
1 lb cooked ham – cut into strips
1 small cos lettuce – washed & shredded
1 bunch of spring onions – trimmed & chopped
½ pint sweet cider
3 tbsp olive oil
1 tbsp balsamic vinegar
1 tbsp wholegrain mustard

1. Boil the cider until reduced by about half. Allow to cool

2. Put it in a screw top jar with the oil, vinegar and mustard. Shake vigorously to mix

3. While the potatoes are still warm mix with all the other ingredients. Season

POTATO & SPRING ONION SALAD

1 lb new potatoes – scrubbed, boiled & halved
1 bunch spring onions – trimmed, washed & sliced
2 tbsp mayonnaise
2 tbsp Greek yoghurt
2 tbsp wholegrain mustard
1 tsp lemon juice

1. Drain the potatoes and allow to cool until just warm. Put all the ingredients in a large bowl, season and mix well

CURRIED POTATO SALAD

1 lb new potatoes – scrubbed & halved
1 tbsp medium curry powder
Juice of 1 lemon
1 oz fresh parsley – chopped
1½ tbsp vegetable oil

1. Pre-heat oven to GM6/200°c/400°f
2. Put the potatoes in a roasting tin, drizzle with the oil then add the curry powder and salt. Mix well so the potatoes are evenly coated. Cook in the oven for 20 mins
3. Remove, allow to cool till just warm, then add the lemon juice and parsley. Season and mix well

PROVENCAL POTATO SALAD

1 lb waxy potatoes – peeled & cubed
½ lb green beans – trimmed & washed
1 red pepper –cored, seeded & chopped
1 courgette – washed, trimmed, boiled & chopped
1 red onion – peeled & chopped finely
1 clove garlic – peeled & chopped finely
1 small head radicchio – washed & cut into bite size pieces
1 tbsp fresh basil
2 tbsp Herbes de Provence
12 black olives
2 tbsp extra virgin olive oil
3 tbsp white wine vinegar
2 tbsp mustard

1. Boil the potatoes and beans together, drain and reserve the water
2. Put oil, vinegar, pepper & mustard in a screw top jar & shake vigorously to mix. Add some of the reserved water and season
3. Put all the other ingredients in a large bowl, mix well, season and pour the dressing over them, sprinkle with torn basil leaves and herbes de provence

SPANISH POTATO SALAD

1 lb new potatoes – scrubbed, halved, boiled & drained
1 medium red onion – peeled & sliced
8 oz cherry tomatoes – halved
6 oz chorizo sausage – cut into small pieces
1 avocado – quartered and sliced
2 tsp paprika
1 tbsp olive oil

Dressing
6 tbsp garlic wine vinegar
6 tbsp olive oil
2 oz sundried tomatoes finely chopped
Seasoning

1. Fry the chorizo until browned, add the paprika and cook for 2 mins. Drain and add to a salad bowl and toss in the other salad ingredients
2. Put all the dressing ingredients into a screw top jar and shake vigourously to mix
3. Pour the dressing into the bowl, season & mix gently

CHEESE & POTATO SALAD (2)

1 lb new potatoes – scrubbed, boiled, drained & diced
6 oz Cheshire cheese – diced
2 carrots – peeled and grated
5 oz cooked ham – diced
6 tbsp mayonnaise

1. Put all the ingredients in a large bowl, season and mix well

TURKEY & POTATO SALAD

1 lb new potatoes – scrubbed & halved
¾ lb cooked turkey - cut into bite size pieces
½ lb sweet peppers in a jar - drained & chopped
10 green olives
4 cloves garlic - papery skin removed
4 tbsp olive oil
1 tbsp white wine vinegar
1 tsp paprika

1. Pre-heat oven to GM6/200°c/400°f

2. Put the potatoes in a roasting tin, add
   1 tbsp of oil and mix well. Season and add
   ½ tsp paprika and the garlic cloves

3. Cook for 20 mins. Remove and allow to
   cool slightly

4. Heat the rest of the oil in a small pan and
   add the vinegar, season, mix well and heat
   very gently until warm

5. Take a large salad bowl and add the
   potatoes, turkey, peppers and olives. Mix
   well, season, and add the remaining paprika
   and pour the dressing on

POTATO SALAD WITH BACON & ASPARAGUS

1 lb new potatoes – scrubbed, boiled & drained
½ lb asparagus tips – washed
3 rashers bacon – cut into pieces
1 tbsp lemon juice
½ tbsp wholegrain mustard
1 tbsp fresh mint – chopped
2 tbsp extra virgin olive oil

1. Heat half the oil and gently fry the
   asparagus until cooked

2. Dry fry the bacon until crispy and drain on
   kitchen paper

3. Put the remaining oil, lemon juice and
   mustard in a screw-top jar. Season and
   shake vigorously to mix

3. Put the asparagus and potatoes in a mixing
   bowl, pour on the dressing and mix.
   Sprinkle with the bacon and mint

POTATO & SALMON SALAD (2)

1 lb new potatoes – scrubbed & halved
1 lb salmon fillets – skinned
½ lb green beans – trimmed & halved
¼ cucumber – peeled & sliced
6 eggs – hard boiled, cooled & quartered
10 cherry tomatoes – halved
6 tbsp extra virgin olive oil
3 tbsp fresh dill – chopped
Juice of 2 lemons
1 tsp mustard

1. Season the salmon and sprinkle with some
   lemon juice and oil. Fry under a pre-heated
   grill until cooked. Cool, then flake the fish

2. Boil the potatoes for 10 mins then add
   the beans and boil for 5 more mins.
   Drain and allow to cool until warm

3. Put the oil, dill, lemon juice and mustard in a
   screw top jar and shake vigorously to mix

4. Put the salad ingredients in a large bowl,
   season and pour over the dressing

QUICK RUSSIAN SALAD

**1 lb new potatoes – scrubbed, boiled, drained
& diced**
½ lb beetroot – cooked & diced
5 fl oz crème fraîche
3 tbsp basil leaves – torn

1. Allow the potatoes and beetroot to cool
   then mix all the ingredients with seasoning
   in a large bowl. Serve

QUICK GREEK POTATO SALAD

**1 lb new potatoes – scrubbed, halved, boiled
& drained**
6 oz tub Tzatziki
¼ cucumber – peeled sliced, then halved
1 bunch wild rocket - torn

1. Allow potatoes to cool then put into a bowl
   and add the other ingredients, season and
   mix well

POTATO & BACON SALAD

1 lb new potatoes – scrubbed, halved, boiled & drained
6 rashers bacon - fat removed, grilled & chopped
5 fl oz soured cream
1 bunch watercress – stalks removed,
leaves chopped

1. *Allow the potatoes to cool slightly then place in a bowl, season and mix in the other ingredients*

POTATO & SAUSAGE SALAD

1 lb waxy potatoes – peeled & cut into bite sized pieces
1 lb cooked smoked sausage – cut into 1" pieces
1 red onion – peeled & thinly sliced
1 tbsp red wine vinegar
1 tbsp wholegrain mustard
3 tbsp vegetable oil
2 tbsp olive oil

1. *Boil the potatoes for 15 mins, drain and allow to cool*
2. *Heat the olive oil and fry the potatoes until crisp*
3. *Add the sausage for the last 2-3 mins. Remove from heat and allow to cool until warm*
4. *Put the vegetable oil, vinegar and mustard in a screw top jar and shake vigorously to mix*
5. *Put the cooled potato and sausage in a large bowl, add the onion, season and pour on the dressing*

TROUT & POTATO SALAD

1 lb small new potatoes – scrubbed & boiled
1 trout
¼ lb green beans – trimmed, washed & boiled
3 spring onions – trimmed & chopped
1 apple – peeled, cored & chopped
6 fl oz crème fraîche
Juice from ½ lemon

1. *Heat the grill and put the trout on buttered tin foil. Grill for about 15 mins until cooked – turning halfway through. Allow to cool, skin, fillet and flake the fish*
2. *Put all the other ingredients in a large bowl, season and mix well*

GREEK POTATO SALAD

1 lb new potatoes – scrubbed, halved & boiled
6 cherry tomatoes – halved
6 black olives – pitted & halved
1 red onion, peeled & sliced
3 oz feta cheese – crumbled
1 clove garlic – crushed
2 tbsp fresh parsley – chopped
3 tbsp extra virgin olive oil
1 tbsp Balsamic vinegar
2 tbsp pine nuts – toasted

1. *Drain the potatoes and allow to cool*
2. *Put in a large bowl and add the onions, tomatoes, olives, cheese and parsley, mix together*
2. *Put the garlic, oil, vinegar and seasoning in a screw top jar and shake vigorously to mix*
4. *Pour over the salad ingredients and toss lightly. Serve topped with the pine nuts*

WARM POTATO & CHORIZO SALAD

1 lb new potatoes – scrubbed, boiled & drained
5 oz chorizo sausage – skinned & sliced
5 oz sundried tomatoes – drained & chopped
2 oz toasted pine nuts
1 bag baby spinach - boiled & drained
6 tbsp extra virgin olive oil
2 tbsp sherry vinegar

1. *Put the oil and sherry in a screw top jar and shake vigorously to mix*
2. *Allow the potatoes to cool until warm then mix with all the other ingredients, season and toss well*

TUNA & NEW POTATO SALAD

1 lb new potatoes – scrubbed, halved & boiled
2 small tins of tuna in oil – drained & flaked
(oil reserved)
2 green peppers (from a jar in oil) – cut into strips
½ lb spinach - washed
2 tbsp green pesto
3 tbsp extra virgin olive oil

1. Mix the fish oil & olive oil with the pesto and season
2. Mix the potatoes with the spinach until the spinach starts to wilt
3. Add the remaining ingredients and mix well

POTATO & SMOKED MACKEREL SALAD

1 lb new potatoes – scrubbed, halved, boiled & drained
2 smoked mackerel fillets – cooked, skinned & flaked
10 asparagus tips – boiled for 10 mins & drained
6 radishes – washed & halved
1 red onion – peeled & finely sliced
4 tbsp French dressing
2 tbsp horseradish
1 tbsp lemon juice

1. Put the dressing, horseradish and lemon juice in a screw top jar, season and shake vigorously to mix
2. Mix all the other ingredients together in a large bowl, season and pour the dressing over

PEPPER & POTATO SALAD

1 lb new potatoes – scrubbed, halved, boiled & drained
3 peppers (1 of each colour) skinned* seeded and cut into strips
2 oz wild rocket
1 tbsp wholegrain mustard
1 tbsp white wine vinegar
3 tbsp extra virgin olive oil

1. Put dressing ingredients in a screw top jar and shake vigorously to mix
2. Put the other ingredients in a large bowl while the potatoes and peppers are still warm. Season and pour over the dressing

To skin peppers – halve them and place them skin side up under a hot grill until they have blistered. Put in a plastic bag for 5 mins then peel off the skin

CLASSIC RUSSIAN SALAD

1 lb new potatoes – scrubbed, boiled, cooled & diced
½ lb carrots – peeled, boiled & diced
½ lb cooked runner beans – diagonally sliced
¼ lb peas – boiled & drained
3 eggs – hardboiled ,separated & chopped
1 tbsp pickled gherkins – drained & chopped
1 tbsp capers – rinsed & drained
2 tbsp fresh parsley – chopped
2 tbsp white wine vinegar
2 tbsp olive oil
½ pint mayonnaise

1. Mix the oil & vinegar together
2. Put the potatoes, carrots, beans, gherkins, peas and capers in a large mixing bowl then pour on the vinegar and oil. Season and mix well. Cover with cling film and refrigerate for 2 hours
3. Remove, add the eggs and parsley then pour on the mayonnaise. Mix well and serve

CRUSHED POTATOES & HORSERADISH SALAD

1 lb new potatoes – scrubbed, boiled & drained
1½ tbsp creamed horseradish sauce
3 fl oz vinaigrette

1. Mix the vinaigrette and horseradish and season
2. Lightly crush the potatoes with the back of a fork and pour on the dressing

POTATO, BACON & AVOCADO SALAD

1 lb new potatoes – scrubbed, halved, boiled & drained
5 rashers bacon – grilled & chopped
½ lb frozen peas – boiled & drained
1 avocado – peeled stoned & sliced
2 cloves garlic – peeled & crushed
6 tbsp mayonnaise
2 tbsp fresh mint – chopped

1. Put the potatoes in a large bowl and add the garlic and mint. Season and leave for a few mins
2. Add all the other ingredients and mix well

POTATO, FISH & BEETROOT SALAD

1 lb new potatoes – scrubbed, boiled & quartered
½ lb cooked fish – skinned & chopped
½ lb cooked beetroot – cubed
3 tbsp creamed horseradish
3 tbsp crème fraîche

1. Mix the horseradish into the crème fraîche. Season
2. Allow the potatoes to cool slightly
3. Put the potatoes, fish and beetroot in a salad bowl. Season, add the horseradish mixture and mix well

BEETROOT, GOATS CHEESE & POTATO SALAD

1 lb new potatoes – scrubbed, boiled & halved
4 oz goats cheese – cubed
½ lb cooked beetroot – drained
5 tbsp extra virgin olive oil
3 tbsp balsamic vinegar
1 tbsp fresh tarragon – chopped
1 bunch rocket – stalks removed

1. Allow the potatoes to cool slightly then place in the bottom of a serving dish. Season then mix with the beetroot
2. Mix the oil and vinegar together in a screw top jar and drizzle half of it over the potatoes and beetroot
3. Season, sprinkle with the tarragon, add the cheese and the rocket then pour on the rest of the oil

SPICY POTATO SALAD

1 lb new potatoes – scrubbed, halved, boiled & drained
1 red pepper – seeded & finely chopped
2 large mild red chillies – seeded & finely chopped
1 small red onion – peeled & finely chopped
5 tbsp extra virgin olive oil
4 tbsp fresh mint – chopped
2 tbsp fresh basil – chopped
2 tbsp lemon juice

1. Heat a little oil and fry the pepper and chillies for 5 mins
2. Mix the lemon juice with the oil
3. Allow the potatoes to cool slightly then put in a large bowl and add the peppers, onions herbs and seasoning
4. Mix well then pour on the oil and lemon dressing

POTATO & TROUT SALAD

1 lb new potatoes – scrubbed, boiled & halved
1 lb trout fillet – skinned
½ lb cooked beetroot – sliced
2 tbsp creamed horseradish
2 tbsp crème fraîche

1. Pre-heat oven to GM6/200°c/400°f
2. Wrap fish in foil and bake for at least 10 mins or until cooked. Drain and reserve the liquid
3. Mix the horseradish with the crème fraîche and the reserved liquid (add a little milk if required).
4. Flake the fish whilst still warm and mix with the cooled potatoes and beetroot. Season and pour on the sauce. Mix well.

ITALIAN POTATO SALAD (2)

**1 lb new potatoes – scrubbed, halved, boiled
& drained**
1 red onion – peeled & thinly sliced
8 green olives – pitted & halved
6 cherry tomatoes – halved
2 cloves garlic – crushed
2 ½ oz feta cheese – crumbled
2 tbsp fresh parsley – chopped
3 tbsp extra virgin olive oil
1 tbsp balsamic vinegar

1. Allow the potatoes to cool slightly then mix with the onion, olives, tomatoes, cheese and parsley. Season
2. Put the garlic, oil and vinegar in a screw top jar, season and shake vigorously
3. Pour the dressing over the potato mixture and mix well.

ITALIAN POTATO SALAD (3)

1 lb potatoes – washed, boiled & drained
½ lb green beans – trimmed, boiled & drained
8 spring onions – trimmed & finely sliced
3 ½ oz crème fraîche
3 ½ oz green pesto

1. Mix the pesto and crème fraîche with the spring onions. Cover with cling film and refrigerate for at least one hour
2. Take a large salad bowl and add all the ingredients, season and mix thoroughly

POTATO & PEPPER SALAD

**1 lb new potatoes – scrubbed, halved, boiled
& drained**
2 red peppers – skinned, seeded & cut into strips
½ lb mozzarella cheese – cubed
5 tbsp extra virgin olive oil
2 tbsp lemon juice
2 tbsp Dijon mustard
1 tbsp olive oil

1. Heat the olive oil and gently fry the skinned peppers for 5 mins. Allow them and the potatoes to cool until warm.
2. Put the extra virgin olive oil, lemon juice and mustard in a screw top jar, season and shake vigorously to mix.
3. Put all the ingredients in a bowl, season and mix well

See 'Pepper & Potato Salad' for how to skin the peppers (page 57)

GREEK POTATO SALAD (2)

**1 lb new potatoes – scrubbed, boiled,
cooled & halved**
½ lb feta cheese – cubed
1 large red onion – peeled & chopped
1 cucumber – trimmed, washed & chopped
4 tomatoes – quartered
12 pitted green olives – halved
7 tbsp extra virgin olive oil
3 tbsp white wine vinegar
2 tbsp fresh oregano – finely chopped

1. Put the oil and vinegar with the oregano in a screw top jar, season & shake vigorously to mix
2. Put all the ingredients except the cheese in a large bowl and pour over the dressing. Season and mix
3. Add the cheese and fold into the salad so as not to break up the cubes

POTATO & CHICKEN SALAD

1 lb new potatoes – scrubbed, boiled & halved
½ lb cooked chicken – cut into bite sized pieces
1 small red onion – peeled & thinly sliced
1 green pepper – de-seeded & cut into thin strips
2 tbsp fresh tarragon – finely chopped
2 tbsp lemon juice
2 tbsp vinaigrette

1. Put the tarragon, lemon juice and vinaigrette in a screw top jar, season and shake vigorously to mix
2. Mix all the other ingredients, season & pour on the dressing

POTATO & HORSERADISH SALAD

1 lb new potatoes – scrubbed, halved, boiled & drained
1 stalk celery – washed & sliced
2 tbsp creamed horseradish
1 tbsp rice wine vinegar
1 tbsp fresh thyme – chopped
2 fl oz extra virgin olive oil

1. *Allow the potatoes to cool slightly then mix with the celery*
2. *Put all the other ingredients in a screw top jar, season and shake vigorously to mix*
3. *Pour over the potatoes and mix well*

BACON & BEAN POTATO SALAD

1 lb new potatoes – scrubbed, halved, boiled & drained
¾ lb bacon – fat removed
½ lb broad beans – boiled & drained
½ iceberg lettuce – shredded
5 fl oz extra virgin olive oil
3 tbsp Dijon mustard
2 tbsp white wine vinegar

1. *Grill the bacon until crisp and cut into pieces. Allow the bacon & potatoes to cool until warm*
2. *Put the oil, mustard and vinegar in a screw-top jar, season and shake vigorously to mix*
3. *Put all the ingredients into a large bowl, season and mix well*

QUICK POTATO SALAD

1 lb new potatoes – scrubbed, halved, boiled & drained
4 tbsp mayonnaise
3 tbsp fresh chives – chopped

Allow the potatoes to cool then place in a large mixing bowl, season and mix with the chives and mayonnaise

PEPPER & SWEETCORN SALAD

1 lb new potatoes – scrubbed, halved, boiled, drained & cooled
1 red pepper – cored, seeded & cut into small squares
1 small tin sweetcorn – drained
6 fl oz mayonnaise
2 tbsp fresh mint – chopped

Put all the ingredients in a mixing bowl, season and mix well

FISH & POTATO MIXED SALAD

1 lb new potatoes – scrubbed, halved, boiled & drained
¼ lb rollmop herrings – chopped
¼ lb gherkins – chopped
¼ lb cooked beetroot – chopped
2 tbsp capers
1 small jar mayonnaise

1. *Allow the potatoes to cool until just warm, then place in a mixing bowl*
2. *Season, spoon on the mayonnaise and add all the other ingredients mixing well*

POTATO & GOAT'S CHEESE SALAD

1 lb new potatoes – scrubbed, boiled & quartered
¼ lb goat's cheese – cubed
½ cos lettuce – shredded
1 clove garlic – crushed
10 cherry tomatoes – halved
4 spring onions – trimmed & chopped
Juice of 2 lemons
½ tsp cayenne pepper
2 tbsp extra virgin olive oil

1. *Put the oil, lemon juice, garlic and cayenne pepper in a screw top jar and shake vigorously until mixed. Season*
2. *Mix all the other ingredients together in a bowl and pour the dressing over. Mix well*

ROCKET & POTATO SALAD

1 lb new potatoes – scrubbed, halved, boiled & drained
¼ lb feta cheese – diced
2 handfuls rocket leaves – washed
2 walnuts – shelled & chopped into small pieces
2 tbsp extra virgin olive oil
1 tbsp runny honey
1 tbsp white wine vinegar

1. *Put the oil, honey and vinegar into a screw top jar and shake vigorously to mix*
2. *Put all the remaining ingredients into a large salad bowl, season, pour on the dressing and mix well*

QUICK POTATO & BEAN SALAD

1 lb new potatoes – scrubbed, halved, boiled & drained
1 small tin pre-cooked broad beans – rinsed & drained
1 small tin pre-cooked kidney beans – rinsed & drained
4 eggs – hard boiled & quartered
10 fl oz yoghurt
2 tbsp lemon juice
4 tbsp wholegrain mustard

1. *Mix the mustard and lemon juice into the yoghurt*
2. *Allow the potatoes to cool until warm then mix with the beans and yoghurt. Serve topped with the egg*

POTATO SALAD WITH HERBS

1 lb new potatoes – scrubbed, halved, boiled & drained
3 tbsp extra virgin olive oil
2 tbsp Dijon mustard
1 tbsp white wine vinegar
1 tbsp fresh parsley – chopped
1 tbsp fresh basil – chopped
1 tbsp fresh rosemary – chopped
1 tbsp fresh chives – snipped

1. *Put the oil, mustard and vinegar in a screw top jar, season and shake vigorously to mix*
2. *Allow the potatoes to cool slightly then put them in a bowl, season and sprinkle with the herbs*
3. *Pour over the dressing and mix together*

ITALIAN POTATO SALAD (4)

1 lb new potatoes – scrubbed, halved, boiled, drained & cooled till warm
1 onion - peeled & thinly sliced
1 green pepper – deseeded & cut into thin strips
2 tbsp tomato purée
2 tbsp lemon juice
1 clove garlic – crushed
¼ lb mozzarella cheese - cubed
2 oz olives
2 tbsp olive oil

1. *Mix the tomato purée, lemon juice and garlic together*
2. *Heat the oil and cook the onion & pepper until softened. Allow to cool slightly*
3. *Put the potatoes in a large bowl, add the peppers and tomato purée mixture. Season and mix well*
4. *Top with the cheese and olives*

POTATO & CAULIFLOWER SALAD

1 lb new potatoes – scrubbed, halved, boiled & drained
1 cauliflower – florets removed (discard the rest)
1 large eating apple – peeled, cored & chopped
¼ lb green beans – washed and trimmed
3 tbsp extra virgin olive oil
2 tbsp tarragon vinegar

1. *Put the cauliflower and beans in boiling water and boil rapidly for 8-10 mins. Drain*
2. *Put the potatoes, cauliflower, beans and apple in a mixing bowl, season*
3. *Blend the oil, vinegar together and pour into the bowl, mix well*

CHICKEN & POTATO SALAD (2)

1 lb new potatoes – scrubbed, halved, boiled & drained
3 chicken breasts – skinned & cut into bite sized pieces
¼ lb green beans – trimmed, boiled & cooled
8 spring onions – trimmed & chopped
8 cherry tomatoes – halved
1 tbsp capers
2 cloves garlic – crushed
5 tbsp lemon juice
2 tbsp mayonnaise
1 tbsp chopped tarragon
2 tbsp extra virgin olive oil

1. *Put the lemon juice and garlic in a screw top jar. Season and shake vigorously to mix. Take a small bowl and add the chicken pour over the juice, cling and refrigerate overnight.*

2. *Heat the oil; remove the chicken pieces with a slotted spoon and fry gently until just cooked. Allow to cool*

3. *Mix the mayonnaise and tarragon*

4. *Mix all the ingredients in a large bowl, season and serve*

BACON, ONION & POTATO SALAD

1 lb new potatoes – scrubbed, halved, boiled & drained
½ lb bacon rashers – fat removed
1 red onion – peeled & thinly sliced
2 tbsp red wine vinegar
2 tbsp extra virgin olive oil
1 tbsp Dijon mustard

1. *Grill the bacon until crisp, drain on kitchen paper and cut into bite sized pieces*

2. *Put the dressing ingredients in a screw top jar, season and shake vigorously to mix*

3. *Put the warm potatoes, bacon and onion in a large bowl, season and mix well. Pour on the dressing, toss to coat*

WARM POTATO & ONION SALAD (2)

1 lb new potatoes – scrubbed, halved, boiled & drained
2 red onions – peeled and finely sliced
3 tbsp extra virgin olive oil

1. *Put all the ingredients in a large bowl, season and mix well*

CURRIED POTATO SALAD (2)

1 lb new potatoes – scrubbed, halved, boiled & drained
3 sticks celery – trimmed & chopped
6 spring onions – trimmed & chopped
2 walnuts – cut into small pieces
1 tbsp Balti curry powder
6 fl oz mayonnaise

1. *Beat the curry powder into the mayonnaise*

2. *Put the potatoes, celery and onions into a bowl. Season and mix*

3. *Add the mayonnaise and stir well to ensure the potatoes are coated. Sprinkle with the walnuts*

GREEN POTATO SALAD

1 lb new potatoes – scrubbed & halved
½ lb fine green beans – trimmed & washed
4 shallots – peeled & finely chopped
3 tbsp white wine vinegar
2 tbsp extra virgin olive oil
2 tbsp fresh mint – chopped

1. *Boil the potatoes for 12 mins. Then add the beans and cook for another 6 mins. Drain*

2. *Heat the oil in a small pan and gently fry the shallots until they start to soften*

3. *Put the potatoes and beans in a serving bowl. Season and add the shallots. Mix well.*

4. *Add the vinegar to the oil, stir well, pour over the potatoes and sprinkle with the mint.*

WARM POTATO & BACON SALAD (2)

1 lb new potatoes – scrubbed, halved, boiled & drained
5 rashers bacon – chopped
4 oz mayonnaise
1 tbsp mustard
1 tsp white wine vinegar

1. *Dry fry the bacon until crispy. Remove with a slotted spoon*
2. *Add the mayonnaise, mustard and vinegar to the fat and whisk together*
3. *Put the warm potatoes in a mixing bowl, season and add the bacon and mayonnaise mixture. Mix well*

NEW POTATO SALAD

1 lb new potatoes – scrubbed, halved, boiled & drained
3 tbsp extra virgin olive oil
5 spring onions – trimmed and sliced
1 tbsp Dijon mustard
2 tbsp lemon juice

1. *Put the oil, lemon juice and mustard in a screw top jar. Season and shake vigorously to mix*
2. *Allow the potatoes to cool until warm then put them in a mixing bowl, season, sprinkle with the chopped onion and pour on the dressing, mixing well. Serve*

ORANGEY PORK & POTATO SALAD

1 lb new potatoes – scrubbed, halved, boiled & drained
1 lb lean pork – cut into bite sized pieces
2 oranges – peeled & separated into segments
¼ pint pure orange juice
2 tbsp orange marmalade
1 small red onion – peeled & thinly sliced
10 cherry tomatoes – halved
1 tbsp olive oil

1. *Put the orange juice in a pint glass, add the marmalade and stir vigorously to mix. Put the meat in a small bowl, pour on the juice, cover with cling film and refrigerate overnight*
2. *Drain the marinade from the pork and reserve the liquid*
3. *Heat the oil and gently fry the pork until cooked*
4. *Boil the reserved liquid in a small pan so any meat residue is cooked and the liquid reduced*
5. *Allow the pork to cool until warm then put in a large bowl with all the other ingredients and pour on the slightly cooled reserved liquid. Mix well*

POTATO SALAD WITH MUSTARD DRESSING

1 lb potatoes – peeled, boiled, drained & cubed
4 sticks celery – washed and sliced
1 onion – peeled and chopped
2 tbsp fresh parsley – chopped
Dressing
2 tbsp single cream
1 tbsp mustard
2 tbsp sugar
2 tbsp cider vinegar

1. *Put the celery, onion and parsley into a blender and mix for 10-15 seconds*
2. *Put all the dressing ingredients, with seasoning into a screw top jar and shake vigorously until mixed*
3. *Put the warm potatoes into a mixing bowl and add the celery mixture. Toss gently to mix then pour the dressing over*

BALSAMIC POTATO SALAD

1 lb new potatoes – scrubbed, halved, boiled & drained
8 spring onions – trimmed & finely chopped
2 tbsp balsamic vinegar

1. *Allow the potatoes to cool until warm*
2. *Add the remaining ingredients, season and mix well*

CRUSHED POTATO SALAD

1 lb new potatoes – scrubbed, halved, boiled & drained
4 oz rocket – leaves only
2 tbsp extra virgin olive oil
2 cloves garlic – crushed
1 tbsp fresh parsley – chopped

1. Heat the oil in a small pan and gently fry the garlic for 1 minute. Add the parsley, season and stir

2. Put the still warm potatoes in a bowl and add the rocket leaves, season

3. Crush lightly with the back of a fork. Drizzle on the oil mixture

POTATO SALAD (3)

1 lb new potatoes – scrubbed, boiled & halved
4 fl oz mayonnaise
½ tbsp white wine vinegar
3 spring onions – trimmed & chopped
2 tbsp extra virgin olive oil
2 tbsp fresh chives – chopped

1. Mix the oil and vinegar

2. Put the potatoes into a salad bowl, season lightly and pour on the oil and vinegar. Toss until coated

3. Add the mayonnaise, onions and chives while the potatoes are still warm. Mix well. Allow to cool then cover with cling film and refrigerate for 3 hours before serving

WARM POTATO & RED PEPPER SALAD

1 lb new potatoes – scrubbed
3 red peppers – cored, seeded & cut into strips
¼ lb mushrooms – halved
1 large red onion – peeled & cut into wedges
2 tbsp walnut oil
1 tbsp Dijon mustard
2 tbsp red wine vinegar
3 tbsp extra virgin olive oil

1. Pre-heat oven to GM6/200°c/400°f

2. Halve the potatoes and boil for 10 mins. Drain

3. Put the potatoes in an ovenproof dish add the peppers, mushrooms and onion. Season and add the olive oil. Mix so that all the vegetables are coated. Bake for 40-45 mins

4. Put the walnut oil, mustard and vinegar in a glass and stir well to mix

5. Remove the vegetables and stir. Allow to cool till warm. Season and pour on the dressing.

POTATO, BACON & AVOCADO SALAD (2)

1 lb new potatoes – scrubbed, halved, boiled & drained
4 rashers bacon – chopped
2 avocados – stoned & sliced
4 iceberg lettuce leaves – chopped
4 tbsp extra virgin olive oil
2 ½ tbsp balsamic vinegar

1. Heat 1 tbsp of oil in a saucepan, add the bacon and fry for 4-5 mins

2. Add the rest of the oil and vinegar and stir. Add the potatoes. Remove from the heat and allow to cool until warm

3. Put the avocado and lettuce in a bowl, mix and add the potato mixture. Season

NEW POTATO SALAD WITH CUCUMBER DRESSING

1 lb new potatoes – scrubbed, boiled and left to cool slightly
½ cucumber – peeled and chopped
3 tbsp white wine vinegar
5 fl oz sour cream
¼ tsp mustard powder

1. Put all the ingredients except potatoes into a blender, season and mix for 20-25 seconds

2. Put the mixture into a bowl, cover with the cling film and chill for 15 mins

3. Pour over the warm potatoes

POTATO & FRENCH CHEESE SALAD

1 lb new potatoes – scrubbed, halved, boiled & drained
3 oz bleu d'Auvergne cheese – diced
½ red onion – peeled and finely sliced
2 tbsp crème fraîche
1 tbsp lemon juice
2 tbsp fresh chives – chopped

1. *Put the crème fraîche in a salad bowl, add the lemon juice and chives. Season and mix well*
2. *Add the potatoes (while still warm), the cheese and onion, mix well and serve*

FISH & POTATO SALAD (2)

1 lb new potatoes – scrubbed, halved, boiled & drained
2 small tins tuna in oil – drained & flaked
6 anchovies – chopped
½ small cos lettuce – shredded
1 red onion – peeled & chopped into small pieces
6 tbsp mayonnaise

Put all the ingredients in a large serving bowl, season and mix well

POTATO SALAD WITH CANARY ISLAND SAUCE

1 lb new potatoes – scrubbed, halved, boiled & drained
5 spring onions – washed and sliced
12 lettuce leaves – washed
2 tbsp fresh coriander – finely chopped
3 tbsp extra virgin olive oil
1 tbsp white wine vinegar
1 clove garlic – crushed

1. *Put the olive oil, vinegar and garlic into a screw top jar with a pinch of salt and shake until mixed*
2. *Pour the mixture over the (warm) potatoes then mix in the spring onion and coriander. Arrange on a bed of lettuce and season*

POTATO & STEAK SALAD

1 lb new potatoes – scrubbed, halved, boiled & drained
1 lb sirloin steak
1 green pepper – cored, seeded & cut into strips
12 cherry tomatoes – halved
4 mushrooms – sliced
1 small red onion – peeled & sliced

1. *Heat the oil in a frying pan and cook the steak until just done. Remove and allow to cool. Cut into strips*
2. *Add the pepper to the oil and fry for 5 mins.*
3. *Add the mushrooms and cook for 5 more mins. Remove and allow to cool. Reserve the oil*
4. *Mix the potatoes and steak with all the other ingredients and pour on the reserved oil. Season*

POTATO, FISH & BEETROOT SALAD (2)

1 lb new potatoes – scrubbed, boiled & quartered
5 cooked mackerel fillets – skinned & chopped
1 lb cooked beetroot – cubed
4 tbsp creamed horseradish
4 tbsp crème fraîche

1. *Mix the horseradish into the crème fraîche. Season*
2. *Allow the potatoes to cool slightly*
3. *Put the potatoes, fish and beetroot in a salad bowl. Season, add the horseradish mixture and mix well*

POTATO & ONION SALAD

1 lb new potatoes – scrubbed, halved, boiled & drained
1 red onion - peeled & chopped into small pieces
5 tbsps salad cream

1. *Put potatoes in a salad bowl, add the onion and salad cream. Season, mix well*

Variations - *You can swap the salad cream for thousand island, mayonnaise etc.*

WARM POTATO & LEEK SALAD

1 lb new potatoes – scrubbed, halved, boiled & drained
1 leek – sliced finely, boiled and drained
1 apple – peeled, cored and diced
2 tbsp mayonnaise
4 fl oz sour cream
1 tbsp capers
1 tbsp fresh chives
1 tbsp lemon juice

1. Put the potatoes in a large bowl and mix in the leek, apple and capers. Season

2. Mix all the other ingredients together and then mix into the salad. Serve whilst warm

FRENCH POTATO SALAD

1 lb new potatoes – scrubbed, halved, boiled & drained
3 fl oz vinaigrette
1 small onion - peeled & finely chopped
1 tbsp fresh parsley - chopped
1 tbsp fresh chives - chopped

1. Add vinaigrette to potatoes while still hot. Mix thoroughly, add onion. Leave to cool

2. Add fresh herbs and season before serving

POTATO & COURGETTE SALAD

1 lb (waxy) potatoes - peeled
1 lb courgettes - washed & sliced
1 onion - peeled & finely chopped
3 eggs - hardboiled & quartered
⅓ pt mayonnaise
6 black olives - stoned
2 oz can achovies - drained

1. Cook the potatoes and courgettes until tender. Drain and allow to cool

2. Dice the potatoes

3. Mix the potatoes, courgettes and onion in a salad bowl. Place the eggs on top, pour on the mayonnaise and garnish with the olives and anchovies

WARM PIQUANT POTATO SALAD

1 lb new potatoes – scrubbed, halved, boiled & drained
5½ oz natural yoghurt
1 tbsp grated parmesan
1 tbsp fresh parsley – chopped
3 oz cherry tomatoes – halved
3 oz diced cucumber
2 tbsp olive oil

1. Pour the oil over potatoes and cool

2. Mix the rest of the ingredients in a bowl and add the potatoes. Mix thoroughly

CRUSHED POTATO SALAD (2)

1 lb new potatoes – scrubbed, halved, boiled & drained
1 tbsp balmasic vinegar
1 small red onion – peeled and finely chopped
4 gherkins – sliced
1 tbsp fresh parsley – chopped
1 tbsp fresh thyme – chopped
2 tbsp olive oil

1. Put the potatoes in a bowl and add the vinegar and oil. Season. Lightly crush the potatoes using a fork

2. Add all the other ingredients and mix gently

NEW POTATO SALAD WITH MINT

1 lb new potatoes – scrubbed, boiled, drained & diced
1½ tbsp fresh mint – chopped
6 fl oz natural yoghurt
4 large lettuce leaves

1. Mix the mint and seasoning into the yoghurt

2. Put the potatoes in a salad bowl and mix with the yoghurt

3. Serve on a bed of lettuce leaves

POTATO SALAD WITH SOURED CREAM

1 lb new potatoes – scrubbed, halved, boiled & drained
2 tsps extra virgin olive oil
1 tsp vinegar
4 tbsp soured cream

1. Mix the oil & vinegar and pour over the potatoes while still warm. Allow to cool
2. Mix in the soured cream and seasoning

POTATO SALAD WITH BACON

1 lb new potatoes – scrubbed, halved, boiled & drained
4 oz bacon - grilled & cut into strips
1 tbsp wholegrain mustard
1 tbsp brown sugar
2 tbsp extra virgin olive oil
2 tbsp wine vinegar - red or white
3 oz red onion - thinly sliced

1. Mix the mustard, sugar, oil and vinegar together, season and add onion
2. Add the potatoes & bacon (still warm). Mix well

POTATO & TUNA MIXED SALAD

1 lb new potatoes – scrubbed, halved, boiled & drained
3 x ¼ lb tuna steaks
¼ lb cherry tomatoes – quartered
¼ lb artichoke hearts – drained
¼ lb french beans – boiled for 4-5 mins and drained
2 oz black olives
4 eggs – hard boiled and quartered
2 tbsp extra virgin olive oil

Dressing
6 tbsp extra virgin olive oil
2 tbsp white wine vinegar
2 tsp wholegrain mustard
2 cloves garlic – crushed
2 tbsp fresh chives – chopped

1. Heat the oil in a pan and gently fry the tuna for about 4-5 mins on each side until cooked
2. Put all the dressing ingredients into a screw top jar and shake until mixed
3. Mix all the other ingredients in a bowl and pour the dressing over. Season
4. Serve with the tuna and egg

NEW POTATO, BACON & BROAD BEAN SALAD

1 lb new potatoes – scrubbed, halved, boiled & drained
½ lb broad beans – boiled
5 rashers bacon – grilled and chopped
2 tbsp olive oil
1 tbsp white wine vinegar
1 tsp mustard
2 tbsp fresh chives – chopped

1. Mix the vegetables and bacon together in a large bowl
2. Put the other ingredients together in a screw top jar and shake vigorously to mix
3. Pour the liquid into the bowl, toss gently and season

POTATO & HERB SALAD

1 lb new potatoes - scrubbed, halved, boiled, allowed to cool slightly
3 fl oz sour cream
1 bunch dill - stalks removed & chopped
2 tbsps fresh parsley - chopped
3 oz Boursin cheese

1. Spoon the sour cream over the potatoes. Season
2. Put the dill, parsley and potatoes in a bowl - mix well
3. Put the cheese on top of the potatoes. (there should be enough heat in the potatoes to melt the cheese)

NEW POTATO SALAD (2)

1 lb new potatoes – scrubbed, halved, boiled & drained
1 leek - washed, trimmed & thinly sliced
1 stick celery - washed & thinly sliced
1 tbsp chopped fresh mint
3 tbsp crème fraîche
1 tsp lemon juice

1. *Combine potatoes with leek, celery & mint*
2. *Mix together the crème fraîche, lemon juice & season. Toss with salad until coated*

POTATO & BACON SALAD (2)

1 lb new potatoes – scrubbed, boiled & kept warm
3 rashers bacon – cooked & kept warm
2 oz baby corn – cooked as directed on pack
2 oz sugar snap peas – cooked as directed on pack
2 spring onions – chopped into small pieces
3 tbsp cream dressing

1. *Slice the potatoes in half & roughly chop the bacon*
2. *Put all the ingredients into a large bowl and mix well. Season*

POTATO SALAD (4)

1 lb new potatoes – scrubbed, boiled, cooled & drained
2 red onions – peeled and chopped
3 eggs – hardboiled and chopped
5 tbsp mayonnaise

1. *Put the potatoes into a large salad bowl, add all the other ingredients. Season and mix well*

How many potatoes do you eat a year?

Nationwide statistics show that on average each person will have tucked into 103 kg that's 500 medium sized spuds

The Spanish claim that Gonzalo Jimenez de Quesada was the first to introduce the potato to Europe in the year 1550. The English say that it was not until 1585 that Sir Walter Raleigh introduced the potato to Europe.

Fish Dishes

FISH CAKES

1 lb potatoes – boiled & mashed
1 lb cooked fish – skinned, boned & flaked
2 eggs – beaten
2 tbsp parsley –chopped
2 oz butter
Fat for cooking
Flour for dusting

1. Mix all the ingredients and seasoning together and mould into flat round cakes. Dust with the flour

2. Fry gently in shallow fat/oil until golden brown. Turn and repeat. Drain on kitchen paper. Serve hot

TUNA FISH CAKES

1 lb potatoes – boiled & mashed
2 small tins tuna in brine – drained & flaked
2 tbsp parsley – chopped
1 tbsp lemon juice
2 eggs – beaten
Flour for dipping
2 tbsp breadcrumbs
Vegetable oil for frying

1. Beat the tuna into the mash then mix in the parsley, lemon juice and 1 egg. Season

2. Divide the mixture into 5 and form into cakes

3. Dust each cake with flour, brush with the remaining egg and coat with breadcrumbs

4. Heat some vegetable oil in a frying pan and cook gently until brown on both sides. Serve hot

POTATOES WITH SPICY COD

1 lb new potatoes – scrubbed & halved
1 lb cod fillets
4 fl oz white wine
1½ tsp allspice
3 rashers bacon
2 bay leaves
1 tbsp fresh thyme leaves
3 tbsp extra virgin olive oil

1. Pre-heat oven to GM6/200°c/400°f

2. Put half the oil in a large roasting tray and add the potatoes. Mix until well coated then roast for 20 mins

3. Mix the rest of the oil with the wine, allspice and thyme. Place the fish in a shallow dish and pour the mixture over

4. Place the fish and juices over the roasted potatoes then put the bacon on the fish and top with the bay leaves

5. Roast for 30 mins, basting occasionally, remove bay leaves & serve

SALMON FISH CAKES

1 lb potatoes – boiled & mashed
1 large tin of salmon – drained, bones removed & flaked
2 oz capers – rinsed & chopped
4 tsp fresh dill – chopped
Juice and zest of 1 lemon
1 egg – beaten
4 oz breadcrumbs
2 tbsp vegetable oil

1. Thoroughly mix the potatoes with the salmon, capers, dill and lemon. Season

2. Roll the mixture flat then mould into 5 cake shapes. Brush each with egg and roll in the breadcrumbs

3. Heat the oil and fry the cakes for 5 mins on each side. Drain on kitchen paper

COD & PESTO PIE

1 lb potatoes – peeled, boiled & mashed
1 lb cod – filleted, steamed & flaked
3 tbsp green pesto sauce
½ pint white sauce - made from a packet

1. Pre-heat oven to GM6/200°c/400°f

2. Add the fish and pesto to the white sauce and heat gently for 10 mins

3. Pour into a casserole dish and season, spread the potato on top and bake for ½ hour until the potatoes are browned

POTATO TUNA & SWEETCORN CRISPBAKES

1 lb potatoes - boiled & mashed
1 small tin tuna – drained & flaked
3 tbsps sweetcorn – drained
1 small onion – thinly sliced
3 tbsp cream dressing
1 egg – beaten
4 oz fresh white breadcrumbs

1. *Fry the onion in vegetable oil for about 3-4 mins until softened*
2. *Put into a large mixing bowl and stir in the dressing. Add the sweetcorn, potato, tuna & onion and mix well. Season*
3. *Divide the mixture in 5 or 6 and press manually into flat round shapes. Brush each with the egg then toss in the breadcrumbs*
4. *Fry each crispbake for 5 mins on each side*

PRAWN & HADDOCK PIE

1 lb (floury) potatoes – peeled, boiled & mashed
1 lb 4oz smoked haddock fillet
½ lb prawns – cooked
1 onion – peeled & sliced
1 pint milk
½ pint double cream
3 eggs – hard boiled, shelled & quartered
4 tbsp parsley – chopped
2 oz butter
2 oz flour

1. *Pre-heat oven to GM6/200°c/400°f*
2. *Wrap the haddock in tin foil and bake for 10 mins. Drain and reserve the liquid*
3. *Melt the butter, stir in the flour and make a sauce with the milk. Add the cream and parsley and reserved liquid. Season well and simmer very gently for 5 mins*
4. *Flake the fish and put it in the base of a casserole dish. Add the prawns and eggs. Season and pour the sauce on top. Allow to cool*
5. *Spoon the potato on top and bake for 45 mins*

SPICY FISH CAKES

1 lb potatoes – peeled & boiled
½ lb smoked haddock fillet – skinned
¼ pint milk
1 onion – peeled & grated
1 tsp fresh ginger – grated
1 tsp paprika
3 tbsp groundnut oil
1 tbsp lemon juice
1 egg – beaten
2 oz brown breadcrumbs

1. *Heat the milk until warm, add the haddock and cook gently for 5 mins. Drain*
2. *Heat 1 tbsp of oil and cook the onion, ginger and paprika for 5 mins*
3. *Mash the potatoes and fish together then add the onion mixture and lemon juice. Season*
4. *Mould into 4 cake shapes and brush with the egg then dip in the breadcrumbs*
5. *Heat the remaining oil and fry the cakes for 6-7 mins on each side*

POTATO & PRAWN NESTS

1 lb potatoes – boiled & mashed
4 oz prawns - cooked
2 tomatoes – sliced
2 eggs – hardboiled & sliced
3 oz cheddar cheese – grated
1 oz flour
3 oz butter
½ pint milk

1. *Mix 2 oz of the butter into the mash*
2. *Divide the mash into 6 individual ovenproof dishes and mould into nests*
3. *Place slices of egg & tomato in the centre of each nest & top with the prawns*
4. *Put the remaining butter, flour, milk and seasoning into a small pan. Heat, whisking continually until the sauce thickens. Add most of the cheese & beat well. Pour the sauce into the centre of the nests*
5. *Sprinkle with the remaining cheese & grill under a pre-heated grill until golden brown*

SALMON FISH CAKES (2)

1 lb potatoes – peeled, boiled & mashed
1 large tin salmon – drained, boned & flaked
2 tbsp fresh parsley – chopped
1 egg

For the coating
2 oz cheddar cheese – grated
6 oz breadcrumbs
1 egg
Vegetable oil for frying

1. *Beat all the main ingredients together in a large bowl, divide the mixture into 4 and shape into 4 cakes*
2. *Mix the cheese and breadcrumbs together*
3. *Brush each cake with the second egg and dip into the breadcrumbs and cheese. Put each cake on a plate, cover with cling film and refrigerate for 30 mins*
4. *Heat plenty of oil in a large frying pan and when fairly hot, place the cakes gently into the pan. Heat each cake for 5 mins on each side or until heated thoroughly. Remove and drain on kitchen paper*

BASS WITH LEMON POTATOES

1 lb (floury) potatoes – peeled & cut into chunks
1 sea bass - washed
1 preserved lemon
2 tbsp white wine
1 tbsp lemon juice
1 tbsp olive oil
1 handful fresh lemon thyme
10 olives

1. *Pre-heat oven to GM6/200°c/400°f*
2. *Mix the wine, lemon juice & oil*
3. *Put the potatoes in a large roasting tin, drizzle with the lemon juice, oil and wine. Roast for 30 mins, tossing occasionally*
4. *Grate the skin of the lemon, combine with the lemon thyme and olives and stuff it into the fish*
5. *Baste the fish with the liquid in the tin and put in the middle of the tin with potatoes on each side. Roast for 30 mins or until the fish is cooked*

COD CAKES

1 lb potatoes – boiled & mashed
1 lb cooked cod – flaked
2 onions – peeled & grated
1 tsp lemon juice
2 tbsp milk
2 tbsp plain flour
2 tbsp vegetable oil

1. *Put the potatoes, cod, onion & lemon juice into a large bowl and beat until mixed thoroughly*
2. *Divide the mixture into 10 and manually shape into cakes. Dust each cake with flour, cover with cling film and put in the fridge for ½ hour*
3. *Heat the oil in a pan and cook the cakes on a medium heat for 10 mins until browned on both sides*

FISH HASH

1 lb potatoes – peeled & cut into small cubes
½ lb cooked fish - flaked
4 rashers bacon – rind removed & roughly chopped
1 onion – peeled & finely chopped
2 sticks celery – wash & finely chopped
¼ lb peas – boiled & drained

1. *Dry fry the bacon in a large pan until crisp. Remove with a slotted spoon and set aside*
2. *Add the onion, celery and potatoes and cook over a medium heat until the potato is browned, stirring continually. Add vegetable oil if needed*
3. *Add the peas, bacon and fish, season and stir fry until heated through*

POTATO & MACKEREL BAKE

1 lb (waxy) potatoes – peeled & boiled for 10 mins
½ lb mackerel fillets – skinned & flaked
1 onion – peeled & sliced
7 fl oz double cream
1½ tbsp olive oil

1. Pre-heat oven to GM5/190°c/375°f

2. Heat the oil and fry the onion until it starts to soften

3. Slice the potatoes while still warm and add to the onion. Stir and season

4. Transfer half the mixture to an ovenproof dish and add the fish. Season and add the rest of the potatoes. Spread the cream evenly on top

5. Cover and bake for 30 mins then remove cover and bake for 20 mins more

CAPER AND HADDOCK FISH CAKES

1 lb potatoes – peeled, boiled, drained & mashed
1 lb smoked haddock – poached, flaked & boned
5 tbsp capers – chopped
2 eggs – hard boiled and finely chopped
2 eggs – beaten
2 tbsp fresh parsley – chopped
Breadcrumbs for dipping
Vegetable oil for frying

1. Put the (warm) potato, haddock, capers, boiled eggs and parsley into a large bowl, season and mix thoroughly

2. Add ½ the beaten egg and mix well. Remove from the bowl and divide the mixture into 15 and mould each piece into a small cake shape

3. Brush each with beaten egg and coat in breadcrumbs

4. Heat the oil to a medium heat in a large pan and fry until golden brown on each side

POTATO & TUNA FRITTERS

1 lb potatoes – peeled, boiled & drained
1 small tin tuna – drained & flaked
2 eggs beaten
1 onion – peeled & grated
1 tbsp dill – chopped
2 oz flour
Vegetable oil for frying

1. Put the tuna in a microwave proof dish and cook until hot

2. Put the potatoes, tuna, onion and dill in a food processor and blend until smooth

3. Put the mixture in a bowl, season and beat in the eggs and flour

4. Heat the oil

5. Divide the mixture into 8 portions and fry until browned. Drain on kitchen paper

TUNA & POTATO BAKE

1 lb new potatoes – scrubbed, sliced & boiled for 10 mins, drained & cooled
2 small tins tuna – drained & flaked
1 small tin sweetcorn – drained
3 oz cheddar cheese – grated
½ pint white sauce - made from a packet
1 tbsp fresh parsley – chopped

1. Pre-heat the oven to GM5/190°c/375°f Add the fish, sweetcorn and parsley to the sauce & heat through

2. Layer the base of a casserole dish with half the potatoes, then pour over the fish mixture. Top with the rest of the potatoes and sprinkle with the cheese. Bake for about 30 mins

HADDOCK WITH POTATO TOPPING

1 lb (waxy) potatoes – peeled & sliced thinly (with a mandolin)
4 smoked haddock fillets
3 tbsp extra virgin olive oil

1. Pre-heat oven to GM6/200°c/400°f

2. Soak the potatoes in water for a few mins and drain. Pat dry with a tea towel

3. Grease a small roasting tin with a little oil and add the fish skin side down. Season

4. Put the potatoes in layers over the fish and season. Drizzle over the oil and bake for 40 mins

5. Remove pour off the excess liquid and serve

POTATO & PRAWN CURRY

1 lb (waxy) potatoes – peeled & diced
10 oz prawns – defrosted & cooked
4 oz frozen peas – defrosted
1 onion – peeled & chopped
2 tbsp mild green curry paste
12 fl oz coconut milk
3 fl oz milk
½ stick lemon grass – finely chopped
1 tbsp coriander leaves – torn
1 tbsp vegetable oil

1. *Heat the oil and fry the potato and onion for 5 mins*

2. *Add the curry paste and lemongrass and fry for 1 min*

3. *Add the coconut milk and the milk. Stir well, bring to the boil and simmer for 20 mins, adding more milk if required*

4. *Add the peas and prawns, season and heat until they are cooked. Serve topped with coriander leaves*

FISHERMANS PIE

1 lb potatoes – peeled & sliced
1 onion - peeled & sliced
½ lb cod steaks – filleted & diced
½ lb salmon fillet – diced
2 oz mushrooms – washed & sliced
3 oz cheddar cheese – grated
3 sun dried tomatoes – chopped
1 oz plain flour
1 tbsp Worcester sauce
¼ pint milk
½ oz butter

1. *Pre-heat the oven to GM6/200°c/400°f*

2. *Toss the cod and salmon in half the flour and mix together*

3. *Put one third of the potatoes in the base of a casserole dish. Cover with half the fish. Top with the sun dried tomatoes, sprinkle with Worcester sauce. Season*

4. *Add half the onions and mushrooms then the rest of the fish and another 1/3 of the potatoes then the rest of the onion and mushrooms*

5. *Make a roux with the butter, flour and milk and heat until thickened then add half the cheese. Pour the sauce into the dish, top with the remaining potato and put into the oven*

6. *Bake for 1 hour, sprinkle over the rest of the cheese and cook for 15 more mins*

SEAFOOD POTATO SLICE

1 lb potatoes – peeled, boiled for 10 mins drained & sliced
1 small can tuna – drained
4 oz prawns – cooked
6 cherry tomatoes – halved
1 level tsp horseradish
1½ tbsp mayonnaise
2 tbsp fromage frais
1 tbsp olive oil
1 tbsp lemon juice

1. *Pre-heat oven to GM5/190°c/375°f*

2. *Brush a baking tray with some oil and lemon and cover the base with potatoes. Brush the potatoes with the rest of the oil and lemon. Bake for 30 mins*

3. *Mix together the tuna, mayonnaise, fromage frais and horseradish. Season then add the tomatoes and prawns*

4. *Layer half the potatoes at the base of a shallow oven proof dish, spoon on the tuna mixture, season & spread it evenly over the potatoes. Add the remaining potatoes, press down with the back of a spoon & bake for 10 more mins*

THAI FISH CAKES

1 lb potatoes – boiled & mashed
2 small tins tuna – drained
2 cloves garlic- crushed
4 eggs – beaten
4 slices bread – toasted & turned into crumbs
1 tsp chilli powder
Plain flour - for brushing
1 tbsp fresh coriander –chopped
1 tbsp parsley – chopped
4 tbsp vegetable oil

1. *Put mash in a large bowl and add the tuna, garlic, herbs and chilli powder - mix well.*

2. *Divide the mixture into 8 cakes and brush each with flour, then dip in egg and breadcrumbs*

3. *Heat the oil and fry each cake for about 5 mins on each side until browned*

NEW POTATOES WITH SALMON

1 lb new potatoes – scrubbed & halved
3 salmon steaks
2 red onions – peeled & chopped
3 cloves garlic
1 lemon – zest & juice
1 lime – zest & juice
2 tbsp fresh parsley – chopped
2 tbsp vegetable oil
5 fl oz vegetable stock

1. *Put the garlic, both zests and lime juice in a food processor. Season and make a purée*

2. *Heat the oil and spread the purée onto the salmon. Cook the steaks for 3 mins on each side. Remove and put aside*

3. *Add the potatoes and fry for about 10 mins*

4. *Add the onion and fry for about 5 mins*

5. *Add the stock and lemon juice. Season and bring to the boil*

6. *Add the fish and parsley then simmer very gently for 5 mins until the fish is fully cooked and the desired consistency is reached*

SPICY FISH CAKES (2)

1 lb potatoes – peeled, boiled & mashed
2 small tins tuna – drained
2 eggs – beaten
3 cloves garlic – crushed
2 tsp crushed chillies
8 oz breadcrumbs
4 tbsp vegetable oil
4 oz flour
2 tbsp fresh coriander – chopped
2 tbsp fresh parsley - chopped

1. *Put the potatoes in a large bowl with the tuna, chillies, garlic and herbs. Mix well and season*

2. *Shape into cakes and coat each one with flour, brush with egg and dip in the breadcrumbs*

3. *Heat the oil in a large pan and fry each cake for about 5 mins on each side until browned*

COD & TOMATO STEW

1 lb potatoes – peeled & cubed
1 lb cod fillet – skinned & cubed
1 large can chickpeas – drained
2 large cans chopped tomatoes
1 large onion – peeled and chopped
3 cloves garlic - crushed
3 tbsp tomato purée
1 tbsp fresh basil – chopped
3 tbsp olive oil

1. *Heat the oil and fry the potatoes for 5 mins*
2. *Add the onion and garlic and fry for 5 more mins*
3. *Add the tomatoes, purée and basil, stir until heated through*
4. *Add the chickpeas and season, stirring well*
5. *Add the fish, mix carefully so as not to break up the fish and heat until the fish is cooked*

POTATO & TUNA CAKES

1 lb potatoes – peeled, boiled & mashed
1 small tin tuna – drained
1 small tin sweetcorn – drained
1 onion – peeled & finely chopped
2 eggs – beaten
2 tbsp parsley – chopped
3 tbsp vegetable oil
2 oz seasoned flour
3 oz breadcrumbs

1. Take a large mixing bowl, mix the potato, sweetcorn, tuna, onion and parsley

2. Shape into cakes and coat each one with flour, brush with egg and dip in the breadcrumbs

3. Heat the oil and fry each cake for 5 mins on each side until browned

CLASSIC FISHCAKES

1 lb (floury) potatoes – peeled, boiled & mashed
1 lb cod fillet – skinned
6 oz white breadcrumbs
1 egg beaten
Juice of 1 lemon
5 tbsp fresh parsley – chopped
3 tbsp fresh chives – chopped
1 tbsp dill – chopped
Sunflower oil for frying

1. *Pre-heat oven to GM6/200°c/400°f*

2. *Wrap the fish in foil and bake for 15 mins. Remove, drain and reserve the liquid*

3. *Allow the fish to cool then add to the mash in a large bowl. Season and add the lemon juice and herbs. Mix well and add the reserved fish liquid if desired*

4. *Form the mixture into 6 cakes and brush with the egg then dip into the breadcrumbs*

5. *Heat the oil and gently fry the cakes for about 10 mins on each side until golden brown.*

QUICK TUNA & POTATO CAKES

1 lb potatoes – peeled, boiled & mashed
3 small tins tuna – drained
6 tsp creamed horseradish
2 tbsp olive oil

1. Mix the potatoes, tuna and horseradish together. Season

2. Form into cakes with your hands

3. Heat the oil in a pan and cook each cake until golden brown – turning regularly

FISH & CHIP PIE

1 lb waxy potatoes – peeled & cut into thin chips
½ lb cod fillet – skinned & cut into wide strips
1 onion – peeled & sliced
5 fl oz double cream
3 fl oz fish stock
1 oz butter

1. *Pre-heat oven to GM6/200°c/400°f*

2. *Lay half the chips at the bottom of a greased ovenproof dish. Season*

3. *Add the onion and fish in two layers. Season then add the rest of the potatoes*

4. *Mix the cream and stock together and pour over*

5. *Season, dot with butter, cover with foil and bake for 30 mins*

6. *Remove the foil and bake for 20 more mins*

FISH PIE

1 lb potatoes – peeled, boiled & mashed
1 lb smoked haddock fillet – skinned
½ pint milk
3 eggs – hard boiled, shelled & chopped
1 tbsp lemon juice
2 oz butter
1 oz flour
2 tbsp fresh parsley – chopped

1. *Pre-heat oven to GM6/200°c/400°f*

2. *Put the fish in a pan and add the milk. Simmer for 15 mins then drain and flake the fish*

3. *Make a white sauce using the butter, flour and milk*

4. *Add the fish, eggs, parsley and lemon juice to the sauce. Season, stir & warm through.*

5. *Put the mixture into a baking dish and spread the mashed potato on top. Bake for 30 mins until browned*

COD & POTATO LAYER BAKE

1 lb (waxy) potatoes – peeled & sliced
1 lb cod fillet
2 onions – peeled & sliced
1 clove garlic - crushed
1 tbsp wholegrain mustard
1 tbsp fresh dill – chopped
2 oz Gruyere cheese – grated
3 oz breadcrumbs
2 oz butter

1. Pre-heat oven to GM5/190°c/375°f
2. Fry the potatoes in the butter for 5 mins, then remove with a slotted spoon
3. Add the onion, garlic, mustard, breadcrumbs and dill. Mix well, fry for 3-4 mins.
4. Grease an ovenproof dish and layer the base with half the potatoes. Add the cod then half the onion mixture
5. Add the rest of the potatoes, top with the remaining mixture and sprinkle with cheese
6. Bake for 30 mins ensuring the fish is cooked

POTATO & FISH PIE

1 lb potatoes – peeled, boiled & mashed
9 oz white fish – filleted & boned
3 oz frozen peas
½ pint milk
3 tbsp fresh parsley - chopped
2 tbsp plain flour
1½ oz butter

1. Pre-heat oven to GM6/200°c/400°f
2. Warm the milk in a small pan and add the fish, simmer for 10 mins
3. Remove the fish and put into an ovenproof dish
4. Add the flour, parsley and butter to the milk and transfer to a blender, blitz for 10 seconds
5. Return to a clean pan and heat gradually over a medium heat, stirring continually
6. When thickened pour the sauce over the fish, add the peas and season. Top with the mash and bake for 40 mins

FISH PIE (2)

1 lb potatoes – boiled & mashed
1 lb cod fillet – cut into bite sized pieces
¼ lb prawns
½ pint packet onion sauce – made up as per instructions
1 small tin mushrooms – drained
1 small tin chopped tomatoes
6 fl oz dry white wine
1 oz butter

1. Pre-heat oven to GM4/180°c/350°f
2. Put the fish in the bottom of a casserole dish. Season and add the mushrooms and tomatoes then the prawns
3. Mix the onion sauce with the wine and pour on top. Season
4. Spoon the potatoes on top and dot with the butter. Bake for 30-40 mins

POTATO & GRAVADLAX BAKE

1 lb potatoes – peeled & thinly sliced
10 oz gravadlax
5 oz courgettes – cut into strips
1 large onion – peeled & finely chopped
7 fl oz double cream
3 fl oz milk
1 oz butter

1. Pre-heat oven to GM5/190°c/375°f
2. Melt the butter and fry the onion for 5 mins
3. Grease a casserole dish and layer $^1/_3$ of the potatoes at the base. Season and add half the fish and onion. Repeat, finishing with a layer of potatoes
4. Mix the cream and milk, season and heat through
5. Pour the cream onto the potato mixture, dot with the butter and bake for 1 hour

SALMON FISH CAKES (3)

1 lb potatoes – peeled, boiled & mashed
½ lb tinned salmon – drained
1 tbsp fresh parsley – chopped
1 tbsp lemon zest – finely chopped
1 oz butter
2 tbsp sunflower oil

1. Beat the salmon, parsley and zest into the mash – season and leave to cool
2. Divide the mixture into 6 cakes and lightly dust with flour
3. Heat the oil and fry the cakes for 5 mins on each side. Drain on kitchen paper before serving

ROSTI FISH PIE

1 lb potatoes – par boiled in their skins for 10 mins & cooled
1 lb smoked haddock
3 oz prawns – peeled
2 eggs – hard boiled & quartered
4 oz tub sour cream
9 fl oz milk
1½ oz butter
1 oz flour
1 oz cheddar cheese – grated
3 tbsp dill – chopped

1. Pre-heat oven to GM6/200°c/400°f

2. Using a little of the milk gently poach the fish for 5 mins. Drain, reserving the liquid and flake the fish

3. Put the fish, prawns and eggs into a casserole dish

4. Make a white sauce using 1oz of the butter the flour and the reserved milk. When the sauce has thickened add the sour cream, dill and seasoning. Pour over the fish

5. Peel and grate the potatoes, squeeze out the excess moisture

6. Melt the rest of the butter and mix with the potatoes

7. Spread the potatoes over the fish and sprinkle with cheese and bake for about 40 mins until browned

POTATO & COD BAKE

1 lb potatoes – peeled, boiled for 10 mins & drained
1 lb cod steaks – skinned & filleted
½ pint cheese sauce - made from a packet
4 tomatoes – sliced
1 tbsp Worcester sauce

1. Pre-heat oven to GM5/190°c/375°f

2. Slice the potatoes and layer them on the bottom of a greased ovenproof dish. Season and add the tomatoes then the cod steaks

3. Mix the Worcester sauce with the cheese sauce, season and pour into the dish. Bake for 20-25 mins until the fish is cooked

SIMPLE FISH PIE

1 lb potatoes – peeled, cooked & diced
1 lb cooked haddock fillet – skin removed & flaked
¾ pint milk
2 oz butter
2 oz flour
2½ tbsp fresh parsley – chopped
puff pastry – thawed if frozen
1 egg beaten

1. Pre-heat oven to GM7/210°c/425°f

2. Make a white sauce with the milk, butter and flour. Season and stir in the parsley

3. Add the potatoes and fish to the sauce and heat gently for 5 mins

4. Pour the mixture into a casserole dish and roll pastry over the top

5. Pinch the edges to seal, brush with the egg and bake for 30 mins

FISH PIE (3)

1 lb potatoes – peeled, cut into chunks, boiled & mashed
1 lb cod fillet – skinned & cut into strips
2 onions – peeled & finely chopped
2 carrots – peeled & finely chopped
6 oz spinach
5 tbsp cheddar cheese – grated
2 eggs – hard boiled, peeled and quartered
2 tbsp mustard powder
3 tbsp lemon juice
3 tbsp parsley – finely chopped
½ pint double cream
2 tbsp olive oil

1. Pre-heat oven to GM7/220°c/425°f

2. Gently heat the oil in a pan and fry the carrots and onions for 5-6 mins. Add the cream and bring to a simmer

3. Remove from the heat then blend in the cheese, lemon juice, mustard powder and parsley

4. Mix the eggs, spinach and fish together then place in an ovenproof dish and season. Pour the sauce over the mixture and spoon the potatoes over the top. Bake for 35-40 mins

TOMATO & FISH PIE

1 lb potatoes – boiled & mashed
1 lb cooked cod fillet – skinned & flaked
1 lb tomatoes – washed & sliced
1 onion – peeled & grated
1 oz butter
2 tbsp cheddar cheese – grated

1. *Pre-heat oven to GM7/210°c/425°f*
2. *Melt the butter and fry the onion for 5 mins*
3. *Mix the onion into the mash, season*
4. *Use ²/₃ of the potato mixture to line the sides and base of a casserole dish*
5. *Layer with half the tomatoes; add the fish and then the remaining tomatoes. Season and top with the rest of the potatoes*
6. *Sprinkle with the cheese, season and bake for 30 mins*

FISH & POTATO CASSEROLE

1 lb potatoes – peeled & thinly sliced
1 lb cod fillet
4 fl oz milk
2 oz butter
1 onion – peeled & thinly sliced
5 fl oz cream
2 tbsp chopped fresh parsley
2 cloves garlic – crushed
4 oz cheddar cheese – grated

1. *Cook the fish gently in seasoned milk for 5 mins. Allow to cool then skin & flake the fish. Keep the liquid*
2. *Heat the oven to GM5/190°c/375°f*
3. *Grease an ovenproof dish. Layer the bottom with ½ the potatoes & onion, then place the fish on top. Sprinkle with half the cheese & parsley & season*
4. *Cover with the remaining potato & onion. Sprinkle with the rest of the cheese & parsley & season*
5. *Mix the cream with the reserved fish liquid & pour over the top. Cover with foil & bake for 50 mins*
6. *Remove the foil & cook for a further 20-30 mins until the potatoes are browned*

COD TIMBALE

1 lb potatoes – boiled & mashed
8 oz cod – cooked & flaked
4 oz cheddar cheese – grated
½ pint milk
1 oz brown breadcrumbs
1 oz plain flour
1½ tbsp parsley – chopped
1 tbsp lemon juice
3 oz butter

1. *Pre-heat oven to GM5/180°c/375°f*
2. *Melt 2 oz of the butter in a pan and add the potatoes & cheese. Season & beat together*
3. *Use some of the rest of the butter to line an ovenproof dish, sprinkle the breadcrumbs in to coat. Line the dish with about ²/₃ of the mash*
4. *Put the remaining butter, flour and milk in a saucepan & season. Heat – stirring continuously until the sauce thickens. Add the fish, parsley & lemon juice & stir thoroughly. Pour into the centre of the dish*
5. *Top with the rest of mash & bake for 35-40 mins*

GRAVADLAX & CELERIAC POTATO PIE

1 lb potatoes – peeled and thinly sliced
½ lb gravadlax
¾ lb celeriac – peeled & thinly sliced
2 onions – peeled & thinly sliced
14 fl oz double cream
Juice of 2 lemons
2 tbsp fresh dill – chopped

1. *Pre-heat oven to GM6/200°c/400°f*
2. *Put the sliced potato and celeriac into a bowl and pour in the lemon juice. Leave for 2 mins*
3. *Put alternate layers of potato, celeriac and fish in a casserole dish. With each layer add a little onion, dill, cream and seasoning*
4. *Finish with a layer of potatoes and top with cream. Cover and bake for 1 hour*
5. *Remove cover and bake for 20 more mins*

POTATOES & FISH WITH ANCHOVY SAUCE

1 lb potatoes – peeled & thinly sliced
12 oz white fish – filleted & cut into chunks
1 tbsp parmesan cheese – grated
1 tbsp olive oil

Sauce Ingredients

2 anchovy fillets – drained & chopped
1 tbsp capers – rinsed, drained & chopped
1 tbsp wholegrain mustard
2 tbsp fresh parsley – chopped
2 tbsp lemon juice
1 clove garlic – crushed
2 tbsp olive oil

1. Pre-heat the oven to GM6/200°c/400°f
2. Put the potatoes into the same pan of boiling water and cook for 10 mins. Drain
3. Put all the sauce ingredients into a blender, season and blitz for 15 seconds
4. Layer half the potatoes in the bottom of an oven proof dish, season and add the fish. Spoon the sauce over the fish and put in the second layer of potatoes. Season and brush with olive oil. Sprinkle with the cheese and bake for 35 mins ensuring the fish is cooked

PRAWN & POTATO CURRY

1 lb potatoes – peeled, diced, boiled for 10 mins & drained
1 lb frozen prawns – defrosted
10 fl oz coconut milk
2 tbsp Thai red curry paste
2 onions – peeled & chopped
1 tbsp sunflower oil

1. Heat the oil and fry the onions until they start to soften
2. Add the curry paste and cook for 1 min
3. Pour on the coconut milk, stir well and heat to a simmer
4. Add the potatoes and prawns, stir well and simmer for about 5 mins ensuring the prawns are cooked and until the desired consistency is reached

SALMON & POTATO PIE

1 lb potatoes – peeled & boiled
12 oz salmon fillet
2 leeks – trimmed & sliced
2 cloves garlic – crushed
1 small onion – peeled & finely chopped
¼ lb prawns – defrosted, cooked & drained
3 tbsp lemon juice
2 tbsp fresh parsley – chopped
1 oz butter
3 fl oz milk
4 tbsp cheddar cheese – grated
1 tbsp olive oil

1. Pre-heat oven to GM5/190°c/375°f
2. Heat the oil and gently fry the leek and onion until they start to soften
3. Add the garlic and cook for a further 2 mins
4. Heat half the milk in a frying pan and gently poach the salmon until just cooked. Reserve the milk
5. Flake the fish and place in an oven proof dish, add the onion, leek, garlic, prawns, parsley, lemon juice and reserved milk. Season and mix well
6. Put the potatoes in a pan and mash with the butter, milk and half the cheese
7. Put the fish mixture in an ovenproof dish, top with the mash and sprinkle with the remaining cheese. Cook for 20-25 mins

SALMON & POTATO BAKE

1 lb (floury) potatoes – peeled & sliced
½ lb smoked salmon fillet
15 fl oz crème fraiche

1. Pre-heat oven to GM6/200°c/400°f
2. Grease an oven proof dish and layer it with one third of the potatoes. Season and add half the salmon, then one third of the crème fraiche, repeat until all the ingredients are used
3. Cover and bake for 45 mins
4. Remove cover and bake for another 15 mins

POTATO & PRAWN BALTI

1 lb new potatoes – scrubbed, halved, boiled & drained
10 oz tiger prawns
1 onion – peeled & finely chopped
3 tbsp balti curry paste
2 tbsp vegetable oil

1. *Heat the oil and fry the onion until it starts to brown*
2. *Turn up the heat, add the prawns and fry until they are cooked*
3. *Add the balti paste and stir well*
4. *Pour on ½ pint of water, add the potatoes and stir. Bring to the boil then simmer gently for about 5 mins*

TUNA & COTTAGE CHEESE POTATOES

1 lb potatoes – peeled, boiled, drained & thinly sliced
1 small tin tuna – drained & flaked
½ lb cottage cheese
3 eggs – beaten
1 oz butter

1. *Pre-heat oven to GM4/180°c/350°f*
2. *Grease an ovenproof dish and layer the base with half the potatoes*
3. *Add the tuna to the cheese and eggs. Season and mix well*
4. *Spoon the mixture onto the potatoes and cover with the rest of the potatoes*
5. *Dot with butter and bake for 30 mins*

QUICK SPICY FISH CAKES

1 lb potatoes – peeled, boiled & mashed
2 small tins tuna in brine – drained
2 Jalapeno peppers – chopped
4 tbsp fresh coriander - chopped
2 tbsp vegetable oil

1. *Heat the oil in a frying pan*
2. *Put all the other ingredients in a large bowl, season and mix manually*
3. *Form into 4 round shapes and fry each one in the pan, turning frequently, until browned on both sides*

Brits are the third largest consumers of potatoes in Europe

Only the Portugese and the Irish eat more than us

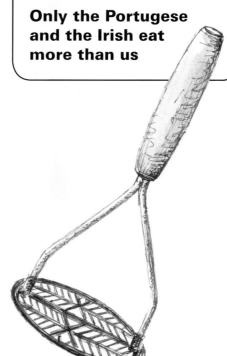

81

Side Dishes

POMMES de TERRE SOUFFLE

1 lb (waxy) potatoes
Vegetable oil

1. Peel the potatoes and slice very thinly; about $1/8$ inch thick. Soak in cold water for 1-1½ hours

2. Drain and pat dry with kitchen paper

3. Heat the oil to 160° and add half the potato slices. Cook until the slices rise to the surface. Remove them and place on absorbent kitchen paper to drain and cool. Repeat with the remaining slices

4. Just before serving heat the oil up to 200° and plunge in the first batch of potatoes. They should puff up immediately and turn golden brown. Remove and drain, then repeat with the rest of the potato. Serve hot

VICTORIAN POTATOES

1 lb potatoes – peeled & par boiled for 15 mins
1½ oz butter
1 oz flour
½ pint milk
2 oz cheddar cheese – grated

1. Pre-heat oven to GM4/180°c/350°f

2. Use ½ oz butter to grease a pie dish

3. Cut the potatoes into thin slices and put into the dish

4. Make a white sauce with the milk, flour and butter and pour over the potatoes

5. Sprinkle with the cheese and bake until the top is golden brown. Serve hot

BROWNED POTATOES

1 lb potatoes - peeled & cut into small pieces
1 oz butter

1. Mash the potatoes (without cooking) and place in a well greased pie dish. Season and dot with the butter

2. Bake for 20 mins at GM6/200°c/400° until browned

SPINACH SAUTE POTATOES

1 lb potatoes – peeled, par boiled & sliced
¼ pint single cream
5 oz frozen leaf spinach – thawed
2 cloves garlic – crushed
2 tbsp vegetable oil
1 oz butter

1. Heat the oil in a frying pan and sauté the potatoes until lightly browned. Remove and drain on kitchen paper

2. Melt the butter in a saucepan and cook the garlic for 1 minute

3. Squeeze any excess liquid from the spinach and cook with the garlic for 1 minute

4. Add the cream, stir and cook for a further minute

5. Season and add the potatoes, toss with the mixture and cook until heated through

SCOTS POTATO FRITTERS

1 lb potatoes – peeled & boiled for 15 mins
3 eggs – beaten
2 tbsp breadcrumbs
2 tbsp lean ham – chopped into tiny pieces
Dripping or foil for frying

1. Cut potatoes into ¼" slices

2. Mix the eggs, breadcrumbs and ham together and beat well

3. Dip each slice of potato into the mixture and coat thoroughly. Fry gently in the dripping for 10-15 mins. Serve hot

BROWNED POTATOES (2)

1 lb potatoes – peeled & sliced
3 oz Dripping

1. Pre-heat oven to GM9/240°c/475°f

2. Heat the dripping in a meat dish and place the potatoes into the hot fat

3. Cook the potatoes for 15 mins until golden brown in colour

NEW POTATOES WITH MINT

1 lb new potatoes – scrubbed, boiled,drained
& halved
¼ pint hot chicken stock
5 fl oz mayonnaise
4 fl oz sour cream
3 tbsp chopped fresh mint

1. *Spoon stock over the potatoes while they are still hot and allow to cool*

2. *Mix all the dressing ingredients together (except 1 tbsp of mint) and toss gently into the potato. Sprinkle with the rest of the mint. Serve cold*

FOIL POTATOES

1 lb potatoes (large potatoes)
2 onions – each cut into 6 thick slices
2 oz butter

1. *Pre-heat oven to GM3/170°c/325°f.*

2. *Peel the potatoes and cut each one crossways into 4 slices. Spread butter thickly between each slice and on top*

3. *Reassemble the potatoes with onion slices between*

4. *Season and wrap each one tightly in a double layer of foil and bake for 1½ hours*

DELICIOUS POTATOES

1 lb potatoes – peeled & sliced into ¹/₈″
thick slices
1 oz butter
2oz cheddar cheese – grated
2 oz double cream

1. *Pre-heat oven to GM6/200°c/400°f.*

2. *Place the potatoes on a large piece of foil, season well, add the cream, sprinkle with the cheese and dot with butter*

3. *Make a secure parcel of the foil, place on a baking tin and bake for about an hour or until the potatoes are soft. Serve hot*

WHOLE SMOTHERED POTATOES

1 lb new potatoes – scrubbed & cubed
4 fl oz natural yoghurt
2 small green chillies – deseeded and chopped
2 tbsp fresh coriander – chopped
½ tsp coriander seeds
¾ tsp turmeric
½ tsp garam masala
2 bay leaves
Vegetable oil for frying

1. *Boil the potatoes for 15 mins, drain and cool*

2. *Mix the spices into the yoghurt, add salt*

3. *Scrape each potato with a fork and dip them in the yogurt mix*

4. *Heat the oil to medium then carefully place the coated potatoes into the pan. Cook for 7-8 mins. Add the chillies and stir in some water to prevent drying*

5. *Mix the coriander into the remaining yogurt, add to the potatoes and cook for 5 mins. Serve hot*

POTATOES & GREEN BEANS IN SAUCE

1 lb new potatoes – scrubbed & cut into chunks
8 oz fine beans – trimmed & cut in half
2 tbsp tomato purée
1 clove garlic – crushed
1 tsp paprika
2 tsp red wine vinegar
½ tsp Tabasco sauce
2 tbsp extra virgin olive oil

1. *Boil the beans for 5 mins in salted water. Drain*

2. *Heat the oil and gently fry the garlic for about 1 minute. Stir in the tomato purée, paprika, wine vinegar and Tabasco*

3. *Toss the hot potatoes and beans into the mixture and mix thoroughly. Season. Serve hot*

FRIED SPICED POTATOES

1 lb new potatoes - scrubbed & cubed
2 onions – peeled & chopped
2" ginger root – grated
3 cloves garlic – crushed
2 tbsp medium curry paste
4 tbsp water
3 oz butter
¼ pint natural yoghurt
¼ pint double cream
3 tbsp fresh mint – chopped
3-4 spring onions – trimmed and sliced
Vegetable oil for cooking

1. *Heat the oil and fry the potatoes for 5 mins until golden brown. Remove and drain on kitchen paper*

2. *Blend the onions, ginger, garlic, curry paste and water together in a food processor until smooth*

3. *Heat the butter, add the onion mixture and fry gently for 2 mins stirring continually. Add the yoghurt, cream and 2 tbsp of the mint and mix well*

4. *Add the potatoes and mix until coated. Heat for 6-7 mins stirring frequently*

5. *Season and sprinkle with the rest of the mint and spring onions*

CHEESE FRITTERS

1 lb potatoes – peeled and finely grated
6 oz cheddar cheese – grated
1½ tbsp self raising flour
Pinch of ground mace
Fat for frying

1. *Mix together the potatoes, cheese, flour, mace and seasoning*

2. *Heat your chosen fat to frying temperature in a saucepan so the fat is at least ½" deep*

3. *Carefully drop tablespoons of the potato mixture into the pan and fry gently until brown on each side*

4. *Lift out carefully and drain on kitchen paper. Serve hot*

NEW POTATOES WITH LEMON SAUCE

1 lb new potatoes – scrubbed, halved & boiled
5 oz spinach – washed
2 tbsp chicken stock
1½ oz butter
Juice of 1 lemon

1. *Add the spinach to the boiled potatoes and leave for 1 minute. Drain*

2. *Add the lemon juice to the stock and slowly bring to the boil. Whisk in the butter and pour over the potatoes & spinach*

COCONUT POTATOES

1 lb potatoes – peeled & cut into chunks
1 large onion – peeled & thinly sliced
3 oz creamed coconut
1 small red chilli – de-seeded & finely chopped
½ pint chicken stock
1 tbsp vegetable oil

1. *Heat the oil and fry the onion until it starts to soften*

2. *Add the chilli and fry for 2 mins*

3. *Drain off as much oil as possible, then add all the other ingredients. Stir well and bring to the boil then simmer for 15-20 mins, until the desired consistency is reached*

SAGE POTATO CRISPS

1 lb (floury) potatoes – sliced fairly thinly
30 fresh sage leaves
3 oz butter

1. *Pre-heat oven to GM4/180°c/350°f*

2. *Line a large baking tray with greaseproof paper brushed with butter*

3. *Place a sage leaf between each pair of adjacent slices of potato and place the pairs of slices on the baking sheet. Brush with butter*

4. *Bake for 20 mins or until crispy*

NEW POTATOES WITH ONIONS & THYME

1 lb new potatoes – scrubbed & halved
2 medium red onions – peeled & cut into
  wedges
1 tbsp extra virgin olive oil
1 tbsp dried thyme
1 slice brown bread – made into crumbs
Lemon rind – grated

1. *Pre-heat oven to GM7/220°c/425°f*

2. *Pour the oil into a roasting tin and place in the oven until hot. Remove and add the potatoes and onion ensuring they are coated in oil. Season and return to the oven for 15 mins*

3. *Remove and mix in the lemon rind and thyme. Sprinkle the breadcrumbs over the top and roast for 15 more mins. Serve hot*

POTATOES WITH RADICCHIO & FENNEL

1 lb (waxy) potatoes – peeled & thinly sliced
½ head of radicchio – sliced thinly
1 bulb fennel – sliced thinly
2 cloves garlic – crushed
Extra virgin olive oil

1. *Pre-heat oven to GM6/200°c/400°f*

2. *Blanch the potatoes and fennel in salted boiling water for 5 mins. Drain and pat dry*

3. *Mix all the ingredients together thoroughly. Season and add enough olive oil to coat. Put the mixture into a baking tray and place in the oven for 25 mins, turning the vegetables once. Serve hot*

LAYERED CHEESE POTATOES

1 lb potatoes – peeled & sliced
1 tomato – thinly sliced
1 small onion – peeled & thinly sliced
3 oz cheddar cheese – grated
1 tbsp flour
Milk

1. *Pre-heat oven to GM6/200°c/400°f.*

2. *Layer the bottom of a small casserole dish with half the potatoes. Season and layer the tomato and onion on top. Sprinkle with 1 oz cheese and top with the rest of the potato*

3. *Add the rest of the cheese. Season and add enough milk to come half way up the dish*

4. *Cover and bake for 45 mins. Remove lid and bake for a further 15 mins*

NEW POTATOES IN CRUMBS

1 lb new potatoes (of similar size) – scrubbed, dried & halved
3 oz butter
1½ oz breadcrumbs

1. *Melt 2 oz of butter gently in a saucepan. Add the potatoes, toss to coat and spread them out so they cover the base of the pan*

2. *Cover and cook under a very low heat for 40-50 mins, turning regularly*

3. *When tender add the rest of the butter, turn the heat up and mix in the breadcrumbs and seasoning. Cook for 4-5 mins stirring continually until the breadcrumbs have absorbed the butter and are crisp and golden. Serve hot*

GREEK POTATOES

1 lb (floury) potatoes – peeled & quartered
3 oz onion – peeled & diced
1 tsp dried oregano
4 fl oz extra virgin olive oil
2 cloves garlic – crushed
Juice of 1 lemon

1. *Pre-heat oven to GM6/200°c/400°f*

2. *Place the potatoes in a roasting tin in which they will just fit*

3. *Scatter with the onion, garlic and oregano. Season*

4. *Pour over the lemon juice and olive oil and add enough water to just cover and bake for 45 mins*

5. *Remove from the oven, turn the potatoes over and bake for a further 45 mins*

LEMONY POTATOES

1 lb new potatoes – scrubbed & halved
Zest of ½ lemon
3 fl oz lemon juice
2 tbsp extra virgin olive oil

1. Boil potatoes with the lemon zest for 18 mins. Drain

2. Heat the oil and lemon juice in a large pan and gently fry the potatoes until lightly browned. remove and drain

SPICY POTATOES

1 lb potatoes – peeled & cubed
1 large tin chopped tomatoes
1 onion – peeled and chopped
2 cloves garlic – crushed
1½ tbsp vegetable oil
1½ tbsp curry paste
1 tbsp cornflour

1. Heat the oil and fry the potatoes, onion and garlic for 5 mins

2. Meanwhile blend the cornflour to a smooth paste with the juice from the tomatoes

3. Stir in the curry paste and fry for 1 more minute

4. Stir in the cornflour paste, tomatoes, and season

5. Cover and simmer for 15-18 mins, stirring occasionally. Serve hot

THICK POTATO CRISPS

1 lb potatoes – peeled and cut into ¼" slices
1 tbsp extra virgin olive oil
1 tbsp butter

1. Pre-heat oven to GM6/200°c/400°f

2. Lay the slices of potatoes in a greased roasting pan, overlapping slightly

3. Melt the butter and mix with the oil. Drizzle over the potatoes. Sprinkle with pepper

4. Cover with foil and bake for 15 mins. Remove the foil and bake for 10 more mins. Season with sea salt. Serve hot

CRISPY POTATO SKINS

1 lb (floury) potatoes - washed & dried
2 tbsp rosemary – chopped
2 tbsp olive oil

1. Pre-heat oven to GM4/180°c/350°f

2. Leave the potatoes in their skins and prick with a fork. Brush with half the oil and put on a baking tray. Place in oven for 40 mins

3. Remove from the oven and cut each potato into 4. Scrape the flesh. Brush with the rest of the oil and put back on the baking tray. Sprinkle with the rosemary and season. Bake for 30 mins. Serve hot. Good with dips

POTATO & CHIVE SAUCE

1 lb potatoes – peeled & chopped
2 onions – peeled & chopped
10 fl oz whipping cream
1 bunch chives – finely chopped

1. Boil the potatoes & onions until potatoes are soft

2. Drain thoroughly, put back into the pan & add the cream. Warm gradually until hot

3. Remove from heat & purée in a food processor, Season well and add the chives then slowly re-heat

BUTTERY POTATOES

1 lb new potatoes – skins scrubbed off, halved
3 oz butter

1. Melt the butter in a small frying pan and add the potatoes. Cover and cook over a medium heat for 20 mins stirring every 5 mins. Serve hot

A potato is about 80% water and 20% solid.

NEW POTATOES WITH ANCHOVY DRESSING

1 lb new potatoes – scrubbed, boiled, drained & halved
6-8 lettuce leaves
4 oz parmesan cheese – grated

Dressing
¼ pint extra virgin olive oil
6 anchovy fillets
2 egg yolks
2 cloves garlic – crushed
1 tbsp red wine vinegar
2 tsp Worcester sauce
1 tsp lemon juice
1 tsp anchovy essence
2 tsp Dijon mustard
1 tsp English mustard powder

1. *Put all the dressing ingredients except the oil in a liquidiser and switch on the motor. With the motor still running drizzle in the oil slowly*
2. *Arrange the lettuce leaves in the bottom of a salad bowl, add the potatoes, season and pour over the dressing. Sprinkle with the cheese. Serve with potatoes still warm*

STIR FRIED POTATOES WITH ONION & PEPPER

1 lb potatoes – peeled & diced
1 onion – peeled & chopped
2 green peppers – peeled, cored & cut into small square shapes
¼ pint beef stock
1 tsp Worcester sauce
3 tbsp vegetable oil

1. *Heat the oil to a medium heat in a wok. Add the potatoes, onion & pepper. Season with a little salt and stir fry for about 5 mins*
2. *Add the Worcester sauce and the beef stock and pour over the potato mixture. Cover and cook for 10 mins stirring occasionally*
3. *Remove cover, raise the heat and stir fry until cooked through and the sauce is sufficiently reduced*

BACON & POTATO MIX

1 lb potatoes – peeled, boiled & diced
5 rashers bacon – rind removed & chopped
1 onion – peeled & chopped
1 handful spinach - washed & chopped
1 tbsp olive oil

1. *Heat the oil and fry the onion gently for 2-3 mins*
2. *Add the bacon and potatoes, continue to fry stirring continually until the potatoes are browned*
3. *Add the spinach and toss the mixture in the pan for 1 minute and serve straightaway*

MINTED POTATOES

1 lb new potatoes – scrubbed & boiled
2 oz butter
2 tbsp fresh mint – chopped

1. *Melt the butter with the potatoes and add the mint*
2. *Toss gently to coat and season with salt only*

HERBY POTATOES

1 lb small potatoes – peeled & cut into small pieces
2 oz plain flour
1 tbsp fresh parsley – chopped
1 tsp fresh rosemary – chopped
1 tsp fresh thyme – chopped
3 cloves garlic (unpeeled)
1 bay leaf
3 tbsp extra virgin olive oil

1. *Pre-heat oven to GM6/200°c/400°f.*
2. *Roll the potatoes in the flour and herbs until they are covered*
3. *Put oil a casserole dish and place the potatoes in it with the garlic and bay leaf. Cover with foil and bake for 45 mins. Remove bay leaf and garlic before serving*

POTATO AND MINCED MEAT

1 lb potatoes – boiled & mashed
¼ lb minced cooked meat (or finely chopped)
1 rasher bacon – chopped
1 small onion – peeled & chopped
1 oz butter
1 tsp wholemeal flour

1. *Pre-heat oven to GM4/180°c/350°f*
2. *Mix the meat, flour and butter into the mash*
3. *Gently dry fry the bacon till the fat runs and add the onion. Cook gently for 3-4 mins*
4. *Mix well into the mash and season*
5. *Bake in a greased pie dish for 30 mins*

POTATOES & ONIONS – INDIAN STYLE

1 lb potatoes – boiled in their skins for 20 mins
10 oz onions – peeled & chopped
2 tbsp ginger – finely chopped
1 green chilli – seeded & finely chopped
1 tsp black mustard seeds
1 tbsp ground coriander
1 tsp turmeric
½ tsp paprika
1 tsp sea salt
1 tbsp lemon juice
3 tbsp fresh coriander – chopped
1 pint water
3 tbsp vegetable oil

1. *Allow the potatoes to cool slightly and cut into bite sized pieces*
2. *Heat the oil to a high temperature in a wok and fry the mustard seeds until they start to pop*
3. *Reduce the heat and add the ginger and chilli. Cook for a further 2 mins*
4. *Stir in the ground coriander, turmeric and paprika then add the potatoes and onions and fry for 10 mins stirring continually*
5. *Add the salt and the water and bring to the boil, stirring continually. Reduce to a simmer and cook for 10 mins or until the desired consistency is reached*
6. *Stir in the lemon juice and add the coriander before serving*

STIR FRIED POTATOES

1 lb potatoes – peeled & boiled for 15 mins
1 clove garlic – crushed
1 tbsp fresh parsley – chopped
1 tsp English mustard
1 tsp Worcester Sauce
1½ tbsp vegetable oil

1. *Allow the potatoes to cool slightly then cut into small cubes, season with salt only*
2. *Heat the oil to a high heat in a wok or heavy saucepan. Add the garlic and stir fry for 30 seconds*
3. *Add the potatoes, stir well, then lower the heat and continue to fry, stirring continually until the potatoes start to brown*
4. *Add the parsley, mustard and Worcester sauce. Stir well and cook for 2 mins*

NEW POTATOES WITH YOGHURT & GARLIC

1 lb new potatoes - scrubbed
1 whole head garlic – separated & peeled
1 small tub Greek yoghurt
4 tbsp extra virgin olive oil
3 bay leaves
1 tsp lemon juice
1 tsp paprika

1. *Half fill a large saucepan with 20 fl oz water. Add the garlic, olive oil and bay leaves and a little salt. Bring to the boil.*
2. *Add the potatoes and bring back to the boil. Reduce to a simmer for 15-18 mins., then remove the potatoes with a slotted spoon and allow to cool*
3. *Boil the liquid until reduced to about a quarter of what it was Remove the bay leaves. Mash the garlic into the liquid and transfer to a bowl. Allow to cool*
4. *Add the yoghurt, lemon juice and seasoning then whisk together*
5. *Slice the potatoes and arrange on a large plate. Season and spoon the sauce over, then sprinkle with paprika. Serve while still warm*

PAPRIKA POTATO PARCELS

1 lb new potatoes - scrubbed & halved
4 oz butter – softened
1½ tsp paprika
1½ tsp coarse sea salt

1. Cut 4 pieces of tin foil about 8 inches square
2. Mix the paprika & the salt into the butter, then rub the mixture evenly into the tin foil
3. Divide the potatoes evenly onto the foil & make into loose parcels
4. Cook under a medium grill for about ½ an hour until the skins are wrinkled

GRILLED BABY POTATOES

1 lb new potatoes – scrubbed, boiled & halved
1 small dried chilli – crushed
2 tbsp extra virgin olive oil
6 stalks rosemary
½ tsp salt

1. Put the chillies, oil and salt into a glass and mix well
2. Thread the potatoes onto the rosemary stalks and brush with the oil mixture
3. Cook on a hot grill (or barbecue) – brushing with oil during cooking

POTATOES WITH LEEKS

1 lb (waxy) potatoes – peeled & cubed
2 leeks – trimmed, washed & sliced
1 pint vegetable stock
1 tbsp fresh thyme – chopped
3 oz butter

1. Melt the butter in a large pan & fry the leeks until softened
2. Add the potatoes & thyme, season and stir well
3. Pour on the stock, bring to the boil and continue to cook until the potatoes are done and the desired consistency is reached

POTATOES WITH CREAM & CHEESE

1 lb new potatoes - scrubbed, halved, par-boiled & drained
3½ oz cheddar cheese – grated
6½ fl oz single cream

1. Preheat oven to GM3/160°c/325°f
2. Put the potatoes into a shallow ovenproof dish. Sprinkle with the cheese, season then cover with cream
3. Bake for ½ hour

POTATOES WITH SPICES

1 lb potatoes – peeled & cut into chunks
1 large tin chopped tomatoes
1″ fresh ginger – peeled and grated
1 tsp chilli powder
1 tbsp ground coriander
2 tbsp fresh coriander – chopped finely
½ tbsp ground turmeric
1 tbsp vegetable oil

1. Heat the oil in a pan and add the ginger, cook for 2 mins
2. Add the tomatoes, ground coriander, turmeric and chilli powder. Heat, stirring continually for about 5 mins until it thickens
3. Add the potatoes and fresh herbs. Heat until boiling then reduce to a simmer and cook for 20 mins, stirring occasionally adding water if desired

INDIAN NEW POTATOES

1 lb new potatoes – scrubbed, halved & boiled for 10 mins
1 tsp coriander seeds
1 tsp chilli flakes
1 tsp crushed cumin seeds
2 tbsp vegetable oil
1 small tub plain yoghurt
1 clove garlic crushed
1 tbsp mint sauce

1. Pre-heat oven to GM7/220°c/425°f
2. Drain the potatoes thoroughly then put in a small roasting tray and mix with the oil and spices. Mix thoroughly and bake for 20-30 mins, stirring once
3. Meanwhile mix the garlic and mint with the yoghurt
4. Serve the potatoes with the yoghurt mixture

SLICED POTATOES WITH ONION

1 lb potatoes – peeled & sliced thinly
2 large onions – peeled & sliced thinly in rings
6 fl oz milk
1½ tbsp fresh parsley – chopped
5 tbsp butter – melted

1. Pre-heat oven to GM5/190°c/375°f
2. Grease an ovenproof dish and layer the bottom with half the potatoes. Spread the onions and parsley onto the potatoes and season. Cover with the rest of the potatoes, season and pour the butter over
3. Pour on sufficient milk to show through the top of the potatoes
4. Bake for 1 hour 15 mins. Serve hot

NEW POTAOTES WRAPPED IN BACON

1 lb new potatoes – scrubbed
½ the number of rashers of bacon as there are potatoes
Springs of fresh thyme
1 tbsp Dijon mustard
4 fl oz chicken stock
1 tbsp olive oil

1. Pre-heat oven to GM6/200°/c400°f
2. Lay out the bacon, spread with mustard, season and cut in half
3. Take a potato and a sprig of thyme and wrap a piece of bacon around them. Secure with a wooden cocktail stick and repeat with each potato

4. Take a small ovenproof dish and brush with oil, add the potatoes, season and pour in the stock. Cook for 45 mins

GRILLED NEW POTATOES

1 lb new potatoes – scrubbed & boiled
2 cloves garlic – crushed
¼ tsp cayenne pepper
1 tbsp olive oil

1. Put the potatoes in a pan of cold water for 2 mins. Remove and drain
2. Heat the oil and gently cook the garlic for 30 seconds. Add the cayenne pepper and a little salt. Remove from the heat
3. Pre-heat the grill
4. Make a couple of slits in each potato and using a butter knife put a little of the garlic mixture into each slit
5. Wrap the potatoes in foil and grill for 15-20 mins

BACON HASH BROWNS

1 lb potatoes – boiled in their skins for 15-18 mins & drained
4 slices bacon – rind removed & chopped
1 onion – peeled & chopped
1 egg – beaten
½ oz plain flour
Vegetable oil for cooking

1. Heat some oil in a pan and gently cook the onion until softened
2. Meanwhile gently fry the bacon in some oil
3. Skin and grate the potatoes. Mix the onion and bacon into the potatoes. Season and mix in the egg then the flour
4. Form into small cake shapes, put on a plate, cover with cling film and refrigerate overnight
5. Heat some oil in a pan and fry the hash browns until browned. Serve hot. Ideal for fry-ups

NEW POTATOES WITH PARSLEY PESTO

1 lb new potatoes – scrubbed, boiled & halved
4 fl oz extra virgin olive oil
3 oz parmesan cheese – grated
2 oz pine nuts – toasted
2 tbsp creamed horseradish
3 tbsp fresh parsley – chopped
1 clove garlic – crushed

1. *Put all the ingredients except the potatoes into a blender and add seasoning. Blitz to a purée*
2. *Spoon the mixture over the potatoes whilst they are still warm*

NEW POTATOES WITH MUSTARD AND HONEY

1 lb new potatoes – scrubbed, halved, boiled & drained
2 tsp Dijon mustard
2 tbsp clear runny honey
Juice of ½ lemon
1 tbsp fresh coriander – chopped
1 oz butter

1. *Melt butter in a pan, add the mustard, honey and lemon juice. Heat very gently*
2. *Add the potatoes and mix well. Season and allow to cool slightly*
3. *Serve warm topped with the coriander*

POTATO & FENNEL MIX

1 lb potatoes – scrubbed, boiled & cubed
½ baby fennel – trimmed & boiled for 8 mins then cut into small pieces
½ lb baby carrots – peeled & boiled for 12 mins
2 oz butter

1. *Put all the hot vegetables into a large bowl, add butter, season, mix well and serve*

FRIED NEW POTATOES AND ONION

1 lb new potatoes – scrubbed, boiled & diced
2 red onions – peeled & thinly sliced
1 tbsp chopped parsley
½ tsp caster sugar
2 tbsp olive oil
3 tbsp butter

1. *Heat the oil and half the butter in a large pan. Fry the potatoes until browned - remove and keep warm*
2. *Add the rest of the butter to the pan and add the onions then sprinkle with the sugar. Stir well and gently fry for about 10 mins until the onions have caramelised*
3. *Mix the potatoes with onions and season. Sprinkle with the parsley and serve*

NEW POTATOES WITH PARSLEY BUTTER

1 lb new potatoes – scrubbed, halved, boiled & drained
3 tbsp fresh parsley – chopped finely
1 large knob butter

Allow the potatoes to cool slightly then add the butter. Toss to mix and as the butter melts sprinkle with the parsley. Season and stir well

QUICK HASH BROWNS

1 lb potatoes – peeled & grated
1 bunch spring onions – trimmed, washed & finely sliced
1 tbsp fresh parsley – chopped
2 tbsp olive oil

1. *Squeeze the potatoes to remove excess water*
2. *Mix the potatoes, onion and parsley manually in a bowl. Season and form into separate shapes*
3. *Heat the oil and fry each one turning frequently until golden*

GARLIC BUTTERED POTATOES

1 lb potatoes – peeled & thinly sliced
4 cloves garlic – crushed
2 oz butter

1. Pre-heat oven to GM5/190°c/375°f
2. Place the potatoes in a bowl of cold water and put aside for 1 hour
3. Beat the garlic into the butter
4. Drain the potatoes and pat dry with a tea towel
5. Grease a cake tin with some of the butter and put a layer of potatoes in the base, season and dot with more of the butter. Repeat until the potatoes are used up
6. Cover and bake for 1 hour
7. Place under a pre-heated grill for 2 mins until golden brown

NEW POTATOES WITH GARLIC SAUCE

1 lb new potatoes – scrubbed, boiled & halved
6 cloves garlic – crushed
½ pint extra virgin olive oil
3 egg yolks
2 tbsp lemon juice

1. Put the garlic in a bowl, add a small amount of seasoning and mix with the egg yolks
2. Gently drizzle in the oil mixing continually. Season and add the lemon juice
3. Allow the potatoes to cool slightly then mix with the sauce

NB If you make the sauce in a blender, ensure the motor is still running while you slowly add the oil

BAKED POTATO & ONIONS

1 lb potatoes – peeled & sliced
2 large onions – peeled & sliced
2 tbsp white wine vinegar
½ pint chicken stock
2 oz butter

1. Pre-heat oven to GM3/170c/325°f
2. Put a layer of potatoes at the base of a small, greased oven proof dish. Season and add a layer of onion. Continue, dotting each layer with butter and seasoning – finishing with a layer of potatoes dotted with butter
3. Mix the vinegar with the stock, and pour onto the potatoes, ensuring the liquid covers the potatoes
4. Cover and bake for 2 hours

NEW POTAOTES WITH GREEN SALSA

1 lb new potatoes – scrubbed, halved, boiled & drained
2 anchovy fillets – finely chopped
1 oz capers – finely chopped
2 cloves garlic – crushed
1 oz fresh parsley – chopped
2 tbsp extra virgin olive oil
1 tbsp lemon juice

1. Put all the salsa ingredients in a small dish, season and mix well. Cover with cling film and refrigerate (preferably overnight)
2. When ready to serve put the warm potatoes in a bowl, add the salsa, adjust the seasoning and serve

NEW POTATOES IN TARRAGON SAUCE

1 lb new potatoes – scrubbed, boiled, drained & halved
3 spring onions – washed, trimmed & chopped
2 tbsp fresh tarragon – chopped
6 fl oz sour cream
½ oz butter

1. Melt the butter, add the onions and cook for 1 minute. Stir in the cream, season and add the tarragon. Heat gently
2. Add the potatoes and mix well. Re-heat gently without boiling. Serve hot

SOUFLÉED POTATOES

1 lb floury potatoes – unpeeled & pierced
3 eggs – separated
2 spring onions – trimmed and chopped
1 oz cheddar cheese – grated
1 tbsp sour cream

1. Pre-heat oven to GM4/180°c/350°f
2. Bake the potatoes for 45 mins
3. Remove the potatoes and cut the top off each
4. Scoop out most of the potato and place in a large bowl. Add the cheese, egg yolks, spring onion and sour cream. Season and mix well
5. Turn the oven up to GM6/200°c/400°f
6. Beat the egg whites until firm and fold into the potato mixture
7. Return the mixture to the potato hollows, place on a baking try and cook for 30 mins until the eggs have risen

NEW POTATOES IN AÏOLI

1 lb new potatoes – scrubbed & quartered
4 cloves garlic – peeled
2 egg yolks
1 tbsp white wine vinegar
10 tbsp extra virgin olive oil

1. Simmer the potatoes for 15 mins and drain
2. Put the egg yolks, garlic and vinegar into a blender and season. Switch on and when the mixture is liquid, slowly pour the oil in while the motor is still running
3. Place the warm potatoes in a bowl and pour on the sauce. Mix well and leave for 15 mins before serving

GRIDDLED POTATOES WITH GARLIC MAYONNAISE

1 lb (waxy) potatoes – peeled, boiled, drained & halved
3 cloves garlic
3 tbsp mayonnaise
Extra virgin olive oil

1. Preheat oven to GM6/200°c/400°f
2. Wrap the garlic in tin foil and bake for 15-20 mins
3. Squeeze out the flesh. Mix with the mayonnaise and season
4. Brush a griddle pan with a little oil and gently fry the potatoes for 10-15 mins. Remove and drain on kitchen paper
2. Mix with the mayonnaise

CRUSHED POTATOES WITH HERBS

1 lb potatoes – peeled, cubed & boiled for 15 mins
1 tbsp fresh dill – chopped
1 tbsp fresh parsley – chopped
1 tbsp fresh thyme – chopped
2 tbsp extra virgin olive oil

1. Pre heat oven to GM7/220°c425°f
2. Drain the potatoes and allow to cool slightly
3. Warm the oil in a small pan and add the herbs. Remove from heat and stir
4. Arrange the potatoes on a plate and crush lightly with the back of a fork. Season and drizzle on the oil and herbs
5. Bake in the oven for 15-20 mins until browned

BUTTERED POTATOES

1 lb potatoes - peeled & thinly sliced
2 oz butter

1. Pre-heat oven to GM5/190°c/375°f
2. Put the potato slices in a bowl of water, cover and refrigerate for 1 hour
3. Drain the potatoes and dry thoroughly with a tea towel
4. Grease a cake tin with some of the butter and put a layer of potatoes at the bottom. Season, dot with butter and repeat until the potatoes are used up
5. Cover and bake for 1 hour then put under a pre-heated grill for 2 mins

SPICY NEW POTATOES

1 lb new potatoes – scrubbed & halved
1 tsp cumin seeds – crushed
1 tsp chilli flakes
1 tsp coriander seeds
2 tbsp vegetable oil

1. *Pre-heat oven to GM6/200°c/400°f*
2. *Put the potatoes in a small roasting tin and sprinkle with the spices. Season and drizzle with the oil – mix well to coat*
3. *Cover with foil and cook for 30-35 mins*

POTATOES WITH LEEKS AND CREAM

1 lb potatoes – peeled & diced
1 lb leeks – trimmed & sliced
1 onion – peeled & chopped
5 tbsp chicken stock
5 tbsp white wine
3 tbsp crème fraiche
2 tbsps olive oil

1. *Heat the oil and fry the leek and onion until they start to soften*
2. *Season and add the potatoes, stock and wine. Bring to a gentle simmer, cover and cook for 30 mins*
3. *Remove from the heat, stir in the crème fraiche, leave for a couple of mins then serve*

POTATO CROUTONS

1 lb potato – unpeeled & diced
2 clove garlic – crushed
3 tbsp olive oil

1. *Pre-heat the oven to GM6/200°c/400°f*
2. *Put all the ingredients into a freezer bag and shake vigorously so the oil covers all the potato*
3. *Put the cubes onto a baking tray and roast for 45-50 mins*
4. *Remove from oven and sprinkle with sea salt*

SPICY CUBED POTATOES

1 lb potatoes – peeled & cubed
2 cloves garlic – crushed
1 red chilli – deseeded & finely chopped
2 tbsp fresh coriander – finely chopped
1 tbsp olive oil

1. *Boil the potatoes for 10 mins. Drain thoroughly*
2. *Heat the oil in a pan and fry the potatoes for 5 mins, stirring frequently*
3. *Add the garlic and chilli and fry gently for 3 more mins*
4. *Remove from the heat and sprinkle with the coriander*

CHEESY NEW POTATOES

1 lb new potatoes – scrubbed, boiled & drained
2 tbsp olive oil
¼ lb Feta cheese – crumbled

1. *Pre-heat oven to GM6/200°c/400°f*
2. *Put the potatoes in a roasting tin and lightly crush with back of a fork*
3. *Season and drizzle with the oil, sprinkle with the cheese and heat until browned*

LIGHTLY CRUSHED POTATOES & PEAS

1 lb new potatoes – scrubbed & quartered
¼ lb frozen peas
1 tbsp fresh mint – chopped
2 tbsp extra virgin olive oil

1. *Boil the potatoes for 12 mins*
2. *Add the peas and simmer for 8 mins. Drain well*
3. *Put the mixture on a large serving plate while still hot, season and crush the potatoes lightly with the back of a fork*
4. *Sprinkle with the mint and drizzle with the oil*

NEW POTATOES WITH STILTON

**1 lb new potatoes – scrubbed, boiled,
drained & halved**
3 oz Stilton cheese – crumbled
3 oz rocket
1 clove garlic – crushed
1 tbsp fresh thyme – chopped
1½ tbsp extra virgin olive oil

1. Mix the oil, garlic and thyme
2. Put the warm potatoes in a bowl and pour
   on the oil mixture. Season and toss until
   coated
3. Sprinkle with the stilton and rocket. Mix
   well. Serve when the cheese starts to melt

NEW POTATOES WITH BACON & SOUR CREAM

**1 lb (large) new potatoes – scrubbed, boiled,
drained & cooled (until warm)**
4 rashers bacon – chopped into small pieces
1 small tub sour cream

1. Dry fry bacon until crisp and drain on
   kitchen paper
2. Cut a hole in each potato and scoop out
   some of the flesh
3. Spoon some sour cream into the hole,
   season and sprinkle with bacon pieces

NEW POTATOES WITH SUN DRIED TOMATOES

**1 lb new potatoes – scrubbed, halved,
boiled & drained**
6 fl oz sour cream
4 sun dried tomatoes – chopped into
   small pieces
1 tbsp fresh basil – chopped

1. Mix the tomatoes and basil with the
   sour cream
2. Put the potatoes in a serving bowl and add
   the cream mixture. Season and mix well

GARLIC BAKED POTATOES

1 lb new potatoes – scrubbed & halved
10 cloves garlic - peeled
3 tsp fresh thyme – chopped
3 tbsp extra virgin olive oil

1. Pre-heat oven to GM6/200°c/400°f
2. Put the potatoes in a mixing bowl, season
   well and add the thyme and then pour on
   the oil. Mix well
3. Lay a large sheet of aluminium foil on a
   surface and put the potato mixture to the
   left of centre. Scatter the garlic on top, fold
   over and seal
4. Bake for 30-40 mins

PESTO POTATOES

1 lb small new potatoes – scrubbed & halved
¼ lb frozen peas
6 fl oz crème fraiche
3 tbsp green pesto

1. Boil the potatoes for 15 mins
2. Add the peas, return to the boil and cook for
   3 mins then drain
3. Mix the pesto with the crème fraiche
4. Put the potatoes in a serving bowl, season and
   add and the cream mixture. Mix well and serve

POTATOES IN MILK

1 lb potatoes – peeled & sliced
1 pint milk
Pinch of nutmeg

1. Put the potatoes in a pan, season and pour
   on the milk. Bring to a gentle simmer (don't
   boil) and cook for 15-20 mins until tender.
   Drain
2. Pre heat oven to GM3/170°c/325°f
3. Place the potatoes in the base of an ovenproof
   dish, sprinkle with the nutmeg. Season and
   add 3 tbsp of the milk. Bake for 15 mins

POTATOES WITH ANCHOVIES

1 lb new potatoes – scrubbed, boiled, drained, cooled & sliced
30 tinned anchovies – drained
6 cloves garlic – peeled and thinly sliced
2 tbsp olive oil
1oz butter

1. Pre-heat oven to GM4/180°c/350°f
2. Heat the oil and fry the potatoes until lightly browned on each side
3. Grease a small round ovenproof dish and put a layer of potatoes in the base. Cover with half the garlic and half the anchovies. Add another layer of potatoes and the rest of the garlic and anchovies, finishing with a layer of potatoes
4. Dot with butter and bake for about 10 mins

FRIED NEW POTATOES WITH LEMON AND THYME

1 lb new potatoes - scrubbed & halved
3 rashers bacon – cut into small pieces
2 cloves garlic – peeled & chopped
½ a lemon - cut into slices
2 tbsp fresh thyme – chopped
1 tbsp olive oil

1. Boil the potatoes for 10 mins and drain
2. Dry fry the bacon until just cooked
3. Add the oil and all the remaining ingredients. Season and mix well
4. Fry gently for about 20 mins stirring frequently. Remove lemon and serve

ITALIAN NEW POTATOES

1 lb new potatoes – scrubbed, halved, boiled & drained
3 sun-dried tomatoes – chopped into small pieces
10 green olives – pitted
4 tbsp vinaigrette

1. Put the potatoes in a mixing bowl, season, add all the other ingredients and mix well

POTATOES WITH BASIL

1 lb new potatoes – scrubbed halved, boiled & drained
3 tbsp fresh basil – chopped
1½ tsp tomato purée
4 oz butter

1. Put the butter in a small bowl, add the basil and the purée. Season and mix with a fork. Cover with cling film and refrigerate for 15 mins
2. Allow the potatoes to cool slightly, place in a serving bowl, season and dot with the butter so it melts as it is served

SAUTEED GARLIC POTATOES

1 lb (waxy) potatoes – peeled, boiled for 10 mins & drained
10 cloves garlic - papery skin removed but not peeled
3 tbsp fresh rosemary
10 tbsp extra virgin olive oil

1. Allow the potatoes to cool slightly then cut into cubes
2. Heat the oil in a small pan, add the potatoes, garlic and rosemary. Fry gently until the potatoes are browned
3. Remove with a slotted spoon, drain on kitchen paper and serve

CRUSHED & MINTED NEW POTATOES

1 lb new potatoes – scrubbed, halved, boiled & drained
2 tbsp fresh mint – chopped
2 tbsp single cream

1. Put the potatoes in a serving dish and using the back of a spoon press the potatoes so they break up
2. Season, sprinkle with half the mint then mix in the cream and sprinkle with the rest of the mint

POTATO & MUSHROOM SAUTE

**1 lb new potatoes – scrubbed, quartered
& boiled**
½ lb button mushrooms – peeled & halved
3 tbsp single cream
2 cloves garlic – crushed
2 oz butter

1. *Melt the butter and gently fry the
   mushrooms for 5 mins or until they start
   to soften*
2. *Add the garlic and potatoes (while they are
   still hot) and stir. Cook for 2-3 mins*
3. *Season and pour on the cream. Stir well until
   the cream is heated through then serve*

NEW POTATOES IN A BUTTER SAUCE

**1 lb new potatoes – scrubbed, halved
& boiled**
½ lb butter
2 shallots – peeled & very finely chopped
3 fl oz white vinegar

1. *Heat the vinegar in a small pan until boiling
   then add the shallots. Boil until well reduced
   then remove from the heat*
2. *Cut the butter into 4 and add one piece at a
   time, beating it into the vinegar as you go*
3. *Slow re-heat until warm (not hot) and pour
   onto the potatoes while they are still warm*

SAUTEED POTATOES

**1 lb potatoes – peeled & cut into ¼" slices,
about 1½ - 2" diameter**
2 oz butter
2 tbsp olive oil

1. *Par-boil the potatoes for 5 mins. Drain and
   allow to cool*
2. *Heat the butter and oil and fry the potato
   slices until lightly browned on each side*
3. *Drain on kitchen paper*

CHEESEY NEW POTATOES

**1 lb new potatoes – scrubbed, halved,
boiled & drained**
4 oz fresh parmesan cheese – grated
2 oz butter
2 tbsp fresh chives

1. *Pre-heat oven to GM6/200°c/400°f*
2. *Melt the butter in a small pan and add the
   potatoes. Season lightly and mix well so the
   potatoes are covered*
3. *Sprinkle with the cheese and toss to coat*
4. *Put the potatoes on a buttered baking tray
   and place in the oven for 10 mins*
5. *Place on a serving dish and sprinkle with the chives*

POTATO NOISETTES

1 lb potatoes – peeled
1 oz butter
2 tbsp sunflower oil

1. *Pre-heat GM6/200°c/400°f.*
2. *Use a melon baller to scoop out the potatoes
   into small round shapes, about 1" across.
   Rinse then dry the potato shapes*
3. *Heat the oil in a small pan and fry the shapes
   until lightly browned. Remove with a slotted
   spoon and place on a greased baking tray*
4. *Cook in the oven for 15 mins. Remove and
   place in a small serving bowl. Season lightly
   and add the butter. Serve once the butter
   has melted*

SALTED POTATOES

1 lb new potatoes - scrubbed
Coarse sea salt

1. *Put potatoes into a pan with enough heavily
   salted water to cover*
2. *Boil hard until the water is gone and then
   shake the dry pan so the salt sets on the
   skins producing a frosted coating*

HASH BROWN POTATOES (2)

1 lb potatoes – peeled & cubed
1 green pepper – seeded and finely chopped
2 tbsp parsley – chopped
2 oz butter

1. *Gradually feed the cubes of potato through the hole in the top of a running blender*
2. *Add the pepper and parsley. Season and blend until thoroughly mixed*
3. *Melt the butter in a large pan. Spread the mixture in the pan, cover and cook gently for 15 mins*
4. *Remove cover and cook for 10 more mins, then put the pan under a grill for 5 mins*

PROVENCAL FRIED POTATOES

1 lb new potatoes – scrubbed, boiled & sliced
1 red pepper – cored, seeded & sliced
1 courgette – trimmed, washed & sliced
1 red onion – peeled & sliced
2 cloves garlic – crushed
2 tbsp fresh basil – chopped
3 tbsp extra virgin olive oil
2 tbsp lemon juice

1. *Heat the oil and fry the potatoes for about 5 mins*
2. *Add all the vegetables and fry until the pepper starts to soften*
3. *Add the lemon juice and basil. Season and serve*

SWEETENED POTATOES

1 lb potatoes – boiled in their skins for 15 mins
1 oz butter
1 oz brown sugar
1 oz water

1. *Pre-heat oven to GM3/160°c/325°f*
2. *Allow the potatoes to cool slightly then cut into slices. Place in layers at the base of a greased casserole dish*
3. *Mix the sugar into the butter until dissolved, add the water and stir well. Pour onto the potatoes and mix well. Cover and bake for 30 mins*

CHEESE & POTATO PIE

1 lb potatoes – boiled & mashed
2 oz mature cheddar cheese – grated
1½ oz butter
Pinch of nutmeg

1. *Pre-heat oven to GM4/180°c/350°f*
2. *Beat half the butter and the nutmeg into the potatoes*
3. *Spread the mashed potato into a shallow casserole dish. Dot with the rest of the butter and sprinkle with the cheese. Bake for 15 mins then place under a pre-heated grill for 3 mins*

POTATO & LEEK PURÉE

1 lb (floury) potatoes - boiled & drained
1 lb leeks - washed, cut into short pieces
  – boiled till tender
¼ pt milk.
1 oz butter
¼ pt double cream

1. *Heat the milk*
2. *Put the leeks and potatoes into a food processor and blitz to a purée. Put the purée into a hot, buttered saucepan, season and place on a low heat*
3. *Add the milk & butter gradually, beating the mixture*
4. *Slowly add the cream and heat through*

FRENCH STYLE POTATOES

1 lb potatoes – peeled, sliced in half lengthwise
1 tbsp butter
Vegetable oil

1. *Preheat oven to GM6/200°c/400°f*
2. *Cut the potatoes into 1"x1"x1½" shapes, cut a piece from each corner so edges are slightly rounded. Cook for 5 mins then drain*
3. *Melt the butter & oil. Add the potatoes. Season. Make sure potatoes thoroughly coated*
4. *Bake for 50-60 mins*

SAUTE POTATOES

1 lb potatoes - scrubbed
1 oz butter
Vegetable oil

1. *Boil the potatoes until tender. Drain & place in cold water until completely cold*
2. *Peel potatoes, & cut into thick slices apx 1½" in diameter. Melt the butter in a large frying pan and add the oil. When the butter starts to froth add the potatoes and turn to ensure an even coating*
3. *Continue cooking under a medium heat, shaking the pan & turning the potatoes occasionally, until they are brown & crisp. Drain off excess fat*

POTATOES WITH GARLIC & CHEESE

1 lb potatoes - sliced thinly
3 oz grated cheese
2 cloves garlic - chopped finely
1½ tbsp double cream
3 oz bacon – cut into ½ " pieces, cooked till crisp
Extra virgin olive oil

1. *Cover the base of a pan with a layer of potatoes. Fill the pan with alternate layers of potato and cheese with sprinkled bacon pieces. Top with garlic*
2. *Cook covered under a medium heat for 30 mins until potatoes are tender*
3. *Pour cream over top, cover and cook for 3 more mins*

POTATO PANCAKES WITH CHEESE

1 lb potatoes - peeled, grated, & squeezed to remove excess moisture
4 oz Cheddar cheese – grated
1 egg
1½ tbsp flour
½ small onion - grated
4 oz cheddar - grated

1. *Mix the cheese, eggs, flour and onion together and season – stir in cheddar & grated potatoes. Form into 3" shapes*
2. *Grill the pancakes until lightly browned on each side*

POTATO FRITTERS

1 lb potatoes– peeled, boiled for 10 mins, drained
3 eggs – beaten
¼ lb cooked ham – cut into small dice
3 tbsp fresh white breadcrumbs
Vegetable oil for cooking

1. *Heat the oil in a large deep pan until fairly hot*
2. *Cut the potatoes lengthways into thick slices*
3. *Brush the potatoes with the egg and dip into the breadcrumbs and ham. Season*
4. *Fry in batches if necessary, until browned*

POTATO & CHICKPEA SIDE DISH

1 lb potatoes – peeled & diced
1 small tin chickpeas
1 tsp chilli flakes
3 tbsp extra virgin olive oil

1. *Heat the oil in a pan and fry the potatoes with the chilli flakes stirring frequently until browned*
2. *Meanwhile heat the chickpeas in a small pan – drain*
3. *Remove the potatoes from the heat and put in a large serving bowl. Add the chickpeas and mix well. Season*

PAPRIKA POTATOES

1 lb potatoes peeled & diced
½ pint beef stock
2 tomatoes skinned & chopped
2 small onions peeled and thinly sliced
1 tbsp olive oil
1 tbsp paprika

1. *Preheat oven to GM4/180c/350f*
2. *Heat the oil in a pan and cook the onions until soft*
3. *Stir in the rest of the ingredients and season*
4. *Bring to a simmer, transfer to a casserole dish and cook for about 1 hour until the potatoes are tender and the stock is reduced*

BATTERED POTATOES

1 lb potatoes – peeled
5 oz seasoned flour
6 sprigs fresh rosemary – leaves removed
Dripping or lard for cooking

1. Pre-heat oven to GM6/200°c/400°f
2. Add enough fat to a baking tin so that when melted it is about 1½" deep
3. Cut the potatoes lengthways down the narrow side and put into a pan of cold, salted water. Bring to the boil and simmer for 10 mins. Drain and dry
4. Mix the rosemary leaves with the flour and add the potatoes. Toss vigorously until evenly coated and the edges of the potatoes are broken
5. Add the potatoes to the fat and cook for 45 mins
6. Remove with a slotted spoon, drain on kitchen paper

POTATOES WITH SPINACH

1 lb potatoes – peeled & thinly sliced
1 lb fresh spinach – trimmed & washed
1 large onion – peeled & thinly sliced
2 cloves garlic – crushed
2 tbsp vegetable oil

1. Simmer the spinach for 5 mins. Drain
2. Heat the oil and gently fry the onion and garlic until the onion is soft
3. Add the potatoes, season and stir. Cook for 1 more minute
4. Add enough water to just cover the potatoes. Bring to the boil then cover and simmer for 10 mins
5. Add the spinach and cook uncovered for about 10 more mins until the potatoes are cooked and the desired consistency is reached

MARJORIE'S CHEESEY POTATOES

1 lb potatoes – peeled & thinly sliced
1 pint white sauce – made from a packet
1 red pepper – deseeded & diced
3 oz Gruyere cheese – grated
3 oz Parmesan cheese – grated

1. Pre heat oven to GM4/180°c/350°f
2. Mix 2 oz of each cheese into the sauce. Season & stir well
3. Grease an ovenproof dish and put a layer of potatoes on the bottom, season and add the peppers. Cover with half of the cheese sauce
4. Add another layer of potatoes and cover with the remainder of the sauce
5. Bake for 45 mins or until the potatoes are soft. Leave to sit 5 mins before serving

TATTIE & BACON GRATIN

1 lb new potatoes – boiled & drained
8 oz button mushrooms – halved
8 oz bacon – diced
2 onions – chopped
8 oz cheddar cheese – grated
2 tbsp olive oil

1. Heat the oil and slowly sauté the bacon & onion – stirring frequently
2. When almost cooked, add the mushrooms – turn up the heat & stir fry for 1-2 mins
3. Halve the potatoes and mix thoroughly with the bacon mixture
4. Transfer to a heat proof shallow dish and season. Sprinkle with the cheese and put under a pre-heated grilled until bubbling

GRILLED GARLIC POTATO KEBABS

1 lb new potatoes – boiled & halved
2 tbsp olive oil
2 cloves garlic – crushed

1. Soak some wooden skewers in water
2. Pre-heat the grill
3. Gently heat the oil and fry the garlic for 3 mins
4. Thread the potatoes onto the skewers and brush with the oil until completely coated
5. Place under the grill and cook for 3-4 mins then turn and repeat. Remove, sprinkle with salt and serve

POTATO & CARROT CHEESE BAKE

1 lb potatoes - peeled & thinly sliced
2 medium onions – thinly sliced
4 medium carrots – grated
2 cloves garlic – crushed
2 oz cheddar cheese – grated
¼ pt single cream
¼ pt milk
½ oz butter

1. *Pre-heat oven to GM4/180°c/350°f*
2. *Lightly butter an ovenproof dish and arrange a layer of one third of the potato slices in the bottom. Cover with half the onion & carrot, plus a sprinkling of garlic. Season*
3. *Add another layer of potatoes, then the onion, carrot, etc*
4. *Finish with a layer of potatoes*
5. *Mix together the cream & milk, pour over the potatoes. Sprinkle the cheese on top. Cook for 90 mins*

WESTERN STYLE POTATO BAKE

1 lb potatoes – peeled & sliced
1 onion – peeled & sliced
1 red pepper – deseeded & sliced
3 fl oz milk
2 oz cheese – grated
½ tin condensed cream of celery soup
1 tsp chill powder
1 clove garlic (crushed)
1½ oz butter

1. *Pre-heat oven to GM4/180°c/350°f*
2. *Melt butter in pan & cook onion, pepper till tender. Add garlic & cook for 1 more minute*
3. *Add soup, milk, chilli powder & 1½ oz cheese & stir until the cheese has melted*
4. *Add the potatoes to a greased baking dish and cover thoroughly with sauce. Cover with foil and bake for 1 hour*
5. *Add remaining cheese 5 mins from the end and cook until golden*

CELERIAC & POTATO GRATIN

1 lb potatoes – peeled & cut into ¼" slices
1 lb celeriac – peeled & cut into ¼" slices
3 oz butter

1. *Pre-heat oven to GM5/190°c/375°f*
2. *Rinse the potatoes in cold water and dry thoroughly*
3. *Melt the butter in a pan and fry half the potato slices for 1 minute on each side. Arrange them in a gratin dish and season*
4. *Fry the celeriac and the rest of the potatoes in the same way. Put the celeriac layer on top of the potatoes, season and add the rest of the potatoes on top of the celeriac. Season again and pour over any remaining butter*
5. *Bake for 1 hour*

GRATED POTATO GRATIN

1 lb potatoes – peeled & grated
6 fl oz double cream
3 oz cheddar cheese – grated
2 cloves garlic – crushed
¼ tsp nutmeg

1. *Pre-heat oven to GM6/200°c/ 400°f*
2. *Mix all the ingredients thoroughly in a mixing bowl and season*
3. *Place in a large ovenproof dish and dot with butter. Bake for 1 hour*

POTATO REMOULADE

1 lb potatoes – peeled & quartered lengthways
6 fl oz mayonnaise
6 fl oz double cream
3 tbsp Dijon mustard
Juice of 1 lime

1. *Boil the potatoes for 15-18 mins, drain and leave to cool. Cut into matchstick shapes*
2. *Beat all the other ingredients together in a large bowl season and stir in the potatoes*
3. *Serve warm*

POTATO & CRAB HASH

1 lb new potatoes – scrubbed, halved & boiled
½ lb tinned crab meat – drained
½ lb frozen peas
1 tbsp olive oil

1. Heat the oil in a pan and fry the potatoes until lightly browned
2. Add the peas and a little water. Season
3. When the water has evaporated add the crab meat and heat until cooked through. Season and serve

CEPS & POTATO GRATIN

1 lb potatoes – peeled & sliced thinly
3 oz dried ceps – soaked for 10 mins in boiled water then drained
5 fl oz milk
1 clove garlic – peeled & cut in half
3½ fl oz double cream
2 oz Gruyere cheese – grated

1. Pre-heat oven to GM6/200°c/400°f
2. Put the potatoes into a large pan, add the milk and bring to the boil. Drain the potatoes – discarding the milk
3. Rub the base of the casserole dish with the garlic
4. Add the potatoes, cream, ceps and season. Mix gently and level. Sprinkle with the cheese and bake for ½ hour
5. Reduce heat to 150° and cook for a further 45 mins

CURRIED POTATO KEBABS

1 lb new potatoes – washed, boiled & drained
1 tbsp curry paste
2 tbsp greek yoghurt

1. Preheat oven to GM4/180°c/350°f
2. Mix all the ingredients until all the potatoes are coated. Season
3. Thread onto wooden skewers and bake for 10-15 mins

HORSERADISH DAUPHINOISE

1 lb (waxy) potatoes– peeled & thinly sliced
¾ pint double cream
¾ pint milk
1 onion – sliced
3 tbsp horseradish sauce
2 cloves garlic – crushed
Pinch of nutmeg
1 tbsp vegetable oil

1. Pre-heat oven to GM6/200°c/400°f
2. Put the milk and cream in a pan and add the horseradish, garlic and a pinch of nutmeg. Season, stir and simmer gently for 15 mins
3. Meanwhile heat the oil in a frying pan and fry the onion for 5 mins
4. Take a greased ovenproof dish and layer half the potatoes in the base then add the onion. Season and add the rest of the potatoes. Pour the cream and milk over the potatoes
5. Bake for about 40 mins until browned on top

THAI STYLE NEW POTATOES

1 lb new potatoes – scrubbed, halved & boiled
1 oz butter
1 red chilli – deseeded & finely chopped
1 stick lemon grass – finely chopped
1 tbsp root ginger – finely chopped
1 tbsp fresh coriander leaves – torn

1. Melt the butter in a small pan and gently fry the chilli, lemon grass and ginger until soft
2. Add the potatoes and mix well. Serve topped with coriander leaves

CURRIED POTATO KEBABS (2)

1 lb small new potatoes – scrubbed & boiled & halved
1 jar curry sauce

1. Mix the potatoes with the curry sauce so the potatoes are thoroughly coated
2. Soak sufficient wooden skewers in water then thread the potatoes onto the skewers. Grill until they start to brown

POTATO GRATIN

1 lb potatoes – peeled & thinly sliced
3 oz bacon – rind removed and chopped
7 oz celeriac – peeled & thinly sliced
5 fl oz double cream
3 fl oz chicken stock
3 oz cheddar cheese – grated
Pinch of nutmeg

1. *Pre-heat oven to GM5/190°c/375°f*
2. *Grill the bacon until golden and crisp*
3. *Layer an ovenproof dish with potatoes, celeriac and bacon. Season*
4. *Mix the cream, stock and nutmeg together and gradually bring to the boil. Pour over the potato layers and bake for 1 hour covered with foil*
5. *Remove the foil, press down and cook for a further 10 mins*
6. *Sprinkle with the cheese, season and bake for 15 more mins*

POTATO & PEA FRITTATA

1 lb new potatoes – boiled & diced
½ lb fresh peas
5 eggs – beaten
2 tbsp fresh mint – chopped
1 oz butter

1. *Pre-heat oven to GM4/180°c/350°f*
2. *Mix together the potatoes, peas, eggs and mint. Season*
3. *Melt the butter in a baking tray and cook over a very low heat for 5 mins without stirring*
4. *Season and transfer to oven and bake for 10 mins until completely set*

POTATO GRATIN WITH LEMON & THYME

1 lb potatoes – peeled & sliced very thinly
5 fl oz milk
Grated zest of ½ lemon
1½ tbsp lemon juice
2 tbsp fresh thyme – chopped
1 oz butter

1. *Pre-heat the oven to GM4/180°c/350°f*
2. *Put half the potatoes at the bottom of a buttered gratin dish, season and sprinkle with half of the lemon zest and half of the thyme*
3. *Add a second layer and repeat. Dot with butter and pour the milk over*
4. *Bake for 50 mins, remove and add the lemon juice*

CHILLI TORTILLA

1 lb potatoes – peeled & thinly sliced
8 eggs – beaten
2 onions – peeled & thinly sliced
1 green pepper – cored, seeded and cut into thin strips
1 yellow pepper – cored, seeded and cut into thin strips
3 cloves garlic – crushed
2 small red chillies – deseeded & finely chopped
3 tbsp extra virgin olive oil

1. *Pre-heat oven to GM6/200°c/400°f*
2. *Heat the oil and fry the potatoes for 10 mins*
3. *Add the onion, peppers, chillies and garlic and cook for 10 more mins*
4. *Remove from heat, season, wait 5 mins then add the eggs and chilli flakes. Stir well*
5. *Allow the mixture to cool then transfer to an ovenproof dish. Cook for 20 mins or until set*

MOROCCAN MASH

1 lb potatoes – peeled & cut into chunks
2 cloves garlic – peeled
2 pinches saffron
1 tsp Harissa paste
2 tbsp fresh coriander – chopped
1 tbsp olive oil

1. *Boil the potatoes with the garlic and saffron. Drain*
2. *Chop the garlic and mash with the potatoes*
3. *Blend in the paste, coriander and oil*

GRATIN POTATOES WITH SAGE & GARLIC

1 lb potatoes – peeled & thinly sliced
¼ pint double cream
3 fl oz milk
2 tbsp fresh sage
2 cloves garlic – crushed
1 oz mozzarella cheese – cut into tiny pieces
1 oz butter

1. Pre-heat oven to GM 3/150°c/325°f
2. Butter a gratin dish and arrange the potatoes in layers putting some garlic, sage and seasoning between each layer
3. Mix the cream and milk together and pour over the potatoes. Dot with cheese and any remaining butter
4. Cover with foil and bake for 1 hour 20 mins, removing the foil for the last 20 mins

BLENDER POTATO PANCAKES

1 lb potatoes – peeled, cubed & divided into 3 lots
1 onion – peeled & finely chopped
4 eggs
4 fl oz milk
2 tbsp fresh parsley – chopped
½ tsp baking powder
3 oz plain flour
5 tbsp lard

1. Put the onion, eggs and milk into a blender and mix for 30 seconds
2. Add ⅓ of the potato through the hole at the top and continue to blend
3. Add a further ⅓ of the potato and the parsley, blend for 10 seconds
4. Add the flour and baking powder and blend or 20 seconds
5. Add the last of the potato and mix for a final 15 seconds
6. Heat the lard in a large pan, roll out the mixture, divide into 15 pieces and fry in batches until brown on each side

POTATO & ANCHCOVY GRATIN

1 lb (waxy) potatoes – peeled & grated
6 anchovy fillets (tinned) – finely chopped
8 fl oz double cream
2 onions – peeled & thinly sliced
1½ oz butter
Oil from the anchovy tin
1 tbsp fresh rosemary – chopped
1½ tbsp breadcrumbs

1. Pre-heat oven to GM6/200°c/400°f
2. Grease a small dish with some of the butter
3. Put the cream, anchovy oil and rosemary in a pan and heat until nearly boiling. Remove from heat and leave to stand for 15 mins
4. Put alternate layers of potato, anchovy and onion in the dish. Season and add cream to each layer – finishing with a layer of potato
5. Pour some cream on top and sprinkle with the breadcrumbs
6. Bake for 30 mins
7. Remove from the oven, add the rest of the cream, dot with butter, season and bake for 20 more mins

BAKED BUBBLE & SQUEAK

1 lb potatoes – peeled, boiled & mashed
½ lb cabbage – chopped & boiled
½ lb carrots – peeled, chopped & boiled
1 large onion – peeled & finely chopped
2 oz cheddar cheese – grated
2 tbsp milk
2 oz butter

1. Pre-heat oven to GM6/200%/400°f
2. Melt half the butter and cook the onion for 5 mins
3. Add the cabbage, milk and half the butter to the mash. Season and mix well
4. Put half the potato mixture at the bottom of a casserole dish. Add the onions and carrots. Season and top with the rest of the potato
5. Sprinkle with the cheese and bake for 45 mins

CREAMY VEGETABLE GRATIN

1 lb waxy potatoes – peeled & thinly sliced
½ lb carrots – peeled & thinly sliced
2 parsnips – peeled & thinly sliced
4 cloves garlic – crushed
12 fl oz double cream
¼ pint milk
1 tbsp fresh thyme – chopped
2 oz parmesan cheese – grated

1. *Pre-heat oven to GM4/180°c/350°f*
2. *Layer the base of a casserole dish with half the potatoes, parsnip and carrot. Season and add half the garlic and thyme then the rest of the vegetables*
3. *Mix the milk and cream in a pan and heat until almost but not quite boiling. Season and pour onto the vegetables*
4. *Cover and bake for 40 mins*
5. *Remove cover, sprinkle with the cheese and bake for 20 more mins*

ASPARAGUS FRITTATA

1 lb new potatoes – scrubbed & quartered
¼ lb asparagus tips – halved
5 eggs – beaten
5 oz goats cheese – crumbled
1 tbsp fresh parsley – chopped
1 tbsp fresh chives – chopped
2 tbsp olive oil

1. *Boil the potatoes for 10 mins*
2. *Add the asparagus and cook for 5 more mins. Drain*
3. *Heat the oil in a pan and fry the potatoes and asparagus for 2 mins*
4. *Season, add the herbs and cheese, stir then add the beaten eggs. Cook gently until almost set then transfer to a pre-heated grill and cook for a few mins until the top is golden brown*

OATMEAL POTATOES

1 lb new potatoes – scrubbed, boiled & drained
2 tbsp pinhead (fine) oatmeal
1 tbsp butter

1. *Toast the oatmeal slightly on a tray in the oven*
2. *Put the potatoes in a small pan and add the butter. Stir so the potatoes are coated then sprinkle with the oatmeal. Stir again*

CHEESEY POTATO SCONES

1 lb potatoes – peeled, boiled & mashed
4 eggs – beaten
½ lb cheddar cheese – grated
6 tbsp butter
5 oz plain flour
Oil/fat for frying

1. *Add the butter and seasoning to the mash*
2. *Mix most of the flour to form a pliable dough then add the cheese and eggs. Season*
3. *Mix well and form into small cakes. Dust the cakes with flour*
4. *Heat the oil or fat and fry until browned on each side*

The Andean Mountains of South America is the birthplace of the white potato.

SIMPLE TORTILLA

1 lb (waxy) potatoes – peeled & cut into slices
1 large Spanish onion – peeled & cut into slices
4 eggs – beaten and seasoned
2 tbsp extra virgin olive oil

1. Heat the oil and fry the potatoes for 10 mins, turning occasionally
2. Add the onion and cook for 5 mins
3. Allow the potatoes and onion to cool then pour in the eggs. Cook for 3-4 mins then turn and repeat

BAKED POTATO TORTILLA

1 lb potatoes – peeled & diced
4 eggs – beaten
1 bunch spring onions – trimmed and cut into small pieces
¼ lb cooked ham – cut into small dice
2 tbsp olive oil

1. Pre-heat oven to GM4/180°c/350°f
2. Heat the oil and fry the potatoes for 10 mins
3. Add the onion and ham. Cook for 2 mins
4. Add the eggs, season and mix well. Cook for 2 more mins then put the pan in the oven and bake for 10 mins

POTATO GALETTE

1 lb potatoes – boiled & mashed
4 oz cheddar cheese – grated
1 onion – peeled & grated
1 egg – beaten
2 tomatoes – sliced
3 oz bacon – rind removed & chopped
2 oz butter
2 tbsp milk

1. Preheat the oven to GM6/200°c/400°f
2. Mix the butter & milk into the mash. Then beat in most of the cheese, the onions, egg & season
3. Place the mixture into a shallow 7 inch oven dish and spread evenly

4. Top the mixture with the sliced tomato & bacon then sprinkle with the remaining cheese. Bake for about 25 mins until the base is firm

POTATO & CELERIAC GRATIN

1 lb waxy potatoes – peeled & sliced
8 oz celeriac – peeled & sliced
2 cloves garlic – crushed
1 large tub double cream
3 oz unsalted butter

1. Pre-heat oven to GM3/175°c/325°f
2. Rub a gratin dish with some of the garlic and 2 oz of the butter
3. Put a layer of potatoes in the base of the dish then half the celeriac and half the garlic. Season and add about one third of the cream
4. Repeat, finishing with a layer of potatoes and pour the remaining cream on top
5. Bake for 1 hour 30 mins
6. Increase heat to GM6/200°c/400°f and dot the potatoes with the remaining butter and cook for 15 more mins

BAKED MASHED POTATOES

1 lb (floury) potatoes – washed & pricked
4 tbsp double cream
2 egg yolks
3 oz unsalted butter
¼ tsp ground nutmeg
1 tsp fresh chives – chopped

1. Pre-heat oven to GM5/190°c/375°f
2. Bake the potatoes for just over an hour until softened
3. Remove, allow to cool slightly, and cut in half lengthways. Scoop out the insides and mash
4. Put the mash in a large bowl, add half the butter and nutmeg. Season
5. Beat in the yolks then add the cream and chives
6. Grease a baking dish and spoon in the mixture
7. Bake for 15 mins. Remove turn the oven up to GM8/230°c dot with the remaining butter and bake for 10 more mins

POMMES SAVOYARDE

1 lb potatoes – peeled & thinly sliced
2 oz gruyere cheese – grated
½ pint. chicken stock
1 clove garlic – peeled & crushed
tsp ground nutmeg
2 oz butter

1. Pre-heat oven to GM4/180°c/350°f
2. Grease a casserole dish with half the butter
3. Mix together the potatoes, half the cheese, the garlic & the nutmeg, seasoning
4. Place in a casserole dish pour on the stock and bake for 50 mins
5. Sprinkle with the rest of the cheese & dot with the rest of the butter. Return to the oven and cook for 15 more mins

MASHED CELERIAC AND POTATOES

1 lb potatoes – peeled & cut into chunks
1½ lb celeriac – peeled & cut into ½ inch cubes
2 oz butter
2 fl oz double cream

1. Put the celeriac & potatoes in separate saucepans & boil each for 20 mins. Drain
2. Purée the celeriac in a blender and mash the potatoes normally
3. Mix the two together and add the cream, butter & seasoning

GRATIN SAVOYARDE

1 lb potatoes – peeled & very thinly sliced
1 large tub double cream
3 tbsp milk
1 clove garlic – peeled & halved
¼ tsp nutmeg

1. Pre-heat oven to GM½ / 130°c/250°f
2. Mix the cream with the milk in a saucepan and heat until nearly boiling. Simmer for about 5 mins

3. Meanwhile rub a small ovenproof dish with the garlic
4. Add the nutmeg to the cream and season with pepper. Add the potatoes, stir well, bring back to the boil then remove the pan from the stove
5. Slowly pour the mixture into the dish ensuring the potatoes are spread out evenly in layers
6. Bake for 45 mins

BACON FLODDIES

1 lb potatoes – peeled & grated
3 onions – peeled & grated
4 eggs – beaten
12 oz bacon – rinds removed & finely chopped
4 oz self-raising flour
Dripping or lard

1. Put the potatoes, onions, bacon & eggs together in a large bowl, sprinkle with the flour & seasoning then mix thoroughly
2. Heat the fat in a large pan and add the mixture in batches & fry until golden brown then turn over and fry the other side. Drain on kitchen paper

POLENTA & POTATO SLICES

1 lb (floury) potatoes – peeled, boiled & mashed
3½ oz polenta
3½ oz butter
6½ oz plain flour
5 tsp baking powder
3½ fl oz milk

1. Pre-heat oven to GM6/200°c/400°f
2. Put the mash in a large bowl and add all the ingredients except the milk. Season and mix together
3. Add the milk gradually and mix manually to form a dough. Knead the dough until smooth
4. Roll the mixture and form it into a large circular shape about ¼ " thick. Trim the edge and cut into 10 slices
5. Place the slices on a tray, score each one with a knife and bake for 20 mins

POTATO & MUSHROOM GALETTE

1 lb potatoes – peeled & very thinly sliced
½ lb wild mushrooms – cleaned thoroughly
   and sliced
3 shallots – peeled & chopped
3 cloves garlic – crushed
2 tbsp fresh parsley – chopped
4 tbsp olive oil

1. *Heat half the oil in a large frying pan and cook the mushrooms until soft. Add the garlic, shallots and parsley. Season and stir*

2. *Heat the remaining oil in a pan and layer the base with half the potatoes in overlapping circles. Pour on the mushrooms and spread evenly. Season and add the remaining potatoes. Fry for 10-15 mins until the underside turns brown*

3. *Use a plate or another pan to flip the galette over and cook the other side until browned*

PERSIAN POTATO OMLETTE

1 lb potatoes – peeled, boiled & mashed
6 eggs – beaten
1 small bunch spring onions – trimmed
   and chopped
2 tbsp fresh coriander – chopped
1½ tbsp fresh parsley – chopped
1 tsp ground cumin
1 oz butter

1. *Put the mash in a bowl with the eggs, onion herbs and cumin. Season and mix well*

2. *Melt the butter in a frying pan, add the mash and cook for about 20 mins until the eggs have set and the base is golden brown*

3. *Slide the pan under a pre-heated grill and heat until the top is browned*

POTATO RAMEKINS

1 lb potatoes – peeled & sliced
Sufficient slices Gruyère cheese
Sufficient pre-made batter (using a packet mix)
Sunflower oil

1. *Using similar size slices of potato make 'sandwiches' using the cheese as the filling. Season each and dip into the batter*

2. *Heat the oil in a deep fat fryer and fry each ramekin until browned*

   (you may want to fix 'the sandwich' with a pre-soaked cocktail stick)

RED TORTILLA

1 lb potatoes – peeled, boiled for 10 mins,
   cooled & sliced
2 red peppers – de-seeded and cut into strips
3 tomatoes – cut into wedges
2 onions – peeled & sliced
8 eggs – beaten & seasoned
3 fl oz olive oil

1. *Pre heat grill*

2. *Heat the oil in a large frying pan and fry the potatoes for 5 mins*

3. *Add the onion and pepper, season and cook until the onion has softened*

4. *Add the tomatoes, stir and cook for 1 more minute*

5. *Pour on the eggs and mix well. Cook gently until the base starts to set*

6. *Place the pan under the grill and cook until the top has set and is golden*

THAI POTATOES

1 lb new potatoes – scrubbed & halved
3 shallots – peeled & finely chopped
6 fl oz coconut milk
3 fl oz light chicken stock
1 small red chilli – finely chopped
2 tbsp vegetable oil

1. *Heat the oil and gently fry the shallot and chilli for 5 mins*

2. *Add the potatoes, stir, then pour on the milk and stock. Stir again, bring to the boil and simmer gently for 15 mins so the potatoes are cooked*

3. *Turn up the heat and boil rapidly, stirring frequently, until the liquid is greatly reduced – but not gone*

4. *Stir in the coriander and serve*

HOISIN POTATOES

1 lb potatoes – peeled & diced
½ lb carrots – peeled & diced
3 cloves garlic – crushed
4 tbsp hoisin sauce
1 tbsp soy sauce
1" piece fresh ginger – grated
4 spring onions
1 tbsp vegetable oil
6 fl oz chicken stock

1. Heat the oil in a wok and add the garlic, ginger and onions. Stir fry for 30 seconds
2. Turn the heat up and add the potatoes and carrots. Stir well then pour in the hoisin & soy sauces and water
3. Cook for 12-15 mins on a high heat, stirring often – until the desired consistency is reached

SKORDALIA MASH

1 lb potatoes – peeled & cubed
1 lb celeriac – peeled & cubed
4 tbsp extra virgin olive oil
5 cloves garlic – crushed

1. Put the celeriac in a pan of lightly salted cold water and bring to the boil. Add the potatoes and return to the boil. Boil for 18-20 mins. Drain
2. Heat the olive oil and gently cook the garlic for 3 mins
3. Mash thoroughly with the oil and garlic. Season

ASIAN POTATOES

1 lb potatoes – peeled, boiled, drained & cubed
1 tsp turmeric
1½ tbsp extra virgin olive oil
2 spring onions – finely chopped

1. Heat the oil in a small pan then add the onions and turmeric. Season and stir and cook for 2 mins
2. Add the potatoes and stir thoroughly until coated

TUSCAN POTATOES

1 lb potatoes – peeled & diced
3 cloves of garlic – crushed
2 tbsp fresh rosemary
2 tbsp olive oil

1. Pre-heat oven to GM4/180°c/350°f
2. Put the oil in an ovenproof dish and heat on the stove
3. Add the potatoes and mix until coated with the oil. Sprinkle with the rosemary, season and add the garlic
4. Bake for 40 mins, stirring once

PORT WINE POTATOES

1 lb new potatoes – scrubbed and boiled for 10 mins
5 fl oz Port
1½ tbsp runny honey
1 tbsp Balsamic vinegar

1. Pre-heat oven to GM5/190°c/375°f
2. Put all the ingredients except the potatoes in a screw top jar and shake vigorously to mix
3. Drain the potatoes and halve them. Place in a small roasting tin, season and pour over the dressing
4. Bake for 30-40 mins

MEXICAN POTATOES

1 lb (waxy) potatoes – peeled, boiled for 15 mins, drained & cut into chunks
2 dried red chillies – finely chopped
½ tsp black mustard seeds
½ tsp turmeric
½ tsp salt
3 tbsp vegetable oil

1. Heat the oil so that a mustard seed pops when put in it. Add the rest of the seeds, the chillies, turmeric and salt. Fry for 1 min. stirring continuously
2. Add the potatoes and fry for 5 more mins, stirring continuously
3. Reduce to a very low heat and cook for 5 further mins, stirring occasionally

CHEESE & EGG CROQUETTES

1 lb potatoes – peeled & mashed
1½ oz butter
3 oz cheddar cheese – grated
1 tbsp milk
4 eggs – hard boiled & chopped
1 red onion – peeled & finely chopped
1 egg – beaten
Breadcrumbs
Fat for deep frying

1. *Mix the cheese, butter & milk into the mash. Season*

2. *Stir in the chopped eggs & onion. Mix well.*

3. *Divide the mixture into 10 and roll into round shapes. Brush with the beaten egg then coat with breadcrumbs*

4. *Fry each portion in hot deep fat until crisp & golden. Dry on kitchen paper*

POTATO & GOATS CHEESE FRITTATA

1 lb potatoes – peeled, diced, boiled for 5 mins & drained
8 eggs – beaten
4 tbsp crème fraiche
5 oz Chevre blanc cheese – crumbled
3½ oz parmesan – grated
2½ tbsp fresh chives – chopped
2 tbsp olive oil

1. *Heat the oil and fry the potatoes for 10 mins*

2. *Add the crème fraiche and chives to the eggs and beat thoroughly. Add the parmesan, season and stir well*

3. *Pour the mixture onto the potatoes, sprinkle with the cheese, stir well and cook over a low heat for about 10 mins until the base begins to set*

4. *Pre-heat the grill*

5. *Put the pan under the grill for about 5 mins until the top has set*

GARLICKY DAUPHINOIS

1 lb potatoes – peeled & thinly sliced
9 fl oz milk
3½ oz crème fraiche
2 oz Gruyere cheese – grated
1 clove garlic – peeled
5 cloves garlic – crushed
2 oz butter

1. *Pre-heat oven to GM4/180°c/350°f*

2. *Put the milk in a large pan and heat slowly. As it reaches boiling point add the crème fraiche, half the cheese and the crushed garlic. Season, stir well and gradually re-heat*

3. *Add the potatoes, stir and cook over a low heat for 10 mins – stirring occasionally*

4. *Take a small ovenproof dish and rub it with the remaining garlic clove then smear it with half the butter and season lightly*

5. *Pour in the potato mixture, top with the rest of the cheese and dot with the rest of the butter*

6. *Cover and cook for 1½ hours. Slide the dish under a pre-heated grill for 5 mins or until the top is golden brown*

POTATOES WITH CHICK PEAS

1 lb potatoes – peeled & cubed
1 large tin chick peas – drained
2 onions - peeled & chopped
3 cloves garlic – crushed
1 in root ginger – peeled & grated
½ tsp chilli powder
3 tbsp olive oil
1 pint chicken stock

1. *Heat the oil in a large pan and fry the onion, garlic and ginger until the onion begins to soften*

2. *Pre-heat oven to GM4/180°c/350°f*

3. *Add the potatoes, chickpeas and chilli powder. Season, stir and cook for 3 mins*

4. *Pour on the stock, stir, bring to the boil and simmer, stirring frequently, until the liquid just covers the potato mixture*

POTATO BRAVAS (2)

1 lb potatoes – peeled & diced
4 rashers bacon – derinded & diced
1 onion – peeled & diced
2 cloves garlic – crushed
1 tbsp chilli oil
2 tbsp extra virgin olive oil

1. *Heat the olive oil and stir fry the potatoes until nearly cooked*

2. *Add the chilli oil and add the onions, bacon & garlic. Season, stir well and fry until the onion starts to soften and the bacon is cooked*

CREAMED COCONUT POTATOES

1 lb potatoes – peeled & cubed
3 oz creamed coconut
9 fl oz vegetable stock
1 onion – peeled & thinly sliced into rings
1 small green chilli – deseeded & finely chopped
1 tbsp vegetable oil

1. *Heat the oil and fry the onion and chilli until the onion starts to soften*

2. *Add all the remaining ingredients, season and stir well. Bring to the boil, then simmer gently for about 15 mins until the liquid has reduced and the potatoes are cooked*

CREAMED PUMPKIN & POTATO

1 lb potatoes – peeled & thinly sliced
1½ lb pumpkin – peeled & thinly sliced
3 cloves garlic – crushed
1 pint double cream

1. *Pre-heat the oven to GM4/180°c/350°f*

2. *Grease a small ovenproof dish and cover the base with a layer of potatoes. Season and add a layer of pumpkin. Continue layering and seasoning finishing with a layer of pumpkin*

3. *Mix the garlic into the cream and pour on top. Cover and bake for 45 mins*

4. *Remove the cover and season. Bake for 15 more mins*

SPINACH & POTATO RED CURRY

1 lb potatoes – peeled & cubed
10 oz spinach leaves – washed
2 onions – peeled & thinly sliced
3 tbsp red curry paste
10 fl oz coconut milk
5 fl oz vegetable stock
3 garlic cloves – crushed
1½ inch fresh ginger – peeled & grated
1 stalk lemon grass – finely chopped
4 tbsp vegetable oil

1. *Put the garlic, ginger and lemon grass in a mortar and crush with a pestle until a paste has formed*

2. *Heat half of the oil and fry the paste for about a minute*

3. *Add the red curry paste and the coconut milk and stock. Stir well and bring to the boil*

4. *Add the potatoes, return to the boil then simmer gently for about 15 mins*

5. *Meanwhile, heat the rest of the oil and fry the onions until browned*

6. *Stir the spinach into the potato mixture and serve once the leaves have melted. Top with the onion*

GARLIC MUSHROOM BAKE

1 lb potatoes – peeled, boiled & mashed
1 lb mushrooms – washed & halved
4 cloves garlic – crushed
2 oz cheddar cheese – grated
2 oz butter

1. *Pre-heat oven to GM5/190°c/375°f*

2. *Melt the butter and gently fry the garlic for 3-4 mins*

3. *Add the mushrooms, mix well so they are coated and cook gently until they start to soften*

4. *Pour the mushrooms into a small ovenproof dish and season. Spread the mash evenly over and sprinkle with the cheese*

5. *Bake for half an hour*

CREAMY CURRIED POTATOES

1 lb (waxy) potatoes – peeled, cubed, boiled for 5 mins & drained
2 onions – peeled & chopped
2 cloves garlic – crushed
1½ inch fresh ginger – peeled & grated
2 tbsp balti curry paste
4 fl oz double cream
4 fl oz yoghurt
2 tbsp fresh mint – chopped
Vegetable oil

1. Heat a little oil and fry the onion until it starts to soften
2. Put it in a blender with the garlic, ginger, curry paste and a little water. Blitz to a purée
3. Heat 2 tbsp of oil in a saucepan and fry the potatoes until browned
4. Add the purée and fry gently for 3 mins
5. Add the cream, yoghurt and mint. Season, mix well and cook gently for 5 mins until fully warmed through

POTATOES WITH SESAME AND GARLIC

1 lb new potatoes – scrubbed & halved
2 cloves garlic – peeled & sliced
1 tbsp sesame seeds
3 tbsp vegetable oil
¼ tsp turmeric

1. Heat the oil and fry the potatoes until lightly browned. Remove with a slotted spoon
2. Add the sesame seeds and garlic to the oil and stir
3. When the garlic starts to brown add the potatoes and turmeric. Season. Stir and fry until the potatoes are cooked

BASIC JACKET POTATOES

1 lb (floury) potatoes – 2 large potatoes
1 tbsp olive oil
1 oz butter

1. Pre-heat oven to GM3/170°c/325°f

2. Wash the potatoes and dry thoroughly
3. Pierce each potatoes a few times with a fork and then place on a lightly oiled baking tray
4. Brush with the oil then sprinkle with a little salt
5. Bake for 1½ hours
6. Cut a cross in the top of each potato and squeeze the base to open it up. Add the butter and serve straightaway

NOTES:
- If you want your potatoes quicker then bake at GM6/200°c/400°f for 1 hour
- If you're really in a hurry, cook each potato for about 8 mins in a microwave. Stand for 2 mins before serving
- Alternatively after baking you may want to cut the potatoes in half lengthways, scrape the flesh with a fork then add the butter
- If you need to remove the potato flesh, ensure you leave enough flesh to hold the skin rigid

SAUSAGEMEAT JACKETS

1 lb (floury) potatoes – washed & pricked
½ lb sausagemeat
2 oz cheddar cheese – grated
2 tbsp double cream
1 oz butter
1 tbsp vegetable oil

1. Pre-heat oven to GM6/200°c/400°f
2. Bake the potatoes for 1 hour
3. With 10-15 mins to go, heat the oil and gently fry the sausagemeat until cooked. Drain off the fat
4. Remove the potatoes and cut each one in half. Scoop out the flesh and put in a bowl. Add the meat and butter, season and mix well
5. Mix the cheese with the cream. Put the potato and meat mixture back in to the potato skins, spoon on the cheese and bake for 10 more mins

COTTAGE PIE JACKETS

1 lb (floury) potatoes – washed & pricked
1 lb minced beef
1 large onion – peeled & chopped
½ pint beef stock
2 cloves garlic – crushed
2 tbsp tomato purée
1 tbsp olive oil
1 oz butter
2 oz cheddar cheese – grated

1. *Heat the oven to GM6/200°c/400°f*
2. *Bake the potatoes for 1 hour. Remove and allow to cool*
3. *Heat the oil and fry the onion and garlic for 5 mins*
4. *Dry fry the mince until browned, remove excess fat and add the onion and garlic. Add the purée and stock. Season and simmer for 20 mins*
5. *Halve the potatoes, scoop out the flesh, add the butter to it, season and mash*
6. *Spoon in the meat mixture, top with the mash and sprinkle with the cheese*
7. *Place under a pre-heated grill until the cheese melts*

CHILLI JACKETS

Make basic jacket potatoes:-
Additional Ingredients
½ lb minced beef
1 large can kidney beans – drained
1 small red chilli – deseeded & finely chopped
4 tbsp sour cream

1. *Dry fry the mince until browned and drain off the fat*
2. *Meanwhile fry the chilli in a small amount of oil until softened*
3. *Add the chilli and beans to the mince, season, cook for 10 mins*
4. *Cut each potato in half lengthways and scoop out half the flesh and place by the jacket*
5. *Fill each jacket with the mince and top each with sour cream*

CHEESEY POTATOES

Make basic jacket potatoes:-
Additional Ingredients
4 oz cheddar cheese – grated
1 egg separated
1 oz butter

1. *Cut the top of each potato and scoop out most of the flesh, mash with the cheese, egg yolk, butter and seasoning*
2. *Whisk the egg white and fold into the mash, replace the mixture into the potato skin, put the top back on and bake for another 5-10 mins*

BAKED BEAN JACKETS

Make basic jacket potatoes:-
Additional Ingredients
1 large can baked beans
1 tbsp wholegrain mustard
1 tbsp Worcester sauce

1. *Heat the beans in pan and stir in the mustard and Worcester sauce, season*
2. *Split the top of each potato and pour half the beans onto each one*

SOUR CREAM & CHIVES

Make basic jacket potatoes:-
Additional Ingredients
6 tbsp sour cream
2 tbsp chives – chopped

1. *Mix the chives with the cream and spoon half the mixture into the top of each split potato*

BACON & ONION JACKETS

Make basic jacket potatoes:-
Additional Ingredients
4 rashers bacon – derinded & chopped
1 onion – peeled & finely chopped
1 tbsp olive oil
1½ tbsp Dijon mustard

1. Dry fry the bacon until cooked
2. Meanwhile, heat the oil and fry onion until browned
3. Scoop out some of the potato and mix it with the bacon, onion and mustard. Season and return to the jacket. Bake for 5 mins

2. Remove most of the flesh from the potatoes and mix with the mushrooms and half the cheese
3. Replace the mixture into the jackets, season and sprinkle with the remaining cheese. Cook under a grill until the cheese is bubbling

PIZZA JACKETS

Make basic jacket potatoes:-
Additional Ingredients
4 tbsp passata
Sliced mozzarella cheese
2 tomatoes – sliced
2 mushrooms – washed & sliced
8 black olives – stoned & halved

1. Pre-heat the grill
2. Slice each potato in half lengthways, scrape with a fork and spread 1 tbsp of passata on each half. Add a layer of cheese and top with tomatoes, mushrooms and olives
3. Season and grill until the cheese has melted

SALMON & BOURSIN JACKETS

Make basic jacket potatoes:-
Additional Ingredients
2 oz Boursin
2 oz sliced smoked salmon
2 tbsp single cream
1 tbsp fresh chives – chopped

1. Mix the cheese, cream and chives together. Season
2. Put half the mixture into the top of each jacket and top with the salmon

MUSHROOM & CHEESE JACKETS

Make basic jacket potatoes:-
Additional Ingredients
¼ lb mushrooms – washed & chopped
3 oz cheddar cheese – grated
1 oz butter

1. Heat the butter and fry the mushrooms until soft

TUNA & MAYO JACKETS

Make basic jacket potatoes:-
Additional Ingredients
1 small tin tuna – drained
1 small tin sweetcorn
6 tbsp mayonnaise

1. Mix the ingredients together and season. Spoon onto the potatoes

GREEK JACKETS

Make basic jacket potatoes:-
Additional Ingredients
8 tbsp Tzatziki
6 spring onions – finely chopped
4 tbsp dried cucumber

1. Mix the ingredients together, season and put half of the mixture onto each potato

Did you know that the Indians in Peru were the first people to cultivate the potato over 4000 years ago?

POTATO CAKES

1 lb potatoes – peeled, boiled & mashed
1 egg - beaten
2 spring onions – finely chopped
2 oz butter
Flour for dusting

1. *Mix into the mash the egg, spring onions & seasoning*
2. *Mould the mixture into round shapes about ½ inch deep by 2 inch diameter on a lightly floured board*
3. *Melt the butter & fry each cake until golden brown on each side*

SAVOURY POTATO PANCAKES

1 lb potatoes – peeled, boiled & mashed
4 eggs – beaten
3 onions – peeled & grated
3 tomatoes – chopped
2 tbsp fresh parsley – chopped
2 tbsp fresh chives – chopped
2 red peppers – chopped
12 tbsp self raising flour
Milk
2 tbsp vegetable oil

1. *Beat the egg into the potatoes and add the flour with enough milk to make a soft batter*

> The potato is now a very common food item worldwide. In the United States, potatoes are grown in all 50 states and in about 125 countries worldwide.

2. *Add the onion, tomatoes, peppers, parsley, chives and season. Mix well*
3. *Heat the oil in a large frying pan and fry the mixture in small batches until each is browned on both sides*

BASIC POTATO PANCAKES

1 lb (waxy) potatoes – peeled & grated
5 oz self raising flour
5 fl oz milk
4 spring onions – trimmed & finely sliced
1 tbsp fresh thyme – chopped
2 tbsp olive oil

1. *Squeeze the potatoes to remove excess liquid*
2. *Sieve the flour into a bowl then slowly pour on the milk stirring continuously and mix to a smooth batter*
3. *Add the potatoes, onions and thyme. Season and mix well*
4. *Heat the oil in a large pan and add the mixture 1 tbsp at a time to the pan – keeping each one separate*
5. *Fry until browned on both sides*

POTATO PANCAKES WITH CREAM CHEESE

1 lb potatoes – peeled & grated
3 eggs – beaten
1 onion – peeled & grated
2 tbsp flour
1 tsp salt
3 fl oz olive oil
Small tub of cream cheese
2 tbsp fresh chives – chopped

1. *Squeeze as much moisture as possible from the potatoes*
2. *Put the potatoes in a bowl and manually mix in the onion, eggs, flour and salt. Season*
3. *Heat the oil and add the mixture one spoonful at a time. Spread each spoonful and cook until the base is golden – turn over and repeat*
4. *Top each pancake with a spoonful of cream cheese and sprinkle with chives*

BANGERS & MASH CAKES

1 lb potatoes – boiled & mashed
½ lb sausages – cooked, cooled & chopped
1 bunch spring onions – washed & chopped
2 eggs beaten
1 tbsp wholegrain mustard
1 slice bread – toasted & made into breadcrumbs
3 tbsp olive oil

1. Mix the mash, sausage, spring onions, mustard and seasoning into a dough
2. Divide into 6 or 8 cakes and place in the fridge for ½ hour
3. Coat the cakes with beaten egg then sprinkle with breadcrumbs
4. Heat oil in a large frying pan and gently fry the cakes until brown on each side and heated through

POTATO PANCAKES

1 lb potatoes – boiled with skins on
3 eggs – beaten
5 fl oz milk
3 oz flour
3 oz unsalted butter – melted
1 tbsp fresh chives – chopped
4 oz clarified butter

1. Drain the potatoes and allow to cool slightly. Peel and mash
2. Beat the eggs, flour, melted butter, chives and seasoning into the potato
3. Heat the clarified butter then spoon in the mixture – 2 desert spoons to each cake, into the pan and flatten to ½ inch height – cook for 5 mins turning halfway through

HAM & STILTON POTATO CAKES

1 lb potatoes – peeled, boiled & mashed
4 oz Stilton cheese – crumbled
4 oz cooked ham – cut into small pieces
3 leeks – trimmed and finely sliced
2 oz butter
2 tbsp olive oil

1. Heat the butter and cook the leeks until soft

2. Remove from the heat and add the ham, potato and cheese. Season and mix well
3. Put the mixture on a lightly floured board and form 4 or 5 separate cakes
4. Pre-heat oven to GM4/180°c/350°f
5. Allow the cakes to cool in the fridge for 15 mins
6. Heat the oil and fry the cakes until lightly browned on each side then bake in the oven for 10 mins

IRISH POTATO CAKES

1 lb potatoes – boiled & mashed
4 oz plain flour
1 oz butter
½ tsp salt
½ tsp baking powder
1 fl oz milk

1. Sieve the flour, salt and baking powder into a bowl
2. Add the potatoes, milk, and 1 oz of the butter. Mix to a smooth paste
3. Knead the dough on a floured board and divide into 4. Roll each piece until ¼" thick and cut into 6 triangles
4. Melt the remaining butter in a pan and cook the triangles until browned on both sides

CARRAWAY POTATO CAKES

1 lb potatoes – peeled, boiled & mashed
1 onion – peeled & finely chopped
1½ tbsp caraway seeds
1 tbsp fresh parsley – chopped
2 oz flour
2 oz butter
2 tbsp olive oil

1. Heat the butter and gently fry the onion till soft
2. Add the onion, butter, caraway seeds, parsley and flour to the mash. Season and mix
3. Divide mixture into 6 and form into cakes, dusting lightly in flour
4. Heat the oil in a frying pan and fry the cakes on a medium heat until browned on both sides. Drain on kitchen paper

117

BOXTY PANCAKES

1 lb potatoes
4 oz self-raising flour
4 fl oz milk
2 oz lard

1. Peel & grate the potatoes & place in a colander. Press down to squeeze out the excess starch
2. Sieve the flour into a bowl and stir in the milk. Mix in the grated potatoes & season
3. Heat the fat in a frying pan until it foams. Add the potato mixture 1 tablespoon at a time and cook for 3 or 4 mins on each side until brown

POTATO & CHEESE CAKES

1 lb potatoes – boiled & mashed
5 oz cheddar cheese – grated
1 oz butter
2 eggs – beaten
2 oz breadcrumbs
1 tbsp plain flour
1 tbsp fresh chives – snipped

1. Pre-heat oven to GM5/190°c/375°f
2. Beat the butter, cheese, chives, flour, 1 egg and seasoning into the potatoes while still hot. Allow to cool
3. Put the mixture onto a surface covered with flour and mix in manually. Form into small round shapes
4. Brush with the remaining egg and coat with the breadcrumbs. Refrigerate for 45 mins then bake for 20-25 mins. Serve hot

SAVOURY BACON POTATO CAKES

1 lb potatoes – boiled & mashed
3 oz bacon – rinds removed & finely chopped
2 oz butter
3 oz flour

1. Add the butter & seasoning to the hot mash
2. Fry the bacon in its own fat for 4-5 mins remove with a slotted spoon. Reserve the fat
3. Beat the flour into the mash and the bacon pieces

4. Allow the mixture to cool slightly then roll out to ¼ inch thickness on a well floured board and cut into circles
5. Heat a little of the bacon fat in a frying pan and cook each cake for 2-3 mins on each side until golden. Drain on kitchen paper

POTATO TUNA & SWEETCORN CRISPBAKES

1 lb potatoes – boiled & mashed
1 small tin tuna – drained & flaked
3 tbsps sweetcorn kernels – drained
1 small onion – thinly sliced
3 tbsp cream dressing
1 egg – beaten
4 oz fresh white breadcrumbs

1. Saute the onion in vegetable oil for about 3-4 mins
2. Put the potatoes into a large mixing bowl and stir in the dressing. Add the sweetcorn, tuna & onion and mix well. Season
3. Divide the mixture in 5 or 6 and press manually into flat round shapes. Brush each with the egg then toss in the breadcrumbs
4. Saute each crispbake for 5 mins on each side until browned

BUBBLE & SQUEAK CAKES

1 lb potatoes – boiled & mashed
5 oz cabbage – washed & shredded
5 oz leeks – washed &shredded
1 onion – peeled & grated
4 oz butter
1 tbsp vegetable oil
Flour for dusting

1. Melt half the butter in a pan and fry the cabbage, leek and onion for about 5 mins, until the onion softens
2. Mix the cabbage, leek and onion into the mash and season
3. Allow to cool slightly then roll out and divide into 10. Mould into cakes and dust with flour
4. Melt the rest of the butter, add the oil and cook the cakes for about 5 mins on each side until browned

VEGETABLE CAKES

1 lb potatoes – boiled & mashed
2 eggs – beaten
¼ lb cooked peas
¼ cooked beans – chopped
¼ lb carrots – cooked & chopped
3 oz cheddar cheese – grated
3 oz breadcrumbs
Vegetable oil

1. *Mix 1 egg into the mash and season*
2. *Beat in the rest of the vegetables and the cheese and mould into patties*
3. *Dip each patty in the rest of the egg mixture and then in the breadcrumbs*
4. *Fry gently in shallow fat until brown then turn and fry the other side. Drain on kitchen paper. Serve hot*

SPICY POTATO PATTIES

1 lb potatoes – peeled, boiled & mashed
6 spring onions – trimmed & finely sliced
3 carrots – boiled & mashed
2 small red chillies – seeded & finely chopped
3 inches fresh ginger – peeled & grated
2 tbsp coconut cream
3 tbsp sour cream
3 tbsp plain flour
1 tbsp ground coriander
2 tbsp lime juice
3 tbsp olive oil

1. *Mix the potato and carrot together in a large bowl*
2. *Heat the oil in a pan*
3. *Add all the remaining ingredients to the bowl and mix well with your hands. Season and shape into 6 patties*
4. *Fry each pattie for 5 mins on each side*
5. *Remove and drain on kitchen paper*

CHEESEY POTATO CAKES

1 lb potatoes – boiled & mashed
4 oz flour
1 egg – beaten
4 oz cheddar cheese – grated
Vegetable oil for frying

1. *Mix the flour and cheese into the mash*
2. *Add the egg, season and beat in thoroughly*
3. *Form the mixture into cakes and fry in the oil until brown on each side. Drain on kitchen paper. Serve hot*

POTATO & PEPPER CAKES

1 lb potatoes – boiled & mashed
3 red peppers – halved & seeds removed
3 spring onions – finely sliced
5 oz cheddar cheese – grated
2 eggs – beaten
2 tsp fresh oregano – chopped
1 tsp fresh basil – chopped
1 tsp fresh rosemary – chopped
Olive oil for cooking
Flour for dusting

1. *Grill the peppers (inside facing down) under a grill until blackened. Place in a freezer bag for 10 mins then remove skins and chop finely*
2. *Mix the peppers and all the other main ingredients into the mash and season*
3. *Roll the mixture out and divide into 6. Shape into cakes and dust with flour*
4. *Heat some oil in a pan and gently fry each side for about 5 mins*

POTATO & OLIVE CAKES

1 lb potatoes – peeled
1 onion – peeled & grated
2 eggs – beaten
2 tbsp olive paste
3 oz self raising flour
3 fl oz olive oil

1. *Grate the potatoes and squeeze in a tea towel to remove moisture*
2. *Put the potatoes in a bowl and mix in the onion, eggs, paste and flour. Mould the mixture manually into 6 cake shapes. Season*
3. *Pre-heat oven to GM2/150°c/300°f*
4. *Heat the oil in large pan and fry until light brown on both sides*
5. *Lightly grease a baking tray and cook for 20 mins in the oven*

BUBBLE & SQUEAK CAKES WITH CHESTNUT & APPLE

1 lb potates – peeled, boiled & mashed
7 oz Brussels sprouts – boiled & finely chopped
5 oz parsnips – boiled & finely chopped
2 oz chestnuts – boiled & finely chopped
1 small apple – peeled, cored & grated
2 tbsp vegetable oil

1. *Mix all the ingredients except the oil in a large bowl. Season*
2. *Divide the mixture into 8 and shape into small cakes*
3. *Heat the oil in a large frying pan and fry the cakes until brown on each side. Reduce the heat and fry for another 5 mins on each side until heated through*

STILTON & BACON POTATO CAKES

1 lb (floury) potatoes – peeled, boiled & mashed
2 oz bacon – fat removed
3 oz stilton – rind removed and crumbled
1 egg yolk
3 spring onions – trimmed and finely sliced
2 tbsp olive oil
3 oz plain flour

1. *Dry fry the bacon until almost crisp*
2. *Add the spring onions and fry for 2 more mins*
3. *Beat all the ingredients into the mash except the oil and a little flour. Form into a dough then separate into cakes. Dust with the rest of the flour*
4. *Heat the oil and fry each cake for about 5 mins on each side, until browned*

BACON & POTATO CAKES

1 lb potatoes – boiled & mashed
½ lb bacon – cut into pieces
2 tomatoes – chopped
2 tbsp fresh sage – chopped
2 tbsp vegetable oil

1. *Dry fry the bacon until browned. Drain*
2. *Put the bacon in a large bowl and add the potatoes, tomatoes and sage. Season and mix well*

3. *Divide the mixture into 6 and form into cakes*
4. *Place each side on a floured surface and refrigerate for an hour*
5. *Heat the oil in a pan and fry the cakes for 5 mins, turning occasionally until browned*

POTATO & HAM CAKES

1 lb potatoes – boiled & mashed
1 lb cooked ham – cubed
1 small tin sweetcorn – drained
5 oz cheddar cheese – grated
1 pint milk
2 oz flour
2 oz butter

1. *Pre-heat oven to GM6/200°c/400°f*
2. *Melt the butter in a saucepan, add the flour and make a roux with the milk*
3. *When thickened add the ham and sweetcorn. Season*
4. *Put the potato into several small baking trays leaving a hole in the middle. Spoon the ham mixture into the hole and sprinkle with the cheese. Season and bake for 15 mins*

CORNED BEEF & POTATO CAKES

1 lb potatoes – boiled & mashed
10 oz tin corned beef – mashed
1 onion – peeled & very finely chopped
3 eggs – beaten
2 oz breadcrumbs
2 tsp mustard
2 tsp Worcester sauce
2 tbsp olive oil

1. *Heat the oil in a frying pan*
2. *In a large bowl, mix all the other ingredients together manually. Season and form into 4 or 5 cakes*
3. *Fry the cakes for about 15 mins turning frequently, until browned. Drain on kitchen paper*

WELSH POTATO CAKES

1 lb potatoes – boiled & mashed
1 egg beaten

4 oz plain flour
1 tsp baking powder
1 oz butter
1 tbsp sugar
Pinch of salt

1. *Pre-heat oven to GM7/220°c/425°f*
2. *Mix together all the ingredients except the butter*
3. *Melt the butter and mix thoroughly*
4. *Roll out the mixture so it is 1" thick and cut into shapes about 1½" diameter*
5. *Place on a baking tray and bake for 20 mins*
6. *Serve hot dotted with butter*

ITALIAN POTATO CAKES

1 lb (floury) potatoes – peeled, boiled & mashed
2 eggs – beaten
2 oz white breadcrumbs
3 sun dried tomatoes in oil – drained and chopped
1 tbsp capers – chopped
1 tbsp fresh parsley – chopped
1 tbsp olive oil

1. *Beat one egg, the tomatoes, capers and parsley into the mash. Season and form into 5 cakes*
2. *Brush with the remaining egg and dip in the breadcrumbs*
3. *Heat the oil and fry until browned on each side*

CHEESEY POTATO CAKES (2)

1 lb potatoes – peeled, boiled & mashed
4 spring onions – trimmed & finely sliced
3 oz mature cheddar cheese
2 tbsp fresh chives – chopped
1 egg – beaten
1 tsp Dijon mustard
Flour for dusting
1 oz butter
2 tbsp olive oil

1. *Melt the butter and gently fry the onions for 3 mins until just softened*
2. *Put the cheese in a mixing bowl; add the egg, mustard and chives. Season*

3. *Mash the potatoes again to form a smooth paste. Add the onions and the rest of the butter*
4. *Mix the potato and cheese mixtures together and form into 4 cakes. Dust with flour and place on a floured plate. Cover with cling film and chill in the fridge for 1 hour*
5. *Pre-heat oven to GM6/200°c/400°f*
6. *Heat the oil until hot and fry each cake for 2 mins on each side. Drain, transfer to a greased tray and cook in the oven for 10 mins*

SPICY POTATO CAKES

1 lb potatoes – peeled & cut into chunks
4 spring onions – chopped
1 small chilli – deseeded & finely chopped
1 red pepper – deseeded & cut into squares
4 oz gruyere cheese – grated
1 egg – beaten
4 tbsp olive oil
1½ tbsp parsley – chopped

1. *Boil the potatoes for 10 mins, drain and mash*
2. *Mix all the other ingredients (except the oil) into the potato and season. Divide into six and form each piece into a small cake*
3. *Heat the oil and fry over a moderate heat for 15 mins turning frequently until brown on both sides*

POTATO PATTIES WITH BACON & CHIVES

1 lb potatoes – peeled & grated
3 rashers bacon-rind removed and chopped finely
2 oz fresh chives – chopped
4 fl oz sour cream
2 tbsp extra virgin olive oil

1. *Pre-heat oven to GM4/180°c/350°f*
2. *Wrap the potatoes in a tea towel and squeeze out excess moisture*
3. *Combine all the ingredients (except the oil) in a bowl. Mix thoroughly and season. Divide into 5 and shape into patties*
4. *Heat the oil and cook the patties until lightly browned on both sides*
5. *Bake for 15 mins*

KIDNEY BEAN PATTIES

1 lb potatoes – boiled, peeled & mashed
1 large tin kidney beans, drained
4 slices white bread crusts removed – crumbled
12 tbsp mango chutney

1. *Mix the potato, beans and breadcrumbs together thoroughly. Season*

2. *Divide the mixture into 12 cakes and put a tablespoon of chutney at the centre of each one. Fold the edges over to seal*

3. *Heat some oil in a large pan and fry the patties in batches, turning when golden brown*

POTATO, CHEESE & BACON CAKES

1 lb potatoes - boiled and drained
1 onion – peeled & finely chopped
5 oz bacon – derinded & diced
4 oz cheddar cheese – grated
1½ tbsp vegetable oil

1. *Heat the oil, add the onion and fry gently until soft*

2. *Add the bacon and fry until crisp. Remove it and the onion with a slotted spoon and drain*

3. *Mash the potatoes in with the cheese. Beat in the onion and bacon then season*

4. *Form the mixture into 5 or 6 flattish shapes then fry in the oil and bacon fat for 5 mins each side till crisp and golden*

POTATO PANCAKES WITH CHEESE (2)

1 lb potatoes – peeled, grated, & squeezed to remove excess moisture
4 oz cream cheese
1 egg
1½ tbsp flour
½ small onion – grated
4 oz cheddar – grated

1. *Mix cream cheese, eggs, flour, onion, season – stir in cheddar & grated potatoes*

2. *Form into 3" patties (make sure no excess liquid)*

3. *Fry pancakes until lightly browned on each side*

COURGETTE POTATO CAKES

1 lb potatoes – peeled,boiled & halved
4 oz courgettes – grated
1 oz butter
1 tbsp crème fraîche
1 egg
1 tbsp capers
2 tbsp fresh chives – chopped
1 tbsp flour
1 tbsp vegetable oil

1. *Put potatoes into bowl with grated courgettes and mash with butter & crème fraîche*

2. *Mix in egg, capers,chives and flour then season. Allow to cool*

3. *Shape into cakes. Heat oil and cook for about 6 mins, on one side only. Then put under a pre-heated grill for about 6 mins*

BUBBLE & SQUEAK CAKES (2)

1 lb potatoes – cooked & mashed
5 oz cabbage – shredded
5 oz leek – shredded
3 oz butter
1 tbsp oil

1. *Fry the cabbage & leeks in melted butter for 5 mins*

2. *Mix the potatoes, cabbage, leeks together. Season*

3. *When cool enough to handle, mould into 10 cakes and dust with flour*

4. *Heat the oil and any butter juices in a frying pan & cook the cakes for 5 mins on each side until crisp & golden*

GRATED POTATO CAKES

1 lb potatoes – peeled & boiled
2 oz butter
2 tbsp olive oil

1. Allow the potatoes to cool slightly then grate them. Squeeze to remove excess moisture

2. Mix the butter with the potatoes while they are still warm. Season

3. Heat half the oil in a frying pan, add the potato and spread it over the base of the pan

4. Fry gently for about 10 mins then remove the cake

5. Heat the rest of the oil then return the cake to the pan cooked side uppermost. Fry for about 10 more mins

SPICED SEED CAKE

1 lb potatoes peeled & halved
1 ½ oz butter
1 tsp cumin seeds
1 tsp fennel seeds
½ tsp onion seeds
1" fresh ginger peeled & finely shredded
1 large onion – halved & thinly sliced
1 tsp ground turmeric
1 tsp ground coriander
1 green chilli – deseeded & sliced
1 pack fresh coriander
3 oz frozen peas
Juice of 1 lime
3 oz filo pastry
4 oz spinach
1 small tub greek yogurt
1 tbsp coconut cream
2 tbsp mint sauce

1. Pre-heat oven to GM4/180°c/350°f

2. Boil the potatoes for 10 mins. Drain, cool slightly and dice

3. Meanwhile melt half the butter in a large pan and fry the cumin, fennel and seeds until they start to crackle. Stir in the ginger and onions and cook for 10 mins, stirring frequently until the onion are soft

4. Stir in the turmeric, ground coriander and chilli, cook for 1 minute then add the potatoes and cook, turning them in the spiced mixture until they start to take on the yellow from the turmeric. Remove from the heat. Chop half the coriander leaves and add to the potato mixture along with salt,

peas and lime juice. Stir well and set aside

5. Melt the remaining butter. Line the base and side of a greased loose based cake tin with filo pastry, brushing each sheet generously with melted butter. Build up the pastry so that you have an even layer all over. Allow pastry to hand over the edge of the tin

6. Cook the spinach and squeeze out as much excess juice as possible. Season

7. Put half the potato mixture into the tin and pack down and cover with the spinach

8. Top with the remaining filling then fold over the excess pastry to cover the filling. Brush with more butter and scatter with remaining onion seeds

9. Bake the cake for 40-50 mins until crispy and golden

10. Tip yogurt, coconut cream and remaining coriander into a food processor with the mint sauce, season and whiz until smooth

11. Serve with the cake

ITALIAN POTATO CAKE

1 lb potatoes – peeled & thinly sliced
1 small onion – peeled & thinly sliced
2 oz mozzarella cheese – grated
1 oz parmesan cheese – grated
2 cloves garlic – crushed
1 ½ oz butter
1 tbsp milk

1. Pre-heat oven to GM7/210°c/415°f

2. Melt 1 oz of the butter and gently fry the onion and garlic until the onion starts to soften

3. Use some of the rest of the butter to grease a small ovenproof dish and layer the base with potato, add half the onion and garlic then half of each of the cheeses. Season and add another layer of potatoes, repeat, finishing with a layer of potatoes. Dot with the rest of the butter and pour on the milk

4. Bake for one hour until the potatoes are cooked and the top is golden brown

PERFECT CHIPS

1 lb Maris Piper potatoes
Sunflower or corn oil for cooking

1. Peel the potatoes removing as little skin as possible

2. Cut into chips using a sharp knife (size is up to the individual but chips should be cut to similar size to ensure they cook evenly)

3. Put the chips into a large bowl of cold water, drain and dry thoroughly on kitchen paper or a clean tea towel

4. Heat the oil in a large, deep pan to exactly 190°c

5. Put the chips into a metal wire basket and carefully lower into the oil. Cook for 5 mins then remove

6. Heat the oil to 200°c and cook the chips for a further 3 mins. Remove and put the chips onto kitchen paper to take away the excess oil

POMMES FRITES

1 lb potatoes – peeled
Sufficient corn oil for frying

1. Slice the potatoes and cut into small sticks. Put in a bowl of cold water and refrigerate for 30 mins. Drain and dry the potato sticks thoroughly on kitchen paper

2. Put sufficient oil in a deep fat fryer and heat to 180°c. Put the potato sticks into the chip basket and lower it into the oil, shaking the basket to stop the chips sticking together

3. When the chips start to rise to the surface, remove the basket for 5 mins

4. Meanwhile bring the oil up to 190° and lower the basket into the oil again and cook for 2 mins

5. Remove the basket, turn the fryer off and drain the oil from the basket. When the oil has stopped dripping, give the basket a shake then tip the chips onto kitchen paper and drain on the paper

6. Put the chips in a serving bowl and sprinkle with a little salt

CHUNKY CHIPS

1 lb (floury) potatoes - washed & dried
3 tbsp olive oil

1. Pre-heat oven to GM7/220°c/425°f

2. Pour the oil into a large roasting tin and place in oven

3 Cut the potatoes into chunky chips

4 Tip the potatoes into the tin and coat with the hot oil. Season. Roast for 30 mins turning twice

SPICY NEW POTATO CHIPS

1 lb new potatoes – scrubbed & halved
1 tsp chilli powder
1 tsp paprika
4 tbsp olive oil

1. Pre-heat oven to GM4/180°c/350°f

2. Mix the spices with the oil, season and warm through in a small saucepan

3. Cut the potatoes into the desired shapes and mix with the oil, ensuring the potatoes are totally covered

4. Place the potatoes in a roasting tin and bake for 30 mins stirring occasionally

BIG CHIPS

1 lb (floury) potatoes – washed but not peeled
1 tsp cumin seeds
1 tsp cayenne pepper
1 tsp coarse sea salt
Olive oil for basting

1. Pre-heat oven to GM6/200°c/400°f

2. Cut each potatoes into large chips and brush each with a good coating of olive oil and place in a bowl

3. Sprinkle with the other ingredients tossing to ensure an even spread

4. Grease a roasting tin with olive oil and bake for about 40 mins

CHIPS & VINEGAR SAUCE

1 lb new potatoes – scrubbed
Oil for frying

For the sauce
2 tbsp white wine vinegar
2 tbsp white wine
2 tbsp malt vinegar
3 oz butter cut into small pieces
4 tbsp whipping cream

1. *Cut the potatoes into chips, wash and dry thoroughly. Cook the chips in hot oil for approx. 3-4 mins. Drain. Re-heat the oil and cook the chips again until crispy and golden brown*

2. *Pour the wine and the vinegars into a pan and bring to a simmer. Allow the mixture to reduce by half. Add the cream and allow to reduce slightly. Add the butter a piece at time and whisk each piece into the mixture. Do not allow the sauce to boil. Season*

3. *Pour the sauce onto lightly salted chips*

FRIED SLICED POTATOES

1 lb potatoes – peeled & thinly sliced
4 oz self raising flour
1 oz cornflour
1 tbsp vegetable oil
1 tbsp lemon juice
Plain flour for dusting
Vegetable oil for frying

1. *Dry the potato slices in a clean tea towel*

2. *Sift both flours and seasoning into a bowl. Slowly add 6 fl oz of water, lemon juice and 1 tbsp of oil. Blend to a smooth paste – adding more water if needed*

3. *Dust the potato slices with plain flour and brush with the paste so each slice is coated*

4. *Half fill a deep pan with vegetable oil and heat to 160°c. Carefully lower the sliced potatoes into the pan (in a chip basket) and fry until golden*

5. *Drain on kitchen paper and serve immediately*

GAME CHIPS (OR KETTLE CHIPS)

1 lb potatoes
Vegetable oil

1. *Peel the potatoes and slice them very thinly with a mandolin. Soak the slices in cold water for ½ hour. Drain well and pat dry*

2. *Heat the oil in a deep pan to about 200°c*

3. *Put half the slices in a frying basket and lower slowly into the oil. Move the slices around to prevent sticking and cook for 5 mins or when brown*

4. *Remove and drain on paper towels. Keep warm under a medium grill while you cook the rest*

5. *Season with sea salt and freshly ground pepper (NB it is important to use the best salt and pepper with this dish as it forms a great part of the overall flavour)*

CURRIED POTATO STICKS

1 lb floury potatoes – peeled & cut into small sticks about 2" x ¼" x ¼"
3 cloves garlic – crushed
1 tsp ground cumin
1 tsp coriander seeds
1 tbsp garam masala
Vegetable oil for frying

1. *Soak the potato sticks briefly in a bowl of cold water then drain, put on a tea towel and pat dry*

2. *Heat some of the oil and gently cook the garlic for 3-4 mins*

3. *Remove from heat, add the spices, stir well and set aside*

4. *Heat the oil in a large deep pan to 190°c/ 375°f and cook the sticks for 6-7 mins. Remove and drain on kitchen paper*

5. *Put in a bowl, season and add the spices. Mix well ensuring the spices are evenly coated over the potato sticks*

FRENCH FRIES

1 lb (floury) potatoes – peeled
Sunflower oil for deep frying

1. Cut the potatoes into chips about $^3/_8$" by 2" long
2. Soak in cold water for 5 mins, change the water and soak for 5 more mins. Drain thoroughly
3. Heat the oil in deep fat fryer or large saucepan to 140° and put the chips in the basket, lower into the oil and cook for approx. 5 mins
4. Remove the chips and drain on kitchen paper

CHEATS CHIPS

1 lb (floury) potatoes – peeled & cut into chips
1 tbsp vegetable oil

1. Put the chips into boiling water for 5 mins, drain and leave to cool for 5 mins
2. Pre-heat the oven to GM4/180°c/350°f
3. Put the oil in a polythene bag and add the chips, shake until the chips are evenly coated
4. Put the chips in a lightly greased baking tray and spread evenly. Cook for 20-25 mins

TWICE FRIED GIANT CHIPS

1 lb (floury) potatoes
Sunflower oil for deep frying

1. Peel the potatoes and cut into large chips. Add to a bowl of water and soak for 5 mins. Drain and dry thoroughly with kitchen paper
2. In a large deep saucepan heat the oil to 140° Put the chips in a basket, lower into the oil and cook for approx. 8 mins
3. Remove the chips and drain on kitchen paper
4. Heat the oil to 190° and cook the chips as before for 2 mins. Shake the basket and cook for 5 mins. Remove and drain
5. Serve sprinkled with sea salt

LOW FAT CHIPS

1 lb (floury potatoes) – peeled & cut into ½" chips
Spray on oil for frying

1. Pre-heat oven to GM6/200°c/400°f
2. Put the chips in boiling water for 5 mins. Remove and drain. Place chips on a tea towel and pat dry
3. Dry the saucepan while still warm and put in the chips. Put the lid on and shake vigorously to rough up the edges of the chips
4. Spray a roasting tin with the oil and put the chips it in. Spray again and shake to coat the chips
5. Bake for 15 mins, remove, spray lightly and bake for 10 more mins
6. Remove, drain and add salt and vinegar

LOW FAT CHIPS (2)

1 lb potatoes – peeled and cut into chips
1 pint chicken stock
1½ tbsp sunflower or corn oil

1. Bring the stock to the boil and add the potatoes. Boil for 5 mins, drain thoroughly
2. Pre-heat oven to GM7/220°c/425°f
3. Put the chips and the oil in a food bag and mix well so the chips are evenly coated. Remove the chips and discard any excess oil
4. Lightly grease a roasting tin with oil and bake the chips for about 15 mins, stirring occasionally
5. Remove from the oven add salt and serve

SHOESTRING CHIPS

1 lb potatoes
Sunflower oil for frying

1. Peel the potatoes and using a mandolin cut lengthways into very thin slices. Then cut the slices into very thin strips
2. Put the potatoes into a sieve and wash with cold running water. Drain and dry on kitchen paper

3. Heat the oil in a large deep saucepan (or deep fat fryer) until hot (170°), carefully add the potatoes and fry until golden. This should take about 2-3 mins. Remove the potatoes with a slotted spoon and drain on kitchen paper

2. Heat the oil and place the matches into a wire basket. Lower the basket into the oil and shake the basket until the potatoes are crisp and golden

3. Lift out and place the potatoes on kitchen paper to drain. Sprinkle with salt. Serve hot

GARLIC & LEMON CHIPS

1 lb (floury) potatoes – peeled & cut into thick chips
2 cloves garlic – peeled & halved
1 lemon – cut into 6 wedges
2 tbsp extra virgin olive oil

1. Pre-heat oven to GM6/200°c/400°f
2. Wash the potatoes and pat dry with a towel
3. Arrange the chips, lemon and garlic in a greased roasting tin, season and drizzle on the oil
4. Bake for 20 mins, remove, shake and cook for 20 more mins

POTATO RIBBONS

1 lb (large) potatoes – peeled
Vegetable oil for cooking

1. Dry the potatoes in a clean tea towel
2. Peel each potato into long ribbons using a potato peeler
3. Take a large pan, half fill it with oil and heat until it reaches 180°
4. Lower the ribbons into the oil in a large chip basket – in batches if necessary and fry for 3-4 mins
5. Drain on kitchen paper

STRAW POTATOES

1 lb potatoes – peeled
Oil for frying

1. Cut the potatoes into shapes like wooden matches. Wash them in cold water and dry them on a clean cloth

HERBY CHIPS & EGGS

1 lb (floury) potatoes – cut into chips
3 cloves garlic – crushed
1 tbsp fresh rosemary leaves
2 tbsp extra virgin olive oil
3 eggs

1. Pre-heat oven to GM7/220°c/425°f
2. Mix the garlic, rosemary and oil together
3. Put the chips in a roasting tin and drizzle with the oil mixture. Season and mix well so the chips are coated
4. Cook the chips for 40 mins, shaking occasionally
5. Remove from the oven, make 3 spaces and break an egg into each. Return to the oven and cook until the eggs are set

POTATO CROQUETTES

1 lb potatoes – boiled & mashed
1 egg – beaten
3 oz breadcrumbs
1 oz butter
Fat/oil for frying

1. Mix the butter, seasoning and half the egg into the potato then form into small cylinder shapes about 2" long by ¾" diameter
2. Brush each shape with the rest of the egg, roll in breadcrumbs and fry in hot fat turning occasionally until golden brown. Drain on kitchen paper. Serve hot

POTATO RISSOLES

1 lb potatoes – peeled, boiled & mashed
4 oz channa dhal (lentils)
1 tsp ground coriander
½ tsp ground cumin
½ tsp chilli powder
Breadcrumbs
Oil for frying

1. Soak the channa dhal overnight in a large bowl of water
2. Rinse the dhal then boil in a large volume of water. Simmer until soft then stir and mash. Mix in the spices and salt
3. Form the potato into 'cup' shapes about 2" in diameter. Divide the dhal mixture accordingly and put into the centre of the potato cup. Enclose each one by squeezing the top and roll in breadcrumbs
4. Fry in oil until brown then turn over and repeat. Drain on kitchen paper. Serve hot

POTATO & POLENTA SLICES

1 lb (floury) potatoes – peeled, boiled & mashed
4 oz polenta
4 oz butter
7 oz flour
4 fl oz milk
5 tsp baking powder

1. Pre-heat oven to GM5/190°c/375°f
2. Put the mash in a large bowl and add all the ingredients except the milk. Season and mix together
3. Add the milk gradually and mix manually to form a dough. Knead the dough until smooth
4. Roll the mixture and form it into a large circular shape about ¼ " thick. Trim the edge and cut into 8 slices
5. Place the slices on a tray, score each one with a knife and bake for 25 mins

BASIC MASHED POTATOES

1 lb potatoes – preferably floury
1 knob butter – approx 1 oz

1. Peel the potatoes removing as little peel as is necessary
2. Cut the potatoes into chunks of similar size, about 2" square
3. Meanwhile, fill a large saucepan ¾ full with cold water, stir in a little salt and bring to the boil
4. Carefully put the potato chunks into the water, stir once and wait until it returns to the boil. Reduce to a simmer and cook for about 16 – 20 mins (stick a knife into one of the chunks and if it slides off easily, the potatoes are cooked)
5. Drain the potatoes thoroughly and return to the pan
6. Add a little pepper and the butter (salt is already in)
7. Mash thoroughly using a potato masher

Variations for basic mash

- Use waxy potatoes instead of floury ones
- Boil the potatoes in their skins then peel later
- Wash the skins thoroughly and don't peel at all (you will need to chop them before mashing)
- Add mint and/or peeled garlic whilst cooking
- Add milk as well as butter when mashing
- Add créme fraîche or double cream when mashing
- Steam the potatoes instead of boiling
- Boil them in milk instead of water
- Mash with a hand held mixer (don't use a food processor)
- Use buttermilk or goat's milk instead of butter

MUSTARD MASH

Make basic mashed potatoes and add
1 ½ tbsp wholegrain mustard (or 2 tbsp Dijon)

1. Add the mustard at the same time as the butter and mash

GARLIC MASH

Make basic mashed potatoes and add
1 whole garlic bulb
1 tbsp olive oil

1. *Pre-heat oven to GM4/180°c/350°f*
2. *Remove the papery skin from the bulb, separate the cloves and place on tin foil*
3. *Drizzle with the oil and wrap the foil to form a parcel. Place in the oven (40 mins before you start the mash) and cook for 1 hour*
4. *Squeeze the garlic flesh from the cloves and mash into the potatoes at the same time as the butter*

PARSLEY MASH

Make basic mashed potatoes and add
3 tbsp fresh parsley – finely chopped

1. *Melt the butter in a very small pan and stir in the parsley. Mash into the potatoes*

PESTO MASH

Make basic mashed potatoes and add
3 tbsp olive oil (instead of butter)
1½ tbsp pesto (green or red)

1. *Warm the oil in a small pan and mix in the pesto*
2. *Add the mash at the same stage as the butter*

CHEESEY MASH

Make basic mashed potatoes and add
2-3 oz grated Gruyere (or Parmesan, Lancashire or Mature Cheddar)

1. *Add the grated cheese onto the mash just after adding the butter and mash together*

CREAM CHEESE & CHIVES

Make basic mashed potatoes and add
2-3 tbsp cream cheese
2 tbsp fresh chives – snipped

1. *Add the cheese and chives at the same time as the butter and mash together*

CORIANDER MASH

Make basic mashed potatoes and add
4 tbsp fresh coriander – chopped
2 tbsp extra virgin olive oil

1. *Heat the oil in a small pan until warm, add the coriander, stir and keep warm for 2 mins. Season*
2. *Add to the mash with the butter*

SPICY FRIED MASH

1 lb potatoes – peeled, chopped, boiled & drained
2 tsp red curry paste
¼ pint single cream
2 tsp fresh ginger
1 tbsp butter
1 tsp vegetable oil

1. *Put the potatoes in a pan, season, add the ginger and mash together*
2. *Melt half the butter in a pan and add the potatoes. Flatten and fry until lightly browned. Remove; add the rest of the butter, then fry the other side. Remove and put on a plate. Keep warm*
3. *Put the cream into a small pan, add the curry paste, stir and heat until hot but not boiling. Pour over the potatoes and serve*

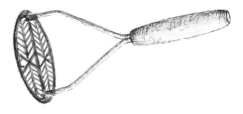

SAFFRON MASH

1 lb potatoes – preferably floury
1 or 2 strands of saffron
1 knob butter – approx 1 oz

1. *Add the strands of saffron to the boiling water then follow the recipe for 'basic mashed potatoe'*

   (for a stronger flavour, boil an additional equal amount of saffron in a little milk and add to the mash)

OLIVE OIL MASH

1 lb potatoes – preferably floury
4 tbsp extra virgin olive oil (or garlic infused olive oil)

1. *Follow the recipé for 'basic mashed potatoes' but when you get to instruction no. 6, add the oil instead of butter*

BACON & LEEK MASH

1 lb potatoes – peeled, boiled & mashed
3 rashers bacon – derinded, grilled & chopped into small pieces
1 leek – trimmed & chopped
3 fl oz milk
1 tbsp olive oil

1. *Heat the oil and fry the leek until browned*
2. *Season the mash while still hot and beat in all the other ingredients*

PUMPKIN MASH

1 lb potatoes – peeled & cut into chunks
2 lbs pumpkin – peeled & diced
1 tbsp crème fraiche
1 oz butter

1. *Boil the potatoes for 10 mins*
2. *Add the pumpkin and boil for 10 more mins*
3. *Drain thoroughly then add the butter and crème fraiche. Season and mash*

LUXURY CELERIAC MASH

1 lb potatoes – boiled & mashed
1 lb celeriac – peeled & cubed
5 fl oz olive oil
2 fl oz lemon juice
2 tbsp fresh parsley – chopped
5 fl oz milk

1. *Put the oil, milk and lemon juice in a screw top jar and shake vigorously. Season and put into a saucepan. Add the celeriac, bring to the boil and simmer for 15 mins*
2. *Mash, drain off any excess liquid and add the parsley. Season and mix into the potato mash*

MASCARPONE CHIVE MASH

1 lb potatoes – peeled, boiled, drained & mashed
7 oz mascarpone cheese
1 bunch of chives

1. *Add the cheese & chives to the potatoes and mix well*

PARSNIP MASH

1 lb floury potatoes – peeled & cut into chunks
2 parsnips – peeled & cut into chunks
4 fl oz milk
2 oz butter
Pinch of nutmeg

1. *Boil the potatoes for 5 mins*
2. *Add the parsnips and boil for 15 more mins*
3. *Drain thoroughly, return to the warm pan and add the butter*
4. *Wait until the butter has melted, season, add the nutmeg and milk then mash until smooth and creamy*

POTATO PUFFS

1 lb potatoes – boiled & mashed
2 oz butter
2 eggs – beaten
1 ½ oz flour
Vegetable oil for deep frying

1. Beat half the butter into the mash
2. Melt the rest of the butter in a saucepan and add 4 fl oz of water. Bring to the boil, remove from heat and beat in the flour. Leave to cool
3. Beat in the eggs, some salt then add the mash
4. Heat the oil to 190°c in a deep fat fryer and put the mixture in one spoonful at a time. Cook for 5 mins. Remove with a slotted spoon and drain on kitchen paper. Serve hot

CRISPY POTATO

1 lb potato – boiled & mashed
1 oz butter
1 tbsp milk
1 egg – beaten

1. Pre-heat oven to GM6/200°c/400°f
2. Add the butter, milk and egg to the mash and whisk until smooth
3. Grease a baking tray and spread the mixture out and bake for 8 mins until crispy

MASHED POTATOES AND CELERIAC

1 lb potatoes – peeled & cut into chunks
1 lb celeriac – peeled & cut into ½ inch cubes
2 oz butter
2 fl oz double cream

1. Put the celeriac & potatoes in the same saucepan & boil for 20 mins. Drain
2. Mash the two together and add the cream, butter & seasoning

RICH PANNED POTATOES

1 lb potatoes – boiled & mashed
2 rashers bacon – rind removed & chopped finely
1 onion – peeled & chopped
2 egg yolks
Dripping or bacon fat or lard for frying

1. Heat a small amount of fat in pan & cook the bacon & onion gently for 5 mins
2. Beat the egg yolks into the mashed potato & mix in the onion & bacon. Season
3. Heat some more fat in a frying pan and put the potato mixture into the pan and flatten to about ½ inch thickness. Divide into separate pieces and fry until well browned underneath. Turn over and brown the other side

5 VEG MASH

1 lb potatoes – peeled & chopped
2 carrots – peeled & chopped
2 parsnips – peeled & chopped
2 celeriac bulbs – peeled & chopped
2 swedes – peeled & chopped
4 oz butter
2 fl oz milk
Pinch of ground nutmeg

1. Boil the potatoes in one pan and all the other vegetables in another, larger pan. Drain
2. Melt the butter in the larger pan, add the milk, nutmeg and pepper
3. Add all the vegetables and mash thoroughly

SNOW POTATOES

1 lb potatoes – peeled, boiled & mashed
¼ pint milk
1 oz butter

1. Mash the potatoes again very finely
2. Heat the milk and butter in a saucepan. When hot (not boiling) add the potatoes and beat until you get a very light consistency. Season

CELERIAC & MUSTARD MASH

1 lb potatoes – peeled, boiled & mashed
1 celeriac – peeled & cut into chunks
Juice of ½ lemon
2 tbsp wholegrain mustard
1½ tbsp double cream

1. *Boil the celeriac in lightly salted water with the lemon juice for 15 mins. Drain*
2. *Add the celeriac to the potatoes and mix well with the mustard and cream. Season*

POTATO & CHEESE BALLS

1 lb potatoes – boiled & mashed
4 oz cheddar cheese – grated
2 eggs – beaten
3 oz breadcrumbs

1. *Pre-heat oven to GM9/220°c/425°f*
2. *Add the cheese and most of the egg to the mash. Season and mix well*
3. *Turn on to a floured board and shape into balls. Brush with the egg and dip in crumbs*
4. *Place on a baking tray and bake in the oven for 15 mins*

CHEESE & HAM CROQUETTES

1 lb potatoes – boiled & mashed
4 oz cheddar cheese – grated
6 oz cooked ham – diced
1 tbsp parsley – chopped
1 egg – beaten
Plain flour for dipping
Breadcrumbs

1. *Mix the cheese, ham and parsley into the mash and season. Mould into 5 cylinder shapes*
2. *Roll each shape in the flour, brush with the egg then roll in breadcrumbs*
3. *Fry gently in vegetable oil until brown all over and hot in the middle*

SAVOURY MASH

1 lb potatoes – boiled & mashed
¼ lb Wensleydale cheese – crumbled
1 clove garlic – crushed
6 oz crème fraiche
2 oz butter

1. *Beat and mash the potatoes in the pan again until you have a purée consistency*
2. *Add seasoning, garlic, butter and crème fraiche. Heat very gently for 1 minute, stirring occasionally*
3. *Add the cheese, stir consistently for a few mins until the cheese has melted and a rubbery consistency is reached*

BASIC ROAST POTATOES

1lb (floury) potatoes - peeled
4 oz goose fat

1. *Cut the potatoes into even sized chunks*
2. *Put the potatoes in boiling water for 5 mins. Drain*
3. *Meanwhile pre-heat oven to GM7/220°c/425°f.*
4. *Return the potatoes to the (warm) pan and put a lid on it. Shake the pan vigorously so the potatoes bash against the sides – in order to rough up the edges*
5. *Put the goose fat in a roasting tin and place in the oven until the fat is very hot*
6. *Remove the tin and carefully add the potatoes, ensuring each one is coated*
4. *Roast for about 25 mins then remove and turn the potatoes. Roast for about 25 mins more*

SAFFRON ROASTIES

1 lb (floury) potatoes – peeled & cubed
1 tsp saffron stamens – crushed to a powder
1 tbsp olive oil

1. *Put the potatoes in a saucepan, sprinkle with salt and half the saffron powder. Add just enough water to cover the potatoes. Cover and simmer for 5 mins*
2. *Drain the water from the pan leaving the potatoes in it*

3. *Clasp the lid to the pan and shake the pan so that the potatoes bash from side to side to create a fluffy surface*

4. *Pre-heat oven to GM7/220°c/425°f*

5. *Mix the oil with the remaining saffron powder and put into a small roasting tin. Heat on a stove*

6. *Carefully add the potatoes and mix with the oil, ensuring the potatoes are completely coated*

7. *Bake for 45 mins*

HONEY ROASTED VEGETABLES

1 lb potatoes – peeled & cut into chunks
1 lb parsnips – peeled & cut into chunks
1 lb celeriac – peeled & cut into chunks
10 cloves garlic – papery skin removed
4 red onions – peeled & roughly chopped
3 tbsp runny honey
3 tbsp fresh thyme – chopped
4 tbsp extra virgin olive oil

1. *Pre-heat oven to GM6/200°c/400°f*

2. *Mix the potato, parsnips and celeriac together and put into a large roasting tin. Add the unpeeled garlic, toss with the oil and season. Bake for 30 mins*

3. *Remove, add the onions, mix well and bake for 25 more mins*

4. *Remove, pour in the honey, add the thyme and bake for 5 more mins. Check seasoning and serve hot*

ROASTED NEW POTATOES

1 lb new potatoes – scrubbed & quartered
6 cloves garlic – papery skin removed
3 sprigs rosemary
4 tbsp extra virgin olive oil

1. *Pre-heat oven to GM6/200°c/400°f*

2. *Put the potatoes in a roasting tin and add the oil, mix until coated, season and add the garlic and rosemary*

3. *Cook for about 30 mins, stirring once, until golden brown*

CURRIED ROAST POTATOES

1 lb (waxy) potatoes - peeled & cubed
2 tsp cumin seeds
2 tsp coriander seeds
1 tsp turmeric
1 tsp black mustard seeds
1 tsp chilli powder
2 cloves garlic – crushed
3 oz butter

1. *Pre-heat oven to GM6/200°c/400°f*

2. *Grind the cumin seeds and coriander seeds together in a pestle & mortar*

3. *Melt the butter slowly in a roasting tin and add the ground seeds and the turmeric, mustard seeds, garlic and chilli powder. Stir well. Place in the oven for 5 mins*

4. *Remove the tin and add the potatoes. Mix well so the potatoes are coated. Return to the oven and cook for 20-25 mins. Serve hot*

ROASTED POTATOES & SPROUTS

1 lb small new potatoes – scrubbed & halved
1 lb small Brussels sprouts – trimmed & washed
5 tbsp balsamic vinegar
2 tbsp runny honey
4 tbsp oil
Sprigs of fresh rosemary

1. *Pre-heat oven to GM5/190°c/375°f*

2. *Boil the sprouts and potatoes for 5 mins in the same pan. Drain and mix together*

3. *Blend the vinegar, honey and oil together and pour over the potatoes and sprouts. Add the rosemary, season and toss the mixture*

4. *Place the mixture on a roasting tray and cook for 20 mins. Serve hot*

SURPRISE POTATO

1 lb potatoes
¼ lb cooked sausage – chopped accordingly

1. *Roast the potatoes normally (see Roasted potatoes)*

2. *When done, cut the end of each potato, scoop out some of the centre and fill with the cooked sausage then replace the end. Serve hot*

ROASTED NEW POTATOES WITH GARLIC & ROSEMARY

1 lb new potatoes – scrubbed & halved
3 cloves garlic – crushed
3 tbsp olive oil
1 sprig fresh rosemary – chopped

1. Boil the potatoes for 10 mins and drain
2. Pre-heat oven to GM6/200°c/400°f
3. Mix the oil and garlic together. Toss with the potatoes
4. Place the potatoes on a lightly oiled roasting tray and sprinkle with the rosemary and seasoning
5. Roast for 25 mins. Serve hot

ROASTED SPICY POTATOES

1 lb potatoes – peeled & cut into chunks
2 cloves garlic – crushed
½ tsp cayenne pepper
¼ tsp chinese 5 spice
2 tbsp olive oil

1. Boil the potatoes for 10 mins. Drain and cool slightly
2. Pre-heat oven to GM6/200°c/400°f
3. Mix the garlic with the olive oil and brush over the potatoes until coated. Pour the remaining oil into a roasting tray and add the potatoes
4. Sprinkle with the cayenne, 5-spice and salt, put the tray in the oven and roast for 40 mins stirring occasionally

ROASTED VEGETABLES

1 lb potatoes – peeled & chopped
½ lb sweet potatoes – peeled & chopped
½ lb celeriac – peeled & chopped
½ lb shallots – peeled
3 cloves garlic crushed
1 tbsp fresh rosemary – chopped
1 tbsp fresh thyme – chopped
2 tbsp olive oil

1. Pre-heat oven to GM6/200°c/400°f
2. Put all the ingredients in a bowl, season and mix together manually so all the vegetables are covered with oil
3. Put on a baking tray and cook for 40 mins

FANNED ROAST POTATOES

1 lb potatoes – peeled
2 fl oz sunflower oil

1. Pre-heat oven to GM5/190°c/475°f
2. Take a sharp knife and make deep cuts into each potato about 5mm apart and about ¾ of the way into the potato
3. Boil a pan of salted water and add the potatoes, simmer for 5 mins and drain
4. Heat the oil in the oven in a small roasting pan and add the potatoes with the cuts facing upwards. Spoon oil over the potatoes and roast for 1 hour basting occasionally
5. Turn oven up to GM7/210°c/425°f and roast for 15 more mins

ROASTIES WITH HERBS

1 lb (floury) potatoes – peeled, par boiled for 5 mins, drained & chopped
1 tbsp fresh thyme – chopped
1 tbsp fresh rosemary – chopped
1 tbsp sea salt
2 tbsp olive oil

1. Pre-heat the oven to GM5/190°c/375°f
2. Drain the potatoes. Return to the pan, put the lid on and shake vigorously
3. Put the oil in a roasting tin and heat in the oven for 5 mins
4. Make cuts in each potato and put in the roasting tin. Coat with oil and sprinkle with the herbs and salt. Roast for 45 mins turning occasionally

HONEY GLAZED ROASTIES

1 lb floury potatoes – peeled & cut into chunks
3 fl oz runny honey
2 oz butter
3 tbsp vegetable oil

1. *Pre-heat oven to GM4/180°c/350°f*
2. *Boil the potatoes for 5 mins. Drain thoroughly*
3. *Put the potatoes on a roasting tray, coat with the oil and dab with the butter. Roast for 30 mins*
4. *Remove the tray, baste the potatoes and spoon the honey on top. Roast for 20 more mins*

MUSTARD ROASTIES

1 lb (floury) potatoes – peeled & cut into chunks
6 tbsp olive oil
3 tbsp wholegrain mustard

1. *Pre-heat oven to GM5/190°c/375°f*
2. *Boil the potatoes for about 10 mins and drain*
3. *Return the potatoes to the pan and put a lid on. Shake the potato so the edges of the potato break up a little*
4. *Pour in the half the oil, mix well and put the potatoes on a baking tray and bake for 40 mins*
5. *Mix the remaining oil with the mustard and mix with the potatoes so they are evenly coated. Cook for 5 more mins*

ROAST BEETROOT & POTATOES

1 lb potatoes – peeled & sliced
1 lb beetroot – peeled & sliced
5 cloves garlic
2 tbsp fresh rosemary
2 tbsp olive oil

1. *Pre-heat oven to GM6/200°c/400°f.*
2. *Put the vegetables in a casserole dish, season and sprinkle with the rosemary.*
3. *Drizzle over the oil and mix well.*
4. *Bake for about 30 mins*

ROASTED POTAOTES WITH BALSAMIC VINEGAR

1 lb new potatoes – scrubbed & halved
8 small white onions – peeled
4 tbsp balsamic vinegar
1 oz butter

1. *Pre-heat oven to GM4/180°c/350°f*
2. *Melt the butter and mix with the vinegar*
3. *Put the potatoes and onions in a baking dish in which they just fit. Season. Pour over the vinegar and butter and toss gently to coat*
4. *Cover with foil and bake for 1 hour stirring every 15 mins. Serve hot*

ROAST NEW POTATOES WITH HERBS

1 lb new potatoes – scrubbed & halved
3 oz full fat butter
2 tbsp fresh rosemary – chopped
2 tbsp thyme – chopped

1. *Pre-heat oven to GM6/200°c/400°f*
2. *Put enough tin foil in a roasting tin to make a parcel. Add the potatoes and dot with the butter*
3. *Sprinkle with the herbs, season and fold the tin foil over all sides*
4. *Bake for 30-40 mins*

ROASTED NEW POTATOES WITH ANCHOVIES

1 lb new potatoes – scrubbed & halved
1 small tin anchovies – drained & chopped
3 cloves garlic – unpeeled
2 sprigs thyme
2 tbsp extra virgin olive oil

1. *Pre-heat oven to GM6/200°c/400°f*
2. *Place all the ingredients on a roasting tray ensuring the potatoes are coated with oil*
3. *Roast for 35 mins. Season with pepper*

BACON & SAGE ROASTIES

1 lb (new) potatoes – scrubbed
8 rashers bacon – rindless
1 bunch sage
2 tbsps olive oil

1. *Pre-heat oven to GM6/200°c/400°f*
2. *Cut rashers in half lengthways. Wrap one around each potato with half a sage leaf underneath and secure with a cocktail stick*
3. *Heat the olive oil in a roasting tin for 2 mins. Add the potatoes, coat with oil and roast for 40 mins*

ROASTIES WITH GARLIC & LEMON

1 lb potatoes – halved and par boiled for 10 mins and drained
3 small parsnips - washed & halved lengthways
½ lemon – sliced
3 cloves garlic - peeled & sliced
3 tbsp lard

1. *Pre-heat oven to GM7/220°c/425°f*
2. *Melt the lard and put into a roasting tin. Add the potatoes and mix well. Put in the oven*
3. *After 20 mins remove and add the parsnips, garlic and lemon. Mix well and cook for a further 15 mins*

NEW POTATOES ROASTED WITH ROSEMARY

1 lb (new) potatoes – scrubbed & halved
2½ tbsp rosemary leaves – chopped
3 tbsps extra virgin olive oil

1. *Pre-heat oven to GM8/230°c/450°f*
2. *Toss the potatoes with the olive oil and rosemary until each potato is evenly covered. Season*
3. *Put into a lightly greased baking tray in a single layer and bake for 35 mins, shaking occasionally to turn the potatoes*

POTATOES & PARSNIPS WITH CARAWAY

1 lb potatoes – peeled, halved & par boiled
1 lb parsnips – peeled, halved & par boiled
2 tbsp caraway seeds
Sunflower oil

1. *Pre-heat oven to GM6/200°c/400°f*
2. *Oil a roasting tin and heat in the oven*
3. *Add all the vegetables, mix with extra oil and sprinkle with the caraway seeds*
4. *Roast for 30 mins turning occasionally*

GOLDEN POTATOES

1 lb (floury) potatoes – peeled & cubed
3 tbsp olive oil
4 sprigs fresh thyme

1. *Pre-heat oven to GM7/220°c/425°f*
2. *Put the potatoes in a bowl with the oil and thyme. Mix well*
3. *Put the contents of the bowl in a roasting tin and bake for 30 mins*
4. *Remove from the oven, shake the tin and season. Cook for 15 more mins*

POTATO & ONION ROAST

1 lb potatoes – peeled & cut into wedges
1 lb red onions – peeled & cut into wedges
4 tbsp extra virgin olive oil
2 tbsp lemon juice
3 tbsp fresh rosemary
3 tbsp fresh oregano

1. *Pre-heat oven to GM7/200°c/425°f*
2. *Put the potatoes and onion in a roasting tin and mix*
3. *Put the rest of the ingredients in a screw top jar, season and shake vigorously to mix*
4. *Pour onto the potatoes and onions, mix well, cover and bake for 1 hour 30 mins*

SEMOLINA ROASTIES

1 lb (floury) potatoes – peeled & cut into small chunks
2 tbsp semolina
4 oz goose fat or lard

1. Pre-heat oven to GM7/200°c/425°f
2. Boil the potatoes for 10 mins and drain
3. Put the fat in a roasting tin and put it in the oven
4. Return the potatoes to the pan and put a lid on. Shake to roughen the edges of the potatoes then sprinkle with the semolina. Shake again to coat
5. Put the potatoes into the roasting tin ensuring that each one is coated with fat. Bake for 45 mins, turning occasionally
6. Remove from the oven, drain off any liquid and bake for 5 more mins

GARLIC ROASTIES

1 lb (floury) potatoes – peeled & cut into chunks
1 head of garlic – papery skin removed & split up
3 sprigs rosemary – leaves removed
Olive oil for roasting

1. Pre-heat oven to GM6/200°c/400°f
2. Boil the potatoes for 10 mins and drain thoroughly
3. Heat the oil in a small roasting tin in the oven. Add the potatoes and sprinkle with the garlic. Mix well. Bake in the oven for 40 mins
4. Remove, season and sprinkle with the rosemary leaves. Mix and bake for 5 more mins
5. Remove and take out the garlic cloves. Squeeze out the flesh and mix some (or all) with the potatoes before serving

GARLIC ROASTIES (2)

1 lb new potatoes – scrubbed, halved & drained
3 cloves garlic – unpeeled
3 tbsp extra virgin olive oil

1. Pre-heat oven to GM5/170°c/435°f
2. Place the potatoes and garlic in an ovenproof dish. Sprinkle with salt , pour on the oil and mix so that that potatoes are covered

3. Bake for 30 mins
4. Remove and squeeze the garlic pulp from the cloves onto the potatoes and mix well. Bake for 10 more mins

BRAISED BAKED POTATOES

1 lb potatoes (waxy) peeled & cut into ¼" slices
6 oz tomatoes – chopped
1 onion – peeled & chopped
½ tsp fresh basil – chopped
½ tsp fresh parsley – chopped
½ tsp chives – chopped
2 tbsp extra virgin olive oil

1. Pre-heat oven to GM7/220°c/425°f
2. Mix all the ingredients together in a roasting pan and season. Bake for 1 hour. Serve hot

HONEY ROASTED POTATOES

1 lb potatoes – peeled & cut into chunks
2oz butter
2 tbsp runny honey

1. Put the potatoes into boiling water for 5 mins. Remove, drain and put into a lightly greased roasting tin
2. Pre-heat oven to GM6/200°c/400°f
3. Slowly melt the butter in a pan, mix with the honey. Pour over the potatoes ensuring the potatoes are evenly coated. Bake for 50-60 mins until crisp and brown. Baste at least twice

ROSEMARY POTATOES

1 lb potatoes – peeled & cubed
6 oz shallots – peeled
2 tbsp fresh rosemary sprigs
2 oz butter
2 tbsp olive oil
2 tsp sea salt

1. Boil potatoes for 5 mins & drain
2. Heat the oven to GM6/200°c/400°f and heat the butter & oil in a roasting tray in the oven
3. Add the potatoes & shallots, coat with oil & sprinkle with 1 tsp salt & half the rosemary. Cook for ½ hour
4. Remove from tin & add the rest of the salt & rosemary

ROSTI POTATOES

1 lb potatoes – peeled
1 small onion – peeled & grated
1 egg beaten
2 oz butter

1. Cut the potatoes into half and boil for 5 mins. Drain and leave to cool
2. Grate the potatoes into a bowl and add the grated onion. Stir in the beaten egg and season
3. Heat the butter in a frying pan and add the mixture, spreading it over the pan. Cook over a medium heat for about 15 mins, turning occasionally until lightly browned throughout and crisp
4. Press the potato together to form a pancake, cook for a further 2-3 mins on each side

ROSTI & TUNA OMELETTE

1 lb potatoes – peeled
1 small can of tuna – drained
1 small tin of sweetcorn – drained
4 eggs – beaten
1 onion – peeled & chopped
2 oz butter

1. Boil the potatoes for 5 mins, drain & cool in cold water. Then grate them, season & put to one side
2. Cook the onion in half of the butter
3. Mix the onion, into the potato and add the tuna, sweetcorn & eggs. Season
4. Heat a small amount of oil in a large frying pan add the mixture & cook on a medium heat until the underside is golden
5. Dot with the remaining butter and cook under a pre-heated grill until golden

LEEK ROSTI

1 lb potatoes
1 leek – finely shredded
1 tbsp vegetable oil

1. Peel & grate the potatoes

2. Heat the oil and fry the potatoes & leeks together for about 3 mins then press the mixture down
3. Reduce the heat & cook until it starts to turn golden
4. Invert the rosti using a plate, slide it back into the pan and cook the other side until golden. Season again

APPLE ROSTI

1 lb potatoes – peeled, boiled for 5 mins &drained
2 eating apples – peeled & cored
1 tbsp whole grain mustard
2 oz butter

1. Allow the potatoes to go cold then grate them, squeezing them to remove excess liquid and put them in a bowl
2. Grate the apples and add to the potatoes, add the mustard, season and mix-well
3. Pre-heat the grill
4. Melt half the butter in a frying pan and add the rosti, pressing down until almost flat. Fry gently until the base starts to brown
5. Dot the top with the rest of the butter and grill until the top is also browned

ROSTI POTATO PIE

1 lb potatoes – peeled & grated
2 onions – peeled & grated
¼ lb mushrooms – sliced
¼ lb green beans – trimmed & boiled
1 large tin chopped tomatoes
2 eggs beaten
1 tbsp Worcester Sauce

1. Pre-heat oven to GM6/200°c/400°f
2. Mix the potatoes with the onions then beat in the eggs
3. Put half the mixture in the bottom of a pie dish and season well
4. Add the mushrooms and beans
5. Mix the tomatoes with the Worcester sauce and pour onto the vegetables. Season
6. Add the rest of the potato mixture and bake for 45 mins

SOUR CREAM ROSTI

1 lb potatoes – peeled, boiled & drained
¼ lb cheddar cheese – grated
1 bunch spring onions – trimmed and chopped
10 fl oz sour cream
1 tsp paprika

1. *Allow the potatoes to cool then grate and place in a mixing bowl*
2. *Pre-heat oven to GM4/180°c/350°f*
3. *Season the potatoes, sprinkle with paprika and manually mix in the onions and half the cheese*
4. *Place in the mixture in a greased ovenproof dish, pour on the cream, sprinkle with the remaining cheese and bake for 30 mins*

BACON ROSTI

1 lb potatoes
4 oz bacon – chopped
1 onion – chopped
3 oz sweetcorn
1 clove garlic – crushed
2 tbsp fresh chives – chopped
2 tbsp olive oil

1. *Boil the potatoes in their skins for 10 mins. Drain and leave to cool then peel and grate*
2. *Fry the bacon, onion and garlic until the onion starts to soften*
3. *Mix in the other ingredients and season. Gently fry for 10 mins then turn over and repeat until browned on both sides*

CHINESE ROSTI

1 lb potatoes – boiled unpeeled for 10 mins & drained
1½" ginger – peeled & grated
8 spring onions – trimmed & shredded
4 tbsp fresh coriander – chopped
2 tbsp olive oil

1. *Allow the potatoes to cool slightly then peel. Grate the potatoes and squeeze to remove the excess liquid. Place in a mixing bowl*

2. *Add the ginger, onions, coriander, season and mix well. Form into 5 or 6 separate pieces*
3. *Heat the oil in a frying pan and cook each rosti until golden brown all over*

LEEK ROSTI (2)

1 lb potatoes - peeled & grated
2 leek – finely shredded
1 tbsp olive oil

1. *Heat the oil and fry the potatoes & leeks together for about 3 mins then press the mixture down*
2. *Reduce the heat & cook on one side for about 10 mins until it starts to turn golden*
3. *Invert the rosti using a plate, slide it back into the pan and cook the other side for about 10 mins until golden. Season again*

ROSTI CRAB CAKES

1 lb (waxy) potatoes
1 lb dressed crab
5 spring onions – peeled & finely chopped
2 tbsp lime juice
2 tbsp grated zest of line
2 tsp parsley – finely chopped
2 tsp capers – chopped
1 tsp cayenne pepper
Olive oil for cooking

1. *Boil the potatoes with skins on for 10 mins Drain and allow to cool. Peel then grate the potatoes*
2. *Mix all the ingredients together in a large bowl. Season*
3. *Divide the mixture into heaps of 2 tablespoons each and mould into shapes. Put on a tray and cover with cling film and refrigerate for 2 hours*
4. *Fry in hot oil for 3 mins on each side until lightly browned*
5. *Drain on kitchen paper*

POTATO & PARSNIP ROSTI

1 lb potatoes – boiled, unpeeled until tender
1 lb parsnips – boiled, unpeeled until tender
1 large onion – peeled & finely chopped
4 tbsp goose fat

1. Drain the potatoes and parsnips and allow to cool slightly then peel & grate them
2. Heat the oven to GM7/220°c/425°f
3. Heat 1 tbsp of fat in a pan and fry the onion until soft. Mix with the potatoes and parsnips in a bowl and season
4. Add 1 tbsp of fat to the pan, add the mixture and press down. Add another tbsp of fat and bake in the oven for 10 mins
5. Remove and turn the cake upside down. Add the remaining fat to the pan and put the cake back in the pan and cook for 5 mins. Return to the oven for 15 mins. Remove, cut into wedges and serve

BACON & CHEESE ROSTI

1 lb floury potatoes
3 oz cheddar cheese – crumbled
3 oz bacon – derinded & chopped
1 onion – peeled & sliced
4 sage leaves
2 tbsp oil

1. Boil the potatoes in their skins for 20 mins. Drain and allow to cool. Peel and grate gently squeezing out any excess liquid
2. Heat 1 tbsp of oil and fry the onion and bacon for 5 mins
3. Add the sage, stir and cook for 1 more minute
4. Mix the contents of the pan into the potato and season
5. Heat the rest of the oil and put half the rosti in the pan, add the cheese, season then add the rest of the potato gently pressing down the rosti
6. Cook for about 10 mins on each side until lightly browned

CURRIED ROSTI WITH EGGS

1 lb floury potatoes – peeled & grated
1 tbsp balti curry powder
2 tbsp vegetable oil
3 eggs

1. Pre-heat oven to GM6/200°c/400°f
2. Squeeze the potatoes to remove excess liquid, then add the curry powder. Season
3. Heat half the oil and gently fry the rosti for 10 mins
4. Take the rosti out of the pan, add the rest of the oil and heat it. Return the rosti, upside down, to the pan and fry until browned
5. Meanwhile poach the eggs and put onto the cooked rosti – breaking each one so the egg runs onto the rosti

WEDGES

1 lb (floury) potatoes – washed thoroughly
Olive oil for brushing

1. Pre-heat the oven to GM6/200°c/400°f
2. Cut each potato in half lengthways and then into wedge shapes
3. Boil the wedges for 5 mins and drain thoroughly
4. Place the wedges on lightly oiled baking try and brush with oil. Bake for 25–30 mins, turning once

CHEESE & BACON WEDGES

1 lb (floury) potatoes – cooked as in 'jacket potatoes'
3 tbsp blue cheese dressing
4 oz bacon – rind removed & chopped
4 spring onions – finely chopped

1. Cut each potato into wedges
2. Scoop out the top half of each of each wedge and spread with the dressing
3. Sprinkle with spring onion and bacon and put under a hot grill for 4-5 mins. Serve hot

QUICK POTATO WEDGES WITH CHEESE & BEANS

1 lb potatoes – washed but not peeled
1 large tin baked beans
4 oz cheddar cheese – grated

1. Prick the potatoes all over and cook in a microwave on full power for 5 mins. Turn the potatoes over and cook for 5 more mins. Cut into wedges

2. Arrange the wedges in a microwave proof bowl, season and pour the baked beans on top and sprinkle with the cheese. Microwave for 4-5 mins until the potatoes are fully cooked and the cheese melted

SALT AND VINEGAR WEDGES

1 lb new potatoes – scrubbed & cut into 6 or 8 wedges
3 tbsp olive oil
3 tbsp balsamic vinegar

1. Pre-heat the oven to GM6/200°c/400°f
2. Brush a little oil on the bottom of a roasting tin and add the potato wedges. Pour the rest of the oil over the top and season generously
3. Cook for 45 mins, turning occasionally
4. Add the balsamic vinegar, stir and cook for 5 more mins
3. Serve sprinkled with salt

WEDGES WITH DILL CREAM

1 lb (floury) potatoes – scrubbed & cut into wedges
4 fl oz sour cream
2 tbsp fresh dill – finely chopped
2 tbsp olive oil

1. Pre-heat oven to GM6/200°c/400°f
2. Mix the dill and the cream, cover with cling film and put in the fridge
3. Put the oil and potatoes in a roasting tin and mix well. Season and cook for 45 mins
4. Serve covered with the dill cream

POTATO WEDGES WITH SAGE & ONION

1 lb potatoes – peeled & diced
4 eggs – beaten
1 onion – peeled & chopped
5 tbsp fresh parsley – finely chopped
2 tbsp sage – finely chopped
4 tbsp olive oil

1. Heat half the oil in a non-stick pan and gently fry the potatoes for 15-18 mins, stirring frequently
2. Add the onion and cook for 8-10 mins, remove pan from heat
3. Add the parsley and sage to the egg mixture, season and mix well
4. Add the potato and onion to the egg and herbs and stir well. Wipe the pan clean
5. Pre-heat the grill
6. Add the rest of the oil and when hot add the potato mixture and spread evenly. Fry for about 10 mins or until the bottom is set
7. Place the pan under the grill and cook for about 5 mins until the top is browned and set. Remove from the heat, transfer to a board and all to cool slightly before cutting into wedges

MEXICAN WEDGES

1 lb potatoes – washed & cut into wedges
8 rashers bacon – fat removed & roughly chopped
2 avocados – peeled, stoned & cut into wedges
6 jalapeno peppers – halved
3 oz cheese – grated
3 tbsp sour cream
2 tbsp extra virgin olive oil

1. Pre heat oven to GM7/220°c/400°f
2. Mix the potatoes with the oil until evenly coated
3. Put the potatoes in a small roasting tin and add the bacon. Season and bake for 30 mins
4. Remove, add the avocado, peppers and cheese. Allow the heat to melt the cheese
5. Transfer to a large bowl. Put the sour cream in the middle

POTATO WEDGES WITH TUNA & TOMATOES

1 lb (floury) potatoes – cut into wedges
1 small tin tuna – drained
2 large tins chopped tomatoes
1 onion – peeled and finely sliced
3 tbsp olive oil
Chilli sauce (or Tabasco) to taste

1. Pre-heat oven to GM7/200°c/425°f
2. Mix the potatoes with 2 tbsp of the oil until fully coated. Bake for 30 mins
3. Meanwhile heat the rest of the oil in a small pan and fry the onion until soft
4. Add the tuna and tomatoes, season and stir well
5. Add your chosen chilli sauce to taste – stir and cook until heated through
6. Put the potatoes in a large dish, season and pour the sauce on. Mix well and serve

PAPRIKA POTATO WEDGES

1 lb baking potatoes – cut into wedges, rinsed and dried
3 tbsp parmesan cheese - grated
1½ tsp paprika
4 tbsp extra virgin olive oil

1. Pre-heat oven to GM6/200°c/400°f
2. Put the potatoes in a large bowl, pour the oil in and mix thoroughly until coated
3. Take a large plastic bag, add paprika and the cheese, season and shake to mix
4. Add the potatoes to the bag and mix until covered
5. Put the potatoes, skin side down on a roasting tray and bake for 45 mins

POTATO WEDGES WITH BACON

1 lb (waxy) potatoes – washed & pricked
¼ lb bacon – rind removed & cut into pieces
¼ lb mozzarella – cut into small pieces
1 tbsp olive oil

1. Pre-heat oven to GM6/200°c/400°f and bake the potatoes on a roasting tray for 1 hour
2. Remove and cut each potato into wedge shapes
3. In a small deep pan fry the bacon in a little oil until crispy. Remove with a slotted spoon and drain on kitchen paper
4. Add the rest of the oil, turn up the heat and fry the potatoes until browned
5. Pre-heat the grill. Put the potatoes on a roasting tray, season and sprinkle with the bacon and cheese and cook until the cheese has melted
6. Serve hot

WEDGES IN BALSAMIC VINEGAR

1 lb (waxy) potatoes – washed, unpeeled & cut into wedges
2 red onions – peeled & cut into wedges
2 fl oz balsamic vinegar
2 tbsp olive oil

1. Boil the potatoes for 15 mins and drain thoroughly
2. Mix with the olive oil so the potatoes are evenly coated
3. Pre-heat oven to GM4/180°c/350°f
4. Put the potatoes on a small baking tray, with the onions, season and pour on the vinegar. Bake for about 20 mins until the vinegar forms a stickly glaze

The potato, a name derived from the American Indian word "Batata", was introduced to Europeans by Spanish conquerors during the late 16th Century

Main Dishes

BLENDER BEEF HASH

1 lb potatoes – peeled & cubed
1 lb cooked beef – cubed
2 large onions – peeled & finely chopped
2 green peppers – deseeded & finely chopped
6 oz beef dripping
Butter for spreading

1. *Line the bottom of a pie dish with butter and pre-heat the oven to GM6/200°c/ 400°f*

2. *Blend the potatoes and onions together in a food processor (in batches if necessary). Place in the bottom of the pie dish and season*

3. *Blend the beef and peppers together and put on top of the potatoes. Season and add the dripping. Cover with foil and bake for 25 mins*

4. *Remove foil and bake for 10 more mins*

BEEF & POTATO HASH

1 lb (waxy) potatoes – boiled & cubed
½ lb roasted beef – cut into small pieces
1 red onion – peeled & chopped
1 yellow pepper – deseeded & cut into cubes
1 large tomato – chopped
4 tsp extra virgin olive oil

1. *Heat the oil in a large frying pan and add the onion, pepper and potatoes. Fry for 20 mins. Season*

2. *Add the tomato and cook for 5 more mins*

3. *Once the liquid has been reduced add the beef and cook gently for 5 more mins until heated through*

SIMPLE BEEF HOT POT

1 lb potatoes – peeled & cut into chunks
1 lb stewing beef – cut into bite sized pieces
3 onions – peeled & chopped
3 carrots – peeled & chopped
1 leek – trimmed and chopped
1 pint beef stock
1 tbsp fresh thyme – chopped

1. *Put all the ingredients into a large saucepan and bring to the boil. Reduce the heat and cook on a low heat for 1–1 ½ hours*

POTATO, VEGETABLE & CORNED BEEF HASH

1 lb potatoes – peeled & sliced
1 large tin corned beef – sliced
2 onions – peeled & sliced
1 small turnip – peeled & sliced
½ lb carrots – peeled & sliced
¼ pint beef stock

1. *Pre-heat oven to GM5/190°c/375°f*

2. *Layer the base of a greased ovenproof dish with $^1/_3$ of the potatoes. Season and add ½ the other vegetables and ½ the corned beef*

3. *Add another $^1/_3$ of the potatoes, the remaining vegetables, season and add the rest of the corned beef, finishing with a layer of potatoes*

4. *Season, pour on the stock and cover. Bake for 1 hour*

5. *Remove the lid and cook for 15 more mins*

STOUT & POTATO STEW

1 lb potatoes – peeled & cubed
1½ lbs stewing steak – cubed
2 onions – peeled & chopped
3 cloves garlic – crushed
2 carrots – peeled & chopped
1 pint Guinness
½ pint beef stock
2 oz flour
1 tbsp fresh thyme – chopped
2 tbsp olive oil

1. *Pre-heat oven to GM5/190°c/375°f*

2. *Heat the oil and fry the beef until sealed Remove with a slotted spoon and set aside*

3. *Add the potatoes, onions, garlic and carrots. Season, stir well and cook for 10 mins*

4. *Add the thyme, steak and flour, stir then pour in the Guinness and the stock. Bring to the boil then remove from the heat and transfer to a casserole dish*

5. *Cover and bake for 2 hours*

CORN BEEF PIE

1 lb potatoes – peeled, boiled & mashed
1 lb corned beef – chopped
1 onion – peeled & chopped
1 red pepper – de-seeded & chopped
½ lb carrots – peeled, boiled & sliced
2 tbsp pickle
1 tbsp olive oil
½ oz butter

1. Pre-heat oven to GM4/180°c/350°f

2. Heat the oil and fry the onion and pepper until they start to soften

3. Grease the base of an ovenproof dish and layer the base with the carrots. Season

4. Mix the corned beef with the onion, pepper and pickle. Spread evenly over the carrots. Season

5. Spread the potatoes on top of the meat and dot with the butter

6. Bake for 30 mins

POTATO GOULASH

1 lb potatoes – peeled, boiled for 10 minutes & drained
2 lb stewing beef – cubed
2 onions – peeled & chopped
3 cloves garlic – crushed
1 large tin chopped tomatoes
1 red pepper – de-seeded & chopped
1½ pints beef stock
1 tbsp paprika
1 tsp caraway seeds
2 tbsp olive oil
2 tbsp sour cream

1. Heat the oil and fry the onion and pepper until they start to soften

2. Add the garlic and fry for one more minute

3. Add the paprika, season and stir

4. Add the beef and caraway seeds, pour on the stock and bring to the boil. Cover and simmer for 1 hour

5. Cube the potatoes and add them to the stew with the tomatoes. Season, stir and cook for 30 more minutes. Serve with small amount of sour cream on the top

LEFTOVER PIE

1 lb potatoes – peeled & sliced
8 oz leftover beef or lamb – minced or very finely chopped
4 oz onions – peeled & chopped
1 tsp dried mixed herbs
2 tbsp tomato purée
1 tsp Worcester sauce
1 large tin chopped tomatoes
1 egg – beaten
5 fl oz natural yoghurt
1 oz butter

1. Preheat oven to GM5/180°c/375°f

2. Melt the butter in a pan and cook the onions gently until soft. Add the meat, mixed herbs, tomato purée and Worcester sauce. Season

3. Take a small casserole dish and lightly butter the bottom and sides. Arrange a layer of potatoes in the bottom, pour in the meat mixture, then the tomatoes and finish with a layer of potatoes. Cover and bake for 30 mins

4. Add the flour and yoghurt to the beaten egg and mix well. Season. Spoon the egg mixture over the pie and return to the oven for a further 30 mins

STEAK, POTATO & PEANUT HOTPOT

1 lb (waxy) potatoes – peeled & cubed
1 lb steak – fat removed & cut into strips
1 large onion – peeled & sliced
3 cloves garlic – crushed
1 green pepper – cored, seeded & cut into strips
5 tbsp crunchy peanut butter
2 oz peanuts
1 pint beef stock
2 tbsp olive oil

1. Heat the oil and fry the beef until sealed

2. Add the onion, pepper and garlic and cook for 2 mins

3. Add the potato and cook for about 5 mins

4. Mix the peanut butter with the beef stock (in a processor if necessary) and add to the potato mixture. Season, add the peanuts and bring to the boil stirring often

5. Reduce to a gentle simmer for 45 mins or until the desired consistency is reached

BEEF AND POTATO STEW

1 lb potatoes – peeled & cut into chunks
1 lb stewing beef
2 onions – peeled & sliced
1 pint beef stock
3 carrots – peeled & chopped
1 small swede – peeled & chopped
1 parsnip – peeled & chopped
10 rashers bacon – derinded & chopped
2 cloves garlic – peeled & crushed
2 tsp Worcester sauce
1 bay leaf
2 tbsp fresh thyme – chopped
2 tbsp fresh parsley – chopped
Vegetable oil

1. Pre-heat oven to GM4/180°c/350°f
2. Heat the oil in a pan and fry the meat until browned. Remove with a slotted spoon
3. Add the onion and garlic and fry gently until soft
4. Fry the bacon until crisp
5. Put the meat, onions, bacon and garlic into a large casserole dish (or slow cooker). Add all the other ingredients and season. Cook for 2½-3 hours on a low heat until the beef and vegetables are tender

BURGER CASSEROLE

1 lb potatoes – peeled & sliced
4 large beef burgers
2 onions – peeled & sliced
1 large tin baked beans
2 tbsp Worcester sauce
1 tbsp tomato purée
½ pint beef stock
2 oz butter
1 tbsp dried oregano

1. Pre-heat oven to GM6/200°c/400°f
2. Heat the butter and fry the onion until it starts to soften
3. Boil the potato slices for 10 mins. Drain and allow to dry
4. Lightly grill the burgers until just cooked. Drain of all excess fat. Slice the burgers in half lengthways to create 8 thinner burgers

5. Layer half the potatoes at the base of a casserole dish, season and add half the onions and half the burgers
6. Add the beans and the rest of the burgers, onion and potatoes in that order. Season
7. Mix the oregano, Worcester sauce, seasoning and purée into the stock and pour onto the potatoes
8. Cover and bake for 20 mins
9. Remove cover and bake for 5 more mins

SPANISH HASH

1 lb new potatoes – scrubbed, halved & boiled
1 tin corn beef – cut into cubes
1 onion – peeled & chopped
1 clove garlic – crushed
1 red pepper – de-seeded & sliced
1 green pepper – de-seeded & sliced
1 small green chilli – de-seeded & chopped
1 tbsp fresh coriander – chopped
1 tbsp olive oil

1. Heat the oil and cook the onion for 3-4 mins
2. Add the garlic and chilli and cook for 3 more mins
3. Add the potato and peppers and cook for 5 mins
4. Add the corn beef, season, mix well and cook for a further 5 mins
5. Remove from the heat and add the coriander

BEEF HASH

1 lb (floury) potatoes – peeled & grated
¾ lb cooked beef – cut into cubes
4 tbsp sour cream
2 tbsp brown sauce
2 tbsp vegetable oil

1. Mix the brown sauce with the sour cream
2. Heat the oil in a wok. Add the potatoes and beef and cook over a high heat, stirring continually until the potatoes are browned
3. Remove and place in a bowl. Season and pour the sauce on top, mixing with a fork

STEAK & POTATO PIE

1 lb potatoes – peeled, cubed, par boiled
& drained
2 lb braising steak – cubed
1 onion – peeled & chopped
1 clove garlic – crushed
½ pint beef stock
3½ oz Roquefort cheese – cubed
1 egg – beaten
1 lb puff pastry
1 tbsp olive oil
2 tbsp fresh thyme – chopped
1½ oz plain flour

1. Heat the oil in a large pan and fry the onion and garlic until the onion begins to soften

2. Add the meat, stir well and cook until it is lightly browned

3. Pre-heat oven to GM5/190°c/375°f

4. Add the thyme, season and stir

5. Sprinkle with the flour, stir then pour on the stock, stir again and bring to the boil. Reduce to a simmer for 15 mins

6. Add the potatoes and the cheese, stir and allow the cheese to melt before transferring to a pie dish

7. Place the pastry on top, trim and brush with the egg. Bake for 30 mins

POTATO HASH

1 lb potatoes – peeled, boiled & mashed
1 tin corn beef – cut into ¾" cubes
6 cabbage leaves – shredded
1 onion – peeled & chopped
2 cloves garlic – crushed
1 tbsp olive oil

1. Heat the oil in a frying pan and gently fry the onion and garlic until the onion starts to soften

2. Add the potato in a thin layer and cook until it is slightly brown

3. Add the cabbage and corn beef, season and cook for 5 mins until lightly browned

4. Cook for a few more mins under a pre-heated grill

BEEF, POTATO & GUINNESS STEW

1 lb potatoes – peeled & cut into bite sized pieces
1 lb beef stewing steak – cubed
2 onions – peeled & cut into wedges
½ lb carrots – peeled & roughly chopped
3 sticks celery – trimmed, washed & chopped
1 tsp Worcester sauce
1 pint Guinness
1 pint beef stock
2 tbsp fresh thyme – chopped
2 tbsp olive oil

1. Pre-heat a slow cooker

2. Heat half the oil in a large pan and fry the meat until browned. Remove with a slotted spoon

3. Add the rest of the oil and cook the onion for 5 mins

4. Transfer to the slow cooker, add the carrots, potatoes, celery, Worcester sauce and thyme. Season well and stir

5. Heat the Guinness and stock until almost boiling. Add to the slow cooker, stir, cover and cook for 3 hours

6. Remove lid and cook for longer if you want to reduce the liquid

BEETROOT, POTATO & CORN BEEF HASH

1 lb potatoes – peeled, boiled, cooled & diced
1 can corn beef – diced
7 oz cooked beetroot – diced
2 onions – peeled & chopped
1 tbsp Worcester sauce
2 tbsp vegetable oil

1. Heat the oil in a large pan and fry the onions for 5 mins

2. Add the potatoes, corned beef and beetroot to the pan. Stir in the Worcester sauce and season

3. Fry gently for about 10 mins stirring occasionally

CORNBEEF HASH WITH EGGS

1 lb potatoes – peeled & diced
½ lb tinned corn beef – cubed
1 onion – peeled & finely sliced
3 eggs
2 tbsp fresh parsley – chopped
2 tbsp olive oil

1. Boil the potatoes for 5 mins and drain
2. Heat the oil and fry the onion for 5 mins
3. Add the potatoes and fry for 10 more mins
4. Add the corned beef, season and fry gently for 5 mins
5. Meanwhile poach the eggs. When done, remove the potato mixture, put on a serving dish and sprinkle with the parsley and top with the eggs – breaking each one

BAKED BEAN HASH

1 lb potatoes – peeled & diced
¾ lb tinned corn beef – sliced
2 onions – peeled & sliced
1 large tin baked beans
1 tbsp Worcester sauce
1 tbsp tomato purée
½ pint beef stock
2 oz butter
1 tbsp dried oregano

1. Pre-heat oven to GM6/200°c/400°f
2. Heat the butter and fry the onion for 3 mins
3. Boil the potato dices for 10 mins. Drain and allow to dry
4. Layer half the potatoes at the base of a casserole dish, season and add half the onions and half the corned beef
5. Add the baked beans then the remaining corned beef, onion and potatoes – in that order. Season
6. Mix the oregano, Worcester sauce, seasoning and purée into the stock and pour over the potatoes
7. Cover and bake for 20 mins
8. Remove cover and bake for 5 more mins

BEEF & POTATOES IN GUINNESS

1 lb (waxy) potatoes – peeled & cubed
1½ lb stewing beef – fat removed & cubed
2 large onions – peeled & chopped
2 large carrots – peeled & chopped
1 pint Guinness
2 cloves garlic – crushed
2 tbsp seasoned flour
1 tbsp Worcester sauce
2 tbsp fresh thyme – chopped
2 bay leaves
3 tbsp olive oil

1. Put the flour in a food bag, add the meat and shake until all the meat is coated.
2. Heat 2 tbsp of the oil in a large saucepan and fry the meat until browned. Remove the meat with a slotted spoon and set aside.
3. Add the rest of the oil and fry the onions until they start to soften.
4. Add the potatoes, carrots and garlic. Stir for 1-2 minutes.
5. Add the beef, season and pour on the (hot) beef stock. Add the thyme and Worcester sauce. Stir well and add the bay leaves.
6. Bring to the boil, then reduce to a very gentle simmer, cover and cook for 1½ hours.
7. Pour on the Guinness, adjust the seasoning, remove the bay leaves and stir well. Turn the heat up and simmer for about an hour, until the desired consistency is reduced.

POTATO, MINCE & PINE NUTS

1 lb potatoes – peeled, boiled & mashed
1 lb minced beef
2 oz pine nuts
2 oz raisins
1 egg – beaten
1 tsp fresh thyme – chopped
1 tsp fresh parsley – chopped
Olive oil for frying

1. Put all the ingredients in a large bowl, season and mix well
2. Form the mixture into small round shapes
3. Heat some oil in a deep heavy saucepan and when hot, carefully add the potato shapes
4. Fry until browned then drain on kitchen paper

MINCED BEEF & POTATO FRITTATA

1 lb new potatoes – scrubbed, boiled for 10 mins, drained
1 lb lean minced beef
1 onion – peeled & thinly sliced
2 cloves garlic – crushed
10 eggs
2 tbsp milk
2 tbsp fresh parsley – finely chopped
1 tbsp Worcester sauce
2 tbsp olive oil

1. *Dry fry the mince with the onion and garlic stirring continually until the meat is browned. Drain and reserve*

2. *Allow the potatoes to cool then slice thinly*

3. *Pre-heat the grill to medium*

4. *Heat the oil in a large frying pan and fry the potatoes until lightly browned on each side*

5. *Add the mince, Worcester sauce, season and stir well, leaving on a very gentle simmer*

6. *Beat the eggs with the milk and parsley and pour onto the potato mixture, season and stir well. Turn up the heat slightly, continue to cook, stirring occasionally*

7. *When the base starts to set, place the pan under the grill until the top sets*

TEXAN POTATO HASH

1 lb potatoes – peeled & diced
1 lb cooked roast beef – cut into bit sized pieces
2 onions – peeled & finely chopped
2 cloves garlic – crushed
1 pint beef stock (made with 2 stock cubes)
2 tbsp olive oil

1. *Heat the oil in a large pan and fry the potatoes and onion until the onion starts to soften*

2. *Add the rest of the ingredients, season and bring to the boil. Simmer until all the liquid is absorbed*

SPICY CHICKEN & POTATO

1 lb potatoes – peeled & cubed
1 lb chicken – cooked & cut into bite sized pieces
2 onions – peeled & chopped
1 large tin chopped tomatoes
2 cloves garlic – crushed
2 small green chillies – chopped
1 tbsp fresh ginger – grated
2 tsp ground cumin
½ tsp ground cinnamon
4 fl oz chicken stock
1 tbsp vegetable oil

1. *Heat the oil in a pan and add the onions, garlic, chillies, ginger, cumin and cinnamon. Fry gently for about 5 mins*

2. *Add the potatoes, chicken, tomatoes, stock and stir well. Bring to the boil then simmer, uncovered for 15-18 mins*

HONEYED POTATOES & CHICKEN

1 lb new potatoes – scrubbed, boiled & cubed
3 large chicken breasts – cut into bite sized pieces
5 tbsp extra virgin olive oil
1 clove garlic – crushed
3 tbsp clear runny honey
1 tbsp Dijon mustard
4 tbsp lemon juice

1. *Put the chicken in a small bowl and season*

2. *Put 2 tbsp of oil, 2 tbsp of lemon juice, garlic and 1 ½ tsp of the honey in a screw top jar, shake vigorously to mix and pour onto the chicken. Mix well, cover with cling film and refrigerate for 2 hours*

3. *Heat 1 tbsp of oil and add the chicken with the marinade. Fry for about 15 mins until the chicken is cooked*

4. *Add the potatoes and cook for 3-4 more mins, until the potatoes are heated through*

5. *Put the remaining oil and lemon juice with the mustard and remaining honey in a screw top jar and shake vigorously to mix*

6. *Remove the chicken and potatoes, put on plate(s) and pour on the dressing*

CHICKEN & POTATOES IN TARRAGON SAUCE

1 lb new potatoes – scrubbed, halved & boiled
1 lb chicken breast – cubed
1 onion – peeled & finely sliced
4 fl oz dry white wine
½ pint double cream
2 tbsp fresh tarragon
1 clove garlic – crushed
2 tbsp olive oil

1. *Heat the oil and fry the onion and garlic for 5 mins*
2. *Add the chicken breasts and fry until the chicken is cooked*
3. *Add the wine, stir well and turn up the heat. Cook until the wine is reduced by half*
4. *Add the tarragon, season and stir then add the cream and potatoes. Reduce the heat and stirring continually, bring the mixture till just, but not quite boiling*

LEMON CHICKEN & POTATO STIR FRY

1 lb new potatoes – scrubbed, halved, boiled & drained
3 chicken breasts – cut into bite sized pieces
2 cloves garlic – crushed
2 tbsp lemon juice
1 tbsp Dijon mustard
5 tbsp extra virgin olive oil

1. *Put 2 tbsp of oil, 1 tbsp lemon juice and the garlic in a screw top jar, season and shake vigorously to mix*
2. *Put the chicken in a small bowl and pour the liquid on top. Cover with cling film and refrigerate overnight*
3. *Heat 1 tbsp of oil in a pan until hot and fry the chicken until lightly browned, stirring continually*
4. *Add the potatoes and cook for 2-3 mins more. Remove from the heat and put into a serving dish*
5. *Boil the reserved liquid until cooked*
6. *Put the remaining ingredients in a screw top jar with the reserved marinade, season and shake vigorously to mix then pour onto the chicken*

CHICKEN & POTATOES IN WHITE WINE SAUCE

1 lb new potatoes – scrubbed & halved
1 whole chicken – cooked, cooled, skinned & boned
3 rashers bacon – rind removed & chopped
10 shallots – peeled
5 fl oz white wine
5 fl oz chicken stock
1 leek – trimmed & chopped
¼ lb carrots – peeled & chopped
3 cloves garlic – crushed
1 tbsp cornflour
2 tbsp milk
1 tbsp fresh parsley – chopped
2 tbsp olive oil

1. *Dry fry the bacon until it starts to brown*
2. *Add the oil and when hot add the onions, leek and garlic. Fry gently until the onion starts to soften*
3. *Meanwhile cut the chicken into bite sized pieces, add to the pan, season and stir*
4. *Add the wine and stock. Stir and bring to the boil, then add the potatoes and carrots. Simmer for about 30 mins*
5. *Blend the cornflour and milk, add to the mixture and bring back to the boil or until the mixture thickens*
6. *Sprinkle with the parsley and serve*

LEMON CHICKEN & POTATO

1 lb potatoes – peeled, halved & slits cut into the top
4 chicken thighs – cut into evenly sized pieces
1 red onion – peeled & thickly sliced
Juice & zest of 1 lemon
1½ tbsp extra virgin olive oil

1. *Pre-heat oven to GM6/200°c/400°f*
2. *Boil the potatoes for 10 mins and drain*
3. *Take a large roasting tin and add the potatoes, chicken and onion*
4. *Mix together the oil, lemon juice and zest. Pour over the potato mixture and bake for 45 mins, stirring occasionally*
5. *Remove from oven, stir and serve*

POTATO & CHICKEN IN MUSHROOM SAUCE

1 lb new potatoes – scrubbed, boiled & halved
1 lb chicken – cut into chunks
1 pint chicken stock
2 cloves garlic – crushed
1 large onion – peeled & chopped
1 lb mushrooms – chopped
½ pint white wine
½ pint double cream
2 oz butter
2 tbsp olive oil

1. Heat the oil in a large pan and cook the potatoes and chicken for 5 mins
2. Add the onion and garlic and cook for 5 more mins
3. Season and add the stock, bring to the boil then simmer for 30 mins, adding more stock if needed
4. Meanwhile melt the butter and gently cook the mushrooms for 3 mins. Add the wine and stir well and bring to the boil. Cook until reduced by half
5. Add the mushrooms to the potatoes and chicken, season and stir well
6. Add the cream until the desired consistency is reached and heat until almost, but not, boiling

VIETNAMESE CHICKEN & POTATO CURRY

1 lb potatoes – peeled & cubed
4 chicken breasts – cut into bite sized pieces
2 carrots – peeled & chopped
2 onions – peeled & chopped
5 cloves garlic – crushed
1 pint coconut milk
1 pint water
1 tbsp lemon grass – finely chopped
1 tbsp onion salt
2 tbsp medium curry powder
1 tsp sugar
4 bay leaves
2 tbsp vegetable oil

1. Mix the curry powder and sugar with plenty of seasoning. Add the chicken and mix thoroughly. Cover with cling film and refrigerate for 2 hours
2. Heat the oil and stir fry the potatoes until lightly browned
3. Add the onion and garlic. Cook for 1 minute
4. Add the chicken and lemon grass and stir fry until the chicken is lightly browned
5. Add a pint of water, carrots and bay leaves, stir well. Bring to the boil and simmer for 15 mins
6. Add the potatoes and coconut milk and simmer for 15-20 mins or until the vegetables are tender and desired consistency is reached

DRUNKEN CHICKEN

1 lb new potatoes – scrubbed & halved
4 chicken breasts – cut into bite sized pieces
4 rashers bacon – de-rinded & chopped
2 onions – peeled & chopped
3 cloves garlic – peeled & crushed
8 shallots – peeled
¼ lb mushrooms – halved
1 pint Guinness
1 tbsp fresh rosemary
1 tbsp mustard powder
1 tbsp Worcester sauce
4 tbsp olive oil

1. Dry fry the bacon. Remove and drain on kitchen paper
2. Heat half the oil and gently fry the onion until it starts to soften. Add the mushrooms, garlic and cook for 1 more minute
3. Heat the remaining oil in another pan, add the shallots and chicken and cook until the shallots have slightly softened and the chicken is slightly browned
4. Add the rosemary, Worcester sauce and mustard powder, stir well and add the bacon bits and onion mixture. Season and stir
5. Add the potatoes, stir and pour on the Guinness. Bring to the boil then reduce to a simmer for 40 mins or until the desired consistency is reached and the chicken is cooked

CHICKEN & POTATOES WITH ROSEMARY

1 lb new potatoes – scrubbed & halved
4 chicken drumsticks
4 chicken thighs
2 red onions – peeled & cut into wedges
4 cloves garlic – crushed
5 oz pitted green olives
¼ pint white wine
3 tbsp clear honey
2 tbsp fresh rosemary – chopped
3 tbsp olive oil

1. Heat the oven to GM5/190°c/375°f
2. Put the potatoes in a large roasting tin and add the chicken, onion and garlic. Season
3. Put the wine, honey, rosemary and oil in a screw topped jar and shake vigorously, pour over the potato mixture
4. Cover with foil and roast for 45 mins
5. Remove the foil, add the olives and stir
6. Cook for another 30 mins

CHICKEN & POTATO GREEN CURRY

1 lb (waxy) potatoes – peeled and cubed
1 ½ lb uncooked chicken – cut into bite sized pieces
3 tbsp green Thai curry paste
20 fl oz coconut milk
2 tbsp lime juice
2 tbsp vegetable oil

1. Heat the oil and fry the chicken until lightly browned. Remove with a slotted spoon and set aside
2. Add the curry paste and heat gently, stirring continually
3. Pour in the coconut milk and stir well so the paste is mixed with the milk. Add the chicken and potatoes
4. Bring to the boil then cover and simmer for 15 mins
5. Remove the cover, add the lime juice and a little salt and heat until the potatoes are cooked and the desired consistency is reached

CHICKEN & POTATO POT ROAST

1 lb new potatoes – scrubbed & halved
4 chicken thighs
2 red onions – peeled & sliced
2 garlic cloves – peeled & sliced
2 tbsp lemon juice
3 tbsp olive oil
2 bay leaves

1. Boil the potatoes for 10 mins, drain
2. Pre-heat oven to GM6/200°c/400°f
3. Put the potatoes in a roasting tin, season and mix with 2 tbsp of oil. Add the bay leaves and roast for 10 mins
4. Heat the remaining oil and fry the chicken until lightly browned
5. Remove the tin from the oven, add the onions and garlic. Stir well. Add the lemon juice and chicken. Season, cover and roast for 40 mins

POT ROASTED CHICKEN AND POTATOES

1 lb new potatoes – washed a& halved
1x 3lb chicken – giblets removed
10 baby carrots – washed
4 leeks – trimmed & chopped
2 bulbs of garlic – papery skin removed
10 fl oz chicken stock
2 cloves garlic – cut into slivers
2 tbsp fresh thyme – chopped
1 tbsp fresh tarragon – chopped
2 bay leaves

1. Pre-heat oven to GM4/180°c/350°f
2. Spike the chicken with the garlic slivers
3. Place the chicken in a large casserole dish, add all the main ingredients, season and sprinkle with the herbs. Pour on the stock to cover and place in the oven
4. Cook for 1 hour 15 mins then remove lid, stir and cook for 20 more mins – ensure the chicken is fully cooked
5. Remove the chicken, bay leaves and garlic
6. Squeeze some of the pulp from the garlic and add it to the sauce. Reduce the sauce if necessary

CHICKEN & POTATO BAKE

1 lb potatoes – peeled, boiled & mashed
1 lb cooked chicken – cut into bite sized pieces
1 onion – finely chopped
2 cloves garlic – crushed
2 carrots – peeled & chopped
3 oz frozen peas
6 fl oz chicken stock
1 tbsp tomato purée
2 oz cheddar cheese
1 tbsp fresh thyme – chopped
1 tbsp olive oil

1. *Pre-heat oven to GM6/200°c/400°f*
2. *Heat the oil and fry the onion, garlic and carrots for 5 mins*
3. *Add the chicken, stir well and cook for 2 mins*
4. *Add the tomato purée, thyme and stock. Season and bring to the boil then simmer for 10 mins*
5. *Add the peas and simmer for 5 more mins*
6. *Put the mixture in an ovenproof dish, spoon the potatoes on top and sprinkle with the cheese. Bake for 20 mins*

LEMON CHICKEN & POTATO CASSEROLE

1 lb new potatoes – scrubbed & halved
1 lb chicken breast – cubed
1 small tin chickpeas – drained
1 onion – peeled & thinly sliced
3 cloves garlic – crushed
Juice of 2 lemons
1 tsp ground cumin
1 pint chicken stock
2 tbsp olive oil

1. *Heat the oil and add the potatoes, chicken, onion and garlic. Fry until the chicken is just cooked*
2. *Add the cumin and lemon juice. Season. Stir and fry for 1 minute*
3. *Pour in the stock, stir well, add the chickpeas, and bring back to the boil. Simmer for 20 mins or longer to achieve the desired consistency*

CHICKEN & NEW POTATO CASSEROLE

1 lb new potatoes – scrubbed & halved
4 chicken thighs
2 onions – peeled & sliced
2 cloves garlic – crushed
¼ lb carrots – peeled & sliced
1 pint chicken stock
6 fl oz white wine
4 fl oz double cream
1 tbsp fresh tarragon – chopped
2½ tbsp olive oil
3 tbsp seasoned flour

1. *Heat the oil in a large pan and fry the chicken for 10 mins. Remove and drain on kitchen paper*
2. *Add the onions, carrots, potatoes & garlic. Cook gently for 5 mins*
3. *Pre-heat oven to GM6/200°c/400°f*
4. *Gradually add the stock and wine, stirring continually. Heat until almost boiling. Add the chicken and tarragon*
5. *Put the mixture in an ovenproof dish, cover and cook for 1 hour*
6. *Remove, add the cream, season and cook for 15 more mins*

ONE-POT POTATO ROAST

1 lb potatoes – peeled & cubed
4 chicken breasts
½ lb carrots – peeled & diced
¾ lb shallots – peeled
2 parsnips – peeled & cubed
3 tbsp lemon juice
3 tbsp fresh thyme
3 tbsp extra virgin olive oil

1. *Pre-heat oven to GM6/200°c/400°f*
2. *Put all the vegetables except shallots in a large mixing bowl and add the lemon juice, thyme and oil. Season and mix*
3. *Arrange the chicken at the base of a greased ovenproof dish and add the vegetables*
4. *Bake for 30 mins, remove, add the shallots, season, stir and bake for 15 more mins*

153

CHICKEN & CHORIZO POTATO STEW

1 lb new potatoes – scrubbed & halved
¾ lb chorizo – sliced
2 large chicken breasts – cut into bite sized pieces
2 onions – peeled & sliced
2 green peppers – cored, seeded and cut
  into squares
4 courgettes – trimmed & cut into chunks
1 large tin chopped tomatoes
¾ pint chicken stock
2 tsp paprika
2 tbsp dried oregano
3 tbsp extra virgin olive oil

1. Heat the oil and fry the chicken and chorizo gently for 6-8 mins until the chicken is lightly browned. Remove with a slotted spoon and set aside

2. Add the peppers and onion and cook until they start to soften

3. Add the paprika and oregano. Season and stir. Cook for 1 minute

4. Add the potatoes, tomatoes and the stock, bring to the boil and simmer for 15 mins

5. Add the courgettes and cook for 5 more mins until the desired consistency is reached and the chicken is cooked

CHICKEN & POTATO CASSEROLE

1 lb potatoes – peeled & cubed
1 lb chicken thighs
5 rashers bacon – chopped
½ lb baby carrots – scrubbed
4 celery sticks – washed and sliced
3 leeks – washed, trimmed and chopped
1½ pints chicken stock
2 tbsp fresh thyme – chopped
2 tbsp olive oil

1. Pre-heat oven to GM4/180°c/350°f

2. Heat the oil and gently cook the bacon, celery and leek for 5 mins

3. Add the potatoes, chicken, carrots and thyme. Season, stir and pour on the stock

4. Bring to the boil and simmer for 20 mins

5. Put in a casserole dish, cover and bake for 30 mins

6. Remove cover, season, stir and bake for 30 more mins

POTATO, CHICKEN & HAM PIE

1 lb potatoes – peeled, boiled for 10 mins, drained & sliced
1 lb cooked chicken – cubed
½ lb cooked ham – cubed
½ lb mushrooms – sliced
2 cloves garlic – crushed
2 onions – peeled & sliced
½ pint chicken stock
½ pint milk
1 tbsp fresh thyme – chopped
1 tbsp parsley – chopped
2 oz plain flour
2½ oz butter
2 tbsp olive oil

1. Heat the oil in a large pan and fry the onions until they start to soften

2. Add the garlic and the mushrooms and cook until the mushrooms start to wilt

3. Pre-heat oven to GM6/200°c/400°f

4. Meanwhile melt 2 oz of the butter in a small pan and add the flour. Stir continually to make a roux

5. Gradually pour in the milk and blend with the roux. Bring to the boil, stirring continuously until it thickens

6. Season, add the stock, stir well and bring to a simmer

7. Add the mushroom mixture and all the other ingredients except the potatoes and remaining butter. Stir well and heat through

8. Put a layer of potatoes in the base of a greased oven proof dish, pour in the mixture, top with the rest of the potatoes and dot with the butter and bake for 30 mins

POTATOES & LEMON CHICKEN

1 lb small (waxy) potatoes – scrubbed & halved
1 whole chicken (2-3 lbs) – giblets removed
  & washed
2 whole lemons – sliced, one peeled
1 whole head of garlic – papery skin removed
4 bay leaves
4 tbsp extra virgin olive oil
Juice of 1 lemon

1. Pre-heat oven to GM6/200°c/400°f
2. Place the chicken in roasting tin. Mix the lemon juice with the oil. Pour it over the chicken and rub all over
3. Place the peeled lemon inside the chicken cavity
4. Arrange the potatoes around the chicken and coat with the lemon liquid. Season and sprinkle with the lemon slices & bay leaves
5. Separate the garlic cloves and scatter them, unpeeled, on the potatoes
6. Cook for about 1½ hours until the chicken is cooked – basting regularly
7. Take the chicken out of the oven, remove the lemon from the cavity and take out the bay leaves and garlic cloves (for extra flavour squeeze out some garlic from the cloves and mix with the juices)

CHICKEN CURRY

1 lb potatoes – peeled & diced
2 chicken fillets – cut into bite sized pieces
2 onions – peeled & chopped
1 small tin chopped tomatoes
2 small carrots – peeled & chopped
4 fl oz chicken stock
1 tsp cumin
1 tsp fresh coriander – chopped
½ tsp chilli powder
½ tsp ground ginger
1 tsp garam masala
¼ tsp ground cloves
2 tbsp vegetable oil
1 tbsp flour

1. Heat the oil in a large pan and fry the onion until soft
2. Add the potatoes, chicken and carrots, season, stir and cook until the chicken is lightly browned
3. Add all the spices and flour, stir well and add the tomatoes
4. Add the stock so that the mixture is just covered, cover and simmer gently for 20 mins (Ensure the mixture does not dry out and stir once or twice to prevent sticking)

POTATO & CHICKEN PIE

1 lb potatoes – peeled & diced
1 lb chicken meat – diced
2 onions – peeled & chopped
10 baby carrots – peeled & halved
3 sticks celery – trimmed, washed & chopped
1½ tbsp fresh parsley – chopped
¼ lb cooked ham – diced
1 pint chicken stock
½ pint milk
2 oz butter
2 tbsp lemon juice
1 lb pack puff pastry
1 egg – beaten

1. Put the stock into a large pan. Add the potatoes, chicken, carrots and celery. Season, stir and bring to the boil. Reduce the heat, cover and simmer for 15 mins. Drain and keep the stock
2. Melt the butter in another large pan and fry the onions until softened
3. Sprinkle with the flour and add the reserved stock slowly – stirring all the time
4. Add the milk and simmer for 3 mins
5. Add the lemon juice and parsley. Season and simmer for 1 min
6. Put the chicken, ham and vegetables in a small pie dish, mix and season well. Pour on the sauce and allow to cool
7. Pre-heat oven to GM6/200°c/400°f
8. Roll out the pastry and place over the dish, trim and seal. Brush with the egg and bake for 30 mins

CHICKEN & POTATO PIE (2)

1 lb new potatoes – scrubbed & sliced
1 lb cooked chicken – cubed
12 asparagus tips – par boiled for 2 mins & drained
1 large onion – peeled and grated
4 tbsp fresh chives – chopped
1 tbsp Worcester sauce
5 tbsp chicken stock
1 lb shortcrust pastry
1 egg – beaten

1. *Pre-heat oven to GM5/190°c/375°f*
2. *Boil the potatoes for 10 mins and drain*
3. *Mix the potatoes with all the other ingredients except the pastry and egg and put in a 10" pie dish*
4. *Roll out the pastry on a floured surface to about 11" or 12" diameter then cut ½" all round*
5. *Brush the edge of the pie dish with water and press the strip of pastry onto it. Add the large piece of pastry and press down to seal. Cut off any excess and brush the pastry with the beaten egg*
6. *Bake for 45 mins until the chicken is cooked*

MOROCCAN CHICKEN & POTATOES

1 lb potatoes – peeled & cut into chunks
1 lb uncooked chicken – cubed
4 cloves garlic – peeled & crushed
2 tbsp lemon juice
2 tbsp extra virgin olive oil
2 tbsp fresh coriander – chopped
1 tbsp runny honey
¼ tsp cumin
½ tsp ground coriander
½ tsp caraway seeds

1. *Put the garlic, coriander leaves, ground coriander, cumin and caraway seeds into a small bowl. Mix together and season. Grind into a paste*
2. *Add the oil, lemon juice and honey. Mix well (add a little water if needed)*
3. *Put the chicken and potatoes in a mixing bowl, season and pour in the marinade. Mix well, cover with cling film and refrigerate for a least 6 hours*
4. *Pre-heat oven to GM4/180°c/350°f.*
5. *Transfer to an ovenproof dish, cover and bake for 1 hour until the chicken is cooked*

CHICKEN & VEGETABLE PIE

1 lb new potatoes – scrubbed & halved
4 chicken breasts – skinned & cut into bite size pieces
½ lb baby carrots
2 onions – peeled & finely chopped
2 cloves garlic – crushed
3 leeks – trimmed, washed & chopped
¼ lb frozen peas
¼ lb broad beans – washed
2 pints chicken stock
1 tbsp flour – seasoned
1½ oz butter
2 tbsp olive oil
1 lb shortcrust pastry (ready made)
1 egg – beaten
3 tbsp fresh parsley

1. *Pre-heat oven to GM5/190°c/375°f*
2. *Heat the oil and gently fry the chicken until slightly brown. Remove with a slotted spoon and discard the oil*
3. *Melt the butter in a large pan and fry the onion and garlic until the onion starts to soften*
4. *Add the flour, stir well, then pour on the stock. Bring to the boil. Add the vegetables, parsley and season. Bring back to the boil and simmer for 10 mins*
5. *Add all the ingredients to a pie dish with enough stock to almost cover the ingredients*
6. *Roll out the pastry, brush with the egg, place on the dish and trim the edges*
7. *Bake for 1 hour*

CHICKEN & POTATO CROQUETTES

1 lb potatoes – boiled & mashed
1 lb cooked chicken – bones removed & minced
2 eggs – beaten
2 oz breadcrumbs
3 tbsp olive oil

1. *Put the mash and the chicken into a large bowl, season and mix well*
2. *Roll the mixture onto a floured board and shape into croquettes. Coat with beaten egg and roll in breadcrumbs*
3. *Heat the oil and fry on a high heat until browned all over*

CHICKEN & POTATO ROAST

1 lb potatoes – peeled & cut into chunks
1 medium chicken – giblets removed
2 onions – peeled & cut into wedges
2 carrots – peeled & chopped
4 sticks celery – trimmed, washed & chopped
1 yellow pepper – deseeded & cut into strips
2 cloves garlic – crushed
½ pint dry white wine
1 pint chicken stock
1 tbsp fresh parsley – chopped
2 tbsp olive oil

1. *Pre-heat oven to GM6/200°c/400°f*

2. *Heat the oil in a large pan and cook the onion and pepper until they start to soften*

3. *Add the garlic and cook for 1 minute*

4. *Add all the remaining vegetables, season, stir and cook for 2 mins*

5. *Add the parsley then pour on the stock and wine, bring to the boil then simmer for 10 mins*

6. *Place the chicken in the middle of a roasting tin and pour on the vegetables and stock so they are evenly spread. Roast for 1 ½ hours until the chicken is cooked and the sauce is reduced to the desired consistency*

CHICKEN & POTATO PIE (3)

1 lb potatoes – peeled & diced
1 lb cooked chicken – diced
½ pint milk
2½ tbsp chopped parsley
12 oz puff pastry – ready made
1 oz flour
1 oz butter

1. *Melt the butter, add the flour and make a roux*

2. *Slowly add the milk, stir and heat until thickened*

3. *Add the potato, chicken and parsley. Season and stir then gradually re-heat*

4. *Pre-heat oven to GM7/ 220°c/425°f*

5. *Line a pie dish with some of the pastry, pour on the sauce, cover with a pastry lid and bake for about 40 mins*

LEMON CHICKEN WITH NEW POTATOES

1 lb new potatoes – scrubbed & thickly sliced
4 chicken breasts
3 red onions – peeled & cut into wedges
1 green pepper – de-seeded & cut into slices
2 courgettes – washed & sliced
4 tbsp lemon juice
6 tbsp extra virgin olive oil
Zest of 1 lemon
1 tbsp fresh oregano – chopped

1. *Put the oil, oregano and lemon zest in a screw top jar, season and shake vigorously to mix*

2. *Put the chicken in a shallow dish, pour over the marinade and coat all of the chicken. Cover with cling film and refrigerate overnight*

3. *Pre-heat oven to GM6/200°c/400°f*

4. *Drain the marinade from the chicken, add the lemon juice, season and stir*

5. *Put the potatoes and onions in a roasting tin and pour half the marinade on top. Mix and roast for 15 mins*

6. *Add the chicken, pepper and courgettes and the rest of the marinade, stir well and cook for 30 more mins ensuring the chicken is fully cooked*

POTATO & CHICKEN FRY

1 lb new potatoes – scrubbed & quartered
4 chicken breasts – cut into strips
2 rashers bacon – cut into strips
1 onion – chopped
2 cloves garlic – crushed
1 glass white wine
2 tbsp fresh tarragon – chopped
2 tbsp olive oil

1. *Boil the potatoes for 10 mins and drain*

2. *Fry the onion in the oil for 3 mins then add the garlic and cook for 1 more minute*

3. *Add the chicken and cook for 5 more mins*

4. *Add all the other ingredients except the wine and cook for 5 more mins*

5. *Turn up the heat, add the wine, season and cook until most the liquid has reduced and the chicken is cooked*

SPANISH CHICKEN & POTATO

1 lb new potatoes – scrubbed & halved
1 lb chicken – cut into bite sized chunks
5 tomatoes – quartered
1 onion – peeled & sliced
2 green peppers – deseeded & sliced
3 tbsp fresh basil – chopped
2 tbsp Worcester sauce
Juice & zest of 1 lime
2 tbsp extra virgin olive oil

1. Boil potatoes for 10 mins and drain
2. Heat the oil in a large pan and fry the chicken gently until lightly browned. Remove with a slotted spoon
3. Add the onion and the peppers and fry for 2 mins
4. Add the potatoes and fry for a further 5 mins
5. Add the chicken pieces, season and add all the other ingredients except the basil. Cook over a low heat for about 20 mins
6. Scatter with the basil and serve hot

CHICKEN & POTATO HASH

1 lb potatoes – peeled & diced
1 lb chicken – cooked & cut into bite size pieces
1 onion – peeled & chopped
1 red pepper – cored, deseeded
2 stalks celery – washed & sliced
2 cloves garlic – peeled & crushed
4 fl oz chicken stock
½ tsp Worcester sauce
1 tsp chilli sauce
1½ oz butter

1. Put the potatoes in boiling salted water for 5 mins then drain
2. Melt the butter and fry the potato for 5 more mins
3. Add the onion, pepper and garlic and cook for a further 5 mins
4. Add the celery and cook for 5 more mins
5. Add all the remaining ingredients, season and stir well. Cook for about 5 more mins or until all the liquid has been absorbed

CHICKEN HASH

1 lb new potatoes, scrubbed, boiled, drained & cubed
1 lb cooked chicken – boned & cubed
1 onion – peeled & chopped
1 green pepper – cored, seeded & finely chopped
2 cloves garlic – crushed
1 beaten egg
2 oz button mushrooms – sliced
5 fl oz single cream
1½ tsp curry powder
1½ tsp Worcester sauce
1½ tbsp fresh parsley – chopped
2 tbsp olive oil

1. Heat the oil in a large pan and gently cook the onion, pepper and garlic for 5 mins
2. Add the chicken, potatoes, mushrooms and parsley. Mix well and season
3. Beat the egg, curry powder and Worcester sauce into the cream and season. Pour over the potato and chicken mixture and continue to cook over a medium heat until golden
4. Put the pan under a hot grill until the top is golden

HERBY POTATO KEBABS

1 lb new potatoes – scrubbed, halved & boiled for 10 mins
1 lb chicken breast – cut into cubes
1 red onion – peeled & cut into wedges
1 tbsp fresh mint – chopped
1 tbsp fresh rosemary – chopped
1 tbsp fresh parsley – chopped
5 tbsp extra virgin olive oil
2 tbsp lemon juice

1. Soak the required number of skewers overnight
2. Mix the chicken, onion and the cooled potatoes in a bowl with the oil, lemon juice and herbs. Season and refrigerate overnight
3. Thread alternate pieces of chicken, potato and onion onto the skewers and cook under a pre-heated grill for 10 mins, turning halfway ensuring the chicken is fully cooked

CHICKEN & POTATO WITH LEMON & THYME

1 lb potatoes – peeled & thinly sliced
3-4 lb chicken – giblets removed
1 large onion – peeled & thinly sliced
½ pint chicken stock
2 cloves garlic – crushed
2 oz butter
1 lemon – rind removed, then finely chopped
2 tbsp fresh thyme – chopped

1. Pre-heat oven to GM6/200°c/400°f
2. Butter a large ovenproof dish and layer it with the potatoes and onion – seasoning each layer
3. Pour over the heated stock and dot with some butter
4. Mix the rest of the butter with the garlic, lemon rind and thyme. Loosen the chicken skin and insert the mixture evenly over the breast area
5. Put the flesh of the lemon in the chicken cavity and place the chicken on the potatoes
6. Cook for 1½-2 hours

CHICKEN & POTATO HASH (2)

1 lb new potatoes – scrubbed & cubed
1 lb cooked chicken – cubed
1 onion – peeled & finely chopped
1 green pepper – cored, seeded & finely chopped
2 cloves garlic – crushed
1 egg beaten
2 tbsp fresh parsley – chopped
5 fl oz single cream
2 tsp curry paste
Vegetable oil

1. Mix together the potatoes, chicken, onion, pepper, garlic, and parsley in a large bowl
2. Put the cream, egg, curry paste and seasoning in a small bowl and mix well. Pour over the potatoes and chicken. Mix well
3. Heat the oil and gently fry the mixture for 20-25 minutes until golden brown and then put under a hot grill for 5 minutes. Serve hot

GARLIC POTATOES (with Lamb)

1 lb potatoes – peeled & thinly sliced
1½ lbs half leg of lamb
1 large sprig fresh rosemary
3 large cloves of garlic – 2 crushed, 1 cut into slivers
2 oz butter

1. Pre-heat the oven to GM5/190°c/375°f
2. Grease a large shallow baking dish. Layer with the sliced potatoes & crushed garlic. Dot with butter & season
3. Pierce the meat in several places with a sharp knife and insert the garlic slivers. Push the sprig of rosemary into the centre of the lamb. Rub the meat with the remaining butter & season
4. Put the dish with the potatoes in it on a shelf in the oven and put the meat (without a dish) directly above the potatoes so that meat juices drip onto the potatoes. Roast for 1½-2 hours

SPICY LAMB & POTATOES

1 lb potatoes – peeled & cubed
1 lb lamb – fat removed & cubed
1 onion – peeled & chopped
1 small red chilli – de-seeded & chopped
1 small tin chopped tomatoes
½ pint lamb stock
1 tbsp ground cumin
1 tbsp ground coriander
1 tbsp turmeric
2 tbsp vegetable oil

1. Heat the oil in a pan and fry the onion and chilli for 3 mins
2. Add the meat and fry until browned
3. Add the potatoes and fry for 5 mins
4. Add all the other ingredients, season and stir well. Gradually bring to the boil stirring continually
5. Reduce heat, cover and simmer gently for about an hour, stirring occasionally
6. Remove cover and continue to simmer until the desired consistency is reached

MOROCCAN LAMB & POTATO BAKE

1 lb new potatoes – scrubbed & halved
4 lamb chops
1 lemon – sliced
4 bay leaves
3 tbsp olive oil
1 oz butter
1 orange pepper – skinned & de-seeded
1 tsp harissa paste
1 oz fresh mint – chopped

1. *Pre-heat oven to GM7/220°c/425°f*
2. *Take an ovenproof dish and layer the potato, lemon and bay leaves at the bottom. Add half the oil, dot with butter, season and cover with foil and roast for 25 mins*
3. *Remove from the oven, take off the foil, stir well and roast for 30 more mins*
4. *Put the skinned pepper, harissa, rest of the oil and mint in a processor, season and liquidise*
5. *Meanwhile grill the chops until almost cooked and add to the roasting tin with 15 mins to go. Remove the bay leaves*
6. *Remove tray from oven and pour the sauce on top*

SIMPLE LAMB STEW

1 lb potatoes – peeled & sliced
1 lb lamb – cut into bite sized pieces
¾ lb onions – peeled & sliced
1 tbsp fresh thyme – chopped
1 tbsp fresh parsley – chopped

1. *Put the meat in a pan, season well, add enough warm water to cover*
2. *Boil and remove any scum from the surface*
3. *Add the potatoes, onions and herbs to the meat. Season. Add enough water to cover then put on a lid, reduce to a very gently simmer and cook for 1½ hours, stirring occasionally*
4. *Remove lid and cook for a further 5 mins or until the desired consistency is reached*

LAMB & NEW POTATO STEW

1 lb new potatoes – scrubbed & halved
1 lb lamb – cubed
1 large onion – peeled & diced
2 leeks – trimmed & sliced
4 carrots – peeled & sliced
1 small tin sweetcorn – drained
1 pint lamb stock
1 tsp dried oregano
1 tsp ground cumin
Juice of 1 lemon
4 tbsp olive oil

1. *Heat half the oil in a large pan and fry the onion, leek and carrot for 5 mins*
2. *Add the potatoes, sweetcorn, lemon juice and oregano. Season and stir well*
3. *Heat the remaining oil in a separate pan, sprinkle the cumin over the lamb, season and fry the meat over a high heat until sealed*
4. *Add the potato mixture, stir well, pour on the stock and bring to the boil. Cover and simmer for 30 mins (or longer if you want a thicker stew)*

POTATO & LAMB STEW

1 lb new potatoes – scrubbed & halved
1½ lb lamb – cut into bite sized pieces
3 onions – peeled & sliced
1½ pints lamb stock
3 cloves garlic – crushed
4 carrots – peeled, sliced and boiled
4 oz frozen peas – boiled & drained
2 tbsp olive oil
1 tbsp fresh thyme – chopped

1. *Heat the oil and fry the onion and garlic for 5 mins*
2. *Add the lamb and fry until meat is sealed*
3. *Season, add the thyme and stock, bring to the boil and simmer for 30 mins*
4. *Add the other ingredients, season and simmer very gently for 1½ hours – stirring occasionally and ensuring it stays at the right consistency*

FRENCH LAMB & POTATO STEW

1 lb new potatoes – scrubbed & halved
2 lb lamb – cut into bite sized pieces
1 lb broad beans
1 lb frozen peas
1 pint lamb stock
½ pint dry white wine
8 shallots – peeled & sliced
4 tbsp olive oil
3 tbsp crème fraiche
1 bouquet garni

1. *Heat the oil and fry the shallots until they start to soften. Remove with a slotted spoon and set aside*
2. *Fry the lamb until lightly browned*
3. *Season and add the stock, wine and bouquet garni. Bring to the boil, then reduce to a very low heat, cover and cook for 1 ½ hours*
4. *Add the potatoes, turn up the heat slightly and cook for 20 mins*
5. *Remove the bouquet garni, season and add the broad beans, peas and shallots. Cook for 20 more mins until the desired consistency is reached*
6. *Stir in the crème fraiche and serve*

LAMB & NEW POTATO STEW (2)

1 lb new potatoes – scrubbed & halved
1 lb lamb – fat removed & cubed
1 large aubergine – trimmed & cut into cubes
2 onions – peeled & chopped
¼ lb spinach – stalks removed & washed
1 large tin chopped tomatoes
4 tbsp fresh rosemary – chopped
1 tsp dried basil
2 tbsp plain flour
2 tbsp tomato purée
½ pint lamb stock
2 tbsp olive oil

1. *Put the lamb in a zip lock plastic bag with the flour and rosemary. Season and shake so the lamb is coated*
2. *Heat the oil and fry the lamb until browned. Remove with the slotted spoon and set aside*

3. *Add the potatoes, aubergine and onions to the pan, adding more oil if needed. Fry for 10 mins*
4. *Add the lamb, basil and purée. Season, stir and pour on the stock. Bring to the boil then reduce to a gentle simmer, cover and cook for one hour*
5. *Remove the cover, season and adjust the stock as required (add more or cook longer to reduce)*
6. *Add the spinach, stir and cook until it softens. Serve*

SLOW COOKED GARLICKY LAMB AND POTATOES

1 lb new potatoes – washed & halved
1 medium size leg of lamb
8 shallots – peeled
8 fl oz dry red wine
¼ lb bacon – rind removed
2 bulbs garlic – papery skin removed
2 cloves garlic – cut into slivers
2 bay leaves
1 tsp turmeric
1 tsp cumin
1 tsp coriander seeds
½ tsp ground cinnamon
½ tsp chilli powder
2 tbsp olive oil

1. *Spike the lamb with slivers of garlic*
2. *Mix the spices and rub into the lamb*
3. *Pre-heat oven to GM3/160°c/325°f*
4. *Heat the oil in a large pan and fry the bacon and shallots for 3 mins. Add the wine, potatoes, garlic and bay leaves. Bring to the boil*
5. *Place the lamb in a large casserole dish and pour on the potato mixture. Adjust the seasoning*
6. *Cover and place in the oven and cook for 3½ hours, check every hour and ensure there is enough liquid*
7. *Remove the cover and cook for 15 more mins*
8. *Remove the lamb, garlic and bay leaves. Squeeze the pulp from the garlic add to the sauce, season, reduce if necessary*
9. *Slice the lamb and serve with the potatoes and sauce*

SPICY POTATO & LAMB

1 lb potatoes – peeled & cut into chunks
1 lb lamb – cubed
4 large onions – peeled & sliced into thin rings
2 cloves garlic – crushed
1" root ginger – grated
1 tsp turmeric
1 tsp ground cumin
1 tsp ground coriander
1 tsp garam masala
3 tbsp vegetable oil

1. *Mix the turmeric, cumin and coriander with the ginger and garlic*

2. *Put the lamb into a bowl, add the mixture of spices and mix well. Refrigerate for 1 hour*

3. *Heat the oil until very hot. Add onions and cook under a high heat for 10 mins, stirring frequently. Remove onions with a slotted spoon and keep warm*

4. *Add lamb and fry until brown on all sides*

5. *Add potatoes and fry for 2-3 mins*

6. *Return onions to pan, stir and add ½ pint water. Season and bring back to the boil. Simmer covered for 1 hour 15 mins. Add the garam masala and adjust seasoning*

7. *Cook uncovered until the desired consistency is reached*

LAMB & POTATO CASSEROLE

1 lb new potatoes – scrubbed, halved & boiled
2 lb lamb – cubed
8 shallots – peeled
1 onion – peeled & diced
3 cloves garlic – crushed
½ lb green beans – trimmed, washed & boiled
8 baby carrots – washed & boiled
1 large tin chopped tomatoes
1½ pints lamb stock
2 tbsp plain flour
2 tbsp olive oil
3 tbsp fresh coriander – chopped

1. *Put the flour in a food bag, season and add the lamb. Shake until the lamb is evenly coated*

2. *Heat the oil and gently fry the lamb until browned. Remove the lamb with a slotted spoon and reserve*

3. *Add the onion and garlic, using more oil if necessary, and gently fry for 2 mins*

4. *Add the vegetables, tomatoes and lamb. Season, stir and pour on the stock. Bring to the boil, reduce to a gently simmer, cover and cook for 1½ hours, stirring occasionally*

5. *Remove the cover, add coriander, stir and cook uncovered until reduced to the required consistency and the lamb is cooked*

BAKED LAMB & POTATO FRICASSEE

1 lb potatoes – boiled & mashed
¾ lb cooked lamb – cut into bite sized pieces
1 packet onion sauce – made up as per instructions on packet
¼ lb frozen peas – boiled & drained
1 large carrot – peeled, sliced, boiled & drained

1. *Pre-heat oven to GM5/190°c/375°f*

2. *Line the base and sides of a casserole dish with the potato*

3. *Add the lamb, peas and carrot to the onion sauce, season and heat gently for 5 mins*

4. *Pour over the potato mixture and bake for 20 mins*

SPICY LAMB & POTATO STEW

1 lb potatoes – peeled & cubed
1 lb lamb – cubed
1 large onion – peeled & thinly sliced
3 cloves garlic – crushed
1 large tin chopped tomatoes
½ pint lamb stock
1 tbsp fresh basil – chopped
1 tbsp tomato purée
1 tsp paprika
3 tbsp fresh coriander – chopped
3 tbsp olive oil

1. *Heat the oil and fry the lamb until just browned. Remove with a slotted spoon and reserve*

2. *Add the potatoes, onion and garlic and fry for 5 mins*

3. Add the basil, purée and paprika. Stir and cook for 1 minute

4. Add the lamb, tomatoes and stock. Season, stir and bring back to the boil. Simmer for 20 mins

5. Add the coriander, adjust seasoning and stir

LAMB & POTATO PASTIES

1 lb potatoes – peeled, boiled & diced
8 oz lamb – cut into dices
1 onion – peeled & chopped
1 tsp turmeric
1 tsp cumin
Grated rind & juice of 1 lemon
1 lb puff pastry
1 egg – beaten
1 tbsp oil

1. Gently cook the lamb & onion in the oil until the onion is soft

2. Stir in the turmeric & cumin and cook for a further minute, then mix in the lemon rind & juice and the potatoes. Leave to cool then season well

3. Pre-heat oven to GM5/190°c/380°f

4. Roll out the pastry thinly and cut as many 6" circles as you can

5. Divide the filling equally among the circles. Moisten the edges with a little milk then fold into pasties & seal

6. Place the pasties on a baking tray & brush with the egg. Bake for 30-35 mins until golden brown

POTATO TOPPED LAMB

1 lb potatoes – peeled, boiled & mashed
½ lb cooked lamb – cubed
¼ lb mushrooms – cleaned & sliced
1 leek – washed and chopped
2 cloves garlic – peeled & crushed
3 fl oz low fat natural yoghurt
Juice of ½ lemon
2 tbsp fresh parsley chopped
1 oz butter
2 tbsp olive oil

1. Pre-heat oven to GM6/200°c/400°f

2. Heat the oil and gently cook the leeks for 5 mins

3. Add the garlic and cook for a further 2-3 mins

4. Add mushrooms and lamb. Season and cook for a further 5 mins

5. Add the lemon juice and yogurt – stir well and put in a oven proof dish

6. Mix the butter, parsley and seasoning with the mash and spread over the lamb mixture

7. Bake for 20-25 mins until the potato is slightly browned

GREEK LAMB & POTATO CASSEROLE

1 lb (waxy) potatoes – peeled & cubed
1 lb lamb – boned & cubed
1 large onion – peeled & chopped
7 oz tomatoes – chopped
¼ pint dry white wine
1 tbsp white wine vinegar
1 cinnamon stick
1 bay leaf
1 tbsp fresh thyme – chopped
1 tbsp plain flour
2 tbsp extra virgin olive oil

1. Heat half the oil in a large pan and fry the potatoes until lightly browned. Remove with a slotted spoon and drain on kitchen paper

2. Fry the lamb and onion until browned

3. Add the flour and stir well, cook for 2 more mins

4. Add the white wine vinegar, tomatoes and white wine. Bring gradually to the boil then add the thyme, cinnamon stick and bay leaf. Season. Reduce heat, cover and simmer on a very low heat for 1 hour

5. Add the potatoes and simmer for 1 more hour. Remove the cinnamon stick and bay leaf. Season

QUICK SHEPHERDS PIE

1 lb potatoes – boiled & mashed
¾ lb minced lamb
1 onion – peeled & chopped
¼ pint lamb stock
1 tbsp Worcester sauce
2 tbsp tomato purée
1 tsp dried oregano
1 tsp dried basil
1 tbsp olive oil
1 oz butter
Pinch fresh nutmeg

1. *Heat the oil and fry the onion until soft*
2. *Add the lamb, mix and fry until browned*
3. *Add the stock, Worcester sauce, purée, herbs and season – stir well*
4. *Bring to the boil and reduce to a simmer. Cook for 5 mins*
5. *Pre-heat oven to GM4/180°c/350°f*
6. *Put the meat in an ovenproof dish. Season*
7. *Mix half the butter and nutmeg into the mash then spoon over the meat and dot with the rest of the butter*
8. *Bake for 40 mins until golden brown*

PIRI-PIRI LAMB STEW

1 lb new potatoes – scrubbed & halved
1½ lbs lamb – cubed
1 small tin chopped tomatoes
3 tsp piri-piri sauce
½ pint lamb stock
1½ tbsp olive oil
2 tbsp fresh coriander – chopped

1. *Heat the oil to a high heat and stir fry the lamb until sealed. Remove with a slotted spoon and dry on kitchen paper*
2. *Put the lamb in a saucepan with a little oil, add the piri-piri, stir and cook for 1 minute*
3. *Add the potatoes, tomatoes, lamb stock, season, stir and bring to the boil. Reduce to a gentle simmer, cover and cook for 1 hour until the desired consistency is reached*
4. *Sprinkle with the coriander before serving*

LAMB & POTATO CURRY

1 lb potatoes – peeled & cubed
1½ lbs lamb – cubed
2 onions – peeled & chopped
5 cloves garlic – crushed
1" piece fresh ginger – grated
1 large tin chopped tomatoes
1 small tin coconut milk
1 pint lamb stock
8 oz plain yoghurt
1 tbsp ground cumin
1 tbsp garam masala
1 tbsp turmeric
1 tbsp milk chilli powder
2 tbsp vegetable oil
1 tbsp plain flour

1. *Heat the oil and fry the lamb until browned. Remove with a slotted spoon and set aside*
2. *Add the onion, garlic and ginger, cook for 3-4 mins*
3. *Add the flour and the spices. Season and stir well to mix. Cook for 2 mins*
4. *Add the tomatoes, coconut milk, stock and potatoes. Stir well, bring to the boil and simmer for about 1 hour until the potatoes are cooked and the right consistency is reached*
5. *Add the yoghurt, stir well and heat through*

LAMB & POTATO FRICASSE

1 lb potatoes – peeled, boiled & mashed
¾ lb cooked lamb – diced
¼ lb frozen peas – boiled & drained
1 packet onion sauce – made with milk
1 egg – beaten

1. *Pre-heat oven to GM5/190°c/375°f*
2. *Cover the base and sides of an ovenproof dish with the potatoes while still hot. Season and brush with the egg*
3. *When the onion sauce is made, add the lamb and peas and heat through. Pour onto the potatoes*
4. *Bake for 15 mins*

LAMB & POTATO CHEESE BAKE

1 lb potatoes – peeled, boiled & sliced
1 lb cooked lamb – diced
1 onion – peeled & chopped
2 cloves garlic – peeled & crushed
1 small tin chopped tomatoes
1 pint cheese sauce (see below)
1 tbsp fresh rosemary – chopped
3 tbsp olive oil
1 oz butter

1. Heat 1 tbsp oil and fry the onion and garlic for 5 mins

2. Add the lamb, tomatoes and rosemary, simmer for 10 mins

3. Fry the potatoes in the remaining oil until lightly browned

4. Pre-heat oven to GM4/180°c/350°f

5. Layer the bottom of a casserole dish with about $^1/_3$ of the potatoes, add ½ the lamb mixture then ½ the cheese sauce. Add another $^1/_3$ of the potatoes, repeat layers and top with the rest of the potatoes. Dot with butter

6. Place in oven and cook for 30-40 mins until browned

Cheese Sauce
2 oz butter
2 oz flour
1 pint milk
3 oz cheese – grated
Seasoning

1. Melt butter, add flour (to make roux) slowly add milk, season, bring to boil and allow to thicken. Add the cheese, season and stir.

POTATOES & LAMB CHOPS

1 lb new potatoes – washed & halved
8 large lamb chops
2 onions – peeled & chopped
2 cloves garlic – crushed
2 tbsp redcurrant jelly
2 tbsp chopped fresh mint

1. Pre-heat oven to GM6/200°c/400°f

2. Rub the jelly onto the lamb and season

3. Heat the oil in a large pan and gently fry the garlic for 2 mins

4. Add the chops and continue to cook until the chops start to brown

5. Remove the chops and add the onion. Cook for 3-4 mins

6. Put the potatoes in a medium roasting tin so they cover the whole base. Season and add the onions and oil (using more if necessary) Stir well so the potatoes are covered, sprinkle with the mint

7. Place the chops on top of the potatoes and cook for 30 mins. Turn the chops half way through cooking

POTATO & MINCE ROLL

1 lb potatoes – peeled, cooked & mashed
10 oz minced beef
1 onion – peeled & chopped
2 cloves garlic – crushed
1 green pepper – peeled, de-seeded & cubed
1 large tin tomatoes
3 tbsp tomato purée
1 tbsp parsley – chopped
1 tsp chilli powder
1 tbsp vegetable oil

1. Heat the oil in a pan and cook the garlic, pepper and onion until soft. Add the mince and chilli powder and cook for 20 mins. Drain off the oil and fat

2. Mix in the potatoes and parsley. Season.

3. Make the sauce – heat the tomatoes and purée together in a small pan until simmering. Season

4. Take a clean damp tea towel and place the mince and potato mixture in the middle. Shape the mixture into a roll and place on a plate and pour the sauce over

QUICK POTATO MINCE

1 lb potatoes – peeled & diced
1 lb lean beef mince
2 onions – peeled & chopped
¼ lb frozen peas
1 large tin chopped tomatoes
2 oz butter
2 tsp curry powder

1. *Melt the butter and fry the onions until softened*

2. *Meanwhile dry fry the mince until browned*

3. *Put all the ingredients in a large pan, season & heat through, then simmer very gently for 45 mins – adding water if necessary*

POTATO TOPPED STUFFED PEPPERS

1 lb potatoes – peeled, boiled & mashed
1 lb minced beef
4 green peppers – halved & de-seeded
2 eggs – separated
1 large tin tomatoes
1 onion – peeled & finely chopped
2 cloves garlic – crushed
2 oz cheddar cheese – grated
1 tbsp dried oregano
1 beef stock cube – crumbled
1 tbsp olive oil

1. *Dry fry the mince until brown, drain the excess fat*

2. *Meanwhile heat the oil and fry the onion until nearly soft, add the garlic and cook for 1 more minute*

3. *Pre-heat the oven to GM6/200°c/400°f*

4. *Add the onion and garlic to the mince, stir, then add the tomatoes, oregano and stock cube. Season and stir. Bring to a simmer then leave to cook on a very low heat*

5. *Place the 8 halves of pepper skin side up in a greased roasting tin and cook for 15 mins*

6. *Meanwhile add the egg yolks and half the cheese to the potatoes*

7. *Whisk the egg whites until stiff and fold into the potatoes*

8. *Remove the peppers, turn them skin side down, add the mince, top with the potato mixture, sprinkle with the remaining cheese and cook in the oven for 20 mins*

MEAT & POTATO BAKE

1 lb potatoes – boiled and mashed
1 lb minced beef
1 medium onion – peeled & finely chopped
1 egg – beaten
1 tbsp breadcrumbs
1 tbsp fresh parsley – chopped
1 oz butter

1. *Pre-heat oven to GM6/200°c/400°f*

2. *Heat the oil and gently fry the onion for about 3 mins*

3. *In a mixing bowl, mix the minced beef, onion, egg, breadcrumbs, parsley and seasoning together. Remove and place in a baking tin. Bake for 20 mins*

4. *Remove and cover with the potato. Dot with butter and bake until the potato starts to brown*

CURRIED MINCE & POTATOES

1 lb potatoes – peeled & cubed
1 lb minced beef
1 onion – peeled & chopped
1 courgette – cubed
4 cherry tomatoes – quartered
3 tbsp curry paste
3 tbsp tomato purée
2 tbsp pickle

1. *Dry fry the mince and drain off the fat. Add the onion and garlic and fry gently for 2-3 mins*

2. *Add all the other ingredients except the tomatoes. Season, stir and heat through. Cover and simmer for 25 mins*

3. *Add the cherry tomatoes, stir. Cook uncovered for a few more mins*

QUICK MEDITERRANEAN BEEF & POTATO PIE

1 lb potatoes – boiled & mashed
1 lb minced beef
4 oz frozen peas – boiled & drained
1 large can Minestrone soup
2 oz cheddar cheese – grated

1. *Pre-heat oven to GM7/220°c/425°f*
2. *Dry fry the beef and drain off the excess fat*
3. *Add the soup and the peas. Season and heat gently for 20 mins*
4. *Put the beef mixture in a casserole dish and spoon the potato mixture on top*
5. *Bake for 15 mins, remove and sprinkle with the cheese and bake for 10 more mins*

QUICK COTTAGE PIE

1 lb potatoes – peeled, boiled & mashed
1 lb minced beef
1 packet minestrone soup
2 onions – peeled & sliced
1 tbsp olive oil

1. *Pre-heat oven to GM5/190°c/375°f*
2. *Dry fry the mince until browned*
3. *Meanwhile heat the oil and fry the onions until they start to soften*
4. *Make up the soup with half the required amount of water*
5. *Mix the soup with the mince, add the onions, season and stir*
6. *Put the mince in an ovenproof dish and spread the potatoes on top. Bake for about 30 mins*

KIDNEYS IN POTATOES

1 lb (2 x large) potatoes – washed & pricked
2 lamb's kidneys
5 oz butter
2 tbsps milk

1. *Rub the potatoes with a small amount of butter and bake for 1 hour at GM4/180°c/350°f*
2. *Skin & core the kidneys keeping each one whole. Season & set aside*
3. *When potatoes are cooked cut a lid from the long side of each one. Put the lids to one side and scoop out the contents. Mix the potato with all the milk and most of the rest of the butter. Season and mix well*
4. *Half fill each skin and place a kidney in each. Put the rest of the potato on top and put the lids back on*
5. *Cook in the oven for another 30 mins*
6. *Put a small piece of butter under each lid before serving*

LIVER & ONION ROSTI

1 lb potatoes – peeled & grated
1 lb liver – cut into cubes
2 onions – peeled & chopped
3 sticks celery – washed, trimmed & chopped
½ pint chicken stock
2 tbsp fresh parsley – chopped
2 oz butter
Seasoned flour

1. *Put half of the liver in a plastic bag with the flour and shake so the liver is coated. Repeat with the remaining liver*
2. *Melt the butter and fry the liver until it is sealed – then remove with a slotted spoon and set aside*
3. *Fry the onion in the butter (add more if necessary) for 5 mins*
4. *Add the liver, potato, celery and parsley. Season and stir and pour on the stock. Mix well and bring to the boil*
5. *Reduce heat, cover and cook very gently for about 45 mins*

POTATO & LIVER CASSEROLE

1 lb potatoes – peeled, boiled, cooled & sliced
½ lb lamb's liver – washed
2 onions – peeled & sliced
4 rashers bacon – chopped
⅓ pint lamb stock
1 oz lard
1 oz seasoned flour

1. Pre-heat oven to GM5/190°c/375°f
2. Blanch the liver for 3 mins, drain and dip in the flour. Chop into pieces
3. Heat the lard and fry the potatoes, onions and liver for 5 mins
4. Put half the potatoes in the base of an ovenproof dish, season and add the other ingredients
5. Add the remaining potatoes, season and pour on the stock. Cover and cook for 35-40 mins

PORK & POTATO IN VINEGAR SAUCE

1 lb potatoes – peeled, boiled, drained & cubed
1 lb pork – cut into bite sized pieces
2 courgettes – cut into chunks
½ lb fine green beans – boiled & halved
4 fl oz balsamic vinegar
1½ oz sugar
3 tbsp olive oil

1. Heat the vinegar in a small pan and add the sugar, stir until the sugar has dissolved.
2. Pre-heat oven to GM6/200°c/400°f
3. Heat the olive oil and fry the pork until lightly browned
4. Brush a little oil into the bottom of a roasting tin
5. Remove the pork with a slotted spoon and put in a roasting tin with the potatoes and courgettes, season and drizzle over the olive oil from the pan. Cook in the oven for 10 mins
6. Add the beans and cook for a further 5 mins
7. Pour over the vinegar and serve

CHEESY PEASY

1 lb potatoes – peeled and cut into chunks
1 lb frozen peas
8 rashers bacon
5 oz cheddar cheese – grated
2 oz butter

1. Boil the potatoes in a large pan as normal then with 5 mins to go add the peas. Return to the boil. When peas are cooked remove and drain
2. Grill the bacon, remove and chop into bits
3. Put the potatoes and peas in a large pan, add the butter, season and mash
4. Add the bacon and half the cheese. Mix well
5. Put the mixture in a roasting tin, put the rest of the cheese on top, season and grill until golden brown

GAMMON & POTATO STEW

1 lb potatoes – peeled & cubed
1 lb whole gammon – soaked overnight
1 large tin cannellini beans – drained
3 onions – peeled & chopped
3 bay leaves
2 tbsp fresh parsley – chopped

1. Drain the meat and wash the pan. Return the meat to the pan and add the bay leaves and onions. Pour on enough water to just cover the meat then slowly bring to the boil. Reduce to a very low heat , cover and cook for about 2 hours until the meat is tender
2. Remove the meat, cut off the rind and cut into bite sized pieces
3. Remove the bay leaves, add the potatoes, gammon, parsley and season. Stir well and bring back to the boil. Simmer for 10-15 mins
4. Add the beans, adjust the seasoning and simmer for about 10 more mins until the potatoes are cooked and the desired consistency is reached

POTATO, BACON & EGG PLATTER

1 lb potatoes – peeled & sliced
10 rashers bacon – fat removed & chopped
2 onions – peeled & sliced
4 eggs – poached
¼ pint chicken stock
1 oz butter

1. Melt the butter and cook the onions for 5 mins

2. Add the bacon and potatoes, season, stir well and cook for 2 mins

3. Add the stock, bring to the boil very briefly then cover and reduce to a very low heat. Cook for 45 mins or until the stock is almost gone

4. Serve topped with the poached eggs

PORK & APPLE BAKE

1 lb potatoes – peeled, boiled & mashed
1 lb pork – fat removed & cubed
2 cooking apples – peeled, cored & sliced
1 onion – peeled & thinly sliced
6 tbsp dry cider
1 tsp mustard
1 tsp fresh sage – chopped
1 oz butter

1. Pre-heat oven to GM4/180°c/350°f

2. Put the pork in an ovenproof dish, add the sage, mustard, onion and apple. Season and pour on the cider. Stir well

3. Cover and bake for 1 hour 30 mins

4. Remove, stir well, season and spread the potatoes on top. Dot with butter and return to the oven for 20 mins

POTATO & BACON HOT POT

1 lb potatoes – peeled & cut into chunks
8 rashers bacon – derinded
1 onion – peeled & chopped
2 sticks celery – trimmed & chopped
2 cloves garlic – crushed
1½ pints chicken stock
½ lb frozen peas
2 tbsp fresh mint – chopped
1 tbsp olive oil

1. Boil the potatoes for 15 mins. Drain

2. Heat the oil and gently fry the celery and onion until the onion starts to soften. Add the garlic and cook for 2 mins

3. Add the peas and mint, season then pour on the stock. Stir and bring to the boil then simmer for 5 mins

4. Transfer half the mixture to a blender and liquidise. Return to the pan, season and re-heat

5. Meanwhile grill the bacon until almost crisp and cut into pieces

6. Add the potatoes and bacon to the pan, stir and continue to heat until the potatoes are warmed through

SPANISH POTATO STEW

1 lb new potatoes – scrubbed
½ lb green beans – trimmed & halved
½ lb frozen peas
¼ lb smoked ham – sliced
5 tomatoes – skinned & halved
1 bunch spring onions – trimmed & chopped
10 baby carrots – washed and halved
10 asparagus tips
3 eggs – hard boiled & quartered
16 fl oz beef stock
3 tbsp extra virgin olive oil

1. Heat the oil in a large pan and fry the onions for 2 mins

2. Add the tomatoes and fry for 2 more mins

3. Add the potatoes and stock. Season and bring to a simmer. Cook for 5 mins

4. Add the beans, peas and carrots and bring to the boil. Simmer for 10 mins

5. Meanwhile par boil the asparagus for 3 mins and drain

6. Add the ham and asparagus to the stew and stir well, continue to simmer until the desired consistency is reached

7. Adjust seasoning and top with the eggs

169

POTATOES COOKED WITH BACON

1lb potatoes
½ lb bacon – in 1 piece
15 small onions – pickling size
8 fl oz chicken stock
¼ pt white wine
1 bouquet garni
1 oz flour
1 oz butter

1. Remove the rind from the bacon and cut into small thick pieces. Blanch in boiling water for 5 mins. Remove with a slotted spoon

2. Peel the onions and blanch them, whole in the same water for 5 mins. Remove with slotted spoon

3. Peel the potatoes and cover with cold water

4. Put the butter in a large saucepan and heat slowly until melted. Remove from the heat, beat in the flour and season. Add all the stock and mix until smooth

5. Return to the heat and add the wine and mix, simmer for 5 mins

6. Add the onions, bacon and bouquet garni

7. Cut the potatoes into thick chips and add to the mixture. Cover and cook very slowly for 45 mins

8. Remove cover and simmer until desired consistency is reached

ITALIAN PORK AND POTATOES

1 lb potatoes – peeled & diced
1 lb pork – cubed
1 large onion – peeled & cut into wedges
2 cloves garlic – crushed
1 small tin chopped tomatoes
1 oz black olives – stoned & halved
6 fl oz chicken stock
2 tbsp tomato purée
3 fl oz dry red wine
2 tbsp flour
1 oz butter
1 tbsp fresh basil – chopped
1 tbsp olive oil

1. Heat the butter and oil in a large pan and fry the potato for 5 mins. Remove with a slotted spoon and drain on kitchen paper

2. Fry the pork until sealed on each side. Remove

3. Add the onion and garlic and cook gently for 5 mins

4. Add the flour and tomato purée and cook for 1 minute

5. Pre-heat oven to GM4/180°c/350°f

6. Mix the wine with the stock and add gradually, stirring continually until a smooth sauce is formed

7. Add the potatoes, pork, tomatoes, olives and basil. Season, stir well and heat through put the mixture in an ovenproof dish, cover and bake for 1 hour

ONE PAN BRUNCH

1 lb new potatoes – scrubbed & quartered
3 eggs
3 tomatoes – cut in wedges
6 rashers bacon – de-rinded & cut into large pieces
1 tbsp olive oil

1. Boil the potatoes for 5 mins and drain

2. Heat the oil in a frying pan and fry the potatoes for about 10 mins

3. Add the bacon and cook until it starts to turn colour

4. Add the tomatoes, stir and cook for 3 mins

5. Break the eggs over the potato mixture and continue to cook until the eggs have set

SPANISH POTATO BALLS WITH BACON

1 lb potatoes – boiled & mashed
4 oz flour
2 eggs – beaten
3 oz butter
3 oz cheddar cheese – grated
½ pint milk
8 rashers bacon – rinds removed
4 tomatoes – skinned

1. Pre-heat oven to GM8/220°c/450°f

2. Put the potatoes in a bowl. Add 3 oz of the flour, beaten eggs & season. Mix well

3. Roll the potato dough on a floured board into round shapes

4. Grease a shallow baking dish with half the butter and spread the potato balls on top

5. Put the rest of the butter, flour, cheese & milk into a saucepan. Heat gently, stirring continually until the sauce thickens. Season. Pour the sauce over the potato balls and bake for 7-8 mins

6. Meanwhile roll each bacon rasher around half a tomato so that the tomato is completely covered. Spear them onto kebab sticks

7. Place the kebabs on top of the potato balls, and cook for another 7-8 mins until the bacon is crisp and tomatoes cooked

BAKED POTATO & EGGS

1 lb potatoes – boiled & mashed
5 eggs
8 rashers bacon – lightly grilled & fat removed
1 oz butter
1 fl oz milk

1. Pre-heat oven to GM6/200°c/400°f

2. Beat 1 egg and mix it and the milk and butter into the mash. Season

3. Line a casserole dish with the potato and make 4 hollows

4. Put 2 rashers in each hollow then carefully break an egg on top of each

5. Bake for 12-15 mins until the eggs are set

BREAKFAST POTATO GRATIN

1 lb potatoes – peeled & very thinly sliced
1 onion – peeled & thinly sliced
2 cloves garlic – crushed
¼ pint vegetable stock
3 rashers bacon – grilled & chopped
4 mushrooms – sliced
2 oz butter
1 tbsp olive oil

1. Pre-heat oven to GM6/200°c/400°f

2. Heat half the butter and oil in a frying pan and fry the onion, garlic and mushrooms for about 5 mins. Add the bacon and stir well

3. Layers half the potatoes at the bottom of a small greased ovenproof dish. Pour in the onion mixture, season and add the rest of the potatoes

4. Pour in the stock, dot with butter and cook for about 45 mins

POTATO STEW

1 lb potatoes – peeled & diced
4 rashers bacon – de-rinded & cut into small pieces
½ lb mushrooms – cleaned & sliced
4 sage leaves – washed
Chicken stock
2 tbsp olive oil for frying

1. Pre-heat the oven to GM4/180°c/ 350°f

2. Heat a little oil in a pan and gently fry the potatoes until slightly brown on each side

3. Remove with a slotted spoon and put in the bottom of a buttered baking dish

4. Briefly fry the mushrooms in the remaining oil then put onto the potatoes with the bacon, sage leaves and seasoning. Pour enough stock to just cover and bake for 1 hour

POTATO, BACON & TOMATO BAKE

1 lb potatoes – peeled, boiled, cooled & sliced
8 rashers bacon – cut in half & derinded
3 tomatoes – sliced
½ pint cheese sauce – made from a packet
2 oz cheddar cheese – grated

1. Pre-heat oven to GM5/190°c/375°f

2. Grease the base of an oven proof dish and layer it with the potatoes. Season and add the bacon and tomatoes

3. Pour on the cheese sauce, season again and sprinkle with the grated cheese

4. Bake for 20 mins

POTATO & BACON PIE

1 lb new potatoes – scrubbed, boiled & halved
½ lb bacon – rind removed
3 courgettes – sliced lengthways
2 eggs
1 egg yolk
7 fl oz double cream
2 tbsp parmesan cheese – grated
2 tbsp olive oil

1. *Pre-heat oven to GM6/200°c/400°f*
2. *Heat the oil and fry the courgettes until soft. Remove and place on kitchen paper to dry*
3. *Put the eggs, yolk and cream in a jug, season and beat until mixed*
4. *Layer half the potatoes in an ovenproof dish, season and sprinkle with the cheese*
5. *Add the courgettes then the bacon. Top with the remaining potatoes*
6. *Pour the egg mixture on top and bake for 30 mins*

NEW POTATO BREAKFAST

1 lb new potatoes – scrubbed & quartered
8 rashers bacon – rind removed & chopped
2 eggs
2 tbsp olive oil

1. *Heat the oil in a frying pan and fry the potatoes for 10 mins*
2. *Add the bacon and fry for 10 more mins*
3. *Meanwhile fry the eggs in another pan*
4. *Remove the potato mixture and put on plate, season and serve topped with fried egg*

POTATO & LEEK PIE

1 lb potatoes – peeled & sliced
2 leeks – trimmed, washed & sliced lengthways
¼ lb ham – chopped
2 oz cheddar cheese – grated
1 oz flour – seasoned
2 oz butter
10 fl oz milk

1. *Pre-heat oven to GM4/180°c/350°f*
2. *Grease a small ovenproof dish and put ⅓ of the potatoes in the bottom. Season*
3. *Add half the leeks and sprinkle with half the flour. Dot with half the butter. Repeat finishing with the ham topped with a layer of potatoes*
4. *Add the cheese, season and pour in the milk. Cover and bake for 35 mins*
5. *Remove cover and bake for 10 more mins*

ITALIAN POTATO CAKE

1 lb (floury) potatoes – boiled & mashed
3 oz pancetta – chopped
2 eggs – beaten
2 cloves garlic – crushed
4 oz fresh parmesan – grated
2 oz mozzarella – diced
2 slices salami – chopped
3 fl oz milk
1 oz butter
1 oz white breadcrumbs

1. *Pre-heat oven to GM5/190°c/375°f*
2. *Beat the milk and butter into the potatoes until you have a really fluffy mash*
3. *Beat the pancetta, eggs, garlic, salami and the cheeses into the mash. Season*
4. *Put the mash in a greased ovenproof dish, and sprinkle with breadcrumbs*
5. *Bake for 1 hour*

POTATO & BACON STEW

1 lb (floury) potatoes – peeled & cubed
10 rashers smoked bacon – rind removed & chopped
5 carrots – peeled & chopped
5 sticks celery – washed, trimmed & chopped
2 onions – peeled & chopped
2 cloves garlic – crushed
1½ pints chicken stock
5 tbsp fresh parsley – chopped
1 tbsp fresh thyme – chopped
3 oz butter
5 tbsp double cream

1. Heat the butter and gently fry the bacon, onions and garlic until the onions soften

2. Add the potatoes, carrots, celery and thyme. Stir well and cook for 5 mins

3. Add the stock, bring to the boil and simmer for 20 mins, reducing slightly

4. Remove from the heat add the cream and parsley. Season, stir well and serve

1. Heat the oil and gently fry the pork, potato, onion and garlic for 5 mins

2. Add the flour and cumin. Season and fry for 2 mins

3. Add the carrots, courgettes, orange juice and water, stir well and heat until nearly boiling. Simmer for 20 mins or until sufficiently reduced

PORK & POTATO BAKE

1 lb potatoes – peeled & sliced
2 pork chops
1 onion – peeled & sliced
3 oz cheddar cheese – grated
1 tbsp wholegrain mustard
5 tbsp milk
1 tbsp extra virgin olive oil

1. Pre-heat oven to GM7/220°c/425°f

2. Heat the oil and fry the onion for 5 mins

3. Put the potatoes in a roasting tin, add the onions and mix well to coat. Add more oil if needed

4. Bake for 20 mins, add the chops and bake for 10 more mins

5. Mix the cheese, mustard and milk together and warm through in a small pan

6. Remove the potatoes and chops from the oven, pour over the sauce and place under a pre-heated grill for 5 mins

PORK, POTATO & ORANGE STEW

1 lb potatoes – peeled & cut into chunks
1 lb pork fillet – cut into bite sized pieces
1 onion – peeled & sliced
2 cloves garlic – crushed
½ lb carrots – peeled & sliced
2 courgettes – peeled & sliced
10 fl oz orange juice
8 fl oz water
1 tsp ground cumin
1 tbsp plain flour
2 tbsp olive oil

POTATO & BACON TORTILLA

1 lb (waxy) potatoes – peeled & diced
5 rashers bacon – diced
6 large eggs – beaten
2 onions – peeled & chopped
1 tbsp fresh parsley – chopped
3 tbsp olive oil

1. Boil the potatoes for 5 mins then drain

2. Heat the oil and fry the onions till soft

3. Add the potatoes and bacon and cook for a further 5 mins

4. Add the parsley and seasoning to the eggs and pour onto the potatoes and onions. Mix together and cook until almost set

5. Finish under a pre-heated grill until browned

BACON & SPRING ONION WITH NEW POTATOES

1 lb new potatoes – scrubbed, halved & boiled
5 rashers bacon – fat removed
6 spring onions – trimmed and chopped
2 oz butter

1. Pre-heat the grill

2. Grill the bacon until crispy, remove from heat and place on kitchen paper. Chop into bite sized pieces

3. Heat the butter in a saucepan and gently fry the spring onion for 2 mins

4. Add the potatoes and bacon to the pan, season and stir well so the potatoes are evenly coated

173

CRUSTY HAM & POTATO

1 lb potatoes – peeled, boiled & mashed
½ lb cooked ham – diced
6 spring onions – trimmed & chopped
1 egg – beaten
1 tbsp fresh parsley – chopped
2 oz butter

1. Put the mash in a large bowl and add all the other ingredients except the butter

2. Season and mix well

3. Cover with cling film and refrigerate for at least 3 hours

4. Heat half the butter in a large pan. Spread out the potato mixture and add it to the pan. Cook over a low heat for 20 mins then turn it onto a plate

5. Melt the rest of the butter and slide the cake back into the pan the other side up. Cook for another 20 mins

APPLE & POTATO PIE

1 lb potatoes – peeled & sliced
1 lb cooking apples – peeled, cored & sliced
½ lb onions – peeled & sliced
½ lb tomatoes – sliced
½ lb cooked ham – diced
2 tbsp dried mixed herbs
½ pint vegetable stock
½ frozen puff pastry – thawed
1 egg – beaten

1. Pre-heat oven to GM5/200°c/400°f

2. Put a layer of potatoes in the base of a casserole dish then add layers of apple, onion, tomatoes and ham – lightly seasoning each layer. Finish with a layer of potatoes

3. Mix the herbs into the stock and pour onto the potato mixture

4. Cover with the pastry, seal the edges and brush with the egg

5. Bake for 45 mins

BREAKFAST GRATIN

1 lb potatoes – peeled
1½ tbsp olive oil
2 small onions – thinly sliced
1 clove garlic – crushed
4 oz bacon – chopped
2 medium tomatoes – sliced
1½ tbsp parsley – roughly chopped

1. Boil the potatoes for 10 mins. Drain & allow to cool slightly. Grate them into a bowl

2. Pre-heat oven to GM5/190°c/375°f

3. Heat 1 tbsp of oil oil in a pan & cook the onions for 3-4 mins. Add the garlic & bacon & cook for 2 more mins

4. Add the onion mixture to the potatoes & mix well return to the pan and cook over a medium heat for 10 mins, stirring frequently

5. Spoon the mixture into a large greased ovenproof dish & top with the sliced tomatoes. Mix the parsley with the remaining oil & sprinkle over the tomatoes

6. Bake for 20 mins

POTATO & BACON GRATIN

1 lb potatoes – peeled & sliced thinly
9 oz bacon – rind removed & chopped
1 small tub soft cheese
2 cloves garlic – crushed
1 medium onion – peeled & sliced
¼ pint milk
3 oz cheddar cheese – grated
1 tbsp dried mixed herbs
1 tbsp extra virgin olive oil

1. Heat the oil in a pan and gently cook the bacon, onion and garlic for 5 mins

2. Pre-heat oven to GM5/180°c/375°f

3. Layer half the potatoes in a lightly buttered ovenproof dish. Pour the bacon mixture over it and sprinkle with the mixed herbs and season. Layer the rest of the potatoes on top

4. Mix the milk and cream cheese into a sauce and pour over the potatoes. Top with the cheddar cheese and bake for 45 mins

BACON & POTATO CASSEROLE

1 lb potatoes – peeled & thinly sliced
½ lb bacon – chopped
½ lb tomatoes – sliced
1 medium onion – peeled & sliced
½ pint milk
1 tbsp sage

1. Pre-heat oven to GM5/190c°/375°f
2. Butter a casserole dish and layer half of the potatoes in the bottom
3. Cover with the bacon, then onion, then tomatoes. Season and sprinkle with some sage
4. Top with the rest of the potatoes. Pour the milk over the top. Dot with butter and bake for 1 hour

BACON, SAGE & ONION CASSEROLE

1 lb potatoes – peeled & sliced
2 medium onions – peeled & sliced
5 rashers bacon – rind removed & chopped
1½ tbsp fresh sage – chopped (or 1 tbsp dried)
2 tbsp vegetable oil

1. Heat the oil and fry the onion gently until it starts to soften
2. Add the potatoes, bacon, sage and season. Mix well
3. Cover and cook on a slow heat for 40 mins, stirring occasionally

BAKED EGGS & POTATOES

1 lb potatoes – boiled & mashed
4 eggs
½ onion – peeled & very finely chopped
¼ lb cooked ham – finely chopped
4 egg yolks
2 oz cheddar cheese – grated
2 oz butter

1. Pre-heat oven to GM5/190°c/375°f
2. Beat the egg yolks and onion into the potato and season
3. Spread the potatoes in a shallow casserole dish and make 4 hollows
4. Line each hollow with ¼ of the ham and carefully break an egg into each one. Sprinkle with the cheese and dot with the butter. Season
5. Bake for 20 mins

POTATOES WITH RICE

1 lb potatoes – peeled & cut into small dices
4 oz basmati rice – boiled & drained
2 rashers bacon – de-rinded & chopped
2 cloves garlic – crushed
1½ oz sun dried tomatoes – drained & chopped
6 fl oz single cream
1 tbsp fresh basil – chopped
1 oz butter
1 tbsp olive oil

1. Heat the oil and butter in a pan and add the potatoes, bacon and garlic. Cook gently until potatoes are tender
2. Add all the other ingredients and simmer for 3-4 mins until heated through

POTATO & BACON SUPPER

1 lb potatoes – peeled, halved, boiled & drained
½ lb bacon – de-rinded
2 onions – peeled & sliced
6 oz button mushrooms
10 fl oz double cream
6 oz cheddar cheese – grated
2 tbsp olive oil

1. Heat the oil in a pan and fry the onion and bacon until the onion is soft
2. Add the mushrooms and cook gently for 5 mins
3. Turn the grill on and transfer the mixture to a flame proof dish
4. Add the potatoes and pour over the cream, add black pepper and cheese. Grill until the cheese bubbles

HAM & CHEESE POTATO CAKE

1 lb potatoes – peeled, boiled & mashed
6 oz sliced smoked ham
6 oz Applewood smoked cheese – grated
2 eggs – beaten
3 fl oz milk
2 oz butter
Pinch of nutmeg

1. *Pre-heat oven to GM6/200°c/400°f*

2. *While the mash is still warm beat in the eggs, milk, butter and nutmeg. Season*

3. *Grease the base of a small round ovenproof dish and layer it with one quarter of the mash. Layer the other ingredients on top of the base in the following order (seasoning each layer of cheese and ham) – half the ham, quarter of potatoes, half the cheese, quarter of potato, rest of the ham, rest of the potato and top with the rest of the cheese*

4. *Bake for about 25 mins*

POTATO & BACON GRATIN (2)

1 lb potatoes – peeled & sliced
10 oz bacon – rind removed & chopped
1 onion – peeled & finely sliced
2 cloves garlic
¼ pint milk
6 oz cheddar cheese – grated
1 tbsp olive oil

1. *Pre-heat oven to GM4/180°c/350°f*

2. *Heat the oil in a pan and gently cook the bacon, onion and garlic for 5 mins*

3. *Put a layer of potatoes in the bottom of the casserole dish. Add half the bacon and onion mixture then repeat the layers finishing with a layer of potatoes*

4. *Heat the milk and stir in half the cheese then season. Once the cheese has melted, pour the sauce onto the potatoes*

5. *Sprinkle with the remaining cheese and bake for 45 mins*

POTATO, LEEK & HAM GRATIN

1 lb potatoes – peeled & thinly sliced
2 leeks – washed & thinly sliced
¼ lb cooked ham – cubed
3 fl oz chicken stock
4 fl oz double cream
6 fl oz milk
2 cloves garlic – crushed
2 bay leaves
2 oz cheddar cheese – grated

1. *Pre-heat oven to GM4/180°c/350°f*

2. *Put the cream, stock, milk, garlic and bay leaves in a pan, season, stir well and heat until nearly, but not, boiling. Remove from heat*

3. *Put the potatoes, leeks and ham in a greased casserole dish, season and pour on the sauce. Season and sprinkle with the cheese*

4. *Cover and bake for 1 hour*

5. *Remove the cover and bay leaves and cook for a further 10 mins*

HERB FRITTATA

1 lb potatoes – peeled, diced & par boiled for 10 mins
10 oz bacon – rind removed & chopped
9 eggs – beaten
2 onions – peeled & diced
2 courgettes – halved lengthways then sliced
1 large red pepper – skinned & diced
1 tsp dried thyme
1 tsp dried sage
5 tbsp milk
2 tbsp olive oil

1. *Heat the oil in a large pan and gently fry the bacon, onions, courgettes and pepper for 5 mins. Add the potatoes and stir, cook for 5 more mins*

2. *Beat together the eggs, milk and herbs. Season and pour the mixture over the vegetables and cook slowly until the base has set*

3. *Put the pan under a pre-heated grill and cook until the top is completely set*

WESTERN HOT POT

1 lb potatoes – peeled & sliced (about ¼" thick)
8 oz onions – peeled & sliced
8 oz bacon – chopped

1. Pre-heat oven to GM3/150°c/325°f
2. Arrange a layer of potato at the bottom of a casserole dish, add a layer of onion followed by the bacon. Season. Repeat the layers seasoning each one and finishing with a layer of potatoes
3. Cover and cook at for 2 hours
4. Remove lid and cook for 20 minutes longer

POTATO & BACON MIX

1 lb potatoes – peeled, boiled, drained & cubed
6 rashers bacon – de-rinded & chopped
1 small onion – peeled & chopped
2 stalks celery – washed & chopped
3 fl oz cider vinegar
4 sprigs parsley – chopped
1 tsp dried sage

1. Cook the bacon until crisp in a frying pan
2. Put the onion, celery, vinegar, parsley and sage into a blender, season and mix for a few seconds
3. Add the mixture to the bacon and gradually heat until boiling
4. Mix the potato cubes and the bacon mixture in a large bowl

BREAKFAST POTATO GRATIN (2)

1 lb potatoes – peeled & thinly sliced
1 red onion – peeled & sliced
¼ pint chicken stock
5 rashers bacon – grilled & chopped
4 mushrooms – sliced
2 oz butter
1 tbsp olive oil

1. Pre-heat oven to GM6/200°c/400°f
2. Heat half the butter and oil in a frying pan

and fry the onion and mushrooms for about 5 mins. Add the bacon and stir well
3. Layer half the potatoes at the bottom of a small greased ovenproof dish. Pour in the onion mixture, season and add the rest of the potatoes
4. Pour in the stock, dot with butter and cook for about 1 hour

POTATO & BACON DAUPHINOIS

1 lb potatoes – peeled & sliced thinly
4 oz bacon – chopped
3 oz Gruyere cheese – grated
1 egg yolk
¼ pint double cream
1 tbsp parsley – chopped

1. Pre-heat oven to GM4/180°c/350°f
2. Boil the potatoes for 2 mins. Allow to cool and pat dry. Arrange the potatoes in the bottom of an ovenproof dish
3. Mix the cream, bacon and egg yolk together and pour onto the potatoes. Season and sprinkle with the parsley and cheese.
4. Cover and bake for 45 mins

POTATO, LEEK & HAM FRITTATA

1 lb potatoes – peeled & sliced
7 oz cooked ham – chopped
4 leeks – trimmed and sliced
10 eggs
2 tbsp fresh parsley – chopped
5 tbsp extra virgin olive oil

1. Boil the potatoes for 5 mins. Drain and allow to cool
2. Heat the oil in a large pan and gently cook the leeks for about 10 mins
3. Add the ham, potatoes and leeks. Mix well, season and cook gently for 2-3 mins
4. Beat the eggs and whisk in the parsley and seasoning
5. Pour in the egg mixture and cook for about for about 10 mins. When the eggs begin to set place the pan under a hot grill until browned

POTATO HAM & GREEN BEAN HASH

1 lb new potatoes – scrubbed & halved
½ lb green beans – trimmed, washed & halved
¼ lb baby carrots – scrubbed & halved
1 bunch spring onions – trimmed, washed & sliced
3 tomatoes – skinned & chopped
½ lb frozen peas
¼ lb smoked ham – cubed
10 asparagus tips – trimmed & blanched
3 eggs – hard boiled, cooled & sliced
1 pint beef stock
3 tbsp olive oil

1. *Heat the oil in a large pan and gently cook the spring onions and tomatoes for 5 mins*
2. *Add the potatoes and the stock and simmer for 5 mins*
3. *Add the beans, carrots, and peas, bring back to the boil then simmer for 10 minutes*
4. *Add the ham, season, warm through and serve topped with asparagus and egg*

MACARONI CHEESE WITH POTATO

1 lb potatoes – peeled & diced
1 lb macaroni
½ lb bacon – rind removed & diced
¼ lb parmesan cheese – grated
8 fl oz whipping cream

1. *Pre-heat oven to GM4/180°c/350°f*
2. *Boil the potatoes and macaroni together for 10 mins. Drain*
3. *Fry the bacon in its own fat until just cooked. Remove from the heat*
4. *Add the cream to the bacon, season and stir*
5. *Add the potatoes and macaroni and mix well*
6. *Put half the mixture into an ovenproof dish, season and sprinkle with half the cheese. Repeat*
7. *Bake for 12-15 mins then slide the dish under a pre-heated grill for 2 minutes or until golden brown*

POTATO & BACON BAKE

1 lb potatoes – peeled & sliced
6 rashers smoked streaky bacon – chopped
1 tbsp fresh thyme – chopped
1 large onion – finely sliced
1 lb turnips – peeled and sliced
4 oz cheddar cheese – grated
3 oz butter

1. *Pre-heat oven to GM4/180°c/350°f*
2. *Heat half the butter in an ovenproof frying pan and add the bacon and cook for a few minutes. Add the thyme and onions, season and cook for a further 8-10 minutes until the onions are soft and golden.*
3. *Put the onions into a bowl, leaving the buttery juices in the pan*
4. *Off the heat, layer the sliced turnips and potatoes in the pan with a scattering of fried onions, a sprinkling of cheese and some dots of butter between the layers. Season with salt and plenty of pepper*
5. *Cover the pan with foil and bake for 1-1½ hours until the turnips and potatoes are tender*
6. *Leave the cake to cool for 5 minutes. Turn upside down onto a plate then cut into wedges*

POTATO SAUSAGES

1 lb potatoes – peeled, boiled & mashed
2 oz Wensleydale cheese – crumbled
2 leeks – washed & shredded
2 eggs – beaten
2 tbsp fresh parsley – chopped
4 tbsp flour
1 oz butter
1 tbsp olive oil
2 oz breadcrumbs

1. *Melt the butter in a pan and cook the leeks for 5 mins*
2. *Remove and allow to cool. Stir in the potato, cheese, parsley, breadcrumbs and one egg. Season and mix well*
3. *Divide the mixture into 6 and roll each one into a sausage shape. Brush the remaining egg onto each sausage and roll in the flour to coat*
4. *Heat the oil in a pan and fry for 10 mins, turning occasionally until browned*

SPICY SAUSAGE & POTATO OMELETTE

1 lb potatoes – peeled & sliced
4 oz spicy sausage – sliced
2 onions – peeled & sliced
1 red pepper – cored & cut into strips
6 eggs – beaten
5 tbsp olive oil

1. Heat the oil in a pan and fry the potatoes for 15 mins. Remove the potatoes with a slotted spoon and keep warm

2. Add the onions and pepper and fry for 5 mins

3. Add the sausage to the onions and pepper, mix and fry for 3 more mins. Add the potatoes and mix well. Season

4. Pre-heat the grill to medium setting

5. Pour the eggs over the mixture and cook until the base has set

6. Place the pan under the grill and cook until the whole mixture is firm and top is golden

POTATO, SAUSAGE & PEPPER FRY

1 lb potatoes – peeled & cubed
1 lb beef sausages
2 red peppers – halved, seeded & cut into strips
2 onions – peeled & chopped
¼ pint dry red wine
2 tbsp tomato purée
2 tbsp fresh oregano – chopped
2 tbsp olive oil

1. Par boil potatoes for 10 mins. Drain

2. Grill the sausages until lightly browned all over. Remove and cut into bite sized pieces

3. Heat the oil and fry the peppers and onion until they start to soften

4. Add the wine, purée and oregano. Season, stir and bring to the boil, add some water if required

5. Add the potatoes and sausages and simmer for at least 10 mins until the desired consistency is reached

MEXICAN SAUSAGE & POTATOES

1 lb new potatoes – scrubbed, halved, boiled & drained
1 lb sausages
½ lb tin sweetcorn – drained
4 oz jar pre-made tomato salsa
1 tbsp olive oil

1. Grill the sausages until browned, then cut into bite sized pieces

2. Heat the oil and add the potatoes, sausage and sweetcorn. Season, stir and cook for 5 mins

3. Remove from the pan and serve topped with the salsa's

MEDITERRANEAN POTATO LUNCH

1 lb new potatoes – scrubbed, halved & boiled
6 sun-dried tomatoes – drained & chopped
8 black olives – pitted
1 Chorizo sausage – peeled & sliced
1 tbsp olive oil

1. Drain the potatoes and allow to cool slightly

2. Heat the oil and fry the sausage until cooked

3. Put all the ingredients in a large bowl and mix together. Season and serve

SAUSAGE & POTATO CASSEROLE

1 lb potatoes – peeled & sliced
1 lb sausages – grilled until lightly browned
1 large tin chopped tomatoes
2 red onions – peeled & sliced
6 fl oz chicken stock
1 tbsp fresh rosemary – chopped
1 tbsp fresh thyme – chopped

1. Pre-heat oven to GM4/180°c/350°f

2. Mix all the ingredients together, season and put in a large roasting tin

3. Cover and bake for 1-1½ hours

SAUSAGE & STOUT BAKE

1 lb waxy potatoes – peeled & sliced
6 beef sausages
2 onions – peeled & chopped
3 cloves garlic – crushed
5 fl oz stout
4 fl oz beef stock
1 tbsp fresh thyme – chopped
1 ½ tbsp olive oil
2 tbsp cornflour
4 tbsp water
3 oz cheddar cheese – grated

1. Boil the potatoes for 10 mins, remove and drain

2. Heat the grill and cook the sausages until browned. Remove and cut into slices

3. Heat the oil in a pan and fry the onion and garlic gently for about 5 mins

4. Add the stout, sausages, stock, thyme and season. Stir well and heat through

5. Pre-heat oven to GM5/190°c/375f

6. Blend the cornflour with the water and add to the mixture. Bring to the boil stirring continually

7. Put the mixture into an ovenproof dish and layer the potatoes on top

8. Season and sprinkle with the cheese. Bake for 30 mins

CHORIZO & POTATO OMELETTE

1 lb potatoes – peeled & thinly sliced
½ lb Chorizo sausage – sliced
9 eggs – beaten
1 onion – peeled & sliced
1 tbsp fresh thyme – chopped
3 tbsp olive oil

1. Heat 1 tbsp of oil and fry the chorizo for 2 mins – turning halfway through

2. Remove the chorizo add the rest of the oil, then the potatoes and onion. Season, add the thyme, cover and cook for about 15 mins

3. Add the chorizo, the eggs and fry gently until the omelette sets

4. Put under a pre-heated grill until the top is set and lightly browned

SAUSAGE & POTATO BAKE

1 lb new potatoes – scrubbed & halved
1 lb sausages
1 red onion – peeled & cut into wedges
2 cloves garlic – crushed
2 tbsp fresh thyme – chopped
3 fl oz red wine
2 tbsp olive oil

1. Heat the grill and cook the sausages until lightly browned. Remove and cut in 1" pieces

2. Pre-heat oven to GM6/200°c/400°f

3. Heat the oil and gently fry the onion for 3-4 mins

4. Add the potatoes, sausage, garlic and thyme. Season stir well and transfer to an oven proof dish

5. Bake for 20 mins. Remove, season, stir and pour on the red wine. Cook for a further 10 mins

POTATOES & PEPPERS

1 lb (waxy) potatoes – peeled and sliced
1 red pepper – cored, deseeded and cut into strips
1 green pepper – cored, deseeded and cut into strips
1 yellow pepper – cored, deseeded and cut into strips
1 large onion – peeled and chopped
3 garlic cloves – crushed
3 bay leaves
1 tbsp fresh parsley – chopped
1 sprig of thyme
5 tbsp olive oil

1. Heat the oil in a large pan and fry the onion for 5 mins

2. Add the peppers, garlic, bay leaves and thyme. Fry for 5 more mins

3. Pre-heat oven to GM4/180°c/350°f

4. Add the potatoes and parsley, season, stir well and cook for 5 more mins, stirring often

5. Transfer to an ovenproof dish and bake for 15 mins

6. Remove from the oven, season, stir and remove bay leaves. Scatter with more parsley and serve

POTATO & EGG PIE

1 lb potatoes – peeled, boiled & mashed
6 eggs – hardboiled, shelled & sliced
3 tbsp double cream
1 oz butter
⅓ pint pre-made parsley sauce – from a packet
1 egg beaten

1. Pre-heat oven to GM4/180°c/350°f
2. Beat the cream and butter into the mash
3. Grease a small ovenproof dish and spread one third of the mash on the base. Season and add half the eggs in a layer. Pour on half the sauce
4. Add another third of potatoes, season and repeat so the final layer is mashed potato
5. Brush with the beaten egg and bake for 30 mins

POTATO & LEEK LAYER

1 lb potatoes – peeled & thinly sliced
8 oz leeks – peeled & thinly sliced
½ pint milk
¼ tsp ground nutmeg

1. Pre-heat oven to GM5/190°c/375°f
2. Take a small casserole dish and place a layer of potatoes at the bottom with a layer of leeks on top. Continue until you have used them both up, sprinkling each layer with the nutmeg & seasoning. Pour the milk over and cover
3. Bake for 1 hour
4. Uncover and cook for a further ½ hour.

CHEESEY POTATO CRUMBLE

1 lb (floury) potatoes – peeled, boiled & mashed
6 spring onions – trimmed & chopped
2 cloves garlic – crushed
2 oz butter
2 fl oz milk
2 oz cheddar cheese – grated
3 oz breadcrumbs
1 tbsp olive oil

1. Pre-heat oven to GM6/200°c/400°f
2. Heat the oil and half the butter and gently fry

the garlic and onions for 2-3 mins
3. Put the mash in an ovenproof dish then mix in the milk, garlic and onions. Season
4. Melt the rest of the butter and add the cheese and breadcrumbs. Season. Mix well and spread on top of the mash. Bake for 20 mins

POTATO & CAULIFLOWER CURRY

1 lb potatoes – peeled & cubed
1 cauliflower – washed, de-stalked and cut into small pieces
2 onions – peeled & chopped
3 cloves garlic – peeled & crushed
6 oz frozen spinach
3 carrots – peeled & chopped
1 large tin chopped tomatoes
12 fl oz vegetable stock
2 oz cashew nuts
2 tbsp tomato purée
2 tbsp curry powder
2 tbsp garam masala
2 tbsp vegetable oil

1. Heat the oil in a large pan and add the onions and garlic and fry for 5 mins
2. Add the curry powder and garam masala and cook for 5 more mins
3. Add all the remaining ingredients except the nuts and the spinach. Bring to the boil and reduce the heat, cover and simmer for 20 mins stirring frequently
4. Add the nuts and the spinach and simmer uncovered for a further 4-5 mins

MEDITERRANEAN POTATO STEW

1 lb potatoes – peeled & cubed
1 large tin chopped tomatoes
1 onion – peeled & thinly sliced
3 cloves garlic – crushed
1 tbsp fresh oregano – chopped
10 green olives – halved & stoned
3 tbsp olive oil

1. Heat the oil and gently fry the onion and garlic until the onion begins to soften
2. Add the potatoes and stir for 1 more minute
3. Add the tomatoes, olives and oregano. Season and stir. Cover and simmer for 20-25 mins

POTATO, SPINACH & TOMATO GRATIN

1 lb potatoes – peeled & sliced
¾ lb spinach – washed
¾ lb tomatoes – thickly sliced
3 cloves garlic – crushed

For the topping
½ pint Greek yoghurt
1 tbsp milk
1 tsp cornflour
1 oz parmesan cheese – grated

1. *Pre-heat oven to GM4/180°c/350°f*
2. *Blanch the spinach in boiling water for 1 minute and drain well. Rinse in cold water then squeeze out excess liquid and chop into small pieces*
3. *Grease an oven proof dish and layer half the potato in the bottom then sprinkle with half the garlic. Season. Add the spinach. Continue with the tomato then add the rest of the garlic. Top with the rest of the potato and season again*
4. *To make the topping combine the cornflour and milk in a pan and stir until smooth. Stir in the yoghurt and heat gradually till bubbling. Allow the mixture to bubble for 1 minute, stirring continually. Remove from heat and season*
5. *Spoon the mixture over the potato and sprinkle with the parmesan. Bake for 1 hour*

WELSH ONION BAKE

1 lb potatoes – peeled & sliced thinly
½ lb onions – peeled & sliced thinly
4 oz butter

1. *Pre-heat oven to GM4/180°c/350°f*
2. *Butter a small casserole dish and line the bottom with potatoes. Add a layer of onion, knobs of butter and seasoning*
3. *Continue the layers, fishing with a layer of potato and dot with butter*
4. *Cover and bake for 1 hour*

SCRAMBLED EGG & POTATOES

1 lb new potatoes – scrubbed, boiled, drained and diced
6 eggs – beaten
1 onion – peeled & finely sliced
⅓ pint milk
1 oz butter
1 tbsp fresh parsley – chopped

1. *Melt the butter and fry the onion till it starts to soften*
2. *Add the potatoes and fry until lightly browned*
3. *Meanwhile add the milk, parsley and seasoning to the eggs, mix well then pour onto the potatoes*
4. *Stir continually until the eggs are scrambled*

VEGETABLE MOUSSAKA

1 lb potatoes – peeled & halved
1 large aubergine – sliced
2 courgettes – sliced
1 large tin chopped tomatoes
1 onion – peeled & sliced finely
4 oz mushrooms – sliced
2 cloves garlic – crushed
¼ pint red wine
3 tbsp tomato purée
1 tbsp fresh basil – chopped
½ pint white sauce made from a packet
2 tbsp olive oil

1. *Pre-heat oven to GM4/180°c/350°f*
2. *Boil the potatoes for 10 mins, drain and slice*
3. *Heat half the oil and fry the aubergine and courgette till cooked. Drain*
4. *Heat the remainder of the oil in a large pan and fry the onion and garlic for 3-4 mins*
5. *Add the mushrooms and cook for 2 mins*
6. *Add the chopped tomatoes, wine, purée and herbs. Season and cook for 10 mins*
7. *Put half the tomato sauce into the bottom of a casserole dish then add half the potatoes, aubergines and courgettes. Pour over half the sauce and then repeat*
8. *Bake for 40-60 mins or until browned on top*

POTATO & LEEK BAKE

1 lb (waxy) potatoes – peeled & thinly sliced
¾ lb leeks – trimmed & sliced
½ pint milk
1 oz butter

1. *Pre-heat oven to GM6/200°c/400°f*
2. *Grease an oven proof dish with half the butter and layer the base with one third of the potatoes. Season well and add half the leeks, repeat layers finishing with a layer of potatoes*
3. *Pour the milk into the dish and dot the top with the rest of the butter. Cover and bake for 1 hour*
4. *Remove the cover and bake for another 15 mins*

WINTER VEGETABLE GRATIN

1 lb potatoes – peeled & sliced
1 lb carrots – peeled & sliced
1 medium celeriac – peeled & sliced
1 clove garlic – finely chopped
½ pint hot vegetable stock
5 tbsp olive oil

1. *Pre-heat oven to GM5/190°c/375°f*
2. *Arrange half the potatoes in a large gratin dish and drizzle with 1 tbsp oil and a little of the garlic. Cover with the celeriac, more oil and garlic , then the carrot and more oil and garlic, seasoning each layer as you go*
3. *Cover with the remaining potatoes and drizzle with the remaining oil*
4. *Pour over the stock and cover the dish and bake for 45 minutes then uncover and bake for a further 35-40 minutes or until the vegetables are golden and tender (This can be made a day ahead and re-heated)*
4. *Remove the cover and bake for another 15 mins*

EASY POTATO CASSEROLE

1 lb potatoes – peeled, thinly sliced & dried with a tea towel
1½ oz butter
4 fl oz milk

1. *Pre-heat oven to GM4/180°c/350°f*
2. *Butter the base of a casserole dish. Place a layer of potatoes on the bottom. Dot with some of the butter and season. Continue until potatoes are used, seasoning each layer*
3. *Pour the milk over and dot with the rest of the butter. Cover and bake for 40-45 mins*

EGG & POTATO BAKE

1 lb potatoes – peeled, diced & boiled
3 eggs – hardboiled, shelled & quartered
1 onion – peeled & chopped
½ pint milk
1 oz flour
1 oz butter
2 oz cheddar cheese – grated

1. *Pre-heat oven to GM5/190°c/350°f*
2. *Heat the butter and cook the onion for 5 mins*
3. *Sprinkle with the flour and gradually add the milk, stirring continually. Bring to the boil, still stirring, season and remove from heat*
4. *Put the potatoes and egg in an ovenproof dish, season and pour the sauce over*
5. *Sprinkle with the cheese and bake for 20 mins*

POMMES DE TERRE AU ROQUEFORT

1 lb (2 x floury) potatoes – scrubbed & pricked
3 oz Roquefort cheese – crumbled
3 fl oz sour cream
1 tbsp fresh chives

1. *Pre-heat oven to GM4/180°c/350°f*
2. *Bake the potatoes for 1½ hours*
3. *Remove and allow to cool slightly. Cut a thin slice, lengthways, from each potato. Scoop out as much potato as possible – leaving enough to keep the shell intact.*
4. *Mix the mash with the cheese, cream and chives. Season and put half the mixture into each potato*
5. *Bake for 10-15 mins*

POTATOES & SPINACH

1 lb potatoes – peeled & cubed
1½ lbs fresh spinach – washed & boiled for 5 mins
2 onions – peeled & chopped
2 small green chillies – de-seeded & chopped
1" piece of ginger – shredded
2 tbsp olive oil
1 tsp turmeric

1. *Drain the spinach and press to remove excess water. Chop into pieces*
2. *Heat the oil and fry the onion, chillies and ginger until the onion is brown*
3. *Add the turmeric, mix well and add the potatoes. Mix well, reduce the heat and cover*
4. *Bake for about 40 mins until the potatoes are tender. Add the spinach and raise the heat. Cook for 5 more mins*

POTATO & COURGETTE BAKE

1 lb potatoes – peeled & thinly sliced
1 lb courgettes – washed & thinly sliced
1 clove garlic – cut in half
8 fl oz single cream
3 oz parmesan cheese – grated
1 oz butter

1. *Pre-heat oven to the GM4/180°c/350°f*
2. *Boil the potatoes for 3 minutes, then drain*
3. *Boil the courgettes for 1 minute then drain*
4. *Rub the cut side of the garlic around the inside of a large ovenproof dish then grease with ½ the butter*
5. *Mix together the cream and parmesan*
6. *Layer the ingredients in the dish starting and finishing with the potatoes & topping each layer with some of the cream/cheese mixture*
7. *Dot with the remaining butter, cover with foil and bake for 1 hour, removing foil after ½ hour*

POTATO & MUSHROOM GALETTE

1 lb potatoes – peeled & very thinly sliced
½ lb mushrooms – cleaned & sliced
3 shallots – peeled & chopped
3 cloves garlic – crushed
2 tbsp fresh parsley – chopped

4 tbsp olive oil

1. *Heat half the oil in a large frying pan and cook the mushrooms until soft. Add the garlic, shallots and parsley. Season and stir. Cook for 2 more mins*
2. *Heat the remaining oil in a heavy pan and layer the base with half the potatoes in overlapping circles. Pour on the mushrooms and spread evenly. Season and add the remaining potatoes. Fry for 10-15 mins until the underside turns brown*
3. *Use a plate or another pan to flip the galette over and cook the other side until browned*

POTATO & SPINACH SAUSAGES

1 lb potatoes – peeled, boiled & mashed
½ lb spinach – washed, finely chopped & boiled
5 spring onions – trimmed & finely chopped
2 cloves garlic – crushed
1 tsp mustard powder
Wholemeal flour (for coating)
2 tbsp olive oil

1. *Heat 1 tsp of the oil and gently fry the onion and garlic for 5 mins.*
2. *Squeeze the spinach and extract as much water as possible. Place it in a large bowl and add the potato and mustard powder. Season, add the onion and garlic and mix well*
3. *Shape the mixture into sausages and dust with the flour until well coated*
4. *Heat the remaining oil and fry the sausages until browned*

VEGETABLE LAYER

1 lb potatoes – peeled & thinly sliced
8 oz carrots – peeled & sliced
4 oz mushrooms – washed & sliced
4 oz green beans – sliced
4 oz cheddar cheese – grated
2 eggs – beaten
½ pint milk

1. *Preheat oven to GM4/180°c/350°f*
2. *Grease a small ovenproof dish. Layer the*

bottom with potato and add layers of all the vegetables and cheese finishing with a layer of potato topped with grated cheese

3. Beat together the eggs and milk and season. Pour onto the vegetables

4. Sprinkle with cheese

5. Bake for 1¼-1½ hours until golden brown on top

SPINACH & POTATO BAKE

1 lb (floury) potatoes – peeled & thinly sliced
¼ lb fresh spinach – washed & chopped
1 onion – peeled & finely sliced
2 oz cheddar cheese – grated
3 fl oz single cream
1 fl oz milk

1. Pre-heat oven to GM5/190°c/375°f

2. Mix the cream and milk together and season

3. Layer one third of the potatoes in a small, buttered ovenproof dish, then season and add half the spinach and half the onion. Pour on half the cream mixture and add another one third of the potatoes. Repeat

4. Top with the rest of the potatoes, sprinkle with the cheese. Cover and bake for 50 mins

5. Remove lid and bake for 10-15 more mins until the potatoes are cooked and the cheese is brown

BAKED PECORINO & POTATO

1 lb new potatoes – scrubbed & boiled for 10 mins
6 spring onions – trimmed & chopped
4 tbsp Pecorino cheese – grated
1 oz butter – melted

1. Pre-heat oven to GM6/200°c/400°f

2. Allow the potatoes to cool slightly then slice thinly

3. Take a small greased ovenproof dish and layer half the potatoes in the bottom

4. Brush with butter and half the onions, half the cheese and season. Add the rest of the potatoes and repeat

5. Bake for 20 mins

POTATO CURRY

1 lb potatoes – peeled & diced
3 oz cauliflower florets
2 oz green beans – sliced
3 oz carrots – peeled & diced
1 onion – peeled & sliced
10 fl oz hot vegetable stock
3 tbsp vegetable oil
1 tsp ground cumin
1 tsp chilli powder
2 tsp ground coriander
1 tsp turmeric

1. Heat the oil in a large saucepan and fry the onion until soft

2. Add the spices and seasoning and cook for a further 2 mins

3. Add the rest of the vegetables, mixing thoroughly until they are coated with the spices

4. Add the stock and cover. Bring to the boil then reduce heat and simmer for 12-15 mins or until the vegetables are tender

DRY POTATO CURRY

1 lb potatoes – peeled & diced
1 onion – finely sliced
2 cloves garlic – crushed
1 x 1" piece ginger – grated
1 fresh green chilli – de-seeded & chopped
1 tsp turmeric
1 tsp mustard seeds
1 tsp ground cumin
½ tsp cayenne pepper
2 tbsp vegetable oil

1. Boil the potatoes until just tender (about 7 mins) then drain & leave

2. Heat the oil and fry the mustard seeds for 30 seconds. Add the onion and fry until it is soft. Stir in the garlic and ginger and fry for 1 more minute

3. Add the potatoes, chilli, turmeric, cayenne pepper, cumin and stir well. Cook uncovered for 4-5 mins until the potatoes are browned and covered with spices

POTATOES WITH CREAM & CHEESE

1 lb new potatoes – scrubbed & halved
3½ oz cheddar cheese – grated
6½ fl oz single cream

1. Preheat oven to GM3/160°c/325°f

2. Put the potatoes into a shallow ovenproof dish. Sprinkle with the cheese, season then cover with cream

3. Bake for ½ hour

POTATO & CHEESE PAN FRY

1 lb potatoes – peeled & sliced
5 oz cheddar cheese – grated
5 oz red Leicester – grated
3 tbsp olive oil
1 bunch chives – finely chopped

1. Boil the potatoes for 5 mins, then drain and dry

2. Heat the oil & fry the potatoes for 15 mins

3. Scatter the cheese onto the potatoes and grill until the cheese is bubbling

4. Sprinkle with the chives & seasoning

POTATO & ONION BAKE

1 lb potatoes – peeled & sliced
2 onions – peeled & sliced in rings
½ pint vegetable stock
2 tbsp white wine vinegar
2 oz butter

1. Pre-heat oven to GM45/180°c/350°f

2. Grease a small ovenproof dish and layer the base with a third of the potatoes. Season and add half the onion

3. Add another third of the potatoes, season then add the remaining onion and top with the rest of the potatoes

4. Add the vinegar to the stock and pour onto the potatoes. Dot with the butter. Cover and bake for 1½ hours

POTATO & CHEESE BAKE

1 lb potatoes – peeled & thinly sliced
3 oz Gouda cheese – grated
6 fl oz vegetable stock
1 clove garlic – crushed
2 tsp fresh thyme – chopped
½ oz butter
1 tbsp plain flour

1. Pre-heat oven to GM6/200°c/400°f

2. Heat the butter in a small pan until it bubbles then stir in the flour. Cook until it starts to go brown then add the vegetable stock, stir well and season. Simmer for 5 mins, stirring often

3. Put 2 oz of the cheese, garlic and thyme in a small bowl , season and mix well

4. Put half the potatoes in a layer at the bottom of an ovenproof dish, season and spread the cheese mix over the potatoes, put the rest of the potatoes in a layer over the top, season and pour the sauce over

5. Cover with foil and bake for 50 mins. Remove foil and bake for 30 mins more, season and sprinkle with the rest of the cheese and bake for 5 mins

LEEK,POTATO & CHICKPEA CASSEROLE

1 lb potatoes – peeled & cut into chunks
5 leeks – trimmed & sliced
1 small can chickpeas – drained
4 cloves garlic – crushed
1 lemon – finely chopped
3 tbsp fresh sage – roughly chopped
1 pint vegetable stock
2 tbsp extra virgin olive oil

1. Heat the oil in a large pan and gently fry potatoes and leeks for 5 mins

2. Add the garlic, lemon and sage and fry for 5 more mins

3. Add the stock, chickpeas, season and bring to the boil. Simmer for 15 mins or until the desired consistency is reached

QUICK POTATO CURRY

1 lb potatoes – peeled & cubed
1 small tin chopped tomatoes
7 oz mushrooms – sliced
7 oz frozen peas
10 fl oz vegetable stock
2 tbsp tomato purée
1 onion – peeled & finely chopped
3 cloves garlic – crushed
1" fresh ginger – peeled & grated
2 tbsp curry paste
¼ tsp ground cinnamon
3 tbsp vegetable oil
2 tbsp fresh coriander – chopped

1. Heat the oil and gently cook the onion, garlic, ginger, cinnamon and curry paste for 5 mins
2. Add the potatoes, tomatoes purée, stock and season, stir well. Bring to the boil and simmer for 20 mins
3. Add the mushrooms, peas and coriander and cook gently for 10 mins

GREEK POTATO HOTPOT

1 lb new potatoes – scrubbed & halved
1 onion – peeled & sliced
1 large can chopped tomatoes
3 cloves garlic – crushed
2 oz black olives – stoned
¼ pint vegetable stock
1 tsp paprika
½ tsp turmeric
1 tsp fresh thyme – chopped
2 tbsp fresh parsley – chopped
2 tbsp olive oil

1. Heat the oil and fry the onion and garlic for 5 mins
2. Add the potatoes, paprika and turmeric. Stir and cook for 2 mins
3. Add the tomatoes, thyme and stock. Season and simmer for about 15 mins (adding water if stew starts to dry)
4. Add the olives and parsley and cook for 5 more mins

HERB & POTATO PIE

1 lb new potatoes – scrubbed, boiled, drained & sliced
1 leek – trimmed & sliced
2 tbsp Gouda cheese – grated
2 tbsp crème fraiche
2 tbsp fresh chives – chopped
2 tbsp fresh parsley – chopped
1 tbsp extra virgin olive oil
½ lb shortcrust pastry
1 egg –beaten

1. Pre-heat oven to GM5/190°c/375°f
2. Par boil the leek for 2 mins then drain
3. Cover the base and sides of a cake dish with the pastry
4. Put half the potatoes and half the leek at the bottom and season. Add half the cheese, crème fraiche, chives and parsley. Mix well and sprinkle with the rest of the cheese
5. Repeat using the rest of the pastry to top the pie. Seal the edges, brush with egg and bake for 40 mins

POTATO & LENTIL CURRY

1 lb potatoes – peeled & cut into chunks
3 oz lentils
1 onion – peeled & chopped
3 carrots – peeled & chopped
1 courgette – washed and chopped
1½ tbsp balti curry paste
1 tbsp vegetable oil
1 pint vegetable stock

1. Heat the oil and cook the onion and garlic for 5 mins
2. Add the potatoes and carrots, stir well and fry for 10 mins
3. Stir in the courgette and curry paste, add the stock, season and bring to the boil
4. Add the lentils, bring back to the boil, then simmer for 20 mins until the desired consistency is reached

POTATO & MARROW CASSEROLE

1 lb potatoes – peeled & cubed
1 marrow – peeled, seeded & cubed
2 onions – peeled & sliced
1 tbsp fresh chives – chopped
1 tbsp fresh thyme – chopped
¼ pint vegetable stock
1 tbsp olive oil

1. Heat the oil and gently fry the onion until it starts to soften
2. Add the rest of the ingredients, season and stir. Cover and cook over a low heat until the potatoes are done, stirring occasionally

SPICY POTATOES & CHICKPEAS

1 lb potatoes – peeled & cubed
1 small tin chickpeas – drained
1 onion – peeled & sliced
2 cloves garlic – crushed
½ tsp paprika
2 tbsp extra virgin olive oil

1. Boil the potatoes for 10 mins and drain
2. Heat half the oil in a large pan and fry the onion for 3 mins
3. Add the rest of the oil, the paprika, potatoes and garlic. Fry until the potatoes are golden
4. Add the chickpeas, stir well and season. Heat through and serve.

POTATO, CHEESE & ONION BAKE

1 lb potatoes – boiled & drained
2 cans condensed onion soup – heated
6 oz cheddar cheese – grated

1. Pre-heat oven to GM6/200°c/400°f
2. Allow the potatoes to cool then cut into slices
3. Put half the potatoes in a layer in the base of a casserole dish. Season and spread 1 can of soup on top then half the cheese. Repeat
4. Bake for 10 mins, then brown the top layer under a pre-heated grill

POTATO, ONION & FENNEL BAKE

1 lb (waxy) potatoes – peeled & cut into wedges
1 lb red onions – peeled & cut into wedges
2 fennel bulbs – peeled & cut into wedges
5 cloves garlic – crushed
3 saffron threads
2 tbsp fresh thyme – chopped
5 fl oz chicken stock
3 tbsp extra virgin olive oil

1. Pre-heat oven to GM5/190°c/375°f
2. Put the saffron in a small bowl, just cover with warm water and soak for 10 mins
3. Boil the potatoes for 10 mins and drain
4. Stir the garlic into the heated stock. Add the saffron and thyme, season and stir well
5. Put all the ingredients in a casserole dish, mix together. Cover and bake for 45 mins
6. Remove the cover, stir and bake for 20 more mins

SPICY RICE & POTATO

1 lb potatoes – peeled & diced
10 oz rice
1 lb peas
2 small green chillies – deseeded and chopped finely
1 tsp cumin seeds
1 tsp garam masala
1 tsp turmeric
1 tsp salt
2 tbsp vegetable oil

1. Heat the oil and fry the cumin seeds until they start to jump
2. Add the potatoes, peas and chillies. Fry for 5 mins
3. Add the rice, stir well and fry for 3-4 mins
4. Add the salt and spices and about 1½ pints of water. Stir once only and bring to the boil. Reduce to a simmer and cooked for about 30 mins or until the rice is cooked and the right consistency is reached

FRIED CHEESE & POTATO SLICES

1 lb potatoes – peeled & cut into ¼" slices, par-boiled & drained
Sliced Gruyere cheese
Pre-made batter (or use a packet)
Vegetable oil for cooking

1. Heat the oil in a large deep saucepan
2. Make sandwiches using one slice of cheese and 2 slices of potato. Season
3. Dip each one in batter and fry in the oil until browned

POTATO & MUSHROOM SAUTE

1 lb new potatoes – scrubbed, quartered & boiled
½ lb button mushrooms – peeled & halved
2 cloves garlic – crushed
3 tbsp single cream
2 oz butter

1. Melt the butter and gently fry the mushrooms for 5 mins or until they start to soften
2. Add the garlic and potatoes (while they are still hot) and stir. Cook for 2-3 mins
3. Season and pour on the cream. Stir well until the cream is heated through then serve

EASY POTATO CASSEROLE (2)

1 lb potatoes – peeled, sliced & dried with a tea towel
1 large onion - peeled and sliced into rings
2 oz butter
5 fl oz milk
1 oz thyme - chopped

1. Pre-heat oven to GM5/180°c/375°f
2. Butter the base of a casserole dish. Layer the base with half the potatoes. Add the onion and dot with some of the butter and season. Sprinkle with the thyme. Top with the remaining potatoes
3. Pour the milk over and dot with the rest of the butter. Cover and bake for 40-45 mins

CURRIED POTATO & AUBERGINE

1 lb potatoes – peeled, boiled & cubed
1 large aubergine – cut into cubes
1 small onion – peeled & chopped
2 cloves garlic – crushed
2 tbsp balti curry paste
1 small tin chickpeas – drained
1 small tin chopped tomatoes
1 tbsp tomato purée
1 tbsp vegetable oil

1 Heat the oil and fry the onion and garlic for 3 mins
2 Add the aubergine and cook for 7 more mins
3 Add the paste, purée, tomatoes and chickpeas. Stir well and heat through for 3 mins
4 Add the potatoes – season and stir well. Add a small amount of water if required
5 Cover and bake for 30 mins

POTATO & CAULIFLOWER BAKE

1 lb potatoes – peeled, boiled & cubed
1 lb cauliflower – broken into florets boiled & drained
1 leek – trimmed & sliced
2 cloves garlic – crushed
1 oz flour
10 fl oz milk
3 oz cheddar cheese – grated
2 oz butter

1. Pre-heat oven to GM5/180°c/375°f
2. Melt the butter and cook the leek and garlic for 2 mins until the leek starts to soften
3. Add the flour and cook for 1 more minute
4. Season and gradually add the milk, stirring continually
5. Add 2 oz of cheese to the sauce and heat until it thickens
6. Put the cauliflower and potato into a casserole, pour on the sauce, sprinkle with the rest of the cheese, season and bake for 20 mins

FENNEL & POTATO BAKE

1 lb potatoes – peeled & thinly sliced
½ fennel bulb – trimmed & thinly sliced
1 clove garlic – crushed
5 fl oz milk
5 fl oz double cream
6 oz Gruyere cheese – grated

1. *Pre-heat oven to GM6/200°c/400°f*
2. *Grease a casserole dish and layer half the potatoes in the bottom*
3. *Add the fennel and garlic, season and top with the remaining potatoes*
4. *Mix the milk and cream with half the cheese, season and pour onto the potatoes*
5. *Bake for 45 mins. Remove, sprinkle with the remaining cheese and put under a pre-heated grill for 5 mins*

CHEESE & POTATO TART

1 lb (waxy) potatoes – peeled
½ lb blue stilton cheese – cut into pieces
½ lb crème fraiche
1 large leek – trimmed & sliced
1 lb pack ready made pastry
3 cloves garlic – crushed
2 oz butter

1. *Pre-heat oven to GM6/200°c/400°f*
2. *Roll out pastry and line a baking tin. Bake until cooked and cool*
3. *Boil the potatoes for 10 mins, drain, cool and thinly slice*
4. *Melt half the butter and gently fry the leek until softened*
5. *Add the garlic and gently fry for 1 more minute*
6. *Spread the cheese pieces onto the pastry case, season and add half the potatoes in a layer. Add the leek, then the crème fraiche and top with the rest of the potatoes*
7. *Season, dot with the remaining butter and bake for 15 mins*

POTATOES WITH EGGS

1 lb potatoes – peeled & boiled & drained
6 eggs – hardboiled, shelled and sliced
1 red onion – peeled & thinly sliced
3 tbsp white wine vinegar
4 oz butter

1. *Pre-heat oven to GM3/170°c/325°f*
2. *Melt 1 oz butter and gently fry the onion until softened*
3. *Allow the potatoes to cool slightly then slice them thinly*
4. *Grease the base of an ovenproof dish and cover the base with half the potatoes then add the egg and onion and top with the remaining potatoes. Season*
5. *Melt the remaining butter in a small pan and add the vinegar. Bring to the boil then pour it onto the potato mixture. Cover and put in the oven for 10 mins*

POTATO & ONION PATTIES

1 lb potatoes – boiled, cooled & diced
1 lb onions – chopped into small pieces
1 packet onion sauce mix – made up as per instructions
6 oz cheddar cheese – grated
1 lb pack of puff pastry
2 oz butter
1 egg – beaten

1. *Pre-heat oven to GM6/200°c/400°*
2. *Melt the butter and cook the onions for 5 mins*
3. *Add the potatoes, onion sauce and cheese. Season. Stir well and cook for 3 more mins*
4. *Flour a board and roll out the pastry and cut into 4 squares. Put ¼ of the mixture at the centre of each square. Dampen the edges of the pastry and fold into triangular shapes*
5. *Press the edges to seal and brush the pastry with the egg. Bake for 15 mins*

CHEESE & ONION POTATO PIE

1 lb potatoes – peeled, boiled & sliced
¼ lb cheddar cheese – grated
1 tin condensed onion soup – made up to ½ pint
by adding milk

1. Pre-heat oven to GM5/190°c/375°f
2. Heat the soup & milk in a small pan
3. Layer the base of an ovenproof dish with one third of the potatoes, pour on half the soup and sprinkle with half the cheese. Season
4. Add another third of the potatoes, the rest of the soup then the rest of the potatoes. Season and add the remaining cheese
5. Bake for 15-20 mins or until the cheese is melted and browned

VEGETARIAN PIE

1 lb potatoes – peeled & thinly sliced
½ lb carrots – peeled & sliced
½ lb swede – peeled & cubed
½ lb parsnips – peeled & cubed
1 large tin chopped tomatoes
2 onions – peeled & sliced
3 cloves garlic – crushed
4 sticks celery – trimmed and chopped
½ pint vegetable stock
2 tbsp fresh parsley – chopped
1 oz plain flour
1 oz butter
3 tbsp olive oil

1. Heat the oil and fry the carrots, swede, parsnips, onions, garlic and celery for 10 mins
2. Pre-heat oven to GM4/180°c/350°f
3. Stir in the flour, seasoning and parsley. Add the stock and tomatoes and bring to the boil. Simmer for 10 mins so the mixture reduces
4. Grease an ovenproof dish and put a layer of potatoes on the base, pour in the vegetable mixture and season. Top with the remaining potatoes, dot with butter and bake for 1 hour

VEGGIE BURGERS

1 lb potatoes – boiled & drained
1 lb swede – boiled & drained
1 large tin sweetcorn – drained
3 red peppers – cored, seeded & cut into small pieces
½ lb cheddar cheese – grated
4 eggs – beaten
3 oz butter
4 tbsp vegetable oil

1. Put the swedes into the pan containing the potatoes, season, add the butter and mash together
2. Heat half the oil & fry the peppers until they start to soften
3. Add the sweetcorn, peppers and cheese to the mash and mix well. Divide into about 20 round burger shapes
4. Heat the remaining oil in a large frying pan, brush the burgers with the egg
5. Fry the burgers in batches, until brown on each side (add more oil if needed)

NEW POTATO CURRY

1 lb new potatoes – scrubbed & cubed
1 small can chickpeas – drained
1 small can chopped tomatoes
¼ lb fresh spinach – stalks removed
1 onion – peeled & finely chopped
3 cloves garlic – crushed
2 tbsp balti curry paste
1 tbsp vegetable oil
10 fl oz chicken stock

1. Heat the oil and gently fry the onion until it starts to soften
2. Add the garlic and curry paste. Stir well and cook for 1 minute
3. Add the potatoes, stir well, season and add the tomatoes, chickpeas and stock. Bring to the boil then gently simmer for 20 mins
4. Turn off the heat, add more stock if needed, then add the spinach. Stir and wait until the spinach has wilted before serving

SIMPLE POTATO STEW

1 lb potatoes – peeled & cubed
2 onions – peeled & chopped
5 celery sticks – trimmed & chopped
1 large tin chopped tomatoes
1½ tbsp vegetable oil
1 pint vegetable stock

1. *Heat the oil and fry the onions till they start to soften*
2. *Add the potatoes and celery, season, stir and cook for 2 mins*
3. *Add the tomatoes then pour on the stock, bring to the boil. Simmer very gently for about 1 hour so the liquid has reduced to the desired consistency*

SPICY COURGETTE & POTATO SLICE

1 lb new potatoes – washed, cubed, parboiled for 10 mins and drained
3 small courgettes – washed, trimmed & cubed
8 eggs beaten
2 cloves garlic – crushed
1 small red chilli – deseeded & finely chopped
8 spring onions – trimmed & chopped
2 tbsp olive oil

1. *Heat the oil in a frying pan and cook the potatoes and courgettes for 8-10 mins*
2. *Pre-heat the grill*
3. *Add the garlic, chilli and onions to the eggs. Season and stir well*
4. *Pour the egg mixture onto the potatoes mixture, stir and cook gently until the base begins to set*
5. *Place the pan under the grill until the top has set and turns golden brown*
6. *Remove, cut into slices and serve*

CHEESE, ONION & POTATO PIE

1 lb (floury) potatoes – peeled, boiled & mashed
2 onions – peeled & thinly sliced
3 oz Stilton – crumbled
1 oz Parmesan – grated
2 oz butter

1. *Pre-heat oven to GM6/200°c/450f*
2. *Melt the butter and fry the onion until completely softened*
3. *Put half the potatoes in a greased casserole dish and top with the onions. Season and add the stilton. Add the rest of the potatoes and sprinkle with the parmesan*
4. *Bake for 30 mins*

ITALIAN POTATO BAKE

1 lb potatoes – peeled & thinly sliced
½ lb tomatoes – sliced
2 red peppers – cored, seeded and cut into strips
2 courgettes – washed, trimmed and sliced
½ pint vegetable stock
1½ oz capers – drained
3 oz parmesan cheese – grated
1½ tbsp extra virgin olive oil
2 cloves garlic – crushed

1. *Pre-heat oven to GM6/200°c/400°f*
2. *Grease an ovenproof dish with some of the oil then layer the base with the potatoes. Season. Pour on the rest of the oil and half the stock. Bake for 20 mins*
3. *Remove and add the peppers, courgettes and garlic. Season and top with a layer of tomatoes. Pour on the remaining stock, sprinkle with the capers and then the cheese. Bake for a further 30 mins*

MUSHROOM & POTATO CURRY

1 lb potatoes – peeled & cubed
1 lb button mushrooms – washed
2 onions – peeled & chopped
1 pint coconut milk
¼ pint chicken stock
3 tbsp red curry paste
1½ tbsp vegetable oil

1. *Heat the oil in a large pan and fry the onions and potatoes for about 5 mins*
2. *Add the mushrooms and cook for 2 more mins*
3. *Add the curry paste, stir well, pour in the stock and coconut milk. Bring to the boil then simmer gently for 12-15 mins on a high heat so the liquid reduces*

CHEESE & POTATO BAKE

1 lb potatoes – peeled, cut into chunks,
  boiled & drained
¼ lb cheddar cheese – grated
1 egg
2 tbsp milk
2 tbsp fresh parsley – chopped
1 tsp mustard powder
1 oz butter

1. *Pre-heat oven to GM7/220°c/425°f*
2. *Put the potatoes in a mixing bowl, add half the cheese and all the remaining ingredients. Season and mash together*
3. *Grease an ovenproof dish and spread the mixture evenly into it. Sprinkle with the rest of the cheese and bake for 15 mins*

ROSEMARY & POTATO TART

1 lb potatoes – unpeeled & thinly sliced
4 oz mozzarella cheese balls
4 oz puff pastry
2 tbsp rosemary – chopped
5 oz grated parmesan
15 pitted black olives – halved
4 tbsp olive oil
Flour for dusting

1. *Smear a small baking tin with oil*
2. *Roll the pastry on a surface dusted with flour until thin*
3. *Put the pastry into the tin so it covers all surfaces, trim the excess and pinch with a fork*
4. *Pre-heat oven to GM6/200°c/400°f*
5. *Put the potatoes in a bowl, season and pour in 3 tbsp of oil. Mix thoroughly until evenly coated*
6. *Arrange the potatoes in overlapping slices over the pastry covering the base. Season*
7. *Sprinkle with the rosemary and drizzle over the remaining oil. Bake for 30 mins*
8. *Sprinkle with the parmesan, dot with the olives and evenly space the cheese balls. Cook for 5 mins or until the cheese balls have melted*

PARSNIP & POTATO BAKE

1 lb potatoes – peeled & thinly sliced
¾ lb parsnips – peeled & grated
1 onion – peeled & sliced
7 fl oz milk
7 fl oz vegetable stock
1½ tbsp flour
1 tbsp vegetable oil

1. *Pre-heat oven to GM5/190°c/375°f*
2. *Heat the oil in a large pan and cook the onion for 3 mins*
3. *Whisk together the flour, milk and stock then mix in all the other ingredients and season generously. Bring to the boil and simmer for 1 minute*
4. *Transfer to an ovenproof dish and bake for ¾-1 hour until you have the desired texture*

ONION & POTATO TART

1 lb (floury) potatoes – peeled, sliced & boiled
  for 10 mins
¾ lb onions – peeled & sliced
2 cloves garlic – crushed
2 eggs – beaten
1 tbsp dried thyme
6 fl oz crème fraîche
2 tbsp wholegrain mustard
10 oz frozen shortcrust pastry – thawed
2 tbsp olive oil

1. *Pre-heat oven to GM7/220°c/425°f*
2. *Heat oil and fry the onions until soft*
3. *Add the garlic and thyme and cook for 2 more mins*
4. *Line the bottom and sides of a cake tin with the pastry, add half the onion mixture and season*
5. *Drain and halve the potatoes then layer on top of the onions, season and add the rest of the onions*
6. *Mix the crème fraiche and mustard with the eggs, season and pour onto the onions*
7. *Bake for 20 mins*

CHEESE AND POTATO PIE

1 lbs potato – boiled & mashed
1 egg yolk
2 oz butter
1 oz flour
½ pint milk
4 oz cheddar cheese – grated
2 eggs – separated
2 oz breadcrumbs

1. Add 1 oz butter and the egg yolk to the mash and season

2. Line a small greased pie dish with the potatoes making a thick coating at the bottom of the dish and building up the sides to form a good edge

3. Pre-heat oven to GM6/200c°/400°f

4. Make a sauce with the flour, butter and milk. Add the cheese, breadcrumbs, egg yolks and mix well

5. Whip the egg whites to a stiff froth and fold them into the mixture then pour the sauce onto the potatoes

6. Bake for 30 mins

POTATO & PARSNIP BAKE

1 lb (waxy) potatoes – peeled & thinly sliced
2 parsnips – peeled & thinly sliced
3 cloves garlic – crushed
4 fl oz double cream
6 fl oz milk
1 bay leaf
2 oz butter

1. Pre-heat oven to GM3/160°c/325°f

2. Put the cream and milk in a saucepan and mix well. Add the potatoes, parsnips, bay leaf and garlic. Season, stir and slowly bring nearly to the boil. Simmer for 2 mins

3. Grease an ovenproof dish with some of the butter. Remove the bay leaf from the potato mixture and put the potato mixture into the dish

4. Dot with the remaining butter and bake for 45 mins

POTATOES WITH BLACK-EYED BEANS

1 lb potatoes – peeled & diced
1 lb black-eyed beans – soaked overnight
3 red onions – peeled & sliced
2 cloves garlic – crushed
3 tbsp lemon juice
3 tbsp olive oil
1 tbsp sesame oil
1 tsp cumin
2 tbsp fresh coriander – chopped

1. Drain the beans and rinse under running cold water. Put in a pan and boil for 1 hour, skimming off any foam. Drain and rinse again

2. Boil the potatoes for 15 mins. Drain

3. Heat both oils, add the onion, cumin and seasoning. Fry until the onion is soft. Add the garlic and lemon juice – bring to a simmer

4. Add the potatoes, beans and coriander. Adjust seasoning and stir well. Cook gently until the potatoes and beans are warmed through

NEW POTATO & CHICKPEA CURRY

1 lb new potatoes – scrubbed & diced
1 large tin chickpeas – drained
¼ lb fresh spinach
1 tbsp curry paste
1 onion – peeled & chopped
2 cloves garlic – crushed
½ pint vegetable stock
1 tbsp vegetable oil

1. Heat the oil and gently fry the onion, garlic and curry paste for about 5 mins

2. Add the potatoes and fry for 1 minute – stirring continuously

3. Pour on the stock, stir well, bring to the boil and simmer for 10 mins

4. Add the chickpeas and simmer for 5 more mins

5. Add the spinach and simmer until the spinach has softened and is cooked

POTATO LAYER BAKE

1 lb waxy potatoes – peeled & thinly sliced
½ lb carrots – peeled & thinly sliced
½ lb parsnips – peeled & thinly sliced
½ lb onions – peeled & thinly sliced
¼ lb celeriac – peeled & thinly sliced
2 cloves garlic – crushed
3 oz butter
Juice and zest of 1 lemon
3 oz Gruyere cheese – grated
2 tbsp dried thyme

1. Pre-heat oven to GM5/190°c/375°f
2. Mix the butter with the garlic, zest, cheese and thyme. Season
3. In a greased roasting tin layer with a third of the potatoes, season add half of the other vegetables and half the butter, sprinkle with half the lemon juice
4. Repeat, finishing with a layer of potatoes
5. Cover and bake for 1 hour
6. Remove cover and bake for a further 30 mins

POTATO CURRY (2)

1 lb potatoes – peeled & cubed
2 onions – peeled & chopped
4 oz peas
1 large tin chopped tomatoes
3 tbsp vegetable oil
1 tsp turmeric
1 tsp ground cumin
1 tsp ground coriander
1 tsp chilli powder
2 tsp garlic powder
2 tsp paprika

1. Boil the potatoes for 5 mins then drain
2. Mix all the spices together with a little warm water to form a paste
3. Heat the oil gently and fry the onion for 2-3 mins then add the paste and fry for another 5 mins
4. Add the potatoes, tomatoes and peas. Season. Simmer for 20 mins adding a little water if required

POTATO & VEGETABLE MIXTURE

1 lb new potatoes – scrubbed & halved
10 baby carrots – washed
3 tinned artichokes – drained
10 asparagus tips – washed
3 tbsp lemon juice
3 tbsp extra virgin olive oil

1. Boil all the vegetables together for 15-18 mins. Drain and allow to cool until just warm
2. Put the lemon juice and oil in a screw top jar, season and shake vigorously to mix
3. Put the vegetables in a salad bowl, pour on the contents of the jar and mix thoroughly

POTATO & SPINACH BAKE

1 lb potatoes – peeled & thinly sliced
4 oz fresh spinach – washed & chopped
5 fl oz single cream
1 onion – peeled & finely sliced into rings
2 oz cheddar cheese – grated

1. Pre-heat oven to GM5/190°c/375°f
2. Season the cream with plenty of freshly ground black pepper
3. Grease a small ovenproof dish and cover the base with half the potatoes, add half the onion and half the spinach season and pour on half the cream. Repeat
4. Sprinkle with the cheese and bake for 1 hour

CHEESE & CELERY BAKE

1 lb potatoes – peeled & sliced thinly
1 tin condensed celery soup
4 oz cheddar cheese – grated
4 fl oz milk

1. Pre-heat oven to GM6/200°c/400°f
2. Mix the soup and milk together
3. Arrange a layer of potatoes at the bottom of a greased oven proof dish. Season. Add a layer of soup and grated cheese and continue each layer seasoning each time. Finish with potatoes topped with grated cheese
4. Bake for 45-50 mins. Serve hot

VEGETABLE BAKE WITH THYME

1 lb new potatoes – scrubbed & cut into thick slices
3 carrots – peeled & cut into thick slices
5 courgettes – trimmed, washed & cut into thick slices
4 tomatoes – cut into wedges
2 sticks celery – trimmed & sliced
4 cloves garlic – crushed
6 tbsp fresh thyme – chopped
6 tbsp olive oil

1. *Pre-heat oven to GM6/200c°/400°f*
2. *Put all the ingredients into a large roasting tin, season well and mix thoroughly and bake for 1 hour*
3. *Remove, stir gently, adjust seasoning and bake for 15 more mins*

NEW POTATO BREAKFAST (2)

1 lb new potatoes – scrubbed & thickly sliced
½ lb mushrooms – sliced
½ lb cherry tomatoes – washed & halved
2 eggs
3 tbsp olive oil

1. *Heat the oil in a large frying pan and fry the potatoes turning often until they start to brown*
2. *Add the mushroom and tomatoes and cook until they start to soften*
3. *Make space in the pan and break in 2 eggs into the potato mixture*
4. *Pre-heat grill*
5. *When the base of the eggs have set, place under grill for a few mins until completely cooked. Season and serve*

POTATO & BRIE BAKE

1 lb (waxy) potatoes – peeled & sliced
4 oz Brie – cut into cubes
2 onions – peeled & sliced
2 cloves garlic – crushed
1 tbsp fresh thyme – chopped
2 tbsp olive oil

1. *Cook the onions in the oil for 2-3 mins*
2. *Add the potatoes and mix in the garlic, thyme and seasoning*
3. *Cover and cook slowly for about 40 mins stirring occasionally*
4. *Place the sliced brie underneath the top layer of potatoes and cook uncovered for 5 mins. Serve once the cheese has melted*

ROAST POTATO & MUSHROOM BAKE

1 lb potatoes – cut into small chunks
4 oz onions – roughly chopped
½ lb mushrooms – roughly chopped
5 oz fresh spinach – roughly chopped
3 oz cheddar cheese – grated
1½ garlic cloves – crushed
3 tbsps tomato purée
5 fl oz white wine
5 fl oz vegetable stock
5 fl oz double cream
5 fl oz Greek yoghurt
1 egg – beaten
3 tbsp olive oil
1½ tsp dried thyme (or 2 tsp fresh, chopped)
2 oz grated parmesan cheese

1. *Pre-heat oven to GM6/200°c/400°f*
2. *Mix potatoes with 1½ tbsp oil in a large roasting pan & cook for 40 mins*
3. *Heat the rest of the oil, add the onion and cook until soft. Add the mushrooms and garlic, turn up the heat and cook for 5 mins*
4. *Stir in the tomato purée and the thyme and wine, bring to the boil and simmer for 2 mins*
5. *Add the stock and cream and simmer for about 20 mins*
6. *Stir in the potatoes, spinach, cheddar and half the parmesan. Season. Pour the lot into a large ovenproof dish*
7. *Combine with yoghurt with the eggs and season. Spoon over the mixture and top with the rest of the parmesan*
8. *Cook for 35 mins*

POTATO CURRY (3)

1 lb potatoes (waxy) – peeled & cubed
1 onion – peeled & finely chopped
3 tsp curry paste
2 oz frozen peas
2 cloves garlic – crushed
1 tbsp fresh parsley – chopped finely
1 tsp lemon juice
3 tbsp vegetable oil

1. *Boil the potato cubes for 12-15 mins in salted water. Drain*
2. *Heat the oil in a saucepan and gently fry the onion and garlic for 3 mins*
3. *Stir in the curry paste and cook for 1 minute*
4. *Add the potatoes and peas. Mix together thoroughly and cook gently for 5 mins*
5. *Add the parsley, lemon juice and seasoning, cover and cook gently for a further 10 mins*

POTATO & CELERIAC ROYALE

1 lb potatoes – peeled & sliced
1 lb celeriac – peeled, quartered & sliced
1 large onion – peeled & thinly sliced
2 eggs – beaten
½ pint milk
¼ pint double cream
½ oz butter
1 tbsp vegetable oil

1. *Par-boil the celeriac and potatoes in separate pans for 5 mins. Drain*
2. *Heat the oil and fry the onion gently until it softens*
3. *Put a layer of potatoes in the bottom of a greased casserole dish, top with a layer of celeriac, some onion and seasoning. Continue layering finishing with a layer of celeriac*
4. *Pre-heat oven to GM6/200°c/400°f*
5. *Whisk the eggs, cream, milk and seasoning together, pour over the vegetables and bake for 30 mins*

CHEESE & ONION POTATO PIE (2)

1 lb potatoes – peeled, boiled & sliced
¼ lb cheddar cheese – grated
2 packets onion soup – made up with 1 pint of milk

1. *Pre-heat oven to GM5/190°c/375°f*
2. *Layer the base of an ovenproof dish with one third of the potatoes, pour on half the soup and sprinkle with half the cheese. Season*
3. *Add another third of the potatoes, the rest of the soup then the rest of the potatoes. Season and add the remaining cheese*
4. *Bake for 15-20 mins or until the cheese is melted and browned*

POTATO & ONION TART

1 lb potatoes – peeled & thinly sliced
3 onions – peeled & sliced
4 eggs – beaten
1 egg yolk
3 fl oz single cream
5 oz butter
2½ oz plain flour
3 tbsp extra virgin olive oil

1. *Sift the flour into a mixing bowl and rub in the butter*
2. *Add the egg yolk and sufficient water to make a dough. Form the dough into a ball and knead until smooth (do not over work). Cover the bowl with cling film and refrigerate for 15 mins*
3. *Line the base and edges of a baking tin with the pastry. Prick the base with a fork and cover with baking paper and bake at a medium heat for 10 mins. Remove the paper and bake for 10 mins more. Remove and leave to cool*
4. *Heat the oil in a frying pan and gently fry the potatoes for about 10-12 mins*
5. *Add the onions and cook till soft. Drain and leave to cool*
6. *Whisk the eggs and cream together with seasoning*
7. *Carefully put the potatoes and onions into the pastry and pour the egg mixture over the potatoes. Bake for 35-40 mins*

POTATO & BABY ONION CASSEROLE

1 lb new potatoes – scrubbed & halved
2 lb baby onions – skins removed
½ lb button mushrooms – washed
2 cloves garlic – crushed
2 sticks celery – chopped into small pieces
4-5 fl oz milk
¼ pint double cream
2½ oz butter
1 tbsp flour mixed with milk to form a paste

1. *Pre-heat oven to GM4/180°c/350°f*
2. *Boil the potatoes for 15 mins. Drain*
3. *Melt the butter and cook the onions until slightly brown*
4. *Add the celery, mushrooms and garlic and cook for 2 mins*
5. *Pour in the milk and flour and cook until the mixture starts to thicken. Season and pour into a casserole dish. Add the potatoes and bake for 45 mins*
6. *Remove from the oven, stir in the cream adjust the seasoning and serve*

MEDITERRANEAN POTATO HOTPOT

1 lb new potatoes – scrubbed& cut into chunks
1 large tin chopped tomatoes
1 large onion – peeled & sliced
¼ pint vegetable stock
2 cloves garlic – crushed
1 tsp paprika
2 tbsp chopped fresh parsley
½ tsp turmeric
2 tbsp extra virgin olive oil

1. *Heat the oil in a large pan and gently fry the garlic and onion for 5 mins*
2. *Stir in the potatoes, paprika and turmeric and cook, stirring continually for 1 minute*
3. *Add the tomatoes and stock and season. Stir and gradually bring to the boil. Reduce the heat and cover. Simmer for 30 mins, stirring occasionally*
4. *Add the parsley and season*

BEETROOT, POTATO & MUSHROOM GRATIN

1 lb potatoes – boiled & mashed
¾ lb beetroot – peeled & diced
5 fl oz vegetable stock
3 tbsp cream
1 small onion – peeled & chopped
2 tbsp horseradish
1½ tbsp flour
½ tbsp white wine vinegar
1 tbsp vegetable oil
5 oz mushrooms – sliced
1 shallot – chopped
2 tbsp parsley – finely chopped
½ oz butter

1. *Heat the oil and cook the onion for 3 mins. Stir in the flour and cook for 1 minute further, then add the stock and simmer for 2 mins then add the beetroot, cream, horseradish and white wine vinegar. Season*
2. *Pre-heat oven to GM5/190°c/375°f*
3. *Spread the mash onto the base of a small, greased ovenproof dish*
4. *Heat the butter and cook the shallot for 3 mins, add the mushrooms and cook until soft. Season and add the parsley*
5. *Pour the beetroot mixture onto the potato and add the mushroom mixture on top. Cover and cook for 30 mins*

PASTA & POTATOES

1 lb new potatoes – scrubbed
1 lb tagliatelle
4 tbsp green pesto
3 oz parmesan cheese – grated
3 tbsp extra virgin olive oil

1. *Boil the potatoes for 15 mins. Drain and slice*
2. *Meanwhile boil the pasta in a separate pan for the time it says on the packet. Drain*
3. *Add the pasta to the potatoes, mix and stir in the oil and pesto. (add more oil if needed). Season and mix in half the cheese*
4. *Serve, sprinkled with the rest of the cheese*

CHEESE, EGG & POTATO BAKE

1 lb potatoes – peeled, diced & boiled for 10 mins
3 eggs – hard boiled & quartered
1 onion – peeled & chopped
1 small can sweetcorn – drained
3 oz cheddar cheese – grated
½ oz butter
½ oz flour
½ pint milk

1. Pre-heat oven to GM4/180°c/350°f
2. Heat the butter and cook the onion for 3-4 mins. Mix in the flour in with the onion and pour in the milk stirring continuously and bring to the boil stirring until it thickens
3. Grease an ovenproof dish and put the potatoes, eggs and sweetcorn in it.
4. Pour over the sauce and sprinkle with cheese. Bake for 20 mins

BAKED POTATO SLICE

1 lb potatoes – peeled & sliced
1 large onion – peeled & sliced
1 clove garlic – crushed
1 tbsp parsley – chopped
1 tbsp oregano
7 fl oz milk
1 oz butter
1 tbsp extra virgin olive oil

1. Boil the potatoes for 7 mins. Drain and place a layer of half the slices in an ovenproof dish
2. Pre-heat oven to GM5/190°c/375°f
3. Heat the oil and cook the onion and garlic for 3 mins. Add half the herbs and cook for 2 more mins
4. Spread the onion over the bottom layer of potatoes and season. Top with potato
5. Sprinkle with the rest of herbs. Season. Dot with the butter and cook for 1 hour 45 mins. Serve hot

DRY POTATO CURRY (2)

1 lb potatoes (waxy) – peeled & cubed
1 onion – peeled & cut into thin rings
2 cloves garlic – crushed
1 inch fresh ginger – grated
1 small green chilli – seeded and chopped finely
1 tsp mustard seeds
1 tsp turmeric
1 tsp ground cumin
½ tsp cayenne pepper
2 tbsp vegetable oil

1. Boil the potatoes for 10 mins. Drain
2. Heat the oil and fry the mustard seeds until they pop
3. Add onion and fry until onions are soft
4. Add garlic and ginger and fry for 1 more minute
5. Add potatoes, chilli, turmeric, cayenne and cumin. Stir well and cook until the potatoes are browned

CHEESE & POTATO CAKE

1 lb potatoes – peeled & thinly sliced
4 oz cream cheese
½ lb tomatoes – sliced
1 egg – beaten
4 oz spinach – with moisture squeezed out
3 fl oz Greek yoghurt
1 oz cheddar cheese – grated
Pinch of nutmeg

1. Boil the potatoes for 5 mins and drain
2. Grease a small cake tin and layer the bottom with half the potatoes
3. Mix the spinach with the cream cheese, nutmeg and season. Spoon over the potatoes. Cover with the rest of potatoes and top with the tomatoes
4. Pre-heat oven to GM6/200°c/400°f
5. Mix the yoghurt and egg together with seasoning and pour over the tomatoes. Cover with foil and bake for 1 hour
6. Remove foil, sprinkle with the cheese and bake for 15 mins

POTATO & CAULIFOWER CURRY (2)

1 lb potatoes – peeled & cubed
1 cauliflower – stalk removed and cut into 1" pieces
2 onions – peeled & finely chopped
3 cloves garlic – crushed
4 oz frozen peas
1 tbsp fresh ginger – finely chopped
2 tbsp curry paste
1 tsp cumin seeds
Juice of 1 lemon
1½ pints vegetable stock
4 tbsp vegetable oil

1. *Heat half the oil and fry the garlic, ginger and onions for 2-3 mins*

2. *Add the potatoes and cauliflower and fry gently for 5 mins*

3. *Add the cumin seeds and cook for 2 mins*

4. *Stir the curry paste into some water and add to the pan, pour on the stock. Bring to a rolling boil and keep on a high temperature until half the liquid is gone*

5. *Add the peas and lemon juice. Season and cook for 5 more mins or until the desired consistency is reached*

VEGETABLE & POTATO MIX

1 lb new potatoes – scrubbed & boiled for 10 mins
8 oz carrots – peeled & cut into match sticks
2 onions – peeled & sliced
10 oz mushrooms – sliced
1 small can sweetcorn – drained
6 oz frozen peas
10 oz cauliflower florets
2 cloves garlic – crushed
1 large can chopped tomatoes
1 tsp dried oregano
1 tsp dried basil
3 tbsp tomato purée
2 tbsp extra virgin olive oil

1. *Drain the potatoes and cut into bite sized pieces*

2. *Boil the carrots for 5 mins and drain*

3. *Heat the oil and gently fry the onions and garlic for 3 minutes*

4. *Add the mushrooms and cook for 3 more minutes*

5. *Add all the other ingredients, season and stir well. Bring to the boil, adding a small amount of water if needed. Reduce heat, cover and simmer for 15 mins*

CHEESE & POTATO BAKE (2)

1 lb potatoes – peeled & thinly sliced
3 oz cheddar cheese – grated
1 onion – peeled & thinly sliced
1 leek – trimmed and sliced
2 oz butter
½ pint milk
1 oz flour
½ tsp mustard

1. *Melt half the butter in a pan, add the flour to make a roux. Gradually add the milk, stirring continually, until it boils and thickens. Add the cheese, mustard and season*

2. *Melt the rest of the butter in a pan and gently fry the potato and onion for 5 mins*

3. *Pre-heat oven to GM4/180°c/350°f*

4. *Grease a casserole dish and layer the bottom with half the potato then add the onions, seasoning each layer. Add the rest of the potato topped with the leek and sprinkled with grated cheese*

5. *Pour over the sauce, cover and bake for 45 mins*

POTATO & PEPPER BALTI

1 lb new potatoes – scrubbed, boiled & halved
1 large jar balti sauce
2 onions – peeled & chopped
2 red peppers – cored, seeded & chopped
5 oz green beans – trimmed & washed
2 tbsp vegetable oil

1. *Heat the oil gently and fry the peppers for 5 mins*

2. *Add the onions and fry for a further 5 mins*

3. *Add the potatoes, then the Balti sauce. Stir well, cover and heat through for 10 mins*

4. *Add the beans and cook for a further 10 mins*

POTATO & GRUYERE BAKE

1 lb (waxy) potatoes – peeled
4 oz Gruyere cheese – grated
1 egg – beaten
3 fl oz double cream
2 cloves garlic – crushed
1 oz butter

1. Pre-heat oven to GM5/190°c/375°f

2. Boil the potatoes for 10 mins, drain, cool and slice thinly

3. Melt the butter and gently cook for garlic for 2 mins

4. Put the garlic and butter in a small ovenproof dish and add one third of the potatoes in a layer, season and half the cheese. Add another layer of potatoes, the rest of the cheese, season and finish with the remaining potatoes

5. Mix the cream with the egg and pour over the potatoes, put a lid on the dish and bake for 15 mins

6. Remove the lid and bake for a further 15 mins

SPINACH & POTATO BAKE (2)

1 lb (floury) potatoes – peeled & thinly sliced
½ lb fresh spinach – washed & chopped
2 oz cheddar cheese – grated
3 fl oz single cream
1 fl oz milk

1. Pre-heat oven to GM5/190°c/375°f

2. Mix the cream and milk together and season

3. Layer one third of the potatoes in a small, buttered ovenproof dish, then season and add half the spinach. Pour on half the cream mixture and add another one third of the potatoes. Repeat

4. Top with the rest of the potatoes, sprinkle with the cheese. Cover and bake for 45 mins

5. Remove lid and bake for 15 more mins until the potatoes are cooked and the cheese is brown

BABY VEGETABLE BALTI

1 lb (small) new potatoes – scrubbed & washed
½ lb baby carrots – scrubbed & washed
¼ lb courgettes – peeled and cubed
¼ lb fine beans – washed, topped and tailed
¼ lb baby corn – washed
10 shallots – peeled
1 small tin chickpeas – drained
10 cherry tomatoes – halved
1 small can coconut milk
2" piece of ginger – peeled and grated
3 tsp Balti curry powder
2 tbsp vegetable oil

1. Heat the oil in a large pan and gently fry the shallots, potatoes and carrots for 5 mins

2. Add the remaining vegetables and cook for 5 more mins

3. Turn up the heat, add the curry powder and ginger then stir fry for 1 minute

4. Add 4 fl oz of boiling water and the coconut milk. Bring to a simmer, cover and leave for 10 mins

5. Add the chickpeas, tomatoes and cook uncovered for 5 more mins until the desired consistency is reached

CHEESE & POTATO DISH

1 lb potatoes
6 oz cheddar cheese – grated
¼ tsp nutmeg
4 tbsp vegetable stock

1. Peel the potatoes and boil for 15 mins. Drain and allow to cool slightly

2. Pre-heat oven to GM6/200°c/400°f

3. Cut into ½" dice and cover the bottom of a small casserole dish with half the potatoes

4. Cover with half the cheese and repeat, seasoning each layer with salt, pepper and nutmeg. Finish with a layer of cheese

5. Pour the stock in cover with a lid and cook for 20 mins

6. Remove the lid and continue to cook until the top layer is golden brown

POTATO AND SQUASH TAGINE

1 lb (waxy) potatoes – peeled & cut into wedges
1 lb butternut squash – peeled, deseeded & diced
1 onion – peeled & chopped
4 cloves of garlic – peeled & crushed
1 small can chickpeas
1 pint vegetable stock
1 tsp turmeric
1 tsp ground cumin
1 tsp chilli powder
1 tbsp ground coriander
1 tbsp olive oil

1. Heat the oil in a pan and cook the onion for 5 mins
2. Add the garlic, all the spices and cook for 2 mins
3. Add the potatoes, squash and cook for 1 more minute
4. Pour in the stock, bring to the boil then simmer for 15 mins
5. Add the chickpeas and simmer for 15 more mins, stir in the coriander

POTATO & CHICKPEA TAGINE

1 lb potatoes – peeled & cubed
2 leeks – trimmed and sliced
1 large tin chickpeas – drained
1 onion – peeled & chopped
4 stick celery – washed and chopped
3 cloves garlic – crushed
1" piece of fresh ginger – grated
1 tbsp cumin seeds – crushed
2 pinches saffron strands – crushed
1 tsp Harissa paste
1 large can chopped tomatoes
1 pint vegetable stock
3 tbsp olive oil

1. Heat the oil in a large pan and fry the onion, garlic and ginger for 5 mins
2. Add the cumin, saffron and harissa. Season, stir and cook for 1 minute
3. Add the leek, celery and chickpeas and stir until well coated
4. Add all the remaining ingredients, stir well and bring to the boil. Reduce to a gentle simmer, season and cook for 1 hour

GRATIN SAYOYARDE WITH WILD MUSHROOMS

1 lb (waxy) potatoes – peeled & thinly sliced
1 lb wild mushrooms – cleaned & chopped
3 oz cheese (Gruyere/Emmental) – grated
1 onion – peeled & finely chopped
1 clove garlic – peeled & cut in half
4 fl oz single cream
4 fl oz butter
1 tbsp fresh parsley – finely chopped

1. Pre-heat oven to GM4/180°c/350f
2. Take an ovenproof dish and rub the inside with the cut half of the garlic clove, then grease with the butter
3. Layer about a third of the potatoes at the base of the dish, season and add half each of the cheese, mushrooms and onion
4. Pour on half the cream
5. Add another third of the potatoes, then the rest of the cheese, mushrooms and onion. Season and top with the rest of the potatoes
6. Pour the rest of the cream on top, dot with the butter and bake for 1 ½ hours

RED ONION & POTATO OMELETTE

1 lb potatoes – peeled & sliced
3 red onions – peeled & sliced
6 eggs – beaten
2 tbsp olive oil

1. Heat half the oil in a large frying pan add the onions and cook for 10 mins. Remove with a slotted spoon
2. Add the rest of the oil and cook the potatoes for 15 mins. Remove with a slotted spoon and mix with the onions. Season
3. Remove most of the oil from the pan, add the potato and onion mixture then pour on the beaten eggs. Mix carefully and cook until the base sets
4. Put the pan under a pre-heated grill until the top sets

Traditional

STOVIES

1 lb potatoes – washed & sliced (not peeled)
½ lb sliced cooked beef
2 onions – peeled & sliced
1 tbsp beef dripping
½ pint beef stock

1. Pre-heat oven to GM6 /200°c/400°f
2. Heat the dripping and fry the onions for 10 mins
3. Add the potatoes and beef. Mix with the onions and cook for 2 mins
4. Season, pour stock over and cover with foil
5. Bake for 30 mins then remove the foil. Cook for another 30-40 mins ensuring the stock is almost absorbed and the potatoes don't stick

EGG HUBBLE-BUBBLE

1 lb potatoes – peeled & diced
¼ lb mushrooms – chopped
¼ lb peas
3 oz cheddar cheese – grated
2 oz butter
4 eggs – beaten & seasoned

1. Gently fry the potatoes in the butter until just tender
2. Add the mushrooms and peas and fry until the mushrooms soften
3. Pour on the eggs and sprinkle with the cheese
4. Cook very slowly with a plate on top until the eggs have set. Serve hot

RUMBLEDETHUMPS

1 lb potatoes – peeled, boiled & mashed
1 lb cabbage – shredded & boiled
4 spring onions – finely chopped
2 oz butter

1. Mix the mashed potatoes and cabbage together
2. Beat in the butter with plenty of salt & pepper then stir in the onions

POTATO SCONES

1 lb potatoes
4 oz butter
8 tsp baking powder
1 tsp salt
12 oz self-raising flour

1. Pre-heat the oven to GM4/180°c/350°f
2. Peel & boil the potatoes in the normal way. Drain & press through a sieve. Reserve
3. Sieve together the baking powder, salt & flour then rub in the butter with your fingers
4. Mix in the potatoes thoroughly, then roll into round pieces about 2 inches across and ¾ inch thick
5. Place on a greased baking sheet and bake in pre-heated oven for 20 minutes

FRITTATA

1 lb potatoes – sliced
1 onion – sliced
1 leek – sliced
1 red pepper – sliced & de-seeded
2 cloves garlic – crushed
3 sundried tomatoes – sliced
3 eggs – beaten
2 tbsp freshly chopped herbs ie parsley, thyme
¼ lb cheddar cheese – grated
2 tbsp olive oil

1. Boil the potatoes for 10 minutes and drain
2. Gently fry the onion, leek, pepper and garlic for 5 minutes in the oil
3. Add the tomatoes & fry for 1 more minute. Then add the herbs & season.
4. Preheat the oven to GM5/190°c/375°f
5. Take an ovenproof dish and grease it lightly. Arrange layers of potatoes & vegetables ensuring that you finish with potatoes.
6. Season the beaten eggs and pour over the top layer. Sprinkle with the cheese and bake for about ½ hour or until eggs have set.

SURREY PIE

1 lb potatoes – boiled & mashed
1 lb minced lamb
2 onions – peeled & chopped
2 cooking apples – peeled, cored and chopped
3 oz sultanas
3 tbsp tomato purée
½ pint beef stock
3 oz cheddar cheese – grated

1. Dry fry the beef and drain off the excess fat
2. Pre-heat oven to GM4/180°c/350°f
3. Fry the onion in a little of the excess fat for a few mins until almost softened
4. Add the beef, apples, sultanas, purée and stock. Season, mix well and cook for 5 minutes
5. Put the mixture into a casserole dish and spoon in the potatoes spread over the mixture. Bake for 30 minutes
6. Sprinkle with the cheese and return to the oven for a further 10 minutes

MARKET DAY CASSEROLE

1 lb potatoes – peeled & sliced
2 onions – peeled & sliced
1 apple – peeled & sliced
3 pork chops
2 pig kidneys – sliced
1 tbsp dried rosemary
¼ pint water

1. Grease a large casserole dish and place a thick layer of potatoes in the bottom
2. Arrange the other ingredients in layers finishing with a layer of potatoes, seasoning each layer
3. Pour over the water, cover and cook slowly for 2½ hours. Serve hot

BYRON POTATOES

1 lb potatoes – washed
2 oz parmesan cheese – grated
3 fl oz double cream
1 tbsp olive oil
2 oz butter

1. Boil the potatoes, unpeeled for 15 minutes. Drain
2. Allow them to cool slightly then peel and roughly mash. Season and form into small cakes
3. Pre-heat oven to GM7/220°c/425°f
4. Heat the oil and butter and fry the cakes until browned
5. Put the cream in the base of an ovenproof dish, add the cakes and sprinkle with cheese
6. Bake for 10-15 minutes

CHEESE & EGG PIE

1 lb potatoes – peeled, boiled, drained & thinly sliced
3 eggs – hard boiled, shelled and sliced
4 oz cheshire cheese – grated
1 tbsp anchovy sauce
½ pint milk
1 oz butter
1 oz flour

1. Pre-heat oven to GM7/220°c/425°f
2. Grease an ovenproof dish and cover the base with the potatoes. Add the eggs and season
3. Melt the butter, add the flour to make a roux and slowly pour on the milk. Heat until the sauce thickens. Add the anchovy sauce, season and stir
4. Pour the thickened sauce onto the potato and eggs. Sprinkle with the cheese and bake for 20 minutes

DARFIN POTATOES

1 lb potatoes – peeled & cut into matchsticks
4 oz butter
1 tbsp olive oil

1. Wrap the matchsticks in a tea towel and squeeze out as much moisture as possible
2. Heat the oil and butter in a large pan and put separate amounts of matchsticks into the pan. Flatten each shape, season and cook until browned on both sides.

POMMES DUCHESSE

1 lb potatoes – peeled, boiled & drained
1 egg – beaten
1 oz butter
Pinch ground nutmeg

1. Mash potatoes until smooth. Mix in the butter, 1 tbsp of the beaten egg, the nutmeg & seasoning
2. Pre-heat oven to GM5/190°c/375°f
3. Put the mixture into a piping bag with a medium size nozzle and pipe it onto a greased baking sheet in large rosettes. Allow to cool.
4. Brush the surface with the rest of the egg then bake for 15 minutes and brown under a hot grill.

CHAMP

1 lb potatoes – peeled, boiled & drained
8 oz leeks
¼ pt milk
2 oz butter

1. Top and tail the leeks and remove outer leaves. Cut into ¾ inch pieces. Put the pieces into a saucepan with just enough milk to cover them. Simmer for 10 minutes.
2. Drain the leeks and reserve some of the milk. Use this milk to mash the potatoes. Add the leeks & season. Mix well & top with a knob of butter.

COLCANNON

1 lb potatoes – peeled, boiled & mashed
¾ lb green cabbage – shredded
1 onion – grated
2 fl oz milk
2 oz butter

1. Par-boil the cabbage until slightly tender, drain
2. Mix well with the potatoes, onion & milk. Season
3. Heat half the butter in a frying pan and add the mixture. Fry until the edges are crisp, dot with the rest of the butter & brown under the grill

IRISH STEW

1 lb potatoes – peeled & cut into chunks
1½ lb mutton or neck of lamb – cut into thin slices
2 large onions – quartered
½ pt cold water
1½ tsp salt
1½ tsp pepper

1. Put a layer of lamb in the bottom of a saucepan and season. Cover with half the onions & season. Cover with potatoes and season again. Repeat, ending with potatoes
2. Pour in the water and bring to the boil, remove any scum, reduce the heat, cover & simmer gently for 2 hours
3. Remove lid and brown the top potatoes under a hot grill

TOURTE DE CHATEAUMEILLANT

1 lb potatoes – peeled & sliced thinly
1 lb puff pastry
10 oz mild goats cheese – cut into small pieces
2 eggs – beaten
4 spring onions – cut into thin rings
3½ oz butter
Pinch of nutmeg

1. Blanch the potatoes in salted boiling water for 5 minutes then plunge into cold water, drain, place on a clean tea towel, pat dry and set aside
2. Briefly fry the spring onion in ½ oz butter. Reserve
3. Butter a 10" tart tin and roll out the pastry and put in the tin covering the edges and base
4. Pre-heat the oven to GM5/190°c/375°f
5. Blend the cheese, eggs, nutmeg and seasoning to a paste
6. Layer the bottom of the pastry with half the potatoes and dot with 2 oz butter. Cover with the cheese mixture then the spring onions. Finish with the rest of the potatoes.
7. Brush the potatoes with the rest of the butter and season
8. Bake for 30 minutes. Serve hot

BASIC LANCASHIRE HOT POT

1 lb potatoes – peeled & sliced
1 lb mutton or neck of lamb – cut into bite sized pieces
2 medium onions – peeled and sliced
1 oz butter
½ pint water

1. Grease a deep casserole dish and put in a thick layer of sliced potatoes (about ½ lb). Add the meat and cover with the sliced onion
2. Season well then pour on the water. Put the rest of the potatoes on top so the meat is completely covered. Dot with the butter
3. Cook slowly for 3-4 hours with the lid on and add more water at various intervals
4. Remove the lid and cook for a further 30 minutes. Serve hot

LATKES

1 lb potatoes – peeled & grated
2 eggs – beaten
½ small onion – peeled & grated
1½ tbsp flour
2 oz butter
2 oz oil
½ tsp salt

1. Squeeze as much water out of the potatoes as you can; place in a bowl with the eggs and mix well
2. Sift the flour with the salt and add to the potato mixture. Stir in the onion and mix well
3. Melt the butter and oil together
4. Form the mixture into 3 " wide cakes and fry them for 5 minutes on each side. Drain on kitchen paper. Serve hot

SAVOYARDE

1 lb potatoes – peeled
3 oz gruyere cheese – grated
2 cloves garlic – crushed
7 fl oz chicken stock
Pinch of nutmeg

1. Pre-heat oven to GM5/190°c/375°f
2. Cut the potatoes into slices ¹/₈" thick and put into a tea towel then press to extract moisture
3. Put into a bowl with 2 oz of the cheese, garlic, nutmeg and season. Mix well together
4. Butter an ovenproof dish and put the mixture in then pour on the chicken stock. Dot the surface with butter and scatter with the rest of the cheese
5. Bake for 45 minutes until golden and bubbling. Serve hot

STELK

1 lb potatoes – boiled & mashed
2 oz butter
2 fl oz milk
1 bunch spring onions – chopped

1. Cook the onions gently in the milk until tender. Beat them into the mash
2. Arrange each serving of mash so there is a well in the centre of the potato. Then place a lump of butter in each well Serve hot

(The idea is to eat from the outside dipping each mouthful into the pool of butter)

BOXTY

1 lb potatoes – peeled, boiled & mashed
2 lb potatoes – grated
2 tbsp plain flour
1 tsp bi-carbonate of soda
1 tsp salt

1. Squeeze the raw potatoes and extract the liquid. Add to the mash with the salt
2. Mix the soda with the flour and mix with the potato mixture
3. Roll out into a circle about ½" thick and cut into 4 quarters
4. Place each one on an ungreased griddle and cook on a gentle heat for 30-40 minutes, turning once, until brown on both sides. Serve hot

(if you don't have a griddle – use a combination of a lightly greased frying pan & a pre-heated grill)

TIAN de MIDI

1 lb (waxy) potatoes
1 onion - peeled & thinly sliced
1 large tomato – thinly sliced
2 oz parmesan cheese – grated
2 tbsps extra virgin olive oil
1 tbsp herbes de provence (or dried thyme)

1. *Peel the potatoes and slice thin. Soak in cold water, then drain & pat dry.*

2. *Heat the oil in a large pan and cover the bottom with a layer of potatoes and season. Add a layer of onions and cheese with a sprinkling of herbs and continue layering until the ingredients are used up.*

3. *Increase the heat and cook. Keep shaking the pan and loosen the sides with a knife for about ½ hour until a crust forms on the bottom. Cover, reduce heat and cook for 15 more minutes.*

4. *Place the tomato over the top layer of potatoes and add seasoning and herbs. Cover and cook for 15 minutes, shaking occasionally.*

GRATIN DAUPHINOIS

1 lb (waxy) potatoes
3 fl oz milk
1 oz butter
3 fl oz double cream
1 clove garlic
2 oz grated cheese
Pinch nutmeg

1. *Preheat oven to GM3/160°c/325°f*

2. *Peel the potatoes & cut into thin slices. Put to one side but not in water.*

3. *Pour the milk into a large saucepan, season, add the nutmeg and then the butter. Beat into a mixture and bring to the boil slowly. Add the potatoes and gradually add the cream. Simmer for 10 minutes.*

4. *Take a large gratin dish and rub the inside with the garlic then thickly butter. Pour in the potato mixture. Top with cheese and bake slowly for 1 ½ hours.*

TIROLER GROSTL

1 lb (floury) potatoes – peeled & thinly sliced
1 onion – peeled & thinly sliced
3 oz smoked pork – cut into small pieces
3 oz smoked Bratwurst – thinly sliced
1 clove garlic – crushed
1 tbsp fresh marjoram leaves – chopped
3 tbsp parsley – chopped
3 tbsp sunflower oil

1. *Heat the oil in a frying pan and cook the pork for 2-3 minutes*

2. *Add the potatoes, onion, bratwurst and cook for 12-15 minutes until the potatoes have browned*

3. *Mix in the garlic and marjoram and cook for 1 minute longer.*

4. *Remove from heat the stir in the parsley. Serve hot*

POMMES PAILLASSON (STRAW POTATO CAKE)

1 lb (floury) potatoes – peeled
1 oz unsalted butter

1. *Put potatoes through a rotary mill fitted with a shredding disc or use the disc on a food processor that gives the longest string possible*

2. *Rinse the strings in cold water, drain in a colander and roll up in a tea towel. Squeeze gently*

3. *Melt half the butter in a small shallow pan and brush to coat the sides. Season*

4. *Press the strings into the pan, leaving a dome in the middle. Season and dot some of the butter around the edge of the pan*

5. *Put a lid on the pan and cook on a low heat for 20-25 mins. Remove the lid every 5 minutes and wipe out any condensation*

6. *Shake the pan occasionally to ensure the mixture doesn't stick to the pan*

7. *Turn the cake upside down on a plate. Melt the rest of the butter and cook the cake for 10 -15 minutes. Season*

CALDO VERDE

1 lb (floury) potatoes – peeled & diced
1 lb Savoy cabbage – thinly shredded
2 cloves garlic – crushed
2 chorizo sausages – cut into ¾" lengths
4 tbsp extra virgin olive oil

1. Boil the potatoes and garlic in 1¾ pints of lightly salted water for 15-18 minutes
2. Add the oil and liquidise to a puree
3. Return to the pan, season and add the cabbage and sausage. Return to the boil and simmer for about 5 minutes. Serve hot

CHASSE

1 lb potatoes – peeled
4 tomatoes
4 slices cooked ham
4 eggs
3 oz cheddar cheese – grated

1. Par boil the potatoes for 3 minutes. Drain and allow cool slightly then slice thinly
2. Pre-heat the oven to GM6/200°c/400°f
3. Blanch and peel the tomatoes. Extract the seeds then dice the flesh
4. Put the potatoes in a large greased oven proof dish and scatter the tomatoes over. Bake for 25-30 minutes.
5. Remove from the oven and make 4 holes to expose the base of the dish. Lay a slice of ham in each hole then break an egg on top of each slice
6. Sprinkle with the cheese. Season and return to the oven for about 5 minutes until the eggs have set. Serve hot

HAIRY TATTIES

lb potatoes – boiled & mashed
lb cod
tbsp parsley – chopped
fl oz milk
oz butter
tsp mustard

1. Cut the fish into small slices and soak overnight.
2. Pre-heat the oven to GM3/170°c/325°f
3. Drain the fish then boil for 10 minutes. Drain again and remove the skin and bones. Flake the fish into bite-size pieces.
4. Beat the fish, parsley and mustard into the mash and moisten with the milk and butter. Season
5. Put the mixture in an ovenproof dish, smooth with a knife and dot with butter. Cook uncovered in the oven until browned and the fish is cooked.

FRIED POTATO SCONES

1 lb potatoes – boiled & mashed
1 oz butter
4 oz plain flour
Vegetable oil

1. Work the butter into the warm potatoes with plenty of seasoning
2. Manually mix in as much of the flour needed to make a pliable dough. Flatten until ½"-¾" thick and cut into circles about 2½"-3" diameter. Prick the surface of each with a fork
3. Heat a heavy frying pan, brush the surface with oil and cook the scones for approximately 5 mins on each side until brown

KALE COLCANNON

1 lb potatoes – peeled & diced
1 lb kale – shredded
2 oz butter
Chicken stock for boiling

1. Put the potatoes in a pan with just enough stock to cover and bring to the boil and simmer for 10 minutes
2. Add the kale and simmer for 5 more minutes. Drain
3. Mash the contents of the pan. Season and beat in the butter

KAILKENNY

1 lb potatoes – boiled & mashed
1 lb cabbage – shredded, cooked & drained
5 tbsp single cream

Mix all the ingredients together thoroughly.
Season

ALIGOT

1 lb potatoes – boiled & drained
1 oz butter
5 fl oz crème fraiche
6 oz cheddar cheese – grated

1. *Return the drained potatoes to the pan and maintain a low heat. Beat in the butter with a wooden spoon*

2. *Add the crème fraiche and mix thoroughly, continue to beat until smooth.*

3. *Add the cheese and beat until the mixture forms ribbons. Season with pepper only*

POTATOES DAUPHINOISE

1 lb potatoes – boiled & mashed
3 eggs
1 oz butter
2 oz flour
4 fl oz water
Vegetable for deep frying

1. *Boil the water and add the butter. When the butter has melted add the flour and stir continuously until the mixture forms a smooth ball*

2. *Put the mixture into a blender, add the eggs and blend well. Add the mixture to the potatoes, season and mix thoroughly*

3. *Heat the oil in a large pan.*

4. *Put the mixture into a piping bag fitted with a ½ inch fluted nozzle. Pipe 2 inch lengths of mixture into the hot oil, snipping with a pair of scissors*

5. *Deep fry until golden, drain on absorbent paper. Serve hot*

PATATAS BRAVAS

1 lb potatoes – peeled & cubed
1 onion – peeled & chopped finely
3 cloves garlic – crushed
1 clove garlic – peeled
1 tbsp red wine
1 tsp chilli powder
1 tsp paprika
½ tsp cumin powder
2 tbsp olive oil

1. *Heat the oil in a pan. Put the peeled garlic clove in the pan and cook until brown, add the potatoes and fry until golden*

2. *Add the onion and the crushed garlic, cook for 3-4 mins*

3. *Add the chilli, paprika, cumin and season. Cook for 2-3 mins and add the red wine. Turn up the heat until the liquid has reduced by half*

FIDGET PIE

1 lb potatoes – peeled & thinly sliced
1 lb 10 oz gammon – fat & rind removed, cut into small pieces
2 large onions – peeled & thinly sliced
3 medium cooking apples, peeled, cored & sliced
½ pint chicken stock
2 tsp dried thyme
2 tsp sugar
12 oz shortcrust pastry
1egg beaten

1. *Arrange ½ the potatoes at the bottom of a pie dish – season. Add half the gammon, onion and apples. Repeat the layers seasoning each one*

2. *Add seasoning, sugar and the thyme to the stock and stir. Pour the stock over the potato mixture*

3. *Pre-heat the oven to GM4 /180°/350f*

4. *Roll the pastry on a floured surface until it is large enough to cover the dish. Lay it on top, trim the edges and make a slit in the centre. Cook for 50-60 minutes*

CLASSIC TORTILLA

1 lb (floury) potatoes – peeled & sliced
1 large onion – peeled & sliced
7 eggs – beaten
Olive oil

1. Take a large frying pan and put oil in to a depth of about ½". Heat the oil and add the seasoned potatoes and onion. Cook gently for 20 minutes
2. Season the eggs and put into a large bowl
3. Remove the potatoes and onion with a slotted spoon and add to the eggs. Mix well
4. Remove the oil from the pan and clean it. Grease the pan with oil, heat and pour in the potato mixture. Cook over a medium heat for about 10 minutes (the base must be set but not dark)
5. Loosen the base of the omelette and remove
6. Clean the base of the pan, add a little oil and replace the omelette top side down. Cook gently for a couple of minutes

WELSH CAWL

1 lb potatoes – peeled & cut into chunks
1 lb stewing lamb – cut into chunks
1 onion – peeled & chopped
3 carrots – peeled & chopped
2 leeks – trimmed, washed & sliced
1 small swede – peeled & cubed
¼ lb sprouts – peeled & halved
2 tbsp fresh parsley – chopped
1 oz butter
2 bay leaves

1. Melt the butter in a large pan and cook the lamb until browned
2. Add all the vegetables except the sprouts. Season and stir well. Cook slowly for 15 minutes stirring frequently
3. Add the parsley, bay leaves and season again before adding enough water to cover the meat and vegetables. Bring to the boil and gently simmer for about 45 minutes
4. Add the sprouts and cook for 15 more minutes. Remove the bay leaves before serving

DUBLIN CODDLE

1 lb potatoes – peeled & cut into ½" cubes
½ lb pork sausages – cut into 1" pieces
1 lb bacon rashers – de-rinded & cut into pieces
½ lb onions – peeled and sliced
¾ pint chicken stock
2 tbsp fresh parsley – chopped
1 tbsp fresh thyme – chopped
2 bay leaves
1 oz butter

1. Pre-heat oven to GM½/130°c/ 250°f
2. Take an ovenproof dish and rub some of the butter on the base then put in a layer of potatoes, mix and season lightly. Layer with bacon then sausage and onion. Lightly season after each layer with salt & pepper. parsley and thyme finishing with a layer of potato. Add the bay leaves
3. Pour over the stock and dot the potato with butter, cover and cook for 3 hours. Remove the bay leaves before serving.

DUBLIN CODDLE (2)

1 lb potatoes – peeled & sliced
½ lb sausages
3 rashers bacon – chopped
1 large onion – peeled & sliced
1 chicken stock cube
2 tbsp parsley – chopped
1 sprig fresh thyme

1. Put the sausages and bacon in a pan and pour in enough water to cover. Bring to the boil. Reduce heat, cover and simmer for 5 mins
2. Remove sausage and bacon with a slotted spoon and cut the sausages into bite sized pieces
3. Pre-heat oven to GM6/200°/400°f
4. Take a shallow ovenproof dish and arrange the potatoes, onion, sausage and bacon in layers, adding the parsley, thyme and seasoning
5. Crumble the stock cube and add it to the reserved liquid. Add some water and pour over the mixture. Cover with foil and cook for 1½ hours. Remove cover and grill the potatoes until browned

CATALAN POTATOES

1 lb new potatoes – scrubbed, boiled, drained & quartered
2 cloves garlic – crushed
1½ tbsp tomato puree
1 tbsp red wine vinegar
2 tsp clear honey
1½ tsp paprika
¼ tsp chilli powder
2½ tbsp extra virgin olive oil
2 tbsp water

1. Heat the oil and fry the potatoes for 5 minutes, turning frequently. Remove with a slotted spoon and drain on kitchen paper

2. Add the garlic and fry for 1 minute. Add all the other ingredients and stir well to make a sauce

3. Heat very slowly and pour over the potatoes

CLASSIC SAUTEED POTATOES

1 lb (floury) potatoes – peeled, rinsed & cut into ½" cubes
4 fl oz melted goose or duck fat
3 oz unsalted butter

1. Drain the potatoes and place on a clean tea towel to dry

2. Heat the fat in a deep saucepan until very hot. Add the potatoes, stir continually to prevent sticking and fry for 4-5 minutes.

3. Remove the potatoes with a slotted spoon and keep warm

4. Remove the fat from the pan, clean it and add the butter

5. Melt the butter, return the potatoes to the pan and heat until browned. Remove with a slotted spoon, drain on kitchen paper, season and serve

NEEPS & TATTIES

1 lb (floury) potatoes
¾ lb turnip – peeled & chopped
1 oz butter
3 tbsp olive oil

1. Pre-heat oven to GM7/220°c/425°f
2. Cut the unpeeled potatoes into small cubes and boil for 5 minutes. Drain and allow to dry
3. Heat the oil in a roasting tin and stir in the potatoes. Roast for about 30 minutes.
4. Meanwhile boil the turnip for about 45 minutes. Drain
5. Put the potatoes and turnip in a bowl, season and mash together, leaving part of the mixture not mashed and allow cool
6. Turn oven down to GM6/200°c/400°f dot the mixture with butter and cook uncovered for 30 minutes

TATTIE DROTTLE

1 lb potatoes – peeled & chopped
1 leek – trimmed & chopped
1 onion – peeled & chopped
½ pint water
½ pint milk
1 oz butter

1. Melt the butter and sauté the potatoes, leek and onion until the onion starts to soften
2. Season, add the water and simmer gently for 15 minutes
3. Liquidise, adding the milk gradually until you have the consistency you desire
4. Return to a clean pan and gradually re-heat. Serve hot

TRUFFADO

1 lb potatoes – peeled & very thinly sliced
5 oz Cantal cheese – diced
3 oz bacon – cut into small pieces
2 cloves garlic – crushed
1 tbsp olive oil

1. Dry fry the bacon in a pan
2. Add the oil, then the potatoes and garlic. Heat gently until the potatoes are lightly browned
3. Remove from the heat and drain off all the oil and fat. Dot with the cheese and serve when the cheese has melted

POMMES BOULANGERE

1 lb (floury) potatoes – peeled & finely sliced
2 onions – finely sliced
¼ pint chicken stock
½ oz butter
1 tbsp fresh thyme – freshly chopped

1. *Pre-heat the oven to GM4/180°c/350°f*
2. *Butter a large shallow ovenproof dish*
3. *Layer the dish with half the potatoes and the onions, adding thyme and seasoning. Finish with a layer of potatoes and press down with your hands*
4. *Pour the hot stock over the potatoes, brush the top layer with butter. Cover with tin foil and bake for 1 hour*
5. *Remove the dish from the oven and take off the foil. Increase oven temp to GM6/200°c/400°f and cook for 30 more minutes*

POT AU FEU

1 lb potatoes – peeled & cubed
2 lb beef (bone in) – fat removed
1 onion – peeled & stuck with a few cloves
2 cloves garlic – crushed
2 carrots – peeled & chopped
2 leeks – washed, trimmed & sliced
2 tbsp fresh parsley – chopped
1 bouquet garni

1. *Put the meat in a large pan and add enough water to cover. Season and bring to the boil. Lower the heat and remove the scum*
2. *Add the onion, more pepper, garlic and the bouquet garni. Simmer gently for 2½ hours. Remove scum if necessary and ensure the water covers the meat and vegetables*
3. *Remove the bone and cube the meat*
4. *Remove the onion and bouquet garni. Add the potatoes, carrots and leeks and simmer for 1 hour*
5. *Bring rapidly to the boil then remove from the heat. Remove any fat, season and sprinkle with parsley*

BANGERS & MASH WITH ONION GRAVY

1 lb potatoes – peeled, boiled & mashed
1 lb sausages of your choice – grilled
2 red onions – peeled & very finely sliced
3 tbsp Balsamic vinegar
1 beef stock cube – crumbled
1 oz butter
½ pint water
1 tbsp olive oil

1. *Heat the oil and fry the onions for 10-12 mins*
2. *Increase the heat and add the vinegar, reduce by half, then add the butter, stock cube and water. Season, stir well and allow to simmer until it reaches the desired consistency*
3. *Pour onto the burgers and mash*

CLAPSHOT

1 lb potatoes – peeled & cut into chunks
10 oz swede – peeled & cut into chunks
2 oz butter
Pinch of nutmeg

1. *Boil the potatoes and swede in separate pans*
2. *Drain each and return to their respective pans*
3. *Mash the potatoes until smooth but mash the swede to leave small pieces*
4. *Beat the two together with the butter and nutmeg and seasoning. Serve hot*

STOVIES (NO 2)

1 lb potatoes – peeled & thinly sliced
1 large onion – peeled & sliced into rings
3 tbsp beef stock
1 oz butter
1 tbsp sunflower oil

1. *Heat the butter and oil and fry the onion for 10 minutes*
2. *Add the potatoes and mix carefully so they are covered in the oil but not broken. Season well and pour in the stock. Heat gently for 5 minutes*
3. *Cover and cook gently for 30 minutes*

BAECKEOFFE

1 lb potatoes – peeled & cubed
¾ lb stewing beef – cubed
¾ lb pork – cubed
1 large onion – peeled & chopped
2 leeks – trimmed & chopped
2 carrots – peeled & chopped
2 sticks celery – trimmed & chopped
3 tbsp fresh parsley – chopped
MARINADE INGREDIENTS
½ pint dry white wine
1 small onion – peeled & finely sliced
2 cloves garlic – crushed
2 tbsp fresh thyme – chopped
2 bay leaves

1. Put the marinade ingredients in a screw top jar, season and shake vigorously to mix. Put the beef and pork in a bowl and pour on the liquid. Cover with cling film and refrigerate overnight
2. Pre-heat oven to GM3/170°c/325°f
3. Remove the bay leaves and put the mixture in an ovenproof dish. Add the rest of the ingredients, season and stir gently to mix. (add water if necessary to ensure the stew is just covered with liquid)
4. Cover and cook for 3-4 hours stirring occasionally.

CORNED BEEF HASH

1 lb potatoes – peeled & diced
½ lb corned beef – cubed
1 onion – peeled and diced
1 red pepper – cored and diced
2 tbsp wholegrain mustard
4 fl oz double cream
1 tbsp olive oil

1. Boil the potatoes for 5 minutes and drain
2. Heat the oil in a large pan and fry the onion and pepper for 5 minutes
3. Add the potatoes and cook for 5 more minutes
4. Add the corned beef and stir well
5. Mix the mustard into the cream, season and add to the mixture. Heat very gently for 3-4 minutes

TRUFFADE

1 lb potatoes – peeled & sliced
½ lb Cheshire cheese – crumbled
3 fl oz sour cream
2 cloves garlic – crushed
1 tbsp fresh parsley – chopped
1½ tbsp vegetable oil

1. Heat the oil and fry the potatoes for about 20 minutes stirring frequently
2. Remove from the heat, season and add the cheese. Mix, cover and leave to stand for 2 minutes or so, until the cheese starts to melt.
3. Add the cream and garlic. Mix well, sprinkle with the parsley and serve

BRANDADE

1 lb potatoes – peeled, boiled & mashed
1½ lb dried salt cod – soaked overnight
10 fl oz extra virgin olive oil
8 fl oz milk
1 onion – peeled and finely sliced
4 cloves garlic – crushed
1 tsp nutmeg
¼ tsp ground cloves
4 tsp lemon juice
3 bay leaves
10 black olives – halved and stoned

1. Drain the cod, rinse and put in a saucepan. Add the bay leaves, cloves, onion and pepper. Pour on enough water to just cover then gradually bring to the boil, reduce to a simmer for 5 minutes then leave to cool
2. Meanwhile heat the milk and oil in separate pans until warm. Add the garlic to the oil
3. Drain the fish (reserve the onion) remove the skin and bones and flake it
4. Put the fish in a large blender add the milk and a little pepper. As you purée the fish and milk, gradually pour in the oil through a gap in the top
5. Put the mixture in a large bowl and add the potatoes, nutmeg and lemon juice. Season and mix thoroughly. Serve in a pyramid shape dotted with the olives

GRATIN DAUPHINOIS (NO. 2)

1 lb (waxy) potatoes – peeled & finely sliced
2 cloves garlic – crushed
2 tbsp crème frâiche
2 oz gruyere cheese – grated
2 tbsp extra virgin olive oil

1. Pre-heat oven to GM4/180°c/350°f
2. Grease the base of an ovenproof dish with some oil
3. Mix the potatoes with the garlic and remaining oil. Season
4. Layer the potatoes in the dish, cover with foil and bake for 1 hour
5. Remove and spoon on the crème fraiche, sprinkle with the cheese and put under a pre-heated grill for 2-3 minutes until the cheese has melted.

RUMBLEDETHUMPS (NO 2)

1 lb potatoes – peeled & cut into chunks
1 lb swede – peeled & cut into chunks
½ lb Savoy cabbage – finely sliced
2 oz cheddar cheese – grated
3 oz butter

1. Pre-heat oven to GM3/170°c/325°f
2. Boil the swede for 5 minutes, add the potatoes and simmer for 20 minutes. Drain
3. Heat half the butter and gently fry the cabbage for 5 minutes
4. Add the cabbage to the potatoes and swede with the remaining butter. Season and roughly mash
5. Transfer to a casserole dish and sprinkle with the cheese. Bake for 30 mins

BANGERS & MASH WITH ONION GRAVY (2)

1 lb potatoes – peeled, boiled & mashed
6 beef sausages
2 onions – peeled & thinly sliced
6 fl oz beef stock
2 fl oz port
1½ oz butter
1 tbsp olive oil

1. Melt the butter in a small pan and gently fry the onion for about 30 minutes until caramelised
2. Pour on the stock and port, season and bring to the boil. Simmer until the gravy is thick and sufficiently reduced
3. Meanwhile heat the oil in a frying pan and gently fry the sausages for at least 20 minutes until fully cooked
4. Put the hot mash on a large plate, add the sausages and pour on the gravy

HIGHLAND COLCANNON

1 lb potatoes – boiled & mashed
1 lb cabbage – washed & shredded
½ lb carrots
½ turnip
2 oz butter

1. Boil the cabbage for 10 minutes. Drain
2. In a separate pan boil the carrots and turnips together for 15-20 minutes. Drain and blend in a mixer
3. Melt the butter in a large pan. Mix all the ingredients together. Season. Add to the pan and cook gently for 20 minutes until browned underneath

GRATIN de POMMES de TERRE

1 lb potatoes – peeled & thinly sliced
3 oz Gruyère cheese – grated
2 shallots – peeled &chopped
2 cloves garlic – crushed
10 fl oz single cream
1½ oz butter
¼ tsp nutmeg
1 clove garlic – peeled & halved

1. Pre-heat oven to GM4/180°c/350°f
2. Take the halved garlic and rub an ovenproof dish well then spread the base with half the butter
3. Layer the base with half the potatoes then add the shallots, garlic, nutmeg and 2 oz of the cheese. Season and add the remaining potatoes
4. Meanwhile warm the cream in a small pan and pour it evenly over the potatoes. Sprinkle with the rest of the cheese and dot with the rest of the butter.
5. Cover and bake for 1 hour
6. Remove the cover and bake for 15-20 more minutes

POTATO GALETTES

1 lb potatoes – peeled & boiled for 15 minutes
1 onion – peeled & very finely chopped
2 eggs – beaten
1 tbsp fresh parsley – chopped
1 tsp chives – chopped
¼ tsp nutmeg
2 tbsp extra virgin olive oil
1 oz butter

1. Drain the potatoes, allow to cool slightly then grate into a mixing bowl.
2. Add the onion, eggs, parsley, chives and nutmeg. Season and mix well
3. Heat the oil and butter in a large pan and put the potato mixture into the pan spreading evenly. Press down and cook on a medium heat, turning frequently until browned on each side

GALETTES de POMMES de TERRE

1 lb potatoes – peeled & thinly sliced
½ lb bacon – rind removed & finely chopped
1 large onion – peeled &finely chopped
1 tbsp fresh thyme – chopped
1 tbsp fresh parsley – chopped
1½ oz butter

1. Pre-heat oven to GM4/180°c/350°f
2. Dry fry the bacon until lightly browned and remove with a slotted spoon. Reserve
3. Add the onion (and a little oil if needed) and cook gently until it starts to soften
4. Use ½ oz butter to grease an ovenproof dish and add the potatoes and thyme. Season then add the bacon and onion (including the cooking fat). Mix well and press the mixture down
5. Dot with the butter and bake for 1 hour. Remove and sprinkle with the parsley. Serve

FIDGET PIE (2)

1 lb potatoes – peeled & sliced
1 lb cooking apples – peeled & sliced
2 onions – peeled & sliced
3 tomatoes – sliced
¼ lb cooked ham – sliced
½ pint vegetable stock
1 tbsp fresh thyme – chopped
½ lb ready made shortcrust pastry

1. Pre-heat oven to GM5/190°c/375°f
2. Grease an ovenproof dish and layer the base with half the potatoes topped with half the apple slices
3. Season and add the onions, tomatoes and ham. Season and sprinkle with the thyme
4. Add the remaining apples then the rest of the potatoes. Season and pour on the stock
5. Cover with the pastry and bake for 45 minutes

POTATO MACAIRE

1 lb (floury) potatoes – pricked & baked (see jacket potatoes)
2 oz butter

1. Pre-heat oven to GM5/190°c/375°f
2. Halve the potatoes and scoop out the flesh, discard the skins
3. Grease a small, shallow ovenproof dish with some of the butter
4. Season the potato and mash. Spread it into the base of the dish and dot with half the butter
5. Bake for about 10 minutes then turn the mixture over, dot with the rest of the butter and bake until golden brown

ALIGOT (2)

1 lb potatoes – peeled, boiled & mashed
6 oz cheese – grated
4 fl oz double cream
1 oz butter

1. Add the butter to the potatoes while they are still hot and mash repeatedly until they are very soft and fluffy
2. Turn the cooker back on to a very low heat and add the cream. Beat into the potatoes using a wooden spoon
3. Turn the heat up a little and gradually add the cheese. Continue beating with the spoon until the mixture forms long ribbons. Season and serve

GRATIN LYONNAISE

1 lb potatoes – peeled & thinly sliced
½ lb swede – peeled & thinly sliced
½ lb celeriac – peeled & thinly sliced
1 clove garlic – peeled & halved
2 pints milk
12 fl oz double cream
4 oz Gruyere cheese – grated
¼ tsp nutmeg
1 oz butter

1. Put 1 pint milk into each of 2 pans. Season
2. Add the swede and celeriac to one and the potatoes to the other. Bring each to the boil and simmer gently for 15 minutes
3. Drain the vegetables and reserve 10 fl oz of milk
4. Pre-heat oven to GM4/175°c/350°f
5. Rub an ovenproof dish with the garlic then add the butter
6. Arrange the vegetables in layers in the dish, seasoning each layer
7. Mix the cream with the reserved milk and nutmeg. Pour it onto the vegetables then sprinkle with the cheese and bake for 30 minutes

Potatoes first became popular when Marie Antoinette paraded in france wearing a crown of potato blossoms.

In the late 1700's Frederick the Great planted potatoes in his pleasure garden in Berlin. He admired the beauty of the potato flowers, and promoted the eating of potatoes because of their high nutritional value.

HASSLEBACK'S

1 lb potatoes – peeled
1 oz butter
5 tbsp cheddar cheese – grated
2 tbsp dried breadcrumbs

1. Pre-heat oven to GM7/220°c/425°f

2. Push a skewer lengthways through the lower part of potato. Slice each potato down to the skewer at ¼ inch intervals.

3. Remove the skewers and place the potatoes in a lightly buttered oven proof dish. Brush with melted butter & sprinkle with salt.

4. Roast for 30-35 minutes then sprinkle over the cheese & breadcrumbs.

5. Roast for another 10 minutes

POTATOES AMANDINE

1 lb potatoes – boiled & mashed
1½ oz almonds – crushed
1 egg yolk
Vegetable oil for frying
1 oz butter

1. Return the mash to the pan and beat in the egg yolk. Fry gently for 2-3 minutes stirring continuously

2. Put the mixture into a mixing bowl, season and mix in the butter and nuts. Form the mixture into small balls

3. Heat the oil in a deep pan until hot. Fry the potato balls until browned. Remove and drain on kitchen paper

STWNS

1 lb potatoes – boiled & mashed
1 lb turnips – boiled & mashed
3 oz butter
2 tbsp milk

Put all the ingredients in a large pan. Season and mash until smooth

POMMES ANNA

1 lb (waxy) potatoes – peeled & thinly sliced
3 oz butter

1. Pre-heat the oven to GM5/190°c/375°f

2. Grease a cake tin. Line the bottom and sides with potatoes & season.

3. Cover the bottom layer with butter and add a layer of potatoes until ingredients are used up. The top layer should be below the top of the tin.

4. Cover with foil & cook for 45 minutes

TORTILLA

1 lb potatoes – boiled & sliced
6 eggs – beaten & seasoned
4 rashers bacon – de-rinded & chopped
1 onion, peeled & finely sliced.
2 tbsps olive oil

1. Heat the oil and cook the onion and the bacon until the onion starts to soften.

2. Add the potatoes and cook for 1 more minute.

3. Pour the eggs into the pan. Cook until set underneath.

4. Put the pan under the grill and cook until the top turns golden

CORN BEEF HASH (2)

1 lb potatoes – boiled & mashed
1 medium sized tin corned beef – diced
1 onion – peeled & finely chopped
3 oz cheddar cheese – grated
1 tbsp olive oil

1. Heat the oil and fry the onion until softened

2. Pre-heat oven to GM5/190°c/375°f

3. Mix the beef and onion into the mash and spread the mixture into the base of a small, greased ovenproof dish. Season and sprinkle with the cheese

4. Bake for 20 minutes

PUNCHNEP

1 lb potatoes – peeled & cut into chunks
1 lb turnips – peeled & cubed
2 oz butter
1 small tub single cream

1. Boil the potatoes and turnips simultaneously in separate pans
2. Drain thoroughly then put both into one pan. Season, add the butter and mash together
3. Serve in mounds on plates and make hollows in the mash. Fill the hollows with cream and serve

PORRUSALDA

1 lb potatoes – peeled & diced
2 lb leeks – washed, trimmed & cut into rings
3 rashers bacon – rind removed & cut into small pieces
3 cloves garlic – crushed
1 bouquet garni
1 tbsp plain flour
1 tbsp lard
5 fl oz water

1. Melt the lard in a large pan and gently fry the bacon for 2-3 minutes
2. Add the potatoes and leeks and cook for 10 more minutes, stirring frequently
3. Sprinkle with the flour, stir well for a few minutes then add the water
4. Add the garlic and bouquet garni, season, stir well. Cover and cook on a low heat for 30 minutes

POTAGE PARMENTIER

1 lb (floury) potatoes – peeled & sliced
1 onion – peeled & thinly sliced
1½ pints milk
2 oz butter
2 bay leaves

1. Melt the butter in a pan and fry the potatoes and onion until the onion is soft
2. Season then pour on the milk. Stir well, add the bay leaves and bring to the boil. Cover and simmer for 15 minutes
3. Remove the cover and throw away the bay leaves. Transfer to a blender and liquidise
4. Return to a clean pan, season and slowly re-heat

POMMES VOISIN

1 lb waxy potatoes – peeled & very thinly sliced
1½ oz butter – melted
2 oz parmesan cheese – grated

1. Pre-heat oven to GM7/220°c/425°f
2. Butter a round cake tin and arrange a layer of potatoes at the base in a circle
3. Season and pour on some of the butter then sprinkle with some of the cheese
4. Continue to layer until the potatoes are gone and top with melted butter
5. Bake for 45 minutes

LYONNAISE POTATOES

1lb (floury) potatoes - cut into ¾ inch slices
2½ lb onions – sliced into thin rings
5 tbsp olive oil

1. Heat half the oil and fry onions till brown.
2. Blanch potatoes for 5 mins, drain.
3. Coat pan with the rest of the oil – cover with potatoes, fry very slowly and leave for 10 minutes.
4. Turn potatoes, (add more oil if needed), cook slowly for ½ hour – turn frequently until each side is crisp & golden
5. Stir in onions and sauté for 2 minutes until heated through

HOMITY PIE

1 lb potatoes – peeled, cubed & boiled for 12 mins
1 lb onions – peeled & chopped
5 oz cheddar cheese – grated
2 cloves garlic – crushed
2 tbsp fresh parsley – chopped
Short crust pastry (to line an 8" tin)
1 oz butter
1 tbsp milk
3 tbsp vegetable oil

1. *Heat the oil and fry the onions until soft*
2. *Add the potatoes, butter, parsley, half the cheese, garlic and milk. Season and mix. Allow to cool*
3. *Pre-heat oven to GM7/200°c/425°f*
4. *Line an 8" baking tin with the pastry, add the mixture, sprinkle with the cheese and bake for 25 mins*

IRISH STEW (2)

1 lb potatoes – peeled & chopped
2 onions – peeled & chopped
2 carrots – peeled & chopped
1½ lb lamb
½ pint lamb stock
1 tsb fresh parsley – chopped
½ a spring of thyme

1. *Blanche the meat, refresh in cold water and cut into bit sized pieces*
2. *Put the meat in a large pan, season and add the thyme and the vegetables. Pour on the stock so it just covers the vegetables (add more if needed) bring to the boil, reduce to a gentle simmer and cover*
3. *Cook for 2 hours – removing scum occasionally*
4. *Remove cover, season, sprinkle with parsley and serve*

TARTIFLETTE

1 lb potatoes – unpeeled, boiled, drained & cooled
2 rashers bacon – chopped
6 oz Emmental cheese – rind removed & thinly sliced
2 shallots – peeled & finely chopped
3 fl oz crème fraiche
1 tbsp fresh thyme – chopped

1. *Peel the potatoes and cut into bite sized pieces*
2. *Gently fry the bacon until the fat starts to run, add the shallots, turn up the heat and fry until they have softened*
3. *Add the thyme, season then add the potatoes and the crème fraiche. Mix well and heat for 2 minutes*
4. *Meanwhile pre-heat the oven to GM6/200°c/400°f*
5. *Transfer the mixture to an ovenproof dish and put the cheese slices on top. Bake for 15 minutes until the cheese has melted*

POMMES BOULANGERE

1 lb (floury) potatoes – peeled, finely sliced & placed in water
¼ lb onions – peeled & sliced
1 clove garlic – peeled & chopped
1½ oz unsalted butter
1tbsp fresh thyme – chopped
1 tbsp fresh parsley – chopped
1½ pints chicken stock

1. *Pre-heat oven to GM5/190°c/ 375°f*
2. *Heat half the butter and add the onion, garlic and thyme. Fry gently for 5 mins.*
3. *Add the parsley and remove the pan from the heat*
4. *Drain the potatoes and dry them on kitchen paper*
5. *Put a layer of potatoes at the bottom of a small ovenproof dish. Add half the onion mixture and then a layer of potatoes, seasoning each layer. Add the rest of the onions and top with a layer of potatoes*
6. *Pour the heated stock over the potatoes and use the remaining butter to dot the top layer*
7. *Bake for about 1 hour until browned*

BOXTY (2)

1 lb potatoes (½ lb peeled, boiled & mashed, ½ lb peeled and grated)
½ lb plain flour
12 fl oz buttermilk
½ tsp bicarbonate of soda
1 oz butter

1. *Put the grated potato into a clean tea towel and squeeze dry*
2. *Put all the ingredients except the butter into a large bowl and mix well. Blend until it forms batter.*
3. *Heat the butter in a non stick frying pan and fry the mixture in small batches until each one is golden on both sides*

BACON STOVIES

1 lb potatoes – peeled & sliced
4 rashers bacon – rind removed & chopped
1 large onion – peeled & sliced
½ oz butter
½ pint hot water

1. *Melt butter in a large pan and fry the onion and bacon for about 5 mins*
2. *Add the potatoes, season and mix well*
3. *Pour in the water, cover and cook on a low heat for about 1-1½ hrs, stirring occasionally*

SKORDALIA

1 lb potatoes - peeled, boiled, cooled
6 garlic cloves - crushed
½ pt extra virgin olive oil
3½ fl oz milk

1. *Blitz garlic and potatoes in blender till pureed*
2. *Continue to process while gradually adding all the olive oil and milk.*
3. *Refrigerate and use as a dip or serve heated as a sauce*

PAN HAGGERTY

1lb potatoes - thinly sliced
8 oz onions - sliced
4 oz cheddar cheese – grated
2 tbsp olive oil

1. *Heat the oil in a small frying pan.*
2. *Remove from heat. Cover base with overlapping potato slices. Layer with the onions, then cheese until ingredients are used up. Finish with layer of potatoes brushed with oil*
3. *Return to a low heat for 20-25 minutes.*
4. *Place under a low grill for about 10 minutes – turn up to maximum for the last minute. Transfer back to the hob for a minute then cut into wedges.*

POTAGE BONNE FEMME

1 lb potatoes – peeled & diced
8 oz leeks - trimmed, washed & sliced
8 oz carrots - chopped
1 oz butter
2 pints warm water
2 bay leaves
2 oz double cream

1. *Melt the butter and cook the leeks & carrots until soft. Add the water, bay leaves, potatoes and season. Simmer uncovered for 45 minutes.*
2. *Remove the bay leaves. Season. Crush the potatoes against the sides and stir in the cream*

ITALIAN GREEN SAUCE

1 lb potatoes – peeled, boiled, cooled & diced
4 bunches fresh parsley – stalks removed
& chopped
12 pickled onions from a jar – drained
10 anchovies – chopped
4 cloves garlic – crushed
1 small onion – peeled & finely chopped
20 tbsp extra virgin olive oil
4 tbsp vinegar

1. *Put the potatoes, parsley, pickled onions, garlic and anchovy fillets in a mortar (in batches if necessary) and pound with a pestle to form a smooth paste.*
2. *Put the paste in a mixing bowl and season. Add the oil a little at a time and beat thoroughly before you add any more. Add the vinegar and mix well*

(ideal as a cold sauce for fish or refrigerate and use as a dip)

CUMBERLAND PIE

1 lb potatoes – peeled, boiled & mashed
½ lb minced beef
1 onion – peeled & chopped
3 carrots – peeled & chopped
4 fl oz beef stock
½ tbsp plain flour
1 tbsp olive oil
1 oz butter

1. *Pre-heat oven to GM4/180°c/350°f*
2. *Dry fry the mince until just browned*
3. *Meanwhile, heat the oil and fry the onion and carrots until the onion starts to soften*
4. *Stir the flour into the stock and pour it onto the mince. Season, add the onions and carrots, stir and simmer for 15 minutes.*
5. *Beat the butter into the mash*
6. *Put the mince in a small ovenproof dish and spread the potato on top. Scrape the potato with a fork*
7. *Bake for 40-45 minutes*

SEETHED POTATOES

1 lb new potatoes – scrubbed
½ oz butter

1. *Put the potatoes in a large saucepan and add a little salt. Add the butter and enough water to reach halfway up the potatoes (potatoes should layer the base – not be stacked)*
2. *Cook, uncovered on a very low heat for 45 minutes, stirring occasionally*

WELSH EGGS

1 lb potatoes – boiled & mashed
6 oz cheddar cheese – grated
4 eggs – hard boiled
1 egg – beaten
1½ oz flour
breadcrumbs
oil or fat for frying

1. *Mix together the potatoes, cheese & flour then season. Divide the mixture into 4 then by hand mould around each hard-boiled egg*
2. *Brush each one with beaten egg then roll in breadcrumbs.*
3. *Fry in hot deep fat until golden & crisp*

STIR FRIED POTATOES

1 lb potatoes – peeled & diced
2 onions – peeled & chopped
1 green pepper – deseeded & chopped
1 large mild red chilli – deseeded & chopped
½ tsp Worcester sauce
3 fl oz beef stock
3 tbsp vegetable oil

1. *Heat the oil in a wok and stir fry the potatoes, onions, pepper and chilli for 5 minutes.*
2. *Reduce the heat, add the stock and Worcester sauce. Cover and cook on a low heat for 10 minutes*
3. *Remove the cover, turn the heat back up and fry until the liquid has gone*

Variations on a theme

POTATO BREAD

1 lb potatoes – boiled & mashed
8 oz flour
2 level tsp baking powder
1 level tsp salt
1 tbsp vegetable oil

1. Pre-heat oven to GM8/230°c/450°f
2. Sift the flour, baking power and salt into a bowl then mix thoroughly with the potato
3. Grease a ½ pint loaf tin
4. Stir the oil and 7 fl oz water into the mixture and put in into the tin. Dust the surface with flour
5. Bake for 25 mins and allow to cool on a rack

POTATO MOUSSAKA

1 lb potatoes – boiled for 10 mins & drained
1 lb minced lamb
1 large aubergine – thinly sliced
2 large onions – peeled & thinly sliced
3 cloves garlic – peeled & crushed
1 large tin chopped tomatoes
3 fl oz vegetable stock
3 fl oz red wine
1 tsp cinnamon
½ tsp all spice
1 tsp dried oregano
1 tbsp fresh parsley – chopped

Topping
18 fl oz milk
2 oz butter
2 oz plain flour
3½ oz cheddar cheese – grated
4 eggs beaten
½ tsp nutmeg

1. Melt the butter in a pan and add the flour. Mix together to make a roux. Add the milk and mix thoroughly. Heat gradually, whisking continually until the sauce thickens. Reduce the heat, season and add the nutmeg, keep on a low heat for about 10 mins then stir in the cheese. Allow to cool slightly then whisk in the eggs
2. Pre-heat the oven to GM4/180°c/350°f

3. Allow the potatoes to cool then cut into ¼ inch slices
4. Heat 4 tbsp of the oil and gently fry the aubergine in batches until golden brown on both sides, adding more oil as necessary. Drain on kitchen paper
5. Using the same pan, heat the rest of the oil and gently fry the onions and garlic until the onion starts to soften
6. Stir in the cinnamon and all spice and cook for 1 minute
7. Add the lamb and mix it thoroughly with the onions and spices. Heat until the lamb is browned. Season
8. Add the tomatoes, oregano and parsley and pour in the stock and the wine. Simmer uncovered for 20-25 mins. Remove from heat and leave to cool
9. Take an ovenproof dish and put a single layer of aubergine in the bottom followed by half of the meat then half of the potatoes. Repeat, finishing with potatoes then pour the sauce on top and bake for 45 mins

POTATO QUESADILLAS

1 lb potatoes – boiled & mashed
9 oz cheddar cheese – grated
2 onions – peeled & finely chopped
4 cloves garlic – crushed
4 green chillies – deseeded & cut into strips
7 oz chorizo sausage – chopped
3 tbsp fresh coriander – chopped
10-15 flour tortillas
2 tbsp olive oil

1. Heat the oil in a saucepan and fry the onion, garlic and chilli until the onion starts to soften
2. Add the sausage and cook for 3 more mins
3. Add the potatoes and mix well
4. Remove from the heat and mix in the cheese and coriander
5. Warm the tortillas (5 seconds in a microwave) spoon some of the mixture into each and fold over. Serve hot – ideally with sour cream

POTATO PIZZA

1 lb (floury) potatoes – peeled, boiled & mashed
½ oz butter
2 cloves garlic – crushed
1 tbsp fresh parsley – chopped
1 egg – beaten
2 fl oz passata
1 tbsp tomato purée
2 large tomatoes – sliced
1 red pepper – cored & cut into thin strips
2 large mushrooms – sliced
3 oz mozzarella cheese – sliced
6 black olives – stoned & chopped

1. *Pre-heat oven to GM7/220°c/425°f*
2. *Mix the butter, garlic, parsley and egg into the mash*
3. *Spread the mash onto a greased and floured 6" pizza tin*
4. *Put the in the oven and cook for 5-6 mins – until the mash begins to set. Remove*
5. *Mix the passata and purée and brush it onto the mash up to ½" from the edge*
6. *Place the sliced tomatoes, pepper, mushrooms and olives on top. Season then add the cheese*
7. *Return to the oven and cook for 20 mins*

POTATO SUSHI

1 lb new potatoes – scrubbed, boiled & drained
3 tbsp mayonnaise
4 tbsp soy sauce
2 tbsp chopped chives
5 tbsp extra virgin olive oil
1 tbsp red wine vinegar
10 slices paper thin raw beef

1. *Mash the potatoes whilst warm then mix in the mayonnaise, chives, 2 tbsp of the soy sauce and season. Leave to cool*
2. *Use 2 desert spoons and form the mixture into egg shapes (there should be enough to make 20 shapes). Place 2 onto each slice of beef*
3. *Mix the remaining soy sauce with the olive oil, wine vinegar and seasoning in a jar and shake thoroughly. Spoon over the sushi. Serve cold*

POTATO PIZZA TOPPING

1 lb new potatoes – scrubbed, boiled, drained and sliced
1 lb brie – rind removed and sliced
1 large pre-made pizza base (with about 15 mins cooking time)
20 black olives – pitted and halved
2 tbsp extra virgin olive oil

1. *Pre-heat oven to GM6/200°c/400°f*
2. *Layer the potatoes and cheese onto the pizza base – sprinkle with the olives and drizzle over the oil. Season*
3. *Bake for 15 mins*

POTATO PIZZA (2)

1 lb (waxy) potatoes – peeled & thinly sliced
1 large pre-made cheese pizza
¾ lb Ricotta cheese
½ lb fine green beans – trimmed, chopped, blanched & drained
2 tbsp green pesto
1 oz parmesan cheese – grated

1. *Cut the potato slices in half and fry in the oil for about 10 mins turning occasionally. Drain on kitchen paper*
2. *Spread the cheese and pesto onto the pizza base. Season*
3. *Spread the potatoes and beans onto the cheese and cook in the oven for 12–15 mins*

POTATO & APPLE STUFFING

1 lb potatoes – boiled & mashed
1 lb cooking applies – peeled, cored & chopped
1 lb onions – peeled & chopped finely
4 oranges – zest removed & juiced
4 tbsps fresh parsley – chopped
2 tbsps fresh thyme – chopped

1. *Mix all the ingredients thoroughly together in a large bowl. Season*
2. *Cover with cling film and refrigerate for 1 hour before use*

POTATO PIZZA TOPPING (2)

1 lb new potatoes – scrubbed, halved and thinly sliced
¼ lb bacon – fat removed
½ lb Gruyere cheese – thinly sliced
6 spring onions – trimmed and chopped
1 large pizza base
1 tbsp extra virgin olive oil

1. *Pre-heat oven to GM7/220°c/425°f*
2. *Grill the bacon until crispy then chop finely*
3. *Boil the potatoes for 10 mins and drain*
4. *Cook the pizza base accordingly to the instructions on the packet but stop 15 mins short of its full cooking time*
5. *Add the potatoes to the pizza, season and drizzle with the oil. Sprinkle with the cheese, bacon and onion*
6. *Cook for 15 mins ensuring the pizza base is fully cooked*

CHEESE & POTATO SCONES

1 lb potatoes – boiled & mashed
8 oz cheddar cheese – grated
4 fl oz milk
6 oz margarine
6 tsp baking powder
9 oz plain flour
½ tsp mustard powder

1. *Put the potatoes in a large bowl and leave to cool*
2. *Sieve the baking powder, flour and mustard into another bowl then rub in the margarine until the mixture resembles breadcrumbs*
3. *Add this to the potatoes and add the cheese. Mix thoroughly with a fork*
4. *Gradually stir in enough milk so you have a mixture which is firm but not dry*
5. *Pre-heat oven to GM7/220°c/425°f*
6. *Flour a board and roll out the mixture to 1" thickness. Cut into circular shapes about 2" in diameter*
7. *Place on a greased baking try and cook for 18-20 mins*

POTATO RATATOUILLE

1 lb potatoes – peeled & diced
1 red pepper – de-seeded and cut into small squares
1 green pepper – de-seeded and cut into small squares
1 yellow pepper – de-seeded and cut into small squares
2 onions – peeled & diced
2 courgettes – washed, trimmed and diced
3 tomatoes – skinned, seeded and chopped
3 cloves garlic – crushed
¼ pint vegetable stock (made with 1 cube)
5 tbsp extra virgin olive oil

1. *Heat the oil and gently fry the potatoes, peppers, courgettes, onions and garlic for 5 mins*
2. *Add the tomatoes, stock, season and stir*
3. *Bring to a gentle simmer, cover and cook for 40 mins*
4. *Remove cover, turn up the heat and continue to cook until the liquid has almost evaporated*

POTATO GUMBO

1 lb potatoes – peeled & diced
1 lb chicken – diced
1 large onion – peeled & chopped
1 leek – trimmed and finely chopped
1 red pepper – cored, seeded and finely chopped
3 cloves garlic – crushed
¾ lb frozen prawns – thawed on kitchen paper
1 large tin chopped tomatoes
1 pint vegetable stock
1 tbsp paprika
2 tsp Tabasco sauce
1 tbsp fresh thyme – chopped
3 tbsp vegetable oil
1 tbsp flour

1. *Heat the oil and stir fry the chicken until just cooked. Remove with a slotted spoon and reserve*
2. *Add the potato, onion, leek, pepper and garlic and fry for 5 mins*
3. *Add the flour, paprika and thyme. Stir and cook for 1 minute*

4. *Add the tomatoes, chicken, Tabasco sauce and stock. Bring to the boil then simmer for 15 mins*

5. *Add the prawns and season. Stir well and simmer for 5 mins more – ensuring the prawns are cooked and until the desired consistency is reached*

POTATO RAVIOLI

1 lb (floury) potatoes – peeled, boiled for 10 mins and drained
¼ lb minced beef
1 small onion – peeled & very finely sliced
2 cloves garlic – crushed
1 tbsp tomato purée
1 small tin chopped tomatoes
1 tsp dried oregano
1 tsp dried basil
5 fl oz beef stock (made with 1 cube)
1 tbsp plain flour
3 egg yolks
3 tbsp olive oil
8 oz plain flour
5 tbsp butter

1. *Dry fry the mince until it starts to brown. Drain off some of the fat. Add the onion and garlic and cook until the mince is browned and the onion starts to soften*

2. *Add the flour (1 tbsp) and the purée, season. Stir and cook for 2 mins*

3. *Add the stock, tomatoes and herbs. Cook on a low heat for 30 mins*

4. *Meanwhile mash the potatoes then add the egg yolks and oil. Season and mix thoroughly*

5. *Sprinkle with 6oz of the flour and mix manually to form a dough*

6. *Use the remaining flour to dust a surface. Roll out the dough, divide it into 20 pieces and flatten each piece into a circular shape*

7. *Spoon some mince onto the right side of each piece of dough and fold the left half over and press down the edges to seal*

8. *Melt the butter in a large pan and gently cook the ravioli for about 10 mins turning occasionally or until they turn golden brown*

POTATO RATATOUILLE (2)

1 lb new potatoes – scrubbed & halved
2 courgettes – washed, trimmed & sliced
1 aubergine – trimmed & chopped
1 onion – peeled & chopped
1 red pepper – seeded & chopped
6 tomatoes – skinned & chopped
3 cloves garlic – crushed
3 tbsp tomato purée
2 tbsp fresh basil – finely chopped
2 tbsp extra virgin olive oil
½ tsp paprika

1. *Heat the oil in a large pan and cook the onion until it begins to soften*

2. *Add the garlic and cook for 2 more mins*

3. *Add all the other vegetables, season, cover and cook over a low heat for 30 mins – stirring occasionally*

4. *Add the basil, paprika and purée, adjust the seasoning, stir well and cook gently for 5 more mins*

POTATO SPRING ROLLS

1 lb potatoes – peeled & cut into match sticks
1 lb carrots – peeled & cut into match sticks
1 lb tinned sweet corn – drained
4 inches fresh ginger – peeled & cut into fine strips
8 tbsp dark soy sauce
1 large packet spring roll wrappers
Vegetable oil for deep frying

1. *Put the potatoes, carrots, sweet corn and ginger in boiling water. Bring back to the boil and blanch for 2 mins. Drain thoroughly*

2. *Put the mixture in a large bowl and add the soy sauce. Mix thoroughly to coat*

3. *Heat the oil in a large pan*

4. *Unwrap the spring roll wrappers and fill each one with the vegetable mixture and seal*

5. *When the oil is really hot, carefully add the rolls to the pan. Fry until browned and crispy*

6. *Remove from the oil and drain on kitchen paper*

BEEF & POTATO MOUSSAKA

1 lb potatoes – peeled & sliced
1 lb minced beef
½ lb onions – peeled & finely chopped
¾ lb aubergine – sliced
3 cloves garlic – crushed
2 tbsp tomato purée
4 floz beef stock
2 tbsp fresh parsley – chopped
¾ pint milk
2 oz butter
4 oz cheddar cheese – grated
4 tbsp olive oil

1. Pre-heat oven to GM6/200°c/400°f
2. Heat half the oil and fry the aubergine until lightly browned. Drain and set aside
3. Add the rest of the oil, heat and fry the potatoes until browned. Remove with a slotted spoon and set aside
4. Fry the onion and garlic for 3-4 mins
5. Add the meat, stir well and cook until browned. Add the tomato purée, stock and parsley. Season and cook gently for 20 mins
6. Make a sauce using butter, milk and flour, adding the cheese at the end. Season
7. Layer a casserole dish with the aubergine and meat alternatively
8. Finish with the potatoes, pour on the sauce then bake for 45 mins

POTATO TAGINE

1 lb new potatoes – washed & halved
½ lb baby carrots – washed
½ lb green beans – trimmed
½ lb baby onions – peeled
4 large tomatoes – quartered
1 small green chilli – deseeded & chopped
½ tsp cumin seeds
½ tsp turmeric
½ tsp cinnamon
3 tbsp fresh parsley - chopped
3 tbsp fresh coriander – chopped
2 pints vegetable stock
2 tbsp extra virgin olive oil

1. Heat the oil in a large pan and gently fry the chilli, cumin, turmeric and cinnamon for 2 mins
2. Add the onions and tomatoes, stir well and cook for 2 more mins
3. Add the parsley and coriander, season and stir
4. Pour on the stock and bring to the boil. Reduce to a gentle simmer for 5 mins
5. Add the potatoes, carrots and beans. Return to the boil then reduce to a simmer for 20 mins and cook until the desired consistency is reached

POTATO MEATBALLS

1 lb potatoes – peeled & grated
1 lb minced beef
2 onions – peeled & chopped
1 egg – beaten
2 cloves garlic – crushed
4 oz breadcrumbs
1 tbsp fresh oregano – chopped
1 tbsp olive oil
Corn oil for frying
Flour for dusting

1. Heat the olive oil and fry the onion until it starts to soften
2. Add the garlic and fry for 1 more minute
3. Squeeze excess moisture from the potatoes then add to the pan. Season and mix well
4. Put the potato mixture in a bowl and add the mince, egg, oregano and breadcrumbs
5. Dust your hands with flour and form the mixture into small round shapes. Cover with cling film and refrigerate for 2 hours
6. Heat the corn oil in a deep fat fryer and cook the meatballs until browned all over
7. Remove with a slotted spoon and drain on kitchen paper

SAUSAGE ROLLS

1 lb potatoes – peeled, boiled & mashed
½ lb minced sausage meat
⅓ lb minced beef
1 onion – peeled & grated

2 cloves garlic – crushed
1 tbsp fresh thyme – chopped
1 tsp Worcester sauce
3 sheets ready rolled puff pastry
1 egg – beaten
1 tbsp olive oil

1. Heat the oil and gently fry the onion until it starts to soften, add the garlic and thyme and cook for a further minute

2. Put the potatoes in a large bowl, add the sausage meat, beef mince, Worcester sauce and onion mixture. Season and mix well

3. Pre-heat oven to GM6/200°c/400°f

4. Cut the pastry sheets in half and divide the potato mixture into 6. Lay each piece of the mixture along the long side of each piece of pastry. Brush the edges with egg and roll the pastry over the mixture to join

5. Cut each roll into 3 pieces and pierce the top of each

6. Place the rolls, pierced side up in a greased roasting tin and bake for 30 mins

POTATO STUFFING

1 lb potatoes – boiled & mashed
1 large onion – peeled & finely chopped
2 oz butter
3 tbsp sage – chopped

1. Heat half the butter and cook the onion till soft

2. Add all the other ingredients, season and mix well

POTATO BHAJEES

1 lb potatoes – peeled, boiled for 10 mins, drained
8 oz garam flour
1 tsp ground turmeric
1 tsp cayenne pepper
1 tsp ground coriander
2 tsp cumin seeds
1½ tsp salt
½ tsp bi-carbonate of soda
16 floz water
Vegetable oil for frying

1. Sift the flour, spices, bi-carbonate of soda and salt into a mixing bowl. Add the cumin seeds

2. Gradually pour in the water, turning continually until a smooth batter is formed

3. Cut the potatoes into shapes about 1½" square by ¼" thick

4. Put the potato into the bowl and mix thoroughly into the batter ensuring the shapes are evenly covered

5. Heat the oil in a deep frying pan until it reaches 180°c/350°f. Then carefully add the potatoes (in batches) Cook for 6-8 mins until golden

6. Remove with a slotted spoon and drain on kitchen paper

POTATO LASAGNE

1 lb new potatoes – scrubbed, boiled & sliced
2 onions – peeled & chopped
2 courgettes – washed & chopped
1 red pepper – seeded & cut into strips
1 green pepper – seeded & cut into strips
5 cloves garlic – peeled & crushed
1 small tin chopped tomatoes
2 tbsp olive oil
1 small jar pasta sauce
¾ pint milk
1 oz butter
1 oz flour
4 oz cheddar cheese – grated
8 sheets pre-cooked lasagne

1. Pre-heat oven to GM6/200°c/400°f

2. Heat the oil and fry the onions, peppers and garlic for 5 mins

3. Add the courgettes, tomatoes and pasta sauce. Season, stir well and heat through

4. Make a sauce using the butter, flour and milk. When thickened add 3 oz of the cheese, season and stir

5. Layer half the potatoes at the base of a greased casserole dish, add half the pasta sauce then 4 sheets of lasagne and half of the cheese sauce

6. Repeat and sprinkle with the remaining cheese. Bake for 40 mins

POTATO SAUSAGE ROLLS

1 lb medium sized potatoes – scrubbed & dried
¼ lb sausage meat
1 onion – peeled & finely chopped
Bacon – 1 rasher for each potato

1. *Pre-heat oven to GM6/200°c/400°f*
2. *Remove the centre of each potato with an apple corer*
3. *Mix the sausage meat and onion and fill each potato cavity with the mixture*
4. *Wrap a rasher of bacon around each potato. Cover with foil and bake for 1 hour*

POTATO PAKORAS

1 lb potatoes – peeled & thinly sliced
½ lb flour
2 egg whites – whisked
1 small green chilli – deseeded and finely chopped
1 tbsp black onion seeds
½ tsp turmeric
1 tsp salt
1 tsp cumin seeds
10 fl oz water
Vegetable oil for frying

1. *Mix the flour with the water and add all the spices and salt*
2. *Fold in the egg whites*
3. *Heat the oil in a large deep pan until very hot*
4. *Dip the slices of potato into the flour mixture ensuring each one is evenly coated. Fry, in batches if necessary, for about 6 mins until lightly browned*

MASHED TATTIES & TURNIPS

1 lb potatoes – peeled & boiled
1 lb turnips – peeled & boiled
2 tbsp chives – finely chopped
3 oz butter or dripping

1. *Mash the potatoes and turnips together*
2. *Mix in the chives, butter and season*

POTATO SPRING ROLLS (2)

1 lb potatoes – peeled & grated
8 sheets filo pastry
1 onion – finely chopped
½ lb bean sprouts
2 tbsp extra virgin olive oil
1 tbsp chopped fresh parsley

1. *Pre-heat oven to GM6/200°c/400°f*
2. *Blanch the potato in boiled water for 2 mins and drain well*
3. *Heat the oil and gently fry the potatoes and onion until golden, add bean sprouts and cook for a further 1 minute*
4. *Remove from heat, stir in the parsley, season and allow to cool*
5. *Divide the mixture into 8 and wrap in the pastry to make 8 spring rolls. Place on a baking sheet*
6. *Brush with the oil and bakefor 10 mins*

POTATO PIZZA BASE

1 lb potatoes – peeled & boiled
1 egg
1 egg yolk
2½ oz plain flour
1 oz butter – melted
1 tbsp fresh parsley – chopped
2 tbsp olive oil

1. *Mash the potatoes thoroughly (until it is more of a purée than a mash)*
2. *Add the egg, egg yolk, flour, butter and parsley to the potatoes, season and mix well with your hands*
3. *Divide the mixture into two and form into a pizza base*
4. *Heat the oil and gently cook each base for 5 mins*
5. *At this point add the topping of your choice eg start with some sliced mozzarella and sliced tomato etc*
6. *Season and cook gently for about 10 mins until the cheese has melted*
7. *Finish under a pre-heated grill if required*

POTATO CHEESECAKE

Base
4 oz plain flour
1 oz lard
4 tbsps water
Pinch of salt

Filling
1 lb potatoes – peeled, grated & soaked in a bowl
of water
10 oz cottage cheese - mashed
3 eggs – separated
1 oz plain flour
1 oz parmesan cheese – grated
¼ pt sour cream
3 spring onions – finely chopped

Topping
¼ pt sour cream
Small packet of ready salted crisps – lightly crushed

The Base

1. Sift the flour and salt into a bowl. Put the water and lard into a saucepan and stir over a gentle heat until melted. Pour onto the flour and mix to a soft dough. Press evenly over the bottom of a greased loose-bottomed 7-8 inch round cake tin working the dough up the sides of the tin to a depth of about 1 inch

The Filling

1. Pre-heat oven to GM3/160°c/325°f

2. Put the cheese in a large mixing bowl and beat in the egg yolks, flour, parmesan, soured cream, spring onions & season. Drain the potato & squeeze dry in a clean cloth. Stir the potato into the cheese mixture. Whisk the egg whites until stiff and fold into the cheese mixture. Spoon the mixture onto the prepared tin and pat level. Bake for 1¼ - 1½ hours until firm but still spongy to the touch

The Topping

3. Heat the soured cream very slowly in a pan. Lift out the cooked cheesecake and spoon the warm sour cream over the top and sprinkle with crisps

QUICK POTATO MOUSSAKA

1 lb potatoes – peeled & sliced
1 lb cooked lamb – cut into small pieces
1 large tin tomatoes
1 onion – peeled & sliced
1 oz flour
½ pint milk
4 oz cheddar cheese – grated
3 tbsp olive oil
4 oz butter
1 clove garlic – finely chopped
½ tsp cinnamon

1. Pre-heat oven to GM5/190°c/375°f

2. Melt 3 oz of the butter in a pan and add the oil. Fry the potatoes until soft. Remove with a slotted spoon

3. Add the onion & fry until soft. Mix in the garlic, lamb, tomatoes and cinnamon. Season

4. Butter a casserole dish and line the bottom & sides with potato. Pour the meat mixture into the middle

5. Put the flour, 1 oz of the butter, the milk, 2 oz of cheese & season in a small pan. Heat, stirring continually, until the sauce thickens

6. Pour the sauce over the meant & sprinkle with the rest of the cheese. Bake for 30 mins

In 1995 potatoes were taken into space aboard the shuttle Columbia, this is the first time food had ever been grown in space

Index

Fish Dishes

Side Dishes

Notes

Notes

Notes

Notes

Notes

Notes